# Freedom in Resistance and Creative Transformation

# Freedom in Resistance and Creative Transformation

Michael St. A. Miller

LEXINGTON BOOKS

Lanham • Boulder • New York • Toronto • Plymouth, UK

Published by Lexington Books
A wholly owned subsidiary of The Rowman & Littlefield Publishing Group, Inc.
4501 Forbes Boulevard, Suite 200, Lanham, Maryland 20706
www.rowman.com

10 Thornbury Road, Plymouth PL6 7PP, United Kingdom



British Library Cataloguing in Publication Information Available

**Library of Congress Cataloging-in-Publication Data**

Miller, Michael St. A.
Freedom in resistance and creative transformation / Michael St. A. Miller.
pages cm
Includes bibliographical references and index.
ISBN 978-0-7391-7352-7 (cloth : alk. paper) -- ISBN 978-0-7391-7353-4 (electronic)
1. Liberty--Religious aspects--Christianity. I. Title.
BT810.3.M55 2013
261.7--dc23

2013004870



Printed in the United States of America

For Diane
I'm grateful for your partnership on this challenging road to freedom

# Table of Contents

# Acknowledgments

It was in the process of developing another project with "liberation" as its central theme that I committed myself to write this text. It started with the recognition that there was not sufficient clarity on the basic concept of freedom in the sources I was examining. Therefore, they would not adequately facilitate my desire to make sense of the wide range of contemporary quests that have freedom as their driving force and would not strengthen my ability to contribute effectively to them. In the early stages of research my colleague Ron Allen challenged me to write a text that in length and style would be accessible to a wide variety of persons. As I proceeded, I recognized that my revisionist intentions could not be effectively pursued under the restrictions I initially placed on myself, especially in regard to length. Still, I hope that thoughtful persons within and outside of the Christian community will find the concepts and discussions of this work so informative and invigorating that they will enthusiastically wrestle with them and be strengthened in their ability to participate in the promotion of freedom that is finite, realistically libertarian, and relational.

A number of other persons contributed to this project through encouragement and/or direct examination of my ideas. Dear friend Diane Jersild Claghorn has been my chief encourager. Academic colleagues Marti Steussy and Clark Williamson were the first to read sections of the manuscript and engage me in challenging and clarifying conversations on its contents. This they continued to do to the very end of the process. Thanks Clark for asking the critical question about the intended audience. Thanks Marti for "poking" me regularly on my writing style. I must also mention my brother Alex who at crucial points challenged me regarding the nature of the responsibility I have when writing on a crucial issue such as freedom and also colleague Frank Burch Brown for helping me restrain my inclination to turn a book proposal into a treatise. Conversation with colleague Bill Kincaid on the ecclesiological proposals of the project reminded me of the ongoing challenge to translate theological ideas into concrete practices within churches in order to strengthen their capacity for just and freedom-enabling contributions to human welfare. Then there is the anonymous reader whose critique of my initial foray into Jacob Arminius's ideas forced me to rethink some of the evaluations I had made. Joyce Krauser corrected some materials, prepared the manuscript for final submission to the publisher, and was always available to give advice. Finally, I mention two young men who contributed significantly to the final form of the project. My son David was the first to read the entire manuscript, and he offered invaluable suggestions for the improvement of both its content and structure. Christian Theological Seminary student Nick Buck did a fine job in helping me identify spelling errors and problems with citations. I look forward to reading books written by both of these intellectually gifted young men.

# Introduction

Freedom, as a general concept, has numerous promoters, and I would hazard a guess that most persons who have opened this text harbor the conviction that they know what it looks like when they see it and know what it feels like when they experience it. It is exactly this quality that makes writing about freedom a very challenging venture. Political theorist Isaiah Berlin puts it well in his celebrated discussion of this concept: "Almost every moralist in human history has praised freedom. Like happiness and goodness, like nature and reality, it is a term whose meaning is so porous that there is little interpretation that it seems able to resist."[1] One could perceive this commentary to be reflecting the recognition that conceptions and concrete expressions of freedom are always influenced by the demands of the contexts in which freedom is pursued and experienced. Being a declared contextualist, I do not resist that perception. Yet it is clear that Berlin's primary intention is to remind us of how difficult it is to fathom this concept. This difficulty is acknowledged by sociologist Orlando Patterson who declares that "freedom, like love and beauty, is one of those values better experienced than defined."[2] Being convinced, as Schubert Ogden is, that "it is in terms of the question of freedom that men and women today typically ask the existential question concerning the ultimate meaning of their existence,"[3] I assert that one needs to have some basic understanding of what characterizes freedom in order to actually experience it. Therefore, in this project I will explicate a kind of freedom that is finite, realistically libertarian, and relational. I am confident that in pursuing this project I am doing exactly what must be done with regard to the very important concept of freedom. This is to examine and reexamine it as often as possible, from as many angles as possible, and in light of the demands of as many contexts as possible.

The background I bring to this discussion of freedom includes my early nurture in a context (the Caribbean) with a long history of colonialism and slavery, in which a small minority curtailed the freedom of the majority of its inhabitants through quite brutal means. Associated with this feature is the painful recognition that it is those who most often used the term freedom in their rhetoric, that is, Christians, who were the chief allies of the economic and socially powerful as they attempted to provide justification for their freedom-suppressing pursuits. Indeed, an important element of the process of Christian evangelization in the Caribbean was the message to the subjugated that they would be most free if they accepted their lot and looked forward to rewards in the Christian heaven. With this background, the project reflects special concern for those who operate in circumstances that do not permit significant degrees of responsible self-expression and self-realization, or in which persons have become convinced that because of theological or socio-political and economic reasons they cannot or ought not to claim or pursue freedom on the basis of their humanity *per se*.

I develop this project with a strong suspicion of rhetoric that promotes freedom through slavery to God and submission to church authority. It might be claimed by some that the one to whom the Christian is expected to be enslaved is the God whose character was revealed in the self-sacrifice of Jesus the Christ. Unfortunately, rather than allowing the vulnerability and risk-taking evident in the life of Jesus to have a significant place in claims made about God's character, many spend great effort establishing God as the absolute, omnipotent, omniscient, and sovereignly free ruler who, being dishonored by human self-assertiveness in the Garden of Eden, could only be "satisfied" through the submission and shed blood of Jesus as the representative "God-man."

With the conviction that it is only in Christ that human nature is acceptable to God, many are intimidated away from adventurous exploration of many potentials inherent in their humanity. This conviction is often associated with the contradictory position that, while the self-existent God is simple, impassible, immutable, that is, perfect (in the classical sense) and does not need human beings, God greatly desires to be loved by human beings and expects us to express devotion through worship and a life of obedience. Usually, it is those who are most highly placed in the hierarchy of power and authority within churches who determine for others what "true" worship and obedience looks like. It is they who provide a constant reminder of the severe consequences: alienation and lostness, which result from being out of line with what is claimed to be God's will.

While these issues are quite problematic, the very fact that they are associated with pronouncements and actions that have freedom as their overarching theme serves to dramatize the degree to which freedom is a driving force of human existence and thus is a preeminent concern that motivates human action. Indeed, prescriptions of freedom I have identified as oppressive are provided by people who are convinced about the integrity of the path to freedom to which they point. Their ideas are informed by worldviews into which they have been socialized or to which they have laid claim, and especially by their understandings of God and God's relation to human beings, as well as other global cohabitants. This is exactly what makes it necessary for the theological underpinning of conceptions of freedom to be re-examined by and for each generation and epoch in light of new insights on the structure of existence in general and the particular needs and aspirations of people in particular contexts.

In this light, I consider the orientation of the project to be revisionist. This orientation begins by taking very seriously the efforts of leaders of thought over the course of the history of Christianity to articulate positions on freedom. It also requires that I critically engage important members of this group in order to emulate their intention to provide the most coherent and relevant understanding of freedom for the era in which I write. Therefore, this text will read like a series of conversations with individual thinkers or groups of thinkers from which the strengths and weaknesses of traditional Christian claims relevant to human freedom emerge and the way is opened for new levels of reflection on the matter. By this means the stage is set for my own positions to emerge.

This project reflects my recognition that in the West ventures in freedom are usually associated with the rapid intensification in the awareness of individuality. I dare say that the pursuit of individuality oftentimes outstrips well-informed consideration of how to express individuality creatively and responsibly. Many grasp personal freedom without adequate guidance for negotiating the terrain that is being opened up in ways that ensure humane existence for individuals as well as communities of individuals. It is exactly because I wish to contribute relevant insights to help guide contemporary human development, in the context of concern for general planetary welfare, that I explore theological alternatives to some traditional ways of understanding and expressing freedom within the Christian community.

Not long ago I re-read the *20/20 Vision of the Christian Church (Disciples of Christ)* by Richard Hamm, in which is described his change from earlier thinking that a move from an ethos of autonomy to one of cooperation was what his denomination needed, to his later conviction that it was actually a culture of interdependence that is necessary. Elaborating on this change, Hamm suggests that there is the need to nurture a culture in which "we really are depending on one another, a culture in which we are really trusting one another, a culture where we make real commitments to one another. . . ."[4] My efforts in this project support the emphasis on interdependence not only within the churches but also for a wide range of religious communities, social organizations, and geographic settings. While in Hamm's general context of operation (the USA), autonomy is often expressed as "self-centered individualism," many groups in this nation and other parts of the world are still burdened by the psychological and spiritual legacy of centuries of coercion (informed, in part, by religious ideas) in which some master class or ruling nation controlled as much of life as it could. In these settings, many people who imbibed Christian indoctrination have come to believe that living for the sake of others through selfless service is the way to realize the self. In actuality, this self is not one's own but Christ's.

I am now convinced that, while the power of service should be celebrated, people also need to be facilitated into emancipating self-engagement leading to a sense of healthy autonomy many have been taught to consider unacceptable. Some of those who have been involved in the oppression of others may well have concluded that any sense of self that is not "in Christ" is inauthentic, and any claim to freedom that is not associated with a specific understanding of submission to God through Christ is *hubris*. This being so, those with what is perceived as inauthentic or misguided self-understandings are not persons who know rightly what freedom is, neither can they handle freedom, and they might not even be capable of freedom. Thus it is clear to me that the foundation for the trust and interdependence Hamm seeks must have as an important element the nurturing of persons to discover themselves as free beings who are willing to work on their own and in concert with others to discern and express what this discovery entails. It is, therefore, hoped that by means of this project many will come to appreciate that it is the development of healthy individuality and the exercise of personal freedom, in as many internal and external manifestations as possible, that will fuel appropriate appreciation of interdependence. Interdependence suggests that each participant in a network of interactions brings something that she/he possesses on their own and has claimed as theirs to contribute, and on which others can rely. This scenario implies not only trust in others, whether human or divine, but also trust in self, resulting in healthy individuality rather than the destructive individualism that is undermining many in Western societies.

Operating within severe social, economic, and political limitations, many become fixated on expressions of freedom in the external sphere of life that constitute the cosmological dimension of freedom. With this in mind, my effort is driven by the conviction that, while any worthwhile consideration of freedom must look for its concrete expressions in the external operations of individuals and communities, there can be no authentic address of social, economic, and political concerns that does not take seriously the deep-structure of the internal life of human beings. It is this internal realm that is the seat of the ontological dimension of freedom, which has to do with the ability of persons to evaluate all features of life in terms of that which is considered ultimate. In the Caribbean, my original home, with its history of colonialism and slavery, painful lessons have been learnt about the consequences that follow when we neglect to nurture appropriately freedom in the internal realm. Therefore, I pursue this project with the echo of the popular lament in that region that it is far easier to remove the shackles from one's feet (physical enslavement) than it is to unshackle the mind and spirit. The need for improved efforts to nurture a healthy correlation between the pursuit of external freedom and that of internal freedom of people in that region is reflected in what Caribbean intellectual and church leader Bill Watty described in 1981 as disturbing "ambiguities in the Caribbean personality."[5]

Ambiguity is an unavoidable feature of finitude, and negotiating life with its uncertainties and in the midst of numerous other decision-makers will certainly have challenging consequences for the mental and spiritual dynamics within each individual. However, considering the long and brutal history of slavery, colonialism, and other forms of disfiguring subjugation in that and other regions of the world, there has been a general failure on the part of contemporary Christian churches to facilitate in those they influence the freedom to know themselves appropriately, to claim themselves in their full humanity, to develop appropriate criteria to judge themselves in their humanity, and to embrace opportunities for expressing their humanity as they engage in worthwhile manifestations of personal and communal freedom. Support for this claim is provided by Chinese theologian Kwok Pui Lan who has spoken of having to shift her thinking on Asian feminist theology when faced with "the fragmented subjectivity or the multiple fractures of the colonized subject's mind and psyche."[6] The language used by Watty and Kwok Pui Lan might appear extreme to some. However, it represents the deep anguish of these thinkers as they work with others to counter the debilitating consequences of the colonial heritage in their respective settings. Supportive of their commitments, I intend in this project to challenge Christian communities to rethink traditional theological positions that have undermined the ability of many in various parts of the world to be effective agents of human liberation.

In pursuing my analysis I will often use the term "unfreedom" to characterize situations in which human freedom is limited in ways and by means that undermine what I consider basic features of what it means to be human. I use this term because, along with the fact that I do not believe that there is an exact combination of elements that characterizes freedom in its perfect state, I do not hold that there is ever a situation in which the human being is so completely without freedom that there is warrant for a term perceived as representing its polar opposite.

The explications, analysis, and proposals involved in this project are directed, in the first instance, to those associated with Christian churches. That being said, it will be evident that I am strongly convinced that, given the historic contribution of Christianity to frameworks of human self-understanding that have both enhanced and undermined yearnings for freedom, the

Christian theologian has an ongoing obligation to facilitate well-informed considerations of freedom in the wider human community. It is my desire to steer people away from subservience to other human beings, even to God, and to provide theological foundation for better cooperation between people and with God for the sake of ongoing humanization. This co-operation involves, among other features, the ability of diverse peoples to dream together and nurture aspirations regarding what human beings might become as co-inhabitants with other species in the world, leading to rational risk-taking as we pursue expanded boundaries of imagination and achievement.

Given the historical legacies with which many wrestle today, the outcome of this process should foster an increased capacity to resist interpretations and actions motivated by the kinds of ignorance, prejudice, and parochialism that have resulted in and continue to lead to various forms of unfreedom in the world. I say all of this knowing very well that human beings are often drawn into promoting and defending issues and causes about which they have little or no understanding. Given the challenges associated with defining freedom, there is a significant risk of this happening with this highly prized ideal. Thus, efforts like mine in this project are highly necessary as we "flesh out" the meaning of freedom and establish the conditions for its appropriate flourishing in diverse settings.

I agree with Paul Tillich's suggestion that the "situation" in which the theologian operates in each epoch is characterized by the scientific, artistic, political, and ethical forms that contribute to humanity's self-interpretation and the interpretation of existence in a special period.[7] Clearly not every possible form of self-interpretation and interpretation of existence will be immediately relevant to each theological project, but the theologian must be ready to utilize those forms that contribute to the coherence, relevance, credibility, and moral plausibility of their endeavor at a particular period. This being so, I utilize representative works from various disciplines in the discussions contained in this project. This is immediately evident in the very first chapter as I place in critical and creative conversation ideas and concepts from thinkers who represent the disciples of theology, sociology, political theory, economics, and philosophy. In this process I identify challenges associated with fashioning a clear definition of freedom even as I lay out important elements necessary for grasping freedom in its natural and ontological dimensions, along with the associated categories personal/individual, social/civic, and sovereignal freedom. Theologian Robert Neville and sociologist Orlando Patterson are primary sources in this endeavor. I also introduce Isaiah Berlin's distinction between negative and positive freedom and the modifications of Amartya Sen that will be crucial to the discussions of chapter 7.

In this project I promote freedom that is finite, realistically libertarian, and relational. This combination of features reflects my critical synthesis of ideas from the thinkers just mentioned, along with Clark Pinnock, Paul Tillich, and others. It also reflects influence from Process-Relational thought. The approach I promote highlights the fact that to be a self is to be unavoidably linked to a world of "others" that influences the context and processes associated with considerations and pursuits of freedom. As used in theological circles libertarian freedom in its most basic sense represents the viewpoint that in decision-making situations, human beings are able to choose one state of affairs or its opposite, and antecedent causal factors will not constitute the sufficient cause for the choices, that is, one will make a choice for reasons that are primarily one's own. My qualifier "realistic" is informed by the recognition that the traditional understanding of the term libertarian presumes a level of independence for decision-makers that does not actually exist. Human beings are psychosomatic wholes who can never avoid influence from other co-inhabitants of an interconnected world and also from God who has ideal aims for each individual in relation to ideal aims for all other individuals and the world as a whole. Therefore, I promote as ideal a situation in which people are able, in the midst of varying causal influences, to exercise sufficient autonomy to be able to make meaningful choices from among viable options. The choices they make will be for reasons that are primarily their own and for which they can accept responsibility.

This project includes critical engagement with the Old and New Testaments and some of the most important figures in the history of Christian thought. My examination of the Scriptures presumes the findings of critical scholarship and this enables me to acknowledge ways in which the historical epochs and cultural settings in which biblical narratives were developed contributed to ambiguities in the treatment of human freedom. In the process of my examination of the Scriptures I substantiate my position that those who utilize them and employ biblical language in contemporary pursuits of freedom cannot afford to overlook the fact that they were developed in epochs generally characterized by acceptance of expressions of unfreedom that included slavery and other forms of oppressive hierarchicalism. My multilayered engagement with theologians highlights the ways contemporary Christian understandings of freedom have been influenced by positions on freewill and on God's character developed by thinkers such as Augustine of Hippo, Martin Luther, and John Calvin. A persistent theme that runs through my evaluation of these theological giants is that human freedom has been compromised in order to protect a concept of God patterned from ancient kings, emperors, and lords who fit the characterization tyrant.

With this position in mind, my examination of free-will raises questions about God that influence discussions over the rest of the project. Is it necessary to belittle humanity in order to elevate divinity? Does appreciation for the significance of God's grace require that any confidence in self by human beings be eradicated? Does a meaningful doctrine of grace require that human beings be stripped of any sense of native worth, even if that worth and ability is claimed to be given by God in the first place? Does the character of God and God's relation to the world portrayed by Christian orthodoxy correspond with the best contemporary understandings of the most effective and humane kinds of governance and the most appropriate uses of power? My approach to answering these questions is in chapters 2 and 3 signaled by the sympathy I show for the heterodox thinkers Pelagius and Desiderius Erasmus as they articulated positions that ran counter to those of Augustine and Luther, respectively.

An important conviction informing my address of all these thinkers is that, contrary to the dominant leaning in the history of Christian thought, human beings are not crippled in their capacity to exercise the will to make choices for good and for God. This position is grounded in rejection of the idea of an original fall by Adam and Eve resulting in corrupted wills in all human beings. Without doubt, human beings are limited by finitude, influenced by the drives of self-protection and self-aggrandizement, and often deliberately resist that which is sensed to be God's will. Yet, as members of a young species, we are learning what it means to be human and are capable of growing in our capacity to exercise free-will for ends that contribute to wholesome global existence. Without doubt, human life, transacted in the midst of ambiguity, includes many missteps. Yet it is not itself a deformity, even though it is defined by limitations. My guarded optimism is consistent with what some call "the enlightenment spirit" insofar as it challenges people to push beyond established "wisdom" and the accompanying fears and anxieties that are stoked by the gate keepers of orthodoxy to keep Christians in their place.[8]

While I enthusiastically embrace the enlightenment spirit for the sake of discovering new things about what it means to be human, it does not mean that I believe that individuals can by the courageous exercise of reason live without some guidance from others. It means, instead, that I take Catholic paleontologist-priest Pierre Teilhard de Chardin seriously when, borrowing an expression from Julian Huxley, he claims that the human species represents evolution conscious of itself.[9] This being so, there is a trajectory in the development of global life as a whole that depends on our willingness to embrace the quest for freedom I encourage, to view it as grounded in the very nature of existence, and in its pursuit seek to realize new ways of being human. It is in light of this fundamental conviction that I challenge the reader to resist teachings and other features of life that undermine the practice of freedom that is finite, realistically libertarian, and relational and take the kind of decisions that contribute to creative transformation within human communities, for the sake of wholesome global existence.

This challenge presupposes the position that if there is to be any pattern, in which the character of human beings who actually inhabit the earth is to be assessed, it should be associated with the consideration of what it means to be born of men and women who, rather than being brought into existence by direct supernatural means, are members of a species that emerged from a complex cosmic process and are still discovering what we are and can be.

An important feature of the process by which I walk away from conventional Christian theology, anthropology, and soteriology is a critical examination of ideas of three celebrated free-will theists. There is Jacob Arminius who reacted to central ideas in the Calvinist theological system, Scottish-American Restorationist Alexander Campbell, and recently deceased Clark Pinnock, who sought to radicalize the Arminian view that the claim that God has exhaustive and infallible knowledge of things necessary, possible, and actual could be reconciled with the claim that human beings have free-will. I show that these free-will theists do not escape the ensnarement of traditional conceptions of God that were designed to protect God's sovereign freedom, even if they threatened claims about human responsibility and were ethically unsustainable when assessed by reasonable human standards. I also show that when Christian thinkers, like Arminius, utilize Scholastic wisdom to establish God as simple, eternal, and having no potential, they undermine their own claims that God is a personal being who participates in the dynamics of global life and has intimate knowledge of human affairs.

The theological high point of the project is reached in a proposal for God-talk that takes seriously the biblical descriptions of God as a personal being—this being a fundamental presupposition of the devotional life of most Christians. While I show appreciation for the process of argument by which Augustine concluded that our measurements and categorizations of time are primarily mental constructs, I reject his understanding of eternity as a state of infinite timelessness or a "stationary now" from which God sees all time as one. Augustine's conception is linked directly with the idea of God as omni-qualitied and sovereignly free. I embrace Schubert Ogden's critique of the strange and confused use of analogy in the development of God-talk by traditional theologians and align myself with Ogden's theological proposals that employ ideas from Martin Heidegger. In this scheme the distinction between God's life and human life is captured not by a distinction between time and eternity but by a distinction between finite temporality and infinite temporality. The privileging of contingency opens the door for the introduction of the di-polar, internally related God of Process-Relational theology that influences and is influenced by the processes that are characteristic of human freedom. Bringing together descriptions from three sources, this is the infinitely temporal and imaginatively creative God that is the self surpassing surpasser of all.

My ability to propose a conception of God such as the one I have presupposes a disposition similar to Schubert Ogden's that human beings are never interminably bound to the "God" to whom we are loyal at any particular period of our life's journey. There are times when faith has to do with freedom from the "God" we have hitherto believed in, for the sake of viable humanness. This position is linked to the recognition that our conceptions of God are always, at least, in part, human constructions. I also operate with the conviction that the denial of freedom, which has characterized life in many parts of the world, has been perpetrated not simply because the oppressors misused theological concepts, especially the grounding concept of God, but because many traditional theological concepts, including that of "God," lend themselves to oppressive use. This being so, my approach to the proposal of a concept of God is an attempt to ensure that the existential meaning of faith in God that is promoted in the name of freedom correlates with appropriate metaphysical thinking.[10] This endeavor should contribute to an understanding of the life of faith that involves authentic choice-making, just accountability, and the healthy affirmation of the goodness of each human being as human, in the context of participation in an interconnected and multidimensional world.

In the closing section of the project I make concrete application of my position on freedom in socio-economic, personal/interpersonal, and ecclesiastical frameworks where people pursue viable existence. I critically identify with the Western liberal tradition and, engaging ideas from Isaiah Berlin, Amartya Sen, Richard Bauckham, Rebecca Todd Peters, and others show that the inclination of many in the West to exercise freedom in individualistic ways will only be countered by the nurturing of a robust doctrine of the common good. My explication of the concept of common good, with special concern for the most vulnerable and oppressed of the world, leads to the proposal of a way that negative and positive freedom as explicated by Berlin and modified by Sen, can work together for their benefit. Behind all these issues is the challenge to enable persons of all kinds who operate in varying circumstances of life to develop increased recognition that they exist in a world that is at root organismic. Therefore, the most viable exercise of individual freedom is pursued with the appreciation that one is always doing so in a community that includes far more than human beings.

It is with the vulnerable and oppressed in mind that I develop my argument for imagination as the last bastion of freedom for the most oppressed. The purposeful exercise of imagination can fuel visions of freedom, plots for freedom, and new expressions of freedom. It is with the support of insights from Process-Relational thought that I move beyond the understandings of imagination proposed by a range of thinkers from Immanuel Kant to Kwok Pui Lan and ground it in the deep-structure of existence, with creativity at its heart. As such, imagination is linked to ontological freedom and is ultimately rooted in the very being of the infinitely temporal and imaginatively creative God that is internally related and all-inclusive. With the help of insights from neuroscientist Ruth Byrne the link between imagination and counterfactual thought is established. And, in dialogue with Emmanuel Levinas, Frantz Fanon, Mayra Rivera, and others, I establish a connection between the dynamics of "recognition," especially "mutual recognition," and imagination in the processes of fashioning wholesome selfhood. I show that embrace of the idea of a God that is available for relationships of mutual recognition is fundamental to the process of re-imagining self, countering the destructive effects of persistent degradation and structuring the kind of personhood that claims the freedom to pursue freedom for self and others.

The explorations of the final chapter, in which ideas from theologians Hans Küng, Jürgen Moltmann, and Letty Russell are very evident, lead to the identification of challenges and possibilities for developing relevant and freedom-enabling ecclesiology in the present era. This ecclesiology includes the formulation of language associated with the concepts of mutuality and partnership to counter the debilitations associated with the language of sovereignty and servitude. The discussion leads to an exploration of the ways an ecclesiology of partnership would influence administrative structures, styles of leadership, and frameworks of relations within and between churches that create opportunities for the practice of partnership as an expression of participatory freedom.

## NOTES

1. Isaiah Berlin, "Two Concepts of Liberty," in *Four Essays on Liberty* (1969; reprint, Oxford: Oxford University Press, 1990), 121.

2. Orlando Patterson, *Freedom in the Making of Western Culture*, vol. I (New York: Basic Books, 1991), 1.

3. Schubert Ogden, *Faith and Freedom: Toward a Theology of Liberation* (1979; reprint, Nashville: Abingdon Press, 1989), 40.

4. Richard Hamm, *20/20 Vision for the Christian Church (Disciples of Christ)* (St. Louis: Chalice Press, 2001), 31. Hamm is former General Minister and President of the Christian Church (Disciples of Christ). He now spends much time training leaders for churches and fostering ecumenical relations.

5. William Watty, *From Shore to Shore: Soundings in Caribbean Theology* (Barbados: Cedar Press, 1981), 6.

6. Kwok Pui Lan, *Postcolonial Imagination and Feminist Theology* (Louisville: Westminster John Knox Press, 2005), 39.

7. Paul Tillich, *Systematic Theology*, vol. I (Chicago: University of Chicago Press, 1951), 4.

8. In the background of this statement is Immanuel Kant's short essay addressing the question "What Is Enlightenment?" This essay is found in Lewis White Beck, trans., *Foundations of Metaphysics of Morals & What Is Enlightenment* (1959; reprint, Indianapolis: The Bobbs-Merrill Company, Inc., 1976), 85–92.

9. Pierre Teilhard de Chardin, *The Phenomenon of Man* (1959; reprint, New York: Harper & Row Publishers, 1975), 221.

10. Ogden, *Faith and Freedom*, 32.

*I*

# Establishing Conceptual Foundations

*Chapter One*

# Freedom as a Concept and Ideal

Over the centuries numerous books of doctrine and practical instruction have focused on the concept of freedom, and a wide range of contemporary theological movements are driven by the promotion of this ideal or its cognate, liberation, on behalf of particular communities seeking to break free from one form of oppression or another.[1] So important is this concept that Orlando Patterson, in his monumental text on freedom, asserts that "no other value or ideal in the West carries such a heavy intellectual burden—one impossible to discard or neglect."[2] In this project I seek to clarify the components and dynamics of this ideal, to help those who pursue or seek to protect freedom focus on the right matters and proceed in an appropriate fashion. This first chapter will explore options for characterizing the structure of human freedom. I will establish a general conceptual foundation by using theologian Robert Neville's distinction between the cosmological and ontological dimensions of freedom, Patterson's triad of personal, sovereignal, and civic freedom, and political theorist Isaiah Berlin's categories of negative and positive freedom as inflected by ideas from economist and philosopher Amartya Sen. This foundation will undergird my engagement of other thinkers in this chapter, with the resulting framework of ideas serving as a guide for the analysis and technical characterizations of freedom pursued in the rest of the project. Patterson's discussion of the emergence of freedom in the socio-cultural dynamics of ancient Greece, in particular the slave system in Athens, contributes a vital element to the fabric of explanation. It opens the way for my claim that human freedom emerged over time from qualities native to human character, and serves as the first layer of historical and sociological explanation that will be carried on throughout the text, by which the relative significance of aspects of the dynamics of freedom will be highlighted.

Through the engagement of ideas from Neville, and other distinguished theologians like Open Theist Clark Pinnock, Thomist David Burrell, Existentialist Paul Tillich, Process-Relational thinker John Cobb, and others, it becomes evident why the priority in this project is the promotion of freedom that is finite, realistically libertarian, and relational. This combination of features reflects my convictions regarding the limitations and possibilities associated with being human in an interconnected world. It is in this context that we exercise the capacity to make choices between options that are significant; that is, antecedent causal constraints will not be so overpowering that one is not able to adopt one of the available options for reasons that are decidedly one's own. This means that as decision-makers human beings have sufficient autonomy to make themselves truly accountable for the choices they make. It should also become clear that and why I consider inner freedom, with the exercise of ontological freedom at its core, to be the grounding for the fullest expression of freedom. Given that ontological freedom has to do with the ability of persons to evaluate the features of life in terms of that which is considered ultimate, its importance for my scheme sets the stage for a struggle that will be front and center throughout the project; that is, the pursuit of an understanding of God compatible with my claim that freedom with the qualities just listed is fundamental to being human.

## EXAMINING THE FOUNDATIONS OF FREEDOM

In a work developed primarily in the interest of Caribbean theology, with "emancipation" as its central theme, Caribbean native and Howard University Professor Kortright Davis grounds his analysis of the features of freedom in convictions about the nature and existence of God. Freedom, he indicates, is not generated by human beings but is grounded in the freedom that is fundamental to the very nature of God who issues the call to freedom. He asserts that "theologically understood, freedom is the gift of God because it is the nature of God." Indeed, freedom is not only the nature of God but also the will of God. He is clear that it is this nature expressed in God's exercise of God's will that is rising up out of and being manifested in Caribbean life. It is the purposeful exercise of freedom by and for the sake of Caribbean peoples and others that is the authentic evidence of divine presence working in and through the historic dynamic of regional life. The capacity to engage in specific acts of freedom is directly related to the capacity to interpret these signs of God's will. Davis lists basic definitions of freedom from Plato, Jean-Jacques Rousseau, and Howard Thurman that correspond with descriptions by his former professor Robert Neville, before moving into a brief discussion of Neville's dimensions of freedom. In the process, Davis highlights the latter's distinction between the personal, social, and religious aspects of freedom that I will say more about later.[3]

As this chapter progresses, it will be seen that as a general idea the connection of human freedom to God is consistent with my position. However, my immediate problem with Davis's treatment of Neville's conceptual structure begins with the recognition that without exploration of the difficulties and/or virtues of that structure, Davis declares that "freedom itself" must transcend categories and dimensions, integrating every aspect of human experience and aspiration and showing itself transparently appropriate to all sorts and conditions of humanity.[4] The notion of "freedom itself" seems to presume that the human mind has some kind of direct and unmodified intuition of essences. But the obvious question is: how exactly does one get hold of "freedom itself" outside of and apart from our struggles in actual situations in which we are challenged to imagine and describe for ourselves and others what the notion of freedom refers to and what it requires of us? Following from this is the related question: how else do we go about this process of discernment and description without identifying and organizing the content of experience and doing so with the use of concepts and categories that best explain the structure and dynamics of freedom? My answer is that there is no way that we can.

## The Cosmological and Ontological Dimensions of Freedom

Neville's distinction between the ontological and cosmological dimensions of freedom seems more helpful for exploring freedom as a concept. The cosmological dimensions of freedom are personal and social freedom, and together they constitute the natural freedom of humankind. Here "natural" refers to "those dimensions of freedom that people have from the simple structures of human society and personality, including those that ordinarily ought to develop in the course of maturation and those that are ideal for moral society."[5] Ontological freedom, which seems to be what Davis labels religious freedom, has to do with how persons "employ all the elements of natural freedom to relate to God as creator, to the world as created, and to themselves as creatures."[6] Stated in more inclusive terms, it is the process by which human beings employ all the elements of natural freedom to develop an understanding of the relationship between self, world, and that which is understood to be ultimate. It would be by means of such a process that one would move from analysis of historical and ongoing endeavors classified as the quest for or the experience of freedom and make claims about "freedom itself," as Davis does.

Neville displays some kinship with Davis in his claim that the utilization of cosmological elements for ontological purposes is a free expression of persons created to be free.[7] Yet he does not, like Davis, risk giving the impression that there is a pure *a priori* form of freedom that human beings are seeking to apprehend. If this were so, his position could only be embraced as an unmitigated contradiction to Orlando Patterson's view, influenced by his explorations in historical sociology, that "valuing freedom is not a part of the human condition, not something we are born with."[8] As it stands, I embrace Neville's claim that human beings were created to be free. This I do in light of my general position that as a species human beings emerged with a disposition toward being centered selves; that is, persons who are able to claim their unique "I-ness" for the sake of meaningful I-Thou relations, and whose growth into authentic selfhood includes the pursuit of self-expression, self-direction, and self-actualization by ways that involve deliberation and decision making. These capacities have engendered yearnings that, given the appropriate constellation of circumstances, resulted in pursuits that would be classified under the concept "freedom."

Given this viewpoint I can accept that there are markers now seen as evidence of freedom that would not have emerged until the necessary constellation of conditions were in place. For Patterson this constellation began with the emergence of a unique form of slavery in Athens, which was associated with other social and economic changes that commenced in the sixth century BCE, and which came to a high point in the late fifth century BCE.[9] Embracing this position as an important element of the story of freedom, I suggest that the evidence of freedom important to Patterson, about which I will elaborate, did cause the basic traits of human character identified above to be manifested in ways that proved decisive for the trajectory of human self-understanding, self-expression, and self-actualization. I am, therefore, able to claim with a wide range of both religious and non-religious people that freedom, which is the concept used to represent yearnings and actions most identified with the new human trajectory, is rooted in the very core of the human self. It is when the features seen as expressive of the cosmological dimensions are, through the dynamics of the ontological dimension, associated with the theological presupposition that God is creator of the world that freedom comes to be seen as derived from God and thus preexisting and transcending all human pursuits of freedom in the world.

My sense is that Davis's desire for Caribbean peoples, with their history of colonialism and slavery, to experience freedom to its fullest extent is so strong that he wishes to avoid approaches to the analysis of freedom that could make them vulnerable to powerful groups that wish to control what the contemporary experience of freedom in the Caribbean should be. Indeed, there are a number of ways in which Neville, being a white American male, could be identified with dominant powers and so be suspect as he explicates freedom in terms of dimensions. Davis's suspicion of Neville's position seems to be implied in his comments about the "priorities of freedom" that he privileges. He suggests that "who determines those priorities, and who presides over their configuration, is the question that lies at the root of human conflict and social discomfort. It is also the question that germinates seeds of revolution and social change."[10] Here Davis does reflect concerns close to that of many whose ancestors were told that acceptance of their lot as slaves was a kind of freedom, especially if they renounced their native cultures and committed themselves to the religion of their masters. On the other side of the same proverbial coin was the self-understanding of slave masters and their associates that they had been given freedom by God to invade, pillage, confiscate, exploit, and enslave in the pursuit of purposes seen as noble simply because they were their purposes. It is quite understandable then, how the brutal history of colonialism and slavery in the Caribbean could lead to skepticism when thinkers from dominant groups attempt to make proposals regarding the way freedom should be analyzed and pursued.

It is my position that, although Davis's intentions are laudable, the path he has taken will limit his ability to contribute to a realistic approach to freedom in his context or elsewhere. My evaluation is based on the recognition that there is nothing in the constitution of the world of which human beings are a part, with its physical structures, biological processes, cognitive, social, and religious dynamics, that enable any legitimate analysis of freedom to overstep the complex dimensions that characterize our life processes and pursuit of freedom. This will be the case for communal and individual existence of all kinds, at every stage of human development, and in every moment in which priorities of freedom are considered. It is therefore quite faulty for Davis to say in an either-or manner that "there are, therefore, priorities for freedom rather than dimensions or categories of freedom."[11]

For those who are religious, and especially for Christians in this instance, there is no avoiding the fact that, regardless of how we come to understand freedom as a concept and ideal, and whatever might be the theological conceptions developed in regard to it, they will, at least in part, be inferences developed from the operations of life experienced and interpreted by human beings in the midst of our struggle for meaning. Apart from this recognition, the notion "freedom as such" is but a vacuous abstraction. With this viewpoint I now explore Neville's dimensions in relation to other thinkers and show that as constructs to frame our thinking about freedom, they serve a very necessary purpose.

First I elaborate on the cosmological dimensions: personal freedom and social freedom. Regarding personal freedom, it is comprised of at least four elements: intentional action, free choice, the capacity to choose on the basis of standards, and external freedom. Neville refers to external freedom as the negative freedom of "not being bound, not being in jail, not being coerced." External elements of freedom "are all relative to what people would want to do and would be capable of doing if there were no external constraint."[12] This understanding of external freedom points directly to social freedom that involves freedom of opportunity to express personal freedom. A socially free setting will be pluralistic; that is, there will be an ongoing struggle to balance "a complicated dialectic of ways of life" or social styles. In such a setting an important means of supporting this plurality is in provisions that enable people to be integrated in their ways of life, informed by an appropriate framework of values. The three elements just mentioned engender a fourth, political freedom, "in which people have the opportunity to influence the conditions under which decisions are made that affect their way of life."[13]

Isaiah Berlin deepens our consideration of these matters with his explication of the concepts of negative freedom and positive freedom in the celebrated essay "Two Concepts of Freedom." Addressing the first, Berlin suggests that "I am normally said to be free to the degree to which no man or body of men interferes with my activity," and he defines political liberty as, in its simplest form, "the area within which a man can do what he wants."[14] If one is prevented by other people from doing what one wants, one is to that degree unfree; and if the framework in which one can operate as she wishes is constricted by others beyond a certain minimum, one can be described as being coerced, or even enslaved. Coercion then involves the deliberate interference of others within the area in which a person wishes to do what she wants, preventing her from attaining her goal.[15] Berlin understands positive freedom to be rooted in the wish of the individual to be their own master, and it is linked to the wish that one's life and decisions be dependent on one's self and not on external forces. It is one's own reason and conscious purposes, among other factors, that will guide one's actions.[16]

Patterson is of the view that any attempt to distinguish between the positive and negative aspects of freedom will not hold up to philosophical scrutiny. He approvingly quotes Bertrand Russell who, he says, clearly saw that "the absence of obstacles to the realization of desires implies, in both logical and practical sociological terms, the attainment of a condition for the satisfaction of our impulses."[17] However, with the recognition that the hindrances to which Berlin referred were external ones, I assert that there is nothing obvious in the notion of "the absence of constraint" that necessarily creates the sufficient condition for the realization of impulses. Neville points us to a concrete consideration that supports my hesitance in following the line of reasoning with which Patterson identifies. As far as Neville is concerned the view that one is free if nothing prevents them from doing what they want represents the simplest understanding of freedom, which on its own, is a naïve view. A person may be "enslaved to narrow ideology or inhibited by deadening psychological pressures." That person "may have a weak image of himself as an agent. He may be ignorant of real opportunities, undeveloped in his taste, alienated from social identifications, or prevented from integrating his separate choices into a coherent personal style."[18] So although not impeded from doing what she/he wants, a person can still be in bondage in all the senses mentioned.

Later in this project I will examine Berlin's complexification of this consideration with his expounding of a scenario that shows how the promotion of positive freedom can have disastrous social, political, and personal implications. Stated in a simplified way for now, whereas negative freedom points to the clearing away of obstacles so that the pursuit of various expressions of freedom will not be hindered, the notion of positive freedom involves the pursuit of a particular prescribed form of life understood to model a particular understanding of freedom. This pursuit is usually associated with a conception of the ideal self that is capable of realizing the prescribed form of life seen as consistent with the status "free." It is important to note that Berlin's use of the categories "negative" and "positive" seems to presume a circumstance in which, along with the nonexistence or minimal presence of the personal "impediments" listed by Neville, there is not just the absence of hindrances to action but the availability of facilities and opportunities that gives one a reasonable chance of accomplishing what one wills. Being sensitive to the circumstance of a large number of the world's population who operate in settings characterized by abject poverty and/or significant oppression, I assert that if these populations privileged only negative freedom, their unencumbered space of personal freedom could be a veritable prison. As such, and not withstanding my identification with Berlin's concerns, I am sympathetic to the more moderate view of positive freedom identified by Amartya Sen, who sees it "in terms of what one is free to do taking everything into account, including interference or help from others, as well as one's own powers and limitations."[19]

## A SOCIOLOGICAL ACCOUNT OF THE EMERGENCE OF FREEDOM

I continue to construct a picture of the character of freedom with an elaboration of Patterson's examination of this concept and ideal from the perspective of historical sociology. Patterson suggests that behind the term's numerous shades of meaning are three ideas of freedom, closely related historically, sociologically, and conceptually. These he lists as personal, civic, and sovereignal freedoms. He pictures these ideas of freedom in terms of the musical metaphor of a chordal triad (a chord with three elemental notes).[20] With this image of a chord we are guided to perceive the three ideas together as a kind of dialectical unity, a harmonious whole having its own unique value. At the same time, within the context of a chord, one is able to emphasize one or another element of expression at a particular time for easier observation and clarity of analysis. While taking the idea of gestalt very seriously, one gets the strong impression when reading Patterson's work that personal freedom has very high premium in his conceptual scheme, as is also the case for Neville and Berlin. Indeed, civic freedom, which is "the capacity of adult members of a community to participate in its life and governance,"[21] is inextricably linked to personal freedom.

Patterson provides elaborate detail to support his position that the process toward the notion of freedom as understood in the West germinated in the desperate yearning of slaves in sixth- and fifth-century (BCE) Greece to negate their inhumane condition. It is within this framework that "the unusual idea developed that being free was not only a value to be cherished but the most important thing that someone could possess."[22] This claim is not a compliment to Greek civilization. While slavery had been everywhere in the ancient world and the yearnings associated with the native human drive for self-expression, self-direction, and self-actualization would have been present in some form wherever slavery existed, it took the extent and intensity of slavery in Greece to bring together the commitment of both a critical mass of the general population and a powerful minority to cause freedom to emerge as a generally prized value.

An important feature of Patterson's discussion is his view that freedom began its journey in the Western consciousness as a woman's value. It is women, he says, "who first lived in terror of enslavement, hence it was women who first came to value its absence. . . ." This was the case for those "who were never captured but lived in dread of it and, even more, for those who were captured and lived in hope of being redeemed or, at the very least, released from their social death by being given the opportunity to operate as free among their captors. . . ."[23] Ironically it was exactly this vulnerability that enabled women to harbor a reasonable hope for freedom. "Not expected to be able to defend themselves, they suffered no irreparable loss of honor in their submission." In fact, there was even "the possibility of the restoration of their status as legitimate members of their master's community or of their own former community." On the other hand, "once a man suffered [the social death of the forced illegitimacy of enslavement] he might as well be physically dead, since there was no prospect of them regaining their honor."[24]

Patterson is of the mind that the aspirations of the female slave would have corresponded with the interests of upper class female citizens. While these upper class women managed the major part of their husband's property, "his household," their lives were restricted to this private sphere, while their husbands were mostly absent from that sphere. In this restricted framework of operation, slaves would be the main adult company for citizen women, and together they had opportunity to influence children in the absence of their fathers. With this as background, I think it is quite noteworthy that in all Greek drama, both tragic and comic, "women stand powerfully and exclusively, for personal independence, for the voice of individual conscience against personal and political tyranny, for universal and natural, as distinct from man-made, justice, and for the freedom to worship their gods and love whom they choose to love."[25] With the recognition that men constituted the audience for Greek drama, this observation suggests that, while these men were generally contemptuous of women,[26] the values and commitments of women would have been influencing the sensibilities of some of them and would be helping to lay the foundation for more explicit adventures in freedom.

The obstacles that served as hindrances to freedom becoming a generally prized value were significant. Indeed, at the obvious levels of assessment, the realm of the household with which women were most associated was not one from which anything pertaining to freedom was expected to emerge—owning a house and other property was important primarily as a prerequisite for men to participate in the affairs of the world. Hannah Arendt furthers our understanding of this issue. She indicates that "the distinctive trait of the household sphere was that in it [human beings] lived together because they were driven by their wants and needs."[27] As such, the activities performed in it were ruled by necessity. On the contrary, the realm of the *polis* was the sphere of freedom. Further, the exercise of force and violence by which one very likely came to own slaves was seen as the justifiable means for one to escape the necessity associated with the private sphere and to become involved in the public sphere. As Arendt put it, "Violence is the prepolitical act of liberating oneself from the necessity of life for the freedom of the world."[28] It was primarily aristocrats and plutocrats who enjoyed this "freedom of the world." As governors of the state (one form of sovereignal freedom) they protected and enhanced the *status quo* as they exercised the self-appointed responsibility to make laws that protected right order; that is, ensuring that persons did what was appropriate to their station, thus contributing to the good of the state.[29]

Patterson's discussion of how civic freedom and sovereignal freedom developed in Athens is for me a reminder of the immense challenges involved in ensuring that freedom is experienced by the most vulnerable in as full a way as possible, rather than having them live with constructions of freedom that primarily serve the interests of the powerful. The picture he paints of life in mid sixth century to later fifth century (BCE) Athens is in some ways quite similar to the contemporary Western scenario. There was growing discontent among non-aristocratic citizens as members of the middle and lower classes pressed for the expansion of the gains won through Solon's reforms.[30] The elites grew increasingly wealthy with the benefits of slave labor as the small farmer was reduced to the status of "self-sufficient, subsistence producer." The latter, therefore, struggled for greater economic equality that, among other things, would include the redistribution of land. The small farmers also had difficulty with the new middle class involved in non-traditional occupations with which *metics* (resident aliens who were not slaves) and freed slaves were associated. This only compounded the anxiety caused by the rapid increase in the number of foreign slaves in their midst.[31]

The reaction of the elite was to pursue programs aimed at drawing disquieted persons into solidarity with them by highlighting the significance of their citizenship over against being slaves. The emergence of civic freedom was nurtured through the provisions made for greater involvement of non-elite citizens in the distribution of justice and the adjustment of the political structure to enable a wider cross-section of persons to be eligible for election as representatives to the Assembly. These efforts were supported by religious reforms that included modifications to the cult of Athena to make more prominent elements that emphasized the common religious foundation of all citizens. It must be noted that, given their design, the regulations governing political service excluded urban free persons of modest means from the political directorate and ensured that most rural persons would be limited in their ability to participate. So, while the development of civic freedom is lauded by many as the early form of democracy, members of the wealthy class ensured they maintained control of executive power, though the executive ruled in cooperation with a popularly elected advisory body called the *boule*. Of even greater significance for me is the fact that citizen women, like slaves and *metics*, were not eligible to exercise civic freedom, as limited as it was.[32]

It seems that the Peloponnesian war (431-404 BCE) was a decisive factor in intensifying the circumstances in Greece that contributed to the development of freedom so that it would become a pervasive social value for which many have struggled and given their lives, and which is a central concept in Christian spirituality. Prior to the outbreak of war, manumission, which has to do with the ability of slaves to buy themselves out of slavery, had been used as incentive for slaves to work hard, especially for those in skilled and demanding occupations. One such industry, craft manufacturing located in Athens, had flourished significantly during the period of economic growth before the war. With war devastating farms, there was even greater dependence on this sector of the economy, thus increasing the need for labor. Given the downturn in their economic situation traditional farm owning masters were more willing to release slaves to find employment elsewhere. This scenario caused the status of manumission to improve significantly.[33] It was during the second phase of the war that Pericles and Sophocles first discussed freedom in terms of a "chordal triad" (personal, civic, and sovereignal freedoms). Patterson says that "for the first time in history, we find not only an unequivocal use of the word freedom in terms entirely comprehensible to a modern person but also its application to the three basic components of the value."[34]

Quotations provided by Patterson from sources like the funeral oration of Pericles are indeed impressive in their celebration of freedom in association with democracy. We hear that all are equal before the law and should enjoy equality of opportunity, and we hear about the freedom of all to enjoy themselves in their own way. We also hear that each person is "lord and owner of his own person."[35] These ideas would have both reflected and contributed to the aspirations for personal freedom harbored by members of the growing class of freed slaves and women. At the same time, there was clearly anxiety over the expressions of freedom and the extent of freedom that different kinds of persons should enjoy. There is also evidence of consternation over how these matters should be determined and who should make the determination. The enlightened Sophocles, while he extolled the virtues of personal, civic, and sovereignal freedoms as a harmonious unit, still revealed his deeply held suspicion of personal and civic freedoms in his claim that, while the freedoms of the people were to be respected, they needed to be held in check.[36] One effect of such an ethos is highlighted by Nicole Loraux's suggestion that the central paradox of political thought in classical Athens was the absence of a democratic way of speaking about democracy. This being so, Pericles' funeral oration was no more than "'an aristocratic eulogy' and discourse on democracy."[37] What was being lauded was certainly not the kind of freedom of participation that Neville perceives as necessary for viable public expressions of personal freedom, without which there is hardly any guarantee that the features that make social freedom viable would be in place.

Without doubt, it is an enormous task to fashion a socially free setting that, being pluralistic, demands what Neville referred to as an ongoing struggle to balance "a complicated dialectic of ways of life."[38] The temptation is strong, even among sensitive souls who care deeply about others, to adopt approaches similar to Plato's notion of "organic freedom." Described by Patterson as "the ultimate Greek refinement of sovereignal freedom,"[39] organic freedom refers to a situation in which people are expected to contribute to "harmonious society" by living their lives in subjection to their superiors. This disposition, in which the external practice of subjection in the name of freedom would be informed by ideological commitment to the state with its established structures, reflects Plato's disdain for democracy. For Plato democracy is actually "the second-to-worst form of imperfect society, ranking only above despotism in the scale of political degeneracy."[40] In the course of discussing the deficiencies of the democratic character, Plato condemns civic freedom "as the main objective of the democratic state . . ." and personal freedom "as the prevailing quality of the typical citizen of such a state." His concern is that this kind of society tends toward "Mob rule, demagoguery, and . . . anarchy," and that personal freedom has a "tendency to become personal license and selfishness." So the democratic person is "one who has 'no order and restraint in his life' and who 'reckons his way of living . . . pleasant, free and happy.'"[41] The way to avoid such a situation is to have a society in which one, supported by a few, governs, and persons accept their given place in the scheme of things. [42]

Coming from Jamaica, with rabid classism and shadeism that reflects the legacy of the country's colonial history, and where the vulgar divide between rich and poor often lead to eruptions of social discontent, I have heard a number of people express sentiments similar to Plato's. Still I encourage resistance to such a temptation for three reasons. First, I am of the view that in contexts where such a scheme is promoted it is usually intended to dignify oppression and lure the unfree into alliance with those whose selfish interests are served by their acceptance of subjugation. Second, it can never be good for a community to be completely reliant on one or a few persons whose ideas and actions will always reflect their limitations, weaknesses, and prejudices, and who are convinced that the fortunes of a diverse community of complex persons rests primarily on their efforts. The latter is the recipe for anxiety-driven extremism. Finally, rebellion of one sort or another is guaranteed if I am correct that an important feature of human nature is the drive for self-expression and self-direction.

As we assess the extent of personal and social freedom enjoyed by Athenians and consider what the character of these freedoms should be in our time, it is important to delve more deeply into Neville's view that freedom involves the ability of persons to influence the conditions under which decisions are made that affect their way of life. In his discussion of the public obligation to provide social and cultural opportunities for the exercise of personal freedom, three striking opportunities are identified. These are "freedom to participate in culture, freedom to participate in organized society, and freedom to participate in historically significant affairs." For all three, "opportunity requires: (1) access to institutions and means of communication (2) the education to be able to take advantage of the access and (3) proximity to the crucial nodes of culture, social organization, and historically significant events." Neville is of the view that "in a society lacking freedom of opportunity, the personal freedom of individuals is greatly frustrated in significance."[43] Conversely the more expressions of this freedom there are the better able persons will be to exercise personal freedom in ways that justify the claim that the capacity for free choice is an important feature of the human nature.

With the challenge of these obligations echoing in my mind, I close this section by returning briefly to Patterson's view that as it emerged among slaves the notion that being free was not only a value to be cherished but the most important thing that someone could possess was a "strange" one. I suggest that Patterson is only able to call this emergence "strange" because, he does not, like I do, consider that which emerged in fifth- and sixth-century (BCE) Greece to be a manifestation of characteristics native to the human being that were brought to the fore by the presence of an appropriate constellation of circumstances. Further, while he identifies religious elements associated with this phenomenon, he, unlike Neville, has not included in his assessment considerations associated with the ontological dimension of freedom. I remind the reader that for Neville, ontological freedom is how people created to be free "employ all the elements of natural freedom to relate to God as creator, to the world as created, and to themselves as creatures."[44] As a theologian myself, I view ontological freedom as a necessary element of any comprehensive consideration of freedom, and so it will be brought into play quite regularly throughout this project. At the same time, I take very seriously Patterson's reminder that whatever might be the other frameworks in which the notion of freedom is analyzed, it must be recognized that freedom has never been divorced from "its primordial servile source."[45] In this light, it must be acknowledged that there is another reminder of this servile source that is prior to and much more striking for many than the Greek example; that is, the biblical account of Israel's slavery in Egypt and their escape (exodus) from that situation. I will argue in chapter 4 that it is a deficiency in Patterson's analysis that this exodus does not figure more in his discussion of Paul's theology of freedom. At the same time I agree with him that the Greek scenario is more relevant for our understanding of personal freedom as it has developed in the West.

## FREEDOM THAT IS FINITE, REALISTICALLY LIBERTARIAN, AND RELATIONAL

The idea of "free choice" is fundamental to freedom as I promote it in this text. In this matter, Clark Pinnock is quite consistent with Neville's leaning when he indicates that the capacity for free choice is one of the noblest of all characteristics with which God endowed the human being.[46] As I embrace it, free choice does not refer to a situation in which a person exercises their will in total independence from other internal or external factors, and my position is associated with the recognition that there is nothing about human life that corresponds to a simple binary distinction between autonomy and heteronomy. Free-will is present where "antecedent causal conditions allow for more than one possible outcome" from a decision-making process. These "antecedent conditions do not have a deterministic causal control over the process of human choice and action . . . although they present the causal materials that the person mixes in decisive ways."[47] Referring to freedom as a perennial commonsense notion that is difficult to deny in practice, Pinnock suggests that "it is the glory of humanity that we act freely and not of necessity. God sovereignly created responsible free beings and wants them to be creative."[48] While he resists any notion of human autonomy, Pinnock is quite enthusiastic in defending significant human agency. He suggests that there is a destiny that is given to us from the past with which we work in the present, but "we bend and reshape it to our particular ends. Destiny only becomes fate when its weight overcomes freedom." Indeed, "we all actualize our own being in the present out of a destiny that comes to us from the past, combined with the possibilities that confront us from the future, as God challenges us to go forward."[49] That which has been described Pinnock classifies as libertarian or contra-causal freedom, and he embraces this approach to freedom in opposition to compatibilist or deterministic freedom in which "God or destiny could be in complete control" of what one wants to do and one could still be said to be free.[50] The qualified notion "realistically libertarian" that I propose is linked directly to the statement just made about free-will. It reflects my attempt to separate from those who make assessments about human freedom presupposing an outmoded anthropology; that is, human beings possess a will that is capable of making determinations with regard to one thing or its opposite in independence from other aspects of the human self and from other any other influence external to the soul. On the other hand, it also reflects my opposition to those who would suggest that libertarian freedom is incompatible with the idea that human beings are creatures of God and that God is a causal agent in human decision-making processes.

We get some sense of the grounding for the first aspect of this outmoded anthropology when, in his *Confessions*, Augustine identifies the self with the soul in distinction from the body. He is, therefore, able to declare: "I, the soul, who am one alone, exercise all these different functions by means of the senses."[51] In this anthropology, the body is properly the servant of the soul to carry out its determinations, and there are operations of the soul that can be carried out with no participation by the body. It is this autonomy of the soul in relation to the body that enables Augustine to claim that with God's guidance he entered into the depth of his soul for direct vision of the Light that never changes, and which reveals truth and eternity.[52] In *City of God*, he does acknowledge that the body and soul together make up a single human whole, but he also asserts that the soul is created by God to be the spiritual-active principle and the body material-passive.[53] Will is the supreme function of the soul.

Twelve centuries later this basic idea was strengthened by René Descartes in a way that would make it very influential in much of the modern era. Descartes is popularly known for his radical ontological dualism whereby the soul, as the unextended thinking substance and the seat of the will, is discrete from the body as extended nonthinking substance.[54] Reflecting on his own experience, Descartes acknowledges that in the exercise of will in judgments he often makes mistakes, and yet without qualification he indicates that as a faculty the will itself is limited by no boundaries. This is because the will, taken precisely as such, is a matter of a person being able to make choices and take decisions, that is, in "being able to do or not do something, that is, being able to affirm or deny, to pursue or to shun." The capacity of the intellect does seem impressive when we hear that the employment of methodological doubt enables one to grasp that there is in one option or another "an aspect of the good and the true" or that "God has disposed the inner recesses of one's thought" in one direction or another, establishing correspondence between clear and distinct ideas and the absolute idea of God's perfect will.[55] Nevertheless, when something is proposed to us by our intellect we are moved to decision-making in such a way that we sense that no external force could have imposed it on us.[56]

David Burrell is quite opposed to positions like Descartes' regarding the character of the will, and he rejects the definition of libertarian freedom that is informed by it. Given his analysis of considerations by Medieval Catholic scholars Duns Scotus and Luis de Molina, Burrell portrays libertarian freedom as implying "a radical 'indifference' before a set of options, so that it is always possible to do otherwise," and the decision one way or another is "a spontaneous act of self-movement";[57] that is, an expression of libertarian freedom is not determined by anything outside of itself. This position, he claims, is incongruous with the understanding of human beings as God's creatures.

Burrell hastens to point out that compatibilist freedom is not the only alternative to libertarian freedom, and he proposes as a third option "'situated freedom.'"[58] This third option presupposes the Thomist position that with human existence being an act (of creation) our specific manner of existing is the source of a distinct power or capacity with a correlative *telos* or perfection. This *telos*, which determines the orientation of human nature, serves as the terminating point for the process of choosing means in relation to ends that characterizes human life. In other words, human existence points toward an end that does not itself serve as means to a more comprehensive goal. Discernment of this end begins with the recognition that in the endeavors of our lives we seek what we consider good for us. This inclination is seen as presupposing an intrinsic intuition of goodness that reflects the character of the creator as the ground of goodness, that is, "the good." In the final analysis then, human beings cannot do anything about our primordial orientation to "the good," and our *terminus ad quem* is God. With one's ultimate goal inscribed in one's nature, freedom cannot be about choice understood as "self-determination of what otherwise remains undetermined," but of consenting to the end that is our proper good. Freedom contains an orientation and a capacity for growth, and consenting freely to the God-given orientation brings one to a greater measure of freedom, whereas refusing it leads one toward enslavement by lesser goods.[59]

My response to this complex of challenges begins with acceptance of recent discoveries in neurobiology that are reflected in Antonio Damasio's declaration that the apparatus of rationality does not seem to work without that of biological regulation. "Nature appears to have built the apparatus of rationality not just on top of the apparatus of biological regulation, but also from it and with it."[60] I appropriate this neuroanatomical insight in terms of explanations provided by Process-Relational thought.[61] It is the latter that informed the claim in my previous full-length work that the human being, which emerged as a result of a multifaceted evolutionary process, is a serially ordered society of occasions of experience that has achieved a level of mentality and subjectivity that enables it to contribute to its own ongoing evolution in intentional ways. Central to this capacity is a level of species development whereby, from the ordered intertwining of societies of occasions with varied defining characteristics, a dominant member has emerged which we call psyche/soul/mind. John Cobb puts it well when he indicates that the accumulation of "surplus psychic energy" in the process of species development separated human beings from other animals and fostered in them a range of mental capacities, including the propensity for the aesthetic and religious life.[62] I now add that among the range of mental capacities are decision-making processes traditionally associated with the will and also indicate that, while the dominant member we call brain/mind is characterized by a high degree of mentality, subjectivity, and autonomy, and exercises downward causation, its existence and operation in intellection and volition is still conditioned by its link to the rich and multifaceted life of the complex system that is the whole person with all its processes and experiences.

So then, as a corrective to outmoded, dualistic anthropological presuppositions of the classic libertarianism critiqued by Burrell, "realistic libertarianism" takes into consideration the normal biological, cultural, linguistic, and the purposively ordered constraints of life that are always present as human beings who are psychosomatic wholes operate in terms of a fundamental self-world correlation. Paul Tillich points to the interesting tension that characterizes this self-world correlation. He indicates that as human beings we experience ourselves as having a world to which we belong.[63] Being particular selves does mean being separated in some measure from everything else, such that we are able to look at and act upon that which is other than one's self, even grasping and attempting to shape the world according to certain norms and ideas. At the same time, when we look at our world we also appreciate that we are "an infinitely small part" of it; and while being the perspective-center, we become a particle of what, from another perspective, appears to be centered in us. It is in the context of this basic structure that we truly encounter ourselves: "There is no self-consciousness without world-consciousness, but the converse is also true."[64] Taking this recognition seriously paves the way for embracing freedom that is finite, realistically libertarian, and relational.

Along with contributing to a critique of a dualistic ontology, these considerations reinforce my earlier suggestion that it is not appropriate to consider the idea of free-will in terms of a simple binary distinction between autonomy (self-determination) and heteronomy (other-determination). What we call free-will is best understood as having to do with the degree and type of self-determination one is able to exercise in different circumstances of life that are always influenced by an array of causal factors. This being so, the idea of libertarian freedom should not be simply linked to the capacity of a will to act indifferently such that to admit influence from God and other causal agents is to render the concept illegitimate. Therefore, I speak directly to Burrell's challenge by asserting that, even if in the context of the fundamental self-world correlation human beings have an innate inclination to "the good," in deciding to perform particular actions or their opposite, we are never completely determined by prior forces: "nature, nurture or even God."[65] This is realistic libertarian freedom, which means that even if because of our grounding in God we engage the issues of life in terms of what we perceive to be good for us, there will always be sufficient space for determinations of what is good that can lead to choices that are contrary to what God may desire in particular instances and influence the degree to which the character of our lives as a whole corresponds to any vision God might have for it.

I agree with Burrell that freedom is not merely about having more than one option. I say it is having options that are significant, and this for me means, as it does for Neville and Pinnock, that antecedent causal constraints on a decision-making process, including God's desires for the decision-maker, are not so overpowering that one is not able to adopt one of the available options for a reason that is decidedly one's own. It is in this way that a person making choices becomes truly accountable. As suggested by Neville, a person could become so fixated on particular stimulations that it results in what is tantamount to unfreedom rather than freedom. As such, vital to the viable expression of our humanity is the capacity for reasonable judgment by which we weigh options in terms of values and standards. Neville has much to say on this matter. He seems quite clear that human beings do have access to a framework by which standards can be established. This conviction is important to his view on what characterizes internal freedom—"the capacity to choose on the basis of standards, to evaluate the standards, and to discern what is truly valuable in order to set standards." Neville indicates that "freedom regarding standards supposes the existence of real values, or of objective rights and wrongs, and that people can have access to them, perhaps not fully or infallibly but with some significant degree of realism." "This dimension of freedom," he suggests, "also supposes that the standards for which we take responsibility can be applied in the process of moral deliberation and choice."[66] Given that Neville is one who believes in a personal God who is good and thus is the ultimate ground of morality, the source of these standards is most probably God's ideals for each life in relation to God's ideal for all life.

With these ideas in mind, I give the reminder that we cannot, in the processes associated with making evaluations, escape the fact that our rational apparatus is grounded in the biological structures of self and the wider biological and social dynamics in which a self operates. Any consideration of human beings as moral agents and of what it means to choose rightly in regard to God must take these into consideration. Therefore, Neville is correct in his claim that "it is always an empirical issue to establish just how wide a person's range of options really is, and just how much control the person has on the consequences of choice. Sometimes we deceive ourselves about both sides."[67] However, it is a fact that human beings are never the total originators of responsible action; there are always antecedents, and nature is far vaster than what we can control. Having said this, Neville is right in not letting us off the hook where the issue of moral responsibility is concerned. He insists that in "the things that are of consequence for the human scale of life—for our moral character, dwellings, society, personal relations, and institutions of cultural life—people are indeed the relevant initiators that decide how things come out."[68]

It is in the exercise of inner personal freedom that people decide what their true values are, not just those to which they will subscribe because they are mandated or are perceived to be necessary for social cohesion. These values will be the constitutive corpus upon which the human being draws in attempts to bring coherence to their lives. As such, these values will inform how one's internal processes dispose one toward the features of life that come under Neville's dimension of natural freedoms. My appreciation of both the call to freedom and the challenge of freedom in decision-making situations is informed by the conviction that what we have from God is not a fixed trajectory with specific mandates but "ideals" entertained by God that constitute a lure in the midst of the variables that characterize the complex processes by which human beings have come to be what we are and in the midst of which we take decisions that partially determine what we will become. So then, even if it is not the *final* cause of freedom, the evolution of the human species to a place where individuality has become a vital form of self-expression and the pursuit of libertarian freedom that involves a desire for and wrestling with meaningful options seems to be vital is certainly revealing what is fundamental to the ongoing development of the species. The intriguing nature of this ongoing humanization is highlighted by the recognition that a decisive element of the outcome from decision-making processes that constitute them as free is produced by the process itself. This element is analogous to what in some quarters is called gestalt; that is, the integration of causal factors and the act of decision-making itself result in an outcome that is never fully explainable by the sum of these factors. This scenario points to an element of novelty that can never be predetermined and which is an expression of creativity that is at the heart of existence.

## Inner Freedom

In my vision of freedom inner freedom is fundamental to personal freedom, and the pursuit of a robust expression of the former should not be simply seen as what one is left with when external forms of freedom are limited or hindered. Inner freedom constitutes the framework in which the dynamics of ontological freedom occur, and I agree with Patterson that important elements of its character are very evident in *The Bacchae of Euripides*.[69] This tragedy was written in approximately 407 BCE while Euripides was exiled in Macedonia, and, as alluded to before, at a time when the tides of war had turned dramatically against Athens. The well-structured social order was under severe threat and the powerful were doing everything feasible to protect their status on the highest rung of the social order.[70]

Depicted in *The Bacchae*, Patterson suggests, "is not so much a world turned upside down as a world turned inside out."[71] As has been suggested by Neville, this inner world can, in important ways, come under the control of influences that support unfreedom in the external realm with this influence remaining long after external expressions of unfreedom are no longer evident. At the same time, inner freedom cannot be monitored in the same way that external freedom can, and, therefore, the perpetrators of unfreedom can never fully assess the impact of the native drives that constitute the deep-structure of all quests for freedom or determine what will be the exact outcome from the dynamics of ontological freedom. This, I suggest, is an important part of the reason why those who wish for dominance and control, would probably perceive *The Bacchae* as portraying what happens when "the deep, dark forces that lie at the root of our souls are set free."[72]

In *The Bacchae* women, "the female force and the symbol of outer personal freedom are also symbols of inner freedom."[73] Significantly, that which in the character of inner freedom some would portray as "the non-rational and passionate in the soul of all persons," I perceive to be primordial drives and the consequent yearnings that result in quests for freedom. Patterson suggests that in the *Bacchae,* Pentheus, the son of Echion and Agave the daughter of Cadmus, who stands for male force and for inner and outer control, comes to accept too late that "women should not be mastered by brute strength."[74]

Recalling Patterson's identification of the important role Greek drama played as social commentary allows me to suggest that the Bacchants, who are women devoted to Bacchus (Dionysus), can be taken to represent rebellion against the kind of order some wish to establish by means of "organic freedom." With this in mind, a subversive capacity can be attributed to *The*

*Bacchae,* even as the portrayal of the Bacchants as out of control and barbaric[75] reflects the way defenders of traditional order typically perceive those who break out of their assigned place in the quest for freedom. Guided by my embrace of its subversive capacity, I interpret this work to be ridiculing and resisting those who enforce external control and who expect that the personal lives of individuals should also be ordered in the manner Plato suggests. It is notable that Cadmus, Pentheus's grandfather and previous King of Thebes, is a Bacchant sympathizer,[76] and even more striking is the recognition that Pentheus' very mother and his aunts are leaders among the Bacchants.[77] Subversion of male oriented sovereignal power is also evident in the fact that Dionysus, who lures Bacchants away, is portrayed as a "feminized" male[78] and the unrecognized cousin of Pentheus. In contrast to the feminized male who has effective power, the stereotypically masculine sovereign Pentheus has an unrealistically high view of his ability to infiltrate the ranks of the Bacchants and to bring them back under control by tried-and-true methods of subjugation: imprisonment, slavery, or domestication.[79] In reality Pentheus is actually quite inadequate in the face of the women's resolute quest for freedom and is vastly more vulnerable than he knows.

Surely this scenario reflects the misguided evaluation the powerful often make of those who have traditionally been subjected to various kinds of unfreedom and also of who they (the powerful) are because they have the capacity to subjugate others.

Dionysus's response is consistent with my surmise, and it serves as a warning to oppressors in any setting: "Your power is mortal, you don't know what you're doing: you don't even know who you are."[80] The subversion continues as Dionysus succeeds in getting Pentheus to dress and behave like a woman,[81] in an attempt to deceive the Bacchants. The high point comes when, after being exposed by Dionysus, it is Pentheus's own mother who makes the first move in the gruesome attack by which he is slaughtered.[82] The tragic character of the play is not overlooked, especially in the closing section that includes the desolation of a mother (Agave) after having killed her son Pentheus.[83] The brutal outburst and later lament are two aspects of the tragedy of many generations, societies, and individuals that fail to recognize that when the native human drive for self-expression and self-determination is persistently beaten down and trapped in static forms of social, political, or ecclesiastical structures, the accumulation of frustrated yearning will eventually break out in ways that will most probably be destructive. As Tillich said in his discussion of the polarity of dynamics and form, we end up with a "continuous flight from law to chaos and from chaos to law."[84]

*The Bacchae* can be seen as an indirect critique on customary perceptions regarding the capacity of those who would restrict the freedom of others and promote what Patterson suggests is a stereotypically male-oriented understanding of rationality, good order, and freedom. *Prometheus Bound,* on the other hand, represents a much more direct expression of the power that resides in the deep interior core of human beings by which we can resist the most extreme limitations to external freedom. One can hardly imagine a more graphic expression of the denial of external freedom than is portrayed by Prometheus chained to the rocks of hell for thousands of years. The popular explanation is that this was the penalty for exercising freedom in a way that violated set boundaries as he stole fire from Zeus to give to human beings. Notably, this is fire that "shines forth: a teacher showing all mankind the way to all the arts there are"[85] —this suggesting a kind of freedom of opportunity.

I am in no doubt that, whatever else it represents, this play confronts sovereignal freedom, and it does so in a way that opens the way for direct theological analysis. Prometheus talks about the willing service he had given to Zeus in his struggle with other gods and how he came to realize that this service had no moderating effect on Zeus's understanding of his sovereignal freedom to do as he pleased with humankind. As Prometheus put it "He makes hierarchies of powers. But for the suffering race of humankind He cared nothing, He planned to wipe out the whole species and breed another, a new one." The immediate point is, rather than accept that sovereignty gave Zeus the freedom to do as he chose—as most would probably have thought, and with some of these fashioning complex arguments of justification— Prometheus claimed the freedom to stand against the god for improper use of sovereignty.[86] Here Prometheus is reminding us that there are certain basic ethical standards that even a God must abide by in order to be perceived as truly loving humankind. This conviction will contribute to my struggle with orthodox Christian thinkers like Augustine, Luther, and Calvin in the chapters ahead, as part of my attempt to make the case that Christians ought to consider whether it is sufficient to declare every kind of action righteous and justified merely because it is attributed to God. In *Prometheus Bound* we find that even though Prometheus's internal organs are eaten over and over by the great eagle and he is burned by lightning and fire, he persists to defy the god he considers unjust and even derides Hermes, the go-between, for his loyalty to Zeus by calling him "Zeus's errand boy [The lackey of the gods]...."[87]

While *Prometheus Bound* is an impressive statement about the importance of inner freedom for the integrity of personal freedom, it must also be acknowledged that it portrays the former in a stereotypically Greek way, as the capacity and the ability to choose not to rely on anyone and anything apart from one's self. Unfortunately, when we examine the presently dominant Western understanding of individuality, especially in the US where I reside, variations of this approach are often associated with the notion of libertarian freedom. It is to this disposition that Christoph Schwöbel points in his reflections on freedom as the modern universal. He does not address the significance of variations in the combinations of dimensions and elements of freedom that are usually evident in actual settings. Nevertheless, his description, which includes the identification of decisive steps in "a progressive process of radicalization in the interpretation of the concept of freedom,"[88] does provide a helpful picture of the possibilities and pitfalls associated with the contemporary Western situation.

We have already said much about the first stage he identifies that involves liberation from external coercion and domination. However, he identifies a feature of that stage that needs to be highlighted. This is the view that the fight for freedom from external domination comes to be seen as "a fundamental human right" and "an inalienable aspect of human dignity." It is a shift that involves embracing the challenge of developing "a strategy for determining one's own goals and means of action." Like Neville, and consistent with aspects of dramatizations in *The Bacchae* and *Prometheus Bound*, Schwöbel associates this process with the discovery of "interiority," and reminiscent of Neville's critique of the naïve view of freedom, he identifies the need for "emancipation from heteronomous determination of our personal identity through internalized authorities."[89] Movement beyond this first stage of interiority brings a dramatically new understanding of freedom. The issues are "no longer liberation from external domination or emancipation from heteronomous determination of our personal identity through internalized authorities." The main question is not, "How can I gain freedom from whatever restricts my freedom?" Instead, it is, "What do I want to be free for?"[90]

Clearly movement from preoccupation with "freedom from" to "freedom for" represents maturation in any quest for freedom. However, given my special concern for the many who are still subjected to the whiles of the perpetrators of unfreedom, I emphasize the need for the continued pursuit of the former even as the latter is embraced. Working concurrently on both aspects of freedom still allows those who experience varying degrees of unfreedom to identify with what Schwöbel suggests is an important outgrowth from the second stage of development. Here there is movement from the use of freedom as a critical concept defined by its opposition against restrictive and oppressive agencies to the use of freedom as a constructive concept where self-interpretation becomes a form of self-expression.[91] It would be unrealistic to understand this process as a movement from one discrete stage to another, and the persistence of situations of unfreedom makes it clear that those privileged to entertain the latter should do so while paying attention to the former, especially for the sake of the downtrodden.

In my framework of consideration, movement toward freedom as a constructive concept is the result of deliberative efforts that are expressions of ontological freedom, in which one develops an understanding of the relationship between self, world, and that which is considered ultimate. It is deficiency at the level of ontological freedom that has contributed to the severe limitation Schwöbel recognizes in the way freedom as a constructive concept has been handled in modern and contemporary Western life. Operating in the legacy of the Kantian epistemological insights, there has been a decided turn to the knowing and experiencing subject. However, this has been done without corresponding regulative principles, such as the Kantian idea of a universal moral law, consensus about the nature and destiny of humanity, or even the notion of cosmic interconnection. This being the case, freedom as self-determination is tantamount to "autonomous self-constitution" in which "'I will be who I choose to be' becomes the new culturally accepted creed."[92] In this way libertarian freedom has in many settings been reduced to self-indulgent individualism as people reach after a condition of life that is not achievable.[93]

In recent times we have seen how this self-indulgent individualism has even ensnared some of the most vulnerable into imitation of the attitudes of the powerful. Without doubt this has contributed to various kinds of economic and social abuses that have plunged the US and other countries into the crisis they are presently experiencing. While people of all kinds have been dismayed by the situation, the already oppressed are being crippled in their capacity to access the opportunities listed by Neville as necessary for both social and personal freedom. This self-indulgence, however, does not eliminate the need for oppressed persons to claim themselves for themselves; that is, to move beyond the self-understanding they have been given and the roles they have been assigned by the powerful, even in instances when these roles have been glamorized with the language of Christian piety and associated with terms such as "calling," "servanthood," "humility," "self-denial," and "long-suffering."

My approach to freedom involves persistent wrestling with what constitutes wholesome levels of self-determination, even as I stand against the ways this pursuit has been corrupted by understandings of power and autonomy developed by the dominant and often adopted by the weak. In many instances these understandings neither reflected Kant's categorical imperative[94] nor Jesus' golden rule,[95] and certainly do not appear to result from serious consideration of what contributes to the common good in an interconnected world. Therefore, a significant contemporary challenge is to contribute to a new framework for understanding what is really occurring in pursuits that carry the name freedom and for guiding these pursuits in any one context so that they enhance rather than undermine the welfare of people in other contexts.

The challenge to nurture libertarian freedom in ways that do not lead to self-indulgent individualism is a major one. It requires the promotion of personal freedom without privileging autonomy (personal sovereignty) over relationality. If there is any scenario that might hint at an optimal expression of freedom, it is that in which there is a mutual and reciprocal relation between internal and external freedoms, grounded in a person's own integrated vision of reality. Contributing to this vision will be a healthy sense of who one is in relation to all else that leads to communal participation for the sake of self and other. I now turn to Tillich who in his explication of freedom as finite freedom addresses the polarities of existence in a way that is very helpful for this endeavor.

Tillich suggests that, informed by the basic self-world structure, our sense of and yearning for freedom take place in terms of the polar character of the basic structure of existence. In this framework, "freedom as such is not the basis of existence, but rather freedom in unity with finitude."[96] The three polarities that undergird finite freedom are Individuality and Participation, Dynamics and Form, and Freedom and Destiny—each pole being meaningful only insofar as it refers by implication to the opposite pole. While it is only in the third of these polarities that freedom is mentioned explicitly in dialectic tension with destiny, together all three help us navigate certain basic features of any meaningful consideration of freedom wherever we might operate in the world. Understanding Individuality and Participation begins with the recognition that "the very term 'individual' points to the interdependence of self-relatedness and individualization"[97] that characterizes a self-centered being. Yet, every individual necessarily participates in her/his environment, their world. It should be noted that Tillich has a bias toward categories that are linked to his intention to establish the ultimacy of Being itself. Therefore, he emphasizes that human beings participate in the universe through the rational structure of mind and reality, even as we participate most fully in that level of life that we are ourselves; that is, we participate in other centered selves (we have communion only with persons). As a contextualist, it is important to add that the participation to which Tillich refers takes place not with persons in general but within the constraints of clan, tribe, nation, ethnicity, geographical location, conceptual frameworks, etc. Having done so, I concur with Tillich that participation is not something an individual might or might not have. It is essential and not accidental; that is, "no individual exists without participation, and no personal being exists without communal being."[98]

For my purposes it is best to move to Tillich's third listed polarity, which is Freedom and Destiny. This third polarity will point us back to the second. In the third polarity is reaffirmed the conviction that human beings as human beings have freedom characterized by the capacity for deliberation (weighing), decision making (cutting off), and responsibility (response/account),[99] but we experience this freedom only in polar interdependence with destiny. The latter pole points to the situation in which, through engagements considered to be expressions of freedom, we find ourselves facing the world as if it were an object available to be shaped by us. Yet there is also the realization that we belong to the world that we think we can shape—this feature of our lives is evident in a range of conditions we cannot avoid from physical laws, through social structures, to the necessary participation in the lives of others. According to Tillich one's destiny is actually the basis of one's freedom, even as one's freedom participates in shaping one's destiny.[100]

Understanding the second polarity, Dynamics and Form, begins with the assertion that being something means having a form: being characterized by a certain content that makes a thing what it is actually. Still, not only does every particular form have the potential to be something—this referring to the dynamics at the heart of that particular form—but it is also true that no particular form fully expresses the dynamics reflected in what it is.[101] Therefore, considering the character of freedom must include the recognition that "every living being . . . drives beyond itself and beyond the given form through which it has being."[102] This is indeed a quest for freedom from restraints that appear to limit one at any point of life. We may use complementary terms like self-transcendence, self-actualization, and progress to describe this drive. However, without appropriate regard for the fact that dynamics are only experienced and expressed in and through the concrete, with all its limitations, this expression of freedom will drive one "in all directions without any definite aim and content. His dynamics are distorted into a formless urge for self-transcendence. . . ." One can speak of the "temptation of the new," Tillich says, "which in itself is a necessary element in all creative self-actualization, but which in distortion sacrifices the creative for the new. Nothing real is created if the form is lacking, for nothing is real without form." One might put this even more starkly by saying that without proper regard for the limiting order of structure and law, the quest for freedom is simply the courting of chaos. On the other hand, if form is embraced without regard for the dynamics in which it is created and of which it is a limited and limiting expression, "it is oppressive and produces either legalism without creativity or the rebellious outbreaks of dynamic forces leading to chaos and often, in reaction, to stronger ways of suppression." This scenario, Tillich suggests, is played out on a regular basis in human history where "there is a continuous flight from law to chaos and from chaos to law."[103]

The idea that freedom involves the tensions associated with pursuing appropriate levels of self-determination in the context of a self-world correlation will be given in-depth theological grounding in chapter 6. Informed by Process-Relational thought, I will elaborate on the idea that, while God relates internally to every person and offers ideals for self-realization that are unique to each person, all this is carried out in relation to God's intimacy with an offering of ideals for every other actuality and the cosmos as a whole. This being so, the overall quality of freedom achievable for each individual is, in important respects, always contingent on that achieved by every other actuality in a world that is at root interconnected. Some insight into this interconnection is provided by Herman Daley and John Cobb, who indicate that persons are constituted by their relationships and have no identity apart from them. Daley and Cobb hastened to indicate that this does not mean that we are nothing more that social products. "People also have some freedom to constitute themselves. Personal responsibility is based on that freedom." However, this transcending of relationships does not introduce something separable from social relationships. Indeed, the quality of personal freedom is linked to the quality of social relations. [104]

## PREPARING FOR FURTHER EXPLORATION OF FREEDOM

Earlier in the chapter it was pointed out how important the ontological dimension of freedom is for this project. I remind the reader that for Robert Neville ontological freedom has to do with how persons employ all the elements of natural freedom to relate to God as creator, to the world as created, and to themselves as creatures. He suggests that "there is nothing mysterious to the dynamics of ontological freedom: it employs external liberties, intentional action, free choice, choice according to standards, social opportunities, pluralistic ways, integration of life, and political action." [105] I reframe Neville's definition in more inclusive terms: it is the process by which we employ all the elements of natural freedom to develop an understanding of the relationship between self, world, and that which is understood to be ultimate. I now go further to suggest how the idea of ontological freedom as understood by the theologian might be re-presented for appropriation beyond the religious realm, so that the possibility of mutually beneficial engagement between the religious and the non-religious might be fostered.

I commence with Tillich's claim that as human beings we have many concerns: spiritual, cognitive, aesthetic, moral, and political, but that which becomes ultimate grasps one in such a way that it demands total commitment and becomes the center from and in relation to which all other concerns are engaged and their significance evaluated. [106] In my framework of thought, it is ontological freedom that describes the dynamic by which all this takes place. At the same time, employing the notion "ultimate concern" allows us to consider how people who do not believe in a personal or nonpersonal divine might be lured to engage in the analysis and constructive pursuits involved in the exercise of ontological freedom. One's ultimate concern does not need to be religious in any conventional sense for it to perform the role described above. As far as Tillich is concerned, whatever is our ultimate concern is our god.

Exactly because one's ultimate concern constitutes one's god, we need to exercise great care regarding what outcomes we accept as legitimate expressions of ontological freedom. For example, Tillich thinks that the extreme nationalism of his homeland Germany that contributed to the Second World

War and the preoccupation with success, social standing, and power he observed in the USA constituted ultimate concerns because, in the respective settings, everything seemed to center in these concerns. Because nationalism and success were not truly ultimate, they were idolatrous forms of ultimate concern and turned out to be demonic. It must also be said that the embrace by the religious of any conception of "God" as if it has a one-to-one correspondence with the ultimate for which it is but a symbol is an equally idolatrous form of ultimate concern. Nevertheless, for Tillich, even idolatrous forms of faith dramatize the unconditional character of ultimate concern. For me, what Tillich calls humanist faith, which expresses itself in secular rather than religious forms and has moral concerns as its central focus, is a quite noble expression of ontological freedom. Its nobility is attested to by Tillich as he identifies its utopian expression in the faith that characterized efforts of the fighters for enlightenment since the eighteenth century, as they resisted "sacramentally consecrated bondage and for justice for every human being." This they have done while holding to "the superior power of reason united with justice and truth."[107] Driven by the "ought to be" as an ethical imperative with humanity as its central focus, humanist faith, like any other form of faith, is characterized by a certain "givenness," to which there must be "surrender."[108] At the same time, it is "a personal, centered act" of the human mind, and, as such, is "a matter of freedom."[109]

Given that as an imperative the "ought to be" of humanist faith is adhered to (chosen) because of its compellingness as a universally valid principle, it can certainly be seen as the closest secular analog to that which ideally results from the exercise of ontological freedom. Without doubt, both humanist faith and religious faith are operations of inner freedom and involve consideration of a universal in relation to self and world.[110] At the same time, successful collaboration between the religious and non-religious for the sake of freedom depends significantly on what results externally from the exercise of internal freedom by the religious. While the secular form of inner freedom will usually result in outward activism of some kind, the religious form can result in external expressions that range from the non-activist to the rebellious. The religious might decide that given what is considered to be the truly ultimate concern, even the most oppressive expressions of freedom in the external realm will not be the significant determinants of the highest quality of freedom human beings are able to experience. What they yearn for is a unique freedom that comes from spiritual intimacy with a personal God, which can be pursued privately and individually. On the other hand, the religious person might be of the conviction that exactly because of their ultimate concern, certain external restrictions on freedom cannot be tolerated, and public acts of resistance are required. It is the people in this latter group who will be available for potentially fruitful collaboration with those who express humanist faith.

It will be seen over the course of this project that I value immensely the capacity enabled by inner freedom expressed in ontological freedom to extend the range of personal freedom and enable people to retain a sense of self and imagine creative ways to address the most severe forms of external unfreedom. At the same time, as human beings who are psychosomatic wholes and members of one interconnected world, there is a level of human viability that is only developed as we engage in efforts along with others to protect and enhance meaningful expressions of external freedom at the personal and social levels.

I proceed to the rest of this project with no definition of freedom that could constitute a strict formula but with a clear sense of vital elements that, if realized in viable combinations, will contribute to rich and wholesome humanity for individuals whose fortunes are always linked to that of other global actualities, both individually and communally. It begins with the recognition of a native drive inherent in every living being that, in one way or another, is always pushing each human being beyond their given form (conditioned by biology, sociology, psychology, economics, etc.) by which they have particular being at any particular point. This representation is in qualified ways consistent with Pinnock's view that freedom is one of the noblest endowments from God, Neville's claim that human beings are created to be free, and Davis's assertion that freedom in human life is grounded in the freedom that is fundamental to the very nature of God who issues the call to freedom. It is this drive that eventually emerged from underground (consciously and externally) in quests for personal freedom; that is, the desire not to be encumbered by restraints that appear to limit one in the pursuit of aspirations for self-governance.

It is nothing else but an expression of this native drive that is evident in the challenging understanding of freedom as self-determination, even where it is distorted and excessive. At the same time I appreciate that the notion of autonomous self-constitution, exemplified in the assertion "I will be who I choose to be," represents a dangerously inadequate regard for the fact that our native drive for self-actualization through self-transcendence (creativity/ dynamics) is only experienced and expressed in and through the concrete and within its limitations. Therefore, the quest for freedom ought to be a creative struggle that must be carried out on a number of levels that are internal and external to the individual, and with acute awareness that every other being ought to have the opportunity to do similarly. It is ontological freedom that will enable one to carry out this struggle in the context of a comprehensive vision of one's self in the broader context of a world with multiple kinds of co-inhabitants who also pursue freedom and who share common grounding in a God who is very much a part of this process and who already has a vision of what it could be at its best.

# NOTES

1. With confidence I can list a number of these: Liberation theology, Womanist theology, Black theology, Feminist theology, Caribbean theology/Caribbean Emancipatory theology.

2. Orlando Patterson, *Freedom in the Making of Western Culture*, vol. I (New York: Basic Books, 1992), 2.

3. Kortright Davis, *Emancipation Still Comin': Explorations in Caribbean Emancipatory Theology* (New York: Orbis Books, 1990), 11-12. Davis references Robert Neville, *The Cosmology of Freedom* (New Haven: Yale University Press, 1974), 8–9.

4. Ibid.

5. Robert Neville, *A Theology Primer* (Albany: State University of New York Press, 1991), 79.

6. Ibid., 82–83.

7. Ibid., 83–84.

8. Patterson, *Freedom*, xi.

9. Ibid., 67–74. Patterson describes a scenario that begins with a labor crisis occasioned by the impressive reforms (*seisachtheia*) spearheaded by the Athenian Solon that abolished all debt and outlawed all forms of debt bondage and enslavement of Athenians for debt. This reform exacerbated the preexistent condition of cash-strapped elite. Added to this problem was the need for additional labor to meet the requirements of a change over to the farming of olives, figs, and viticulture "to meet the needs of the aristocrats for imports and also because of declining marginal productivity in grain agriculture." There was a dramatic turn to the use of foreign slaves, with this increasing even more as sectoralization led to the growth of an urban craft goods sector and an expanded mining sector. For the first time in history a society was transforming itself through the use of slaves causing the elite to become completely dependent upon slaves for their economic survival. Over time there was the accumulation of large numbers of slaves (by the late fifth century BCE one out of every three persons in Athens was a slave) and people of slave ancestry who were at the center of the economy and social life, even if they could never be rulers.

10. Davis, *Emancipation*, 9.

11. Ibid.

12. Neville, *Primer*, 78. Neville discusses the four elements on pages 77–81.

13. Ibid., 82.

14. Isaiah Berlin, "Two Concepts of Liberty," in *Four Essays on Liberty* (1969; reprint, Oxford: Oxford University Press, 1990), 122.

15. Ibid.

16. Ibid., 131.

17. Patterson, *Freedom*, 3.

18. Robert Neville, *The Cosmology of Freedom* (New Haven: Yale University Press, 1974), 91.

19. Amartya Sen, *Rationality and Freedom* (Cambridge: Harvard University Press, 2004), 509. In this interpretation, "a violation of negative freedom must also be—unless compensated by some other factor—a violation of positive freedom, but not vice versa." In note 5, he indicates that in Berlin's scheme each can be violated without violating the other (586).

20. Patterson, *Freedom*, 3.

21. Ibid., 4.

22. Ibid., 9. Patterson identifies three important aspects of the condition of slavery that form the background for the appreciation of the character of freedom as he understands it. First, slavery was a form of personal domination. One individual was under the direct power of another or of another's agent. This power usually involved the power of life and death over the slave. Second, the slave is always an excommunicated person, alienated from family or origin and having no right to establish a life-long union with a partner, and if they have children they can/will also be slaves to be bought and sold. Expressed differently, slavery implied the loss of ties of birth in both ascending and descending generations. The male slave, more often than the female, does not belong to the legitimate social and moral community. He has no independent social existence. He exists only through and for the master, i.e. a perpetual condition of dishon-

or and social death. What is more, the master and his group parasitically gain honor by degrading the slave.

23. Ibid., 51.

24. Ibid., 54.

25. Ibid., 109–110. The reader should take note that Patterson utilizes Greek tragedy, in which the tragic heroine is often a slave, as cultural evidence. He suggests that Greek drama was a kind of natural poll of fifth-century Athenian values and ideals. On pages 108–109 we hear that, "in Greek drama we find a unique body of socio-historical material in which dramas, skillfully selected for their expression of the most profound cultural and social ideals, by persons whom we would today call cultural experts, are preserved precisely because they have won the popular approval of the Athenian audience." Note should also be taken of Patterson's telling analysis of the *Antigone* that identifies gender conflict as primary and that leads to the view that the play in its moral aspects is a study in the nature and limits of freedom. This he discusses on page 120 onward and on page 127.

26. Ibid., 108. Patterson reminds us that Greek literature was written by authors living in a world of confined women for an audience of males who seemed to hold women in contempt.

27. Hannah Arendt, *The Human Condition* (Chicago: The University of Chicago Press, 1958), 30.

28. Ibid., 31.

29. In *Freedom* Patterson reminds us that, while in theory sovereignal freedom has to do with the perceived right or privilege to act as one pleases regardless of the wishes of others, it was not normally pursued in this way in the ancient world. Rather, people sought to be linked to powerful others or to groups that powerful people represented or led. We hear on page 44 that "Such bonds existed within the context of a network of countervailing powers that constrained the power of individual despots." Yet, in Greece we see a quite effective variation of sovereignal freedom. The enslavement of foreigners would certainly have allowed for the "best" expression of this freedom by their masters who had the power of life and death over them, and we learn more from Patterson about the ideology that informed its more nuanced expression in the broader socio-cultural life of Greece, and Athens in particular. On pages 84–87 we hear that Greek victory in warfare, beginning with the Persian war, provided an opening for sovereignal freedom to be associated with "*arete*—glory, manliness, and valor in warfare and athletics." While broadened to include those who distinguished themselves in warfare, this "freedom for the virtuous aristocrats and plutocrats meant freedom to rule over others." On one hand, this involved protecting the independence of the state and/or becoming dominant over other states. On the other hand, it involved the maintenance of the state order that served their purposes best.

30. Note 9 above has given an idea of how these well-intended reforms led to the intensification of slavery in Athens.

31. Patterson, *Freedom*, 70–72.

32. Ibid., 73–75.

33. Ibid., 134–135. Here again we have a situation in which the powerful would benefit most; a fourfold benefit Patterson suggests. The slave worked diligently with the hope of one day being free; the master received from the slave at the end of the period of service enough money to purchase a brand-new slave; the master was relieved of any responsibility to provide for the slave in old age; and the master had a freed slave obliged to remain eternally grateful for the privilege of buying his/her freedom.

34. Ibid., 99–103.

35. Ibid. This claim should be placed in juxtaposition with Patterson's indication that the freed slave gained minimally from manumission.

36. Ibid., 170–171.

37. Ibid., 104. Patterson's reference is Nichole Loraux, *The Invention of Athens: The Funeral Oration of the Classical City* (Cambridge: Harvard University Press, 1986), 52.

38. Neville, *A Theology Primer*, 82

39. Patterson, *Freedom*, 160.

40. Ibid., 158.

41. Ibid.

42. Ibid., 159. Patterson suggests that Plato's position is understandable given the horrors experienced during the Peloponnesian war and the extent of civil strife it engendered.

43. Neville, *Primer*, 82.

44. Ibid., 82–83.

45. Patterson, *Freedom*, 9.

46. Clark Pinnock, *Most Moved Mover: A Theology of God's Openness* (Grand Rapids, MI: Baker Academic Press, 2001), 126.

47. Neville, *Primer*, 78–79.

48. Pinnock, *Most Moved Mover* , 126 – 127.

49. Ibid., 127.

50. Ibid., 128.

51. Augustine, *Confessions*, trans. R. S. Pine-Coffin (London: Penguin Books, 1961) [X.7], 213–214.

52. Ibid., VII.10, 146–7.

53. Augustine, *City of God*, trans. Gerald Walsh et al. (New York: Image Books, 1958), [IX.9], 1 [XII.24], 525.

54. René Descartes, *Meditations on First Philosophy*, trans. Donald Cress (Indianapolis, Cambridge: Hackett Publishing Company, 1979), [med. 3], 23. See Meditation VI for a focused discussion on the existence of the body and its distinction from the mind.

55. Ibid., [med. IV], 37, 38–40.

56. Ibid.

57. David Burrell, *Faith and Freedom — An Interfaith Perspective* (Malden, MA: Blackwell Publishing, 2004), 106.

58. Ibid., 107. Burrell cites as the source of this expression Joseph Incandela, "Aquinas' Lost Legacy: God's Practical Knowledge and Situated Human Freedom" (PhD dissertation, Princeton University, 1986).

59. Ibid., 106–110.

60. Antonio Damasio, *Descartes' Error: Emotions, Reason and the Human Brain* (New York: Putnam's Sons, 1994), 128.

61. This framework of thought, which is influential in many disciplines, has as its chief inspiration Alfred North Whitehead's speculative philosophy that attempted to fashion "a coherent, logical, necessary system of general ideas in terms of which every element of our experience can be interpreted." This quotation is from Alfred North Whitehead, *Process and Reality*, corrected edition, David Ray Griffin and Donald W. Sherburne (New York: The Free Press, 1978), 3.

62. John Cobb, Jr., *The Structure of Christian Existence* (Philadelphia: Westminster Press, 1967), 39.

63. Tillich alludes to the fact that his discussion of human belonging to the world reflects his attempt to apply ideas developed in Heidegger's *Being and Time* to his theological project. This allusion is found in Paul Tillich, *Systematic Theology,* vol. I (Chicago: University of Chicago Press, 1951), 168. Heidegger's explication of the relation between Being and time contributes to the conception of God I propose.

64. Ibid., 171.

65. Pinnock, *Most Moved Mover* , 127.

66. Neville, *A Theology Primer* , 81.

67. Ibid., 80.

68. Ibid.

69. Patterson, *Freedom*, 171.

70. By the time this play was performed in Athens in 405 BCE the city was on the verge of collapse.

71. Patterson, *Freedom*, 171.

72. Ibid.

73. Ibid.

74. Ibid.

75. C. K. Williams (ed.), *The Bacchae of Euripides* (New York: Farrar, Straus and Giroux, 1990), 4. As is pointed out on page 19, the women have not only "abandoned" home, they have broken out of the City, the sphere of right order, rationality, and civilization.

76. Ibid., 20.

77. Ibid., 44.

78. Ibid., 23, 30. When sending the guards to apprehend Dionysus, Pentheus refers to him as "the girlish stranger." Later he ridicules Dionysus with the words: "What a mane of hair you have, very seductive. Look at it falling down your cheeks. Good hand holds for a wrestler. And how white your skin is: you must be careful about staying out in the sun."

79. Ibid., 19, 33.

80. Ibid. 30–33.

81. When the suggestion is initially made, he asks: "Do I have to be demoted to a woman?" See Ibid., 50–52.

82. Ibid., 70.

83. Ibid., 81–82.

84. Paul Tillich, *Systematic Theology,* vol. II (Chicago: University of Chicago Press, 1957), 64.

85. Aeschylus, *Prometheus Bound,* trans. James Scully and C. J. Herington (New York: Oxford University Press, 1975), 35.

86. Ibid., 40–41.

87. Ibid., 75.

88. Christoph Schwöbel, "Imago Libertatis: Human and Divine Freedom," in *God and Freedom—Essays in Historical and Systematic Theology,* ed. Colin E. Gunton (Edinburgh, UK: T&T Clark, 1995), 58.

89. Ibid. Here Schwöbel echoes Neville in his indication that "when the external forces of oppression have been removed there still remain internal authorities to be dealt with, the heteronomous determination through authorities, which we internalize. . . ." These internal authorities are "traditions, customs, perspectives, concepts and behavior code which may restrict our freedom just as oppressively as external agencies."

90. Ibid., 59.

91. Ibid.

92. Ibid., 62–64.

93. Later in this project I will explicate the link between this individualism and substance metaphysics. At this point the reader might be interested to hear from my colleague Carol Johnston who hints at how substance metaphysics was manifested in the orientation of early modern physics, from which flowed influence that would affect socio-political and economic dispositions. She suggests that enlightenment individualism was based on Newtonian physics, "which assumed that the world is composed of discrete, independently existing individual entities. In this atomistic individualism, relations between entities are strictly external—they exist as they are whether they have any relationships or not." These ideas are from Carol Johnston, *The Wealth or Health of Nations: Transforming Capitalism from Within* (Cleveland: The Pilgrim Press, 1998), 24.

94. Immanuel Kant, *Grounding for the Metaphysics of Morals,* trans. James W. Ellington (Indianapolis: Hackett Publishing Company, 1980), 14. In Kant's words: "I should never act except in such a way that I can also will that my maxim should become a universal law."

95. The "Golden Rule" found in Matthew 7:12 (and Luke 6:31) says, "In everything do to others as you would have them do to you." Except when otherwise indicated, my Scripture quotations are from the *Harper Study Bible,* Revised Edition (New York: Harper Collins Publishers, 2006).

96. Tillich, *Systematic Theology,* vol. I, 165.

97. Ibid., 175.

98. Ibid., 176.

99. Ibid., 184.

100. Ibid., 185.

101. Ibid., 178.

102. Tillich, *Systematic Theology,* vol. II, 64.

103. Ibid.

104. Herman Daley and John Cobb Jr., *For the Common Good: Redirecting the Economy toward Community, the Environment, and a Sustainable Future* (Boston: Beacon Press, 1994), 161.

105. Neville, *Primer*, 83.

106. Paul Tillich, *Dynamics of Faith* (New York: Harper and Rowe Publishers, 1957), 1–3. Tillich suggests that for those of the Jewish and Christian traditions, that which is ultimate is best represented biblically by the *Shema* (Deut. 6:4-9) especially the section that reads, "Hear, O Israel: The Lord is our God, the Lord alone. You shall love the Lord your God with all your heart, and with all your soul, and with all your might."

107. Ibid., 69.

108. Ibid., 7. This process of surrender I associate with the ecstatic character of faith, in which one is overtaken and driven beyond self and stands outside of self without ceasing to be a self.

109. Ibid., 5.

110. I do recognize that Tillich, and quite probably Neville, would classify that which is associated with humanist faith as deficient.

*II*

# Clearing a Path for Freedom

*Chapter Two*

# Free-will Established as a Christian Problematic

Many contemporary considerations on freedom reflect the continued influence of Augustine's theological anthropology, including his views on the character and capacity of the human will. His earlier discussions presupposed the fundamental goodness of the human being as God's creature, and it was his understanding that God's just judgment when we do evil necessitated the human capacity to choose both good and evil. Over time, he moved to a more pessimistic stance, suggesting that because of "the fall" all humanity lost its ability not to sin. The will, as an aspect of the soul, was incapacitated in its ability to keep the body in check and sustain undiluted communion with God. Augustine's resistance to the ideas of British monk Pelagius pushed him to articulate his most extreme position in his doctrine of predestination in which he proposed that, not only are human beings dependent of prevenient grace for the ability to choose good and God, but God had predetermined who would accomplish the latter. Pelagius rightly insisted that, while tainted by the fall of the first human, the capacity given by God to choose in two directions has not been lost. He leans in the direction of freedom that is finite, realistically libertarian, and relational as he wrestles with the tension between what human beings often choose to do and what we are capable of accomplishing in relation to the possibilities created for us by God. This leaning is also evident in his insistence that God's way of acting cannot be characterized by the overwhelming omnipotence presupposed by Augustine's doctrine of predestination, but by the gift of the ability for good.

## AUGUSTINE AND HIS CHANGE OF MIND

While many are aware of Augustine's views on freedom of the will, which emerged in the course of his conflict with the monk Pelagius, the text *On Free Choice of the Will* represents his earlier thinking on the matter. In this work we find that, while being convinced that it was the very providence of God expressed in the creation of the world that would determine its end, Augustine was of the view that free-will is an important characteristic of the human being as she/he operates in the world as a rational creature. Understood in its most basic sense, free-will involves the ability to evaluate, take decisions, and make choices. At another level, it represents the capacity to choose that which is good, that is, what is consistent with God's will. Expressed in qualitative terms, human beings are good by virtue of being God's creatures; so too is the will good because it is a necessary feature of the human being, as the means by which we determine both good and evil. Augustine hastens to make clear that one should not infer from this capacity that God gave free-will so that human beings should sin. The very fact that God punishes those who use the will to sin shows that free-will was given for us to live rightly; otherwise God could be accused of injustice for punishing us. Augustine speaks clearly on the matter:

> For the goodness that we admired in God's justice—his punishing sins and rewarding good deeds—how could it even exist if human beings lacked free choice of will? No action would be either a sin or a good deed if it were not performed freely by the will, and so both punishment and reward would be unjust if human beings had no free-will. But it was right for there to be justice in both reward and punishment, since this is one of the goods that come from God. Therefore, it was right for God to give free will to human beings. [1]

Prior to this statement, Augustine had spent time explicating the characteristics of sin as opposed to living rightly. He is clear that human beings did not learn to sin, since learning is a good. [2] He engages the alternative proposal of whether we can trace back our sins to God, since our souls come from God. Is it possible that our sins indirectly come from God? It is in the process of answering this question that Augustine defines evildoing as "inordinate desire or cupidity," which is "the love of those things that one can lose against one's will." We are able to determine what constitutes inordinate desire by assessing actions in light of the two sets of laws given to us by God: eternal law and temporal law. Both laws are good: "an unjust law is no law at all," and both are important to perfect order. [3] Augustine's conclusion seems to have been that sin, or actions not in accord with eternal law or temporal law, is the result of free choice, since it could not have been learned or come from God. In his own words: "only its own will and free choice can make the mind a companion of cupidity." By so doing, "inordinate desire rules the mind" and "the mind is dragged by inordinate desire into ruin and poverty."[4] It is only the right exercise of reason (mind-spirit) that enables us to make those judgments that ensure its dominance over the lower impulses of the soul (emotions-passions-desires-fears-anger) that feed inordinate desire. When reason operates rightly, one can be said to have good will, which is a will that desires to live uprightly and honorably and to attain the highest wisdom, that is, the eternal truth that is in God.[5]

Significantly for Augustine, the very fact that God punishes us when we get carried away into sinful deeds is testimony to our capacity to will that which is good. It is God saying to us that we haven't used our will for the purpose for which it is given to us, that is, for living rightly. His interlocutor Evodius asks an interesting question: "But don't you think that if free will were given to us for living rightly, we ought not to have been able to pervert it and use it for sinning? It should have been like justice, which was also given to human beings to enable them to live well." He continues: "No one can use justice to live wickedly. In the same way, it ought to be the case that no one could use the will to sin, if indeed the will was given for acting rightly." Augustine responds by engaging Evodius in a way that gets him to affirm that God is indeed the giver of free-will, and in the process it becomes clear that the fact that a thing can be misused does not itself negate that thing's essential goodness. Given the acknowledgment that free-will is God's gift, Augustine declares: "If it is quite certain that God gave us freewill, then we must admit that it ought to have been given, and in exactly the way it was given; for God gave it, and his deeds are utterly beyond reproach."[6] Later in book three of this work he argues that free-will is not negated by God's foreknowledge, since to know that a person would act in a certain way in the future does not mean that the one who knew predetermined what was done. Indeed, God would have foreknown the act as an expression of the doer's will. So then, while the earlier Augustine, like other orthodox thinkers, viewed the human as seriously compromised, he at this point in his considerations does not appear to view it as crippled or intrinsically (in its inherited nature) disposed to sin. Nothing in the *Confessions* overturns this basic position. There he states that wickedness is "not a substance." Instead, it is "perversion of the will" when it turns aside from God,[7] and turning aside most certainly presupposes having been turned toward God previously.

Unfortunately Augustine's problems with materiality and the body caused him to be excessive in his assessment of this matter, resulting in expectations of self and others that were not achievable. Nevertheless, even in the supposed corruption of will, his love and desire for God persisted. Of great significance is that the memory of God, continued appreciation for beauty, and ability for correct judgment in temporal matters set the stage for his reason to turn him toward God in such a way that "in an instant of awe, my mind attained to the sight of the God who IS. Then, at last, I caught sight of your invisible nature, as it is known to your creatures."[8] That he could not sustain such an undiluted vision and was again distracted by "things of this world"[9] is not surprising to me. I am of the view that human beings are not constituted to persist in a state of undiluted vision of God that is unaffected by the body in its interaction with its surroundings.

Admittedly, the chief coordinator of the human body is the mind, and the mind is central to our capacity to prehend God. However, if neuroscientist Antonio Damasio and Process-Relational thinker John Cobb are correct,[10] a properly functioning mind cannot help but be attuned to, and in significant degree conditioned by, the aspects of the human self that Augustine considers of lower status and "a drag on the soul." Thus Augustine was on a healthier and more productive path when, sensing God in ordinary things, he allowed the mind to be stimulated to reflections on God rather than on the things themselves. However, his concern that preoccupation with the things themselves easily led to one being overpowered by the body with its desires resulted in persistent attempts to attain freedom for abstracted intimacy with God. The frustration, even despair, he experienced was born not from arrogance but from ignorance. Indeed, his inability to manage the impulses of the body was, at least, in part, because he was unable to appreciate their full legitimacy as elements of the God-given biological structure that grounds and conditions reason in human beings who are psychosomatic wholes. Ignorance of this holistic state of humanity resulted in an unrealistic position in regard to the dynamics of willing. Augustine, therefore, persisted in the expectation that the mind should be able to order itself and to "will" in the sense of giving a command that is obeyed. Constant failure in this matter he attributed to a disease of the mind.[11]

The limitation in Augustine's conceptualization of soul/mind in relation to body on one hand, and, on the other hand, soul/mind in relation to will is highlighted by comments from political philosopher Hannah Arendt, who wrote her doctoral dissertation on love (*caritas*) in Augustine's thought. It was in the interest of the ways Augustine's ideas could be beneficial to meaningful public action that she carried out her evaluation of his thought. Her view was that authentic freedom results from public action that initiates "beginnings," not from a preoccupation with interiority. She suggests that "intercourse between me and myself," which in Augustine's case was internal conflict caused by a corrupted will, would not have made sense to persons of classical antiquity. Without doubt they perceived a dualism between soul and body, with the soul seen as designed to move both itself and the body. However, Augustine's "hot contention" within the soul would have made no sense, for the struggle in which Augustine had become engaged was not between the two different human faculties of reason and passion, between understanding and appetite (*thumos*) but a conflict within the will itself. Arendt suggests that such an inner conflict of the will "paralyzes and locks it within itself," and "willing in solitude is always *velle* and *nolle*, to will and not to will at the same time." She suggests that Augustine's paralysis is all the more surprising since, by her understanding, the very essence of the will is to command and be obeyed. "Hence it appears to be a 'monstrosity' that human beings may command themselves and not be obeyed, a monstrosity which can be explained only by the simultaneous presence of an I-will and an I-will-not."[12]

Arendt recognizes that Augustine's analysis of the condition of the will was not at all new, and she alludes to Paul's lament in Romans 7:21-23 when she indicates that "the historical fact is that the phenomenon of the will originally manifested itself in the experience [of Paul] that what I would I do not, that there is such a thing as I-will-and-cannot."[13] She is clear that if this is where our evaluation of the human situation leaves us, it represents a crippling stalemate that proves tragic for any position that human freedom is linked to a free-will. The exercise of will-power, which for the ancients was the path to liberating the self from passions and intentions, is now seen as defeated in the struggle with the self. This being the case, the will-to-power now corresponds to a will-to-oppression. Given her concern, Arendt points to a fatal consequence of Augustine's and Paul's viewpoint for political theory and suggests that "it was one of the causes why even today we almost automatically equate power with oppression."[14] In Arendt's estimation, the sense of being crippled and oppressed, born from preoccupation with a will in conflict with itself, is only overcome when we step away from the framework of analysis that associates human freedom with the dynamics of willing and immerse ourselves in the cut-and-thrust of the external sphere—that is, the political life. Being situated in this sphere one is overtaken by some "principle," enabling I-will to coincide with I-can, thus promoting freedom.[15]

Augustine's later theological construction eventually addressed what Arendt describes as the desired movement from I-will to I-can. In the *Confessions*, Augustine's dramatic transition took place in association with his reading of Romans 13:13. His claim is that "it was as though the light of confidence flooded into my heart, and all the darkness of doubt was dispelled."[16] However, his struggles with his "unruly" being did not cease. He looked toward the day when God would free him from his conflicts, and until then he intended to focus on God's mercies toward him.[17]

Clearly Augustine had come to a place of assurance that his relationship with God would not be broken by his ongoing struggles because God was merciful, but he was not at the point where he saw the need to disparage the human will in order to establish the power of grace. Earlier in the text he used the term "necessity" in regard to sin, but the associated discussion suggests that it referred not to the logical sense of the word, which would mean that to think of a human being without sin would be a contradiction in terms. Instead it referred to the hardening of habits willfully and persistently indulged in over time. In his precise words: "When I gave in to lust habit was born, and when I did not resist the habit it became a necessity";[18] that is, his habit became a stubborn and dominant feature of his life. Augustine did not seem to be claiming that human beings are totally bereft of the capacity to exercise their will to avoid sinning. As mentioned before, having turned away from God his reason had enabled him to turn toward, travel to, and abide for a while in the very presence of God. Surely, as the mind wills itself (inadequately) in regard to the body, so it would have willed itself in regard to this venture toward God, even though success was only temporary.

This capacity is suggestive of a good will with significant limitation. This goodness is also evident in Augustine's claim that even as he struggled with the old will a "new will" emerged in him to serve God. Obviously, the inability of the new will to overcome the old will, which had more practice, occasioned great agony in him. I, however, recognize in his description a stronger inclination toward that which was perceived to be good—that is, judgments, choices, and behaviors that were consistent with the will of God. Therefore, he not only recognized himself on both sides of the conflict between what he considered "the impulses of nature and the impulses of the spirit," but, as he put it: "I took the part of that which I approved in myself rather than the part of that which I disapproved."[19] I say that this is an example of a will that is exercising freedom in tension, which will probably always be the case because human freedom is finite freedom. It may well be that some things Augustine disapproved of were fixations that undermined freedom, but there were probably also many inclinations that would now be considered gifts of embodiment. Some elements of the agonizing expressions of finite contra-causal freedom evident in the *Confessions* actually positioned Augustine's will in such a way that the appropriate conditions emerged for the kind of breakthrough that led to confidence and the dispelling of doubt.

It is well known that Augustine, unfortunately, did not remain in the theological stance just described, which recognized human impediments but honored human capacity not only for free-will as judging and choosing but also as the capacity to choose that which is good and of God—this being an expression of finite, realistically libertarian, and relational freedom. Instead, he progressed to an insistence that the human will is so corrupted by the consequence of Adam's sin that it lost the capacity to exercise itself to do any good on its own. Arendt suggests that Augustine's emphasis on an internal struggle was a reaction to the decline of freedom in the Roman Empire and thus gives a hint regarding the commerce between one's external circumstance and one's internal considerations. In this general framework, she says, the Christian approach to political freedom arose out of suspicion of and hostility toward the public realm from which they demanded to be released in order to be free. This approach exhibited a hope for civic freedom for the sake of salvation.[20] This evaluation reminds one of Neville's idea of internal freedom and the space it provides for the expression of ontological freedom, which includes the exercise of both intellect and will.

In regard to Augustine's theological shift, four additional factors should be taken into consideration. The most obvious and immediate factor was his theological struggle with Pelagius (and his followers), whose ideas I will soon explicate. However, other layers of concern would have existed beneath this conflict. The first would have been his ongoing struggle to live what he considered as the disciplined life, along with the need for assurance that despite his ongoing failure his salvation was secure. He also would have been affected by his struggle to settle the Donatist controversy.[21] On one hand, there were the church leaders who had renounced the faith in the face of Diocletian persecution, and, on the other hand, there were those who in their very attempt to protect the purity of the faith had acted arrogantly and unforgiving, and were even willing to undermine the unity of the body. It is probable that, given the behavior of both sides and Augustine's own ongoing struggle, an increased sense of the extent of human deficiency came home to him. Compounding his theological challenge was the accelerated demise of the Roman Empire, which reached a high point in the sack of Rome by the Visigoths in 410 CE. These crises together very likely suggested to Augustine, among other things, that human reason, the pursuit of self-discipline, super-piety, or even a life spent testifying to God's mercies could not thwart the overpowering influence of certain base impulses at the personal level. Military, political power and even ardent religiosity could not redirect the march of certain historical forces that influenced the rise and fall of nations. As a result, the most vital things necessary for the happiness and fulfillment often pursued by means of human judgment and choice (expressions of will) or sought by human beings through personal and/or institutional pursuits are actually beyond human capacity to attain. Indeed, they are completely in the hand of God, and this is the almighty God that "has the power to do whatever He wills to do."[22]

Augustine's developed sense of human deficiency expresses itself in a theological anthropology that is very evident in *City of God*. There we hear that as soon as our first parents disobeyed God by going against that which was good (was being willed by God) "they were immediately deprived of divine grace," and "the soul which had taken perverse delight in its own liberty and disdained the service of God, was now deprived of its original mastery over the body; because it had deliberately deserted the Lord who was over it, it no longer bent to its will the servant below. . . . From this moment then, the flesh began to lust against the spirit." Now "man corrupted by choice and condemned by justice, has produced a progeny that is both corrupt and condemned."[23] With sin now firmly anchored in human beings, we are left with a dilemma we cannot resolve: while we retain the power of free-will, we are now not capable of using this power to choose that which is good. Human will is corrupted and is no longer able not to sin and, thus there can no longer be any degree of confidence in good result from human struggle.[24] As such, those who are available for freedom through slavery to Christ are so not because of their free exercise of will but because they are made able by being specifically directed by God according to a predetermined plan. This general position is further developed in *Predestination of the Saints,* which emerges from his struggle with Pelagianism. In this work he acknowledges and explicitly renounces his previous position that human beings have a natural capacity for faith—this being the retention of a capacity inherent in us as creatures created by God in God's image.[25] He now ventures into important explication of the relation between grace and predestination, suggesting that while grace is the gift from God that enables faith, predestination is the preparation for grace. This being so, even the appearance of free-will in the midst of Augustine's struggles in the *Confessions* could be understood as having been predetermined by God to be a capacity through which grace would be bestowed on Augustine. He calls on Ephesians 2:9-10 and suggests not only that the believer is God's workmanship created in Christ for good works but also that the good works were prepared beforehand by God. Predestination cannot exist without foreknowledge, although there can be foreknowledge without predestination. "By predestination God indeed foreknew that which he himself was going to do, whence it was said: 'He has made that which shall be.'"[26] So then, the elect are chosen not because they have believed, but "they are chosen so that they may believe."[27]

Among the many ways Augustine dramatizes his claim is with a brief exposition of Ephesians 1:3-4. This he does in response to the position attributed to Pelagians that God foreknew who would be holy and spotless through the choice of their free-will, "and on that account chose them before the foundation of the world in his foreknowledge, by which he knew that they would be such." Augustine points out that the apostle Paul did not say God chose persons in Christ "'because we were going to be' so [holy and spotless]" but "'that we should be so." He continues: "It is evidently certain; it is evidently manifest. Clearly, we were going to be holy and spotless, because God chose us, predestining us that we might be such through his grace."[28] He is therefore in no doubt that "faith . . . both in its beginning and its completion is a gift of God," and that the believer should not be disturbed about the fact that the gift of faith was given only to some. This is because the sin of "one man" made all human beings condemned anyway, and so those not delivered got what they deserved. To the query by some regarding why God delivers some and not others, Augustine answers by quoting Romans 11:33: "'How incomprehensible are his judgments, and how unsearchable his ways.'" He continues: "For it is better for us here to listen or to say 'O man, who are you that replies against God?' than to dare to explain, as if we knew, what God has chosen to keep a secret—God who in any event could not will anything unjust."[29]

Some residue of his earlier disposition does show up in the later work *Grace and Free Will,* and so there seems to be a little space for free-will. In the closing section of chapter 2 Augustine acknowledges that in many passages in the Scriptures there are commands that God's precepts should be kept, and he asks: "How can He command if there is no free choice?" Pointing to Psalms 1:2 in which the psalmist indicates that his will has been according to the law of God, Augustine asks: "Does he not make it clear that it is by the will that man takes his stand on the side of God's law?" He points to a number of other passages and proceeds to the following question: "What do such numerous passages from the Books of the Old Testament show, except that man's will is possessed of free choice?"[30] At the same time the overwhelming emphasis of the book portrays the consequences of depending on our own capacities and devices, and the reader is reminded that God's grace is the central element in conversion and in the ability to choose good.[31] In this later work Augustine continues to battle Pelagianism and often frames his pronouncements in the form of a response to claims attributes to them, such as, that there is a form of grace that corresponds to human merits. In relentless argument and with copious references from the Scriptures, Augustine makes the case that if a person lives a good life "it is nothing more than the grace of God. Even more then, is eternal life, the recompense for a good life, without any doubt, also a grace of God; for it is freely given in recompense for that which has been freely given."[32]

I imagine then, that given opportunity to speak to Arendt, Augustine might well indicate to her that the insight he, like Paul before him, was given had not been granted to the ancients of Greece with whom she contrasts his stance, because they continued to live out the arrogance of the first human beings by thinking that they had the capacity through rational processes to gain freedom by means of self-mastery. Arendt, he might suggest, is woefully mistaken in thinking that freedom will come through submission to some general principle in the course of activity in the earthly city—this realm being one of deception because of conjectures like Arendt's or because of demons. As suggested by the general situation of a collapsing Roman Empire in which *City of God* was written, there is no guarantee that those called to be Saints will experience any form of external freedom so that one's "happy" life in relationship with God will translate into obvious external freedoms. Instead, the immediate boon for the person connected to God through God's gracious intervention in Christ is that in the midst of any category and level of unfreedom, she or he will still be enabled to make choices that are consistent with God's will and thus experience wholeness in its most authentic sense. To those like Arendt who are focused on the political arena, Augustine might suggest that only as the state (to the degree that it can) reflects the values of the heavenly city to which those predestined for Christ belong can it be rightly ordered and be a framework in which responsible freedom and peace prevail.

Augustine's recognition of human limitation and the consequent need for modesty in the assessment of our capacity to operate in correspondence to God's way should be taken seriously. A the same time, Augustine's extreme reactions to his internal and external life-situation progressively undermined his ability to recognize the importance and unavoidability of the human struggle for discernment, communion, and self-development—activities that are not necessarily antithetical to the valuing of grace as an ongoing feature of human lives that are complex-dynamic works in progress. This struggle is compounded by Augustine's limited understanding of the character of the human mind and the human body and thus the proper relation between them,[33] leading him to unrealistic expectations in regard to the ordering of one's life. More significantly, his doctrine of predestination seems to have been born of his desire for ultimate security in the midst of existential struggles. Whether or not Adam (and Eve) had sinned, only certain human beings would have had the privilege of wills oriented to right choice—that is, choice that results in salvation, inclination to the good, and authentic happiness.

## PELAGIUS—A HERETIC WITH GREAT INSIGHT

Human freedom, as finite freedom, will always be experienced within the strictures of established factors beyond the control of any individual or group of human beings. Along with limited brains and perceptual apparatus, these factors include the legacy of good and bad choices by generations of human beings and their consequences. Speaking to those like the later Augustine who took extreme positions on the extent of limitations on human freedom, Descartes suggested: "It would be absurd, simply because we do not grasp one thing [preordination], which we know must by its very nature be beyond our comprehension, to doubt something else [free-will] of which we have an intimate grasp and which we experience within ourselves."[34] As I've already suggested, the ideas of Pelagius were very influential in Augustine's change of mind on free-will. Martien Brinkman and John Ferguson help to make it clear that Pelagius's position was not the polar opposite of Augustine's as is sometimes suggested. Indeed, his views ought to be seen as a development of Augustine's earlier thought, showing how the integrity of the human being and the gracious authority of God can be honored together. At the same time, their obvious differences on crucial points might encourage even those who hold to the orthodox position that human beings have inherited a crippling deformity of the will to reconsider the extent of this deformity and explore ways in which the assessment of the implications might be nuanced. Pelagius's emphasis is not so much on freedom lost but on the inherited challenges that affect our ability to realize the promise of freedom inherent in our humanity.

Pelagius's theological pursuits seem to have been associated with his attempt to promote the uniqueness of Christian identity among those who were flocking to the church during the looming collapse of Rome. In his thinking, the image of God in human beings implies primarily a certain way of acting, rather than how humankind actually is ontologically. *Imago Dei* represents the goal of humankind made possible by God; that is, we are children of God not by nature but through imitation. This imitation is the imitation of God's justice. Of course there is always a tension between the possibilities created for us by God for imitation and what we actually choose to imitate as a result of our freedom.

Interestingly, Pelagius seems somewhat supportive of the "situated freedom"[35] discussed in chapter 1 when he asserts that, because man was created in the image of God, he is free, that is, free to realize our destiny: the image of God in himself. To that end God gives to human beings "'the gift of [their] own freewill.'" So then, freedom is an expression of grace, and it has everything to do with "leaving one free," that is, giving room or space, which allows for choice-making.[36] However, he is very clear that God's way of acting is not characterized by overwhelming omnipotence but by the gift of the possibility of imitating God in justice. The freedom human beings are given is therefore always a qualified freedom as to content. Here he sounds somewhat libertarian in his indication that "freedom is always implied by 'the choice between two ways.' It is always 'a freedom in two directions.'"[37] This freedom does not preclude the possibility of choosing evil, which is the reverse of the good that is the destiny of human beings given in creation.[38]

By way of elaboration, we hear that "the possibility of not sinning (the *posse non peccare*) belongs to true freedom and this human capacity (*posse*) is a possibility for the good that is supported by God but can be perverted by human beings." So then, "the human possibility to choose good is not an 'empty' possibility but a capability that tends towards good and therefore is not to be identified with indifference or unqualified autonomy."[39] John Ferguson reminds us that vitally important to Pelagius is that while God wished human beings to choose to do right, it was important to God that our fulfillment of God's way should come from our wills, not from God's will. This position presupposed what Ferguson terms "a natural holiness" in human hearts that was evident even in the lives of many pagan philosophers and patriarchs.[40]

Brinkman does well to remind us that Pelagius was clear that our experience and expression of freedom is indeed corrupted by sin. Yet Pelagius, seeming to echo Augustine's position in the *Confessions*, wisely insisted that "sin was not a substance which could be handed on and itself act upon human nature, but a quality to be discerned in individual action."[41] Not disagreeing with this view, Brinkman reminds us that Pelagius held that Adam's actions not only set a bad example but left deep traces on the human race. "Through Adam's sin a new, normative example was created which exerts a negative pull, just as the image of God exerts a positive pull." So then:

> In the case of Adam as image of God we are dealing with something that has to do directly with nature, the essence, of humankind, in the case of Adam as predecessor in sin we are dealing with a cause, an occasion (*occasio*) that has nothing to do with the destiny of human beings but which does have sweeping consequences.[42]

Here we are up against one of Augustine's significant points of contention with Pelagius, as is quite explicit in his *Treatise on the Grace of Christ and Original Sin*. In that work Augustine accuses Pelagius of subterfuge. Augustine's claim is that, while Pelagius publicly condemned those who held that God's grace is not associated with individual actions but consists of free-will and the gift of laws and teaching and also those who affirm that the grace of God is bestowed in proportion to merits, his books suggest that he holds the same positions. Pelagius, we are told, thinks that God helps us turn away from evil and do good by revealing and showing us what to do, not, as Augustine claims, by pouring love into us so that we do what we know we are to do.[43] Augustine identifies Pelagius's distinction between ability that is bestowed by God, and will and action that proceed from ourselves. Acknowledging that Pelagius did indicate that it is with the help of God's grace that human beings have the ability to turn away from sin, he hastens to indicate that "[Pelagius] does not believe that either our will or our action is aided by God's help, but only the ability for willing and for acting." This leads to the accusation that Pelagius is implying that the element that God places in human beings (that is, ability) is weak and needs help, while the elements Pelagius attributes to human beings (that is, will and action) are so strong and self-sufficient that they do not need help. This accusation reflects Augustine's desire to portray Pelagius as intent on diminishing the status of God's grace and exalting the status of human beings.

That Pelagius arrogates to human beings greater capacity than we actually have is seen by Augustine to be supported by a declaration in which praise is given to human beings when they exercise good will and good action, and only in a second clause is praise given to God for giving human beings the ability for good will and good action.[44] Pelagius is said to be in opposition to the apostle Paul's claim that while Christians are to work out their own salvation, it is God who works in us to produce the willing and the accomplishing. For Augustine, the root of the issue is that instead of recognizing that it is God who pours into the human will "the fire of love" so that we might will appropriately, Pelagius places this ability of the will in sinful human nature.[45]

My own reading of Augustine's representation of Pelagius's ideas suggests that Pelagius was attempting to carry out tasks that are vital for my approach to human freedom. He was acknowledging obvious features of the life-processes of human beings: we judge, we make choices, we act on choices. Quite appropriately Pelagius celebrates the fact that there are instances in which these tasks are successfully exercised in accomplishing good things and in pursuing a right relationship with God. There is the correct presumption that a genuine relationship must have been freely chosen by all the participants, even if one participant is more/most powerful. Given his Christian faith, Pelagius also wishes to give due praise to God, whom he considers the gracious creator that gave to human beings the capacity to grow in maturity through judgments and choices for which we are able to take responsibility and who, desiring genuine relationship with human beings, gave us the ability to seek after good and choose God by our own volition.

To Pelagius, the fact that human beings are able to will and effect any good work comes from God alone. Therefore, willing and acting are at root expressions of grace, and any gracious contribution God makes to human ability has direct implications for the character of willing and acting. Pelagius explicates the logic of the matter by indicating that while willing and acting are not necessary to God's gift of ability to human beings—that is, God could have given ability without including willing and acting, willing and acting necessarily presuppose ability. Augustine's suggestion that Pelagius's position implies that ability (which comes from God) is weak seems to be quite erroneous. Indeed, contrary to Augustine's allegation, Pelagius is testifying to the power of ability when he indicates that "I am free, therefore, to have neither my will nor my action good." He seems to be saying that in his exercise of that which depends on him, he may fail to use it as God desires; "but I cannot fail to have ability for good." Try as he might he cannot eliminate what God bestowed on him so that in its right exercise he might live as God desires. The ability for good, he insists, "is present in me, even if I do not want it, nor does nature ever take a holiday from itself in this respect."[46] Here it should be obvious that the use of "nature" is not an attempt to establish human beings as fundamentally autonomous but simply to refer to that which characterizes human beings *per se,* with the clear presupposition that we have been made so by God.

It is not illegitimate to interpret the claim in Philippians 2:13, attributed to Paul by Augustine, to be suggesting that it is God who works in persons to produce the willing and the accomplishing, meaning that God uses many expressions of grace to strengthen human ability to will and act in accordance with what God desires. It is also understandable that Pelagius was of the conviction that among the gracious means God uses would be law, given in order to provide guidance for the just ordering of life. It is also telling that by Augustine's representation Pelagius added that God helps us "through his teaching and revelation, in opening the eyes of our heart, in disclosing to us what is to come so that we may not be absorbed with what is present, in exposing the snares of the devil, in enlightening us by the manifold and ineffable gift of his heavenly grace." Nothing said here leaves the impression that Pelagius is locating God's grace solely in "the law and teaching," as Augustine suggests.[47] Neither is it plain, as Augustine later claims it should be, that when Pelagius speaks of "the grace by which God produces in us the willing that is good," he means "precisely the law and teaching,"[48] that is, nothing else but the law and the teaching.

Without doubt, Pelagius seems to have high regard for law and teaching, but he seems also to be highlighting the significance of the ongoing communion, which attunes the human to what God desires to be achieved through law and teaching. So, as human ability, which involves willing, acting, and the capacity for good, are expressions of God's grace, so are law and teaching and God's ongoing communion with human beings by which hearts are opened, minds are illumined, and the desire to do God's will is fueled. Therefore, I have great difficulty with Augustine's reaction to Pelagius in which he asserts that knowledge of the law unaccompanied by the assistance of grace is prejudicial and avails for producing the transgression of the commandment.[49] I understand Pelagius to be suggesting that the law, along with other means of guidance, is an expression of God's grace, and allowing this and other means of grace to facilitate appropriate response to law will enable the grace of the law to be manifested. Holding this position is not necessarily contradictory to the position that our attempts to live in accordance to the law help us to appreciate our need for grace.[50] So, there is righteousness in the law because it is, in the first place, an expression of God's grace and also because it opens us to our need for grace. At the same time, it is important for Pelagius that no means of grace can so dominate the human will that we lose our capacity to legitimately exercise our own will in the matter of good or evil, and in the final analysis, to genuinely choose to be in relationship with God.

Pelagius might well have been driven to excess in his enthusiasm to defend free-will, as when he is represented by Augustine to suggest that human beings merit the divine grace by doing the will of God. At the same time, it is Augustine who indicates that this suggestion should be understood "in the sense that additional grace is given to those who believe and live good lives." In the Pelagian scheme, any ability to do the will of God will be, in the first place, grounded in an unmerited gift given from God, and, in the second place, influenced by the associated capacity for good that human beings cannot eliminate. In addition, there are the various lures Augustine sought to reduce to law and teaching. Why then should Pelagius's apparently excessive position on human merits not be interpreted to be suggesting that it is those who use their free-will to choose what God wills who show themselves worthy of God's expressions of grace in initial gifts and ongoing lures? This declaration can additionally be interpreted to be suggesting that when we dispose ourselves to live in accordance with what God desires, we become more receptive to God's gracious activities in and around us. It might be argued that any view that human beings can be seen as worthy is excessive, but this would not be so in the way Augustine represents it.[51]

Actually, the words of Pelagius referred to by Augustine immediately after those just addressed do not seem to portray Pelagius as one who is promoting salvation by merit. It seems to be both an active response to a powerful lure and an acknowledgement of great need that "those who have recourse to the Lord and desire to be ruled by him, that is, who make their will dependent upon his will, who by constantly clinging to him become, as the apostle said, one spirit with him, achieves this simply by the freedom of choice."[52] Indeed, while some of Pelagius's language feels uncomfortable, it seems somewhat consistent with contemporary theologian Robert Neville's position that generally speaking "free choice" represents a scenario in which antecedent causal conditions allow for more than one possible outcome, and any actual outcome depends on the choice of the personal agent.[53] In other words, while conditions (ability, law, teaching, lures, circumstance of life, etc.) antecedent to a decision to "have recourse to the Lord" will be very influential, they will not have exercised deterministic causal control over the decision. The decision remains with the exercise of the will by the person making the decision.[54]

Pelagius did entertain the possibility of human beings living without sin,[55] and he seemed to have had difficulty giving confident support for it. This reticence is evident in Ferguson's description of an encounter between Pelagius and Orosius, one of Augustine's disciples. We are told that Orosius asked Pelagius directly to explain what he meant by the possibility of sinlessness. Pelagius replied: "'I did not mean that human nature has a natural endowment of sinlessness; I meant that the person who is prepared to toil and strive to avoid sin and to walk in the commandments of God on behalf of his own salvation, is granted by God the possibility of so doing.'" When there were further murmurings that Pelagius gave no place to the grace of God, Pelagius answered with scriptures that portrayed Paul's self-assessment: "'I laboured (*sic*) more abundantly than they all, yet not I but the grace of God which was within me,'" and again, "'It is not of him that willeth nor him that runneth but God that showeth mercy.'" He also quoted Psalm 127:1: "Except the Lord build the house they labour in vain that build it."[56] While Pelagius may have been excessive and unrealistic in regard to the human capacity to achieve sinlessness, his response to Orosius gives some idea of what is meant by Brinkman's claim that Pelagius attempted to find "a middle way between speaking of evil as 'only' a possibility and of evil as a compelling necessity."[57]

We gain more insight into Pelagius's attempt at a middle way through Brinkman's discussion of his commentary on Romans 7 where he distinguishes the power of sin from our real nature. Sin, he suggests, "only reigns *quasi naturaliter* as an intruder, and unwelcome guest, in our lives. Sin is therefore never a force that *naturale* belongs to human existence but an 'extra' (*accidens*) force."[58] So while Pelagius, like Augustine, does not believe that human beings start from an ethically neutral point in every new situation in our lives, he does not, like Augustine, adopt "a collectivist, fatalistic position in which sin is considered to be so firmly anchored in human nature that we have no choice but to do evil and are incapable of any good."[59]

Without doubt, Pelagius insisted that only in Christ could one be free of the vexing reality of the power of sin, and this freedom has nothing to do with any merit on our part. We embrace God's gift of grace when in faith (which involves active assent and will) we accept Christ. Pelagius emphasized this position by using the paradoxical expression: "'Only by faith (grace), and yet not without faith (one's own assent).'"[60] This two-pronged approach is maintained in his claim that it is the continuation of grace in the life of the Christian that enables one "to do in freedom what human beings are destined to do. In that way, grace opens 'the secret treasures of nature.'"[61] By this faith and grace the potential of humanity given at creation can once again be realized in full. On the other hand, as freedom in "the concrete" is unthinkable without grace, so is it "unthinkable without personal responsibility and personal decisions. Hence freedom is not only a gift but also a task."[62]

As a result of this approach Pelagius does not have to resort to predestinationism, which disparages humanity *as such* and raises challenges in regard to God's justice, or to association with the kind of position on God's sovereignty that seems to incline many Christians to an ethic of coercive power in which might makes right.

As suggested above, Pelagius was misguided in his view that human beings had the ability to achieve sinlessness. At the same time, his overall position on free-will protects the integrity of natural human processes that involve making judgments on the basis of criteria grounded in general principles, and focused according to the demands of "situation." This exercise of judgment often leads to decisions on matters evaluated as less, more, or most important, and at times may even go against what one finds most comforting or pleasurable. Indeed, that which Arendt characterizes as the will conflicted in itself is most striking in situations where the difference between greater goods and lesser goods is evident in aspects of issues or situations rather than between issues or situations as a whole and in shades and degrees of difference that make qualitative distinctions difficult to assess. With the internal struggle represented as above, there can indeed be stalemates within the will as one is caught between *velle* and *nolle*, and this quandary may or may not be resolved when one arrives at a periodic or long-lasting position that results in concrete choices.

When contrasted with Augustine's extreme position of predestinationism, that which results from Pelagius's framework better reflects human experience. No doubt, some will agree with Ferguson that where Pelagius's analysis is inadequate is in its failure to distinguish between the nature of an action and the moral quality of the motive from which it springs.[63] My own view on this issue is that neither Pelagius nor Augustine, nor any other human, ever really knows the deep motives of any other human being; often there is even difficulty knowing one's own motives. However, by honoring the ongoing human struggle to make correct decisions in the midst of competing and compelling interests and in light of the ambiguity that characterizes the life of human beings born of woman and man, and by presupposing a sufficient degree of personal autonomy contingent on freedom of will, Pelagius and others like him contribute to the ability to justifiably attribute personal accountability as a meaningful feature of ongoing efforts at social organization on a general level and in determining the concrete implications of living as a Christian.

## NOTES

1. Augustine, *On Free Choice of the Will*, trans. Thomas Williams (Indianapolis: Hackett Publishing Company, 1993), [2.1], 30.
2. Ibid., [1.1], 1.
3. Ibid., [1.3-4, 1.4, 1.5], 6-8.
4. Ibid., [1.11], 17.
5. Ibid., [1.8, 1.12], 19.
6. Ibid., [2.1, 2.2], 30-31.
7. Augustine of Hippo, *Confessions*, trans. R. S. Pine-Coffin (London: Penguin Books, 1961) [7.16], 150.
8. Ibid. [7.16, 17], 151-152.
9. Ibid.
10. In chapter 1 I mentioned relevant insights from Damasio's *Descartes' Error* and from Cobb's *The Structure of Christian Existence*.
11. Augustine, *Confessions*, [8.9], 172.
12. Hanna Arendt, *Between Past and Future* (New York: Viking Press, 1961), 158-9.
13. Ibid. Arendt's evaluation still has relevance even if Paul was not talking about himself but utilizing "speech in character," a literary device allowing an author to identify with an audience.
14. Ibid., 162.
15. Ibid., 160.
16. Augustine, *Confessions*, [8.12], 178.
17. Ibid. [10.34], 241.
18. Ibid. [8.5], 164.
19. Ibid., 164-165.

20. Arendt, *Between Past and Future*, 158.

21. This controversy is named after Donatus, who became bishop of Carthage in 313 CE and leader of a rigorist group that had broken away from the church over the consecration of one Caecilian as bishop of Carthage in 311. One of the consecrators, Felix of Aptunga, was accused of having surrendered copies of the Scriptures to the civil authorities during the Diocletian persecution. In the assessment of Donatists, the resulting contamination corrupted not only Caecilian and his successors, but anyone who maintained communion with them. This is found in J. N. D. Kelly, *Early Christian Doctrine,* rev. ed. (New York: Harper San Francisco, 1978), 410.

22. Augustine, *City of God,* trans. Gerald Walsh et al. (New York: Image Books, 1958), [21.7], 500.

23. Ibid., [13.13], 278.

24. Augustine's extreme struggle with his own sexuality is evident in his claim that before the fall human procreation would not have required sexual excitation, but by deliberate choice the seminal fluid would have gone from the male to the female, even without rupture of the hymen. Ibid. [14.26], 318.

25. Augustine, "On the Predestination of the Saints," in *Four Anti-Pelagian Writings*, trans. John Mourant and William Collinge, vol. 86. Fathers of the Church: A New Translation (Patristic Series). (Washington DC: The Catholic University of America Press, 1992), 224. Earlier on page 223 Augustine indicated that pronouncements by Cyprian were influential in his change of mind.

26. Ibid., 241.

27. Ibid., 258.

28. Ibid., 262.

29. Ibid., 238.

30. Augustine, "Grace and Free Will," in *The Teacher, Free Choice of the Will, Grace and Free Will*, ed. Roy Joseph Deferrari (editorial director emeritus), trans. Robert P. Russell, The Fathers of the Church (Washington, DC: The Catholic University of America Press, 1968), 253.

31. Ibid., 266.

32. Ibid., 272.

33. I am simply stating this as a fact, and not trying to suggest that Augustine should have had information that only became available in later times.

34. Rene Descartes, "Principles of Philosophy," section 1.40- 41, in *The Philosophical Writings of Descartes*, vol. I, trans. John Cottingham, Robert Stoothoff, and Dugald Murdoch (Cambridge: Cambridge University Press, 1985), 206.

35. Recall the discussion of "situated freedom" in chapter 1 of this work, from Burrell, *Faith and Freedom*, 106.

36. Martien Brinkman, *The Tragedy of Human Freedom: The Failure of the Christian Concept of Freedom in Western Culture*, trans. Harry Flecken and Henry Jansen (New York: Rodopi, 2003), 117. Brinkman's reference is Pelagius, *Expositions* 87 (PLS I, 1160).

37. Ibid., 117-118. Brinkman's reference is Pelagius, *Espitola ad Demetriadem* 3 (PL 30,17c).

38. Ibid., 118.

39. Ibid. The latter quotation is from G. Greshake, *Gnade als Konkrete Freiheit. Eine Untersuchung zur Gnadenlehre des Pelagius.* (Mainz, 1972), 64.

40. John Ferguson, *Pelagius—A Historical and Theological Study* (Cambridge: W. Heffer and Sons Ltd., 1956), 60. On page 59 Ferguson mentions contemporary personalities, notably one of Pelagius's female students, Demetrias.

41. Ibid., 160. From Augustine, *De Natura et Gratia*, xix, 21.

42. Brinkman, *The Tragedy of Human Freedom*, 118-119.

43. Augustine, *Treatise on the Grace of Christ and Original Sin*, in *Works of Augustine: A Translation for the 21st Century [Answer to Pelagius]*, ed. John E. Rotelle O.S.A., trans. Ronald J. Teske, S.J. (New York: New City Press, 1997), 404.

44. Ibid., 405.

45. Ibid., 406.

46. Ibid., 405.
47. Ibid., 407.
48. Ibid., 409.
49. Ibid., 407.
50. Ibid.
51. Ibid., [chapt. 24],415.
52. Ibid.
53. Robert Neville, *A Theology Primer* (Albany: State University of New York Press, 1991), 78-79.
54. Ibid.
55. Augustine, *Confessions*, [chapt. 5], 405.
56. Ferguson, *Pelagius*, 84. These quotes are from 1 Cor. 15:10, Romans 9:16, and Psalm 127:1, respectively.
57. Brinkman, *The Tragedy of Human Freedom*, 119.
58. Ibid. Brinkman's reference is Pelagius, *Expositiones* 59-60 and 90 (PLS I, 1144 and 1162).
59. Ibid., 119-120.
60. Ibid., 120. Brinkman's reference is Pelagius, *Expositiones* 353 (PLS I, 1293).
61. Ibid., 121. Brinkman's reference is Pelagius, *Epistola ad Demetriadem* 6 (PL 30, 22a).
62. Ibid. Brinkman's reference is Greshake, *Grande als konkrete Freiheit*, 150-52.
63. Ferguson, *Pelagius*, 161.

*Chapter Three*

# Reformed, but Not Free

The doctrine of justification by grace through faith alone has been paraded as the centerpiece of the freedom-enabling disposition of the broad Reformation tradition. However, this doctrine covers over a framework of thought that in the final analysis undermines the integrity of human beings by portraying as insignificant their role in matters of faith and reinforces a concept of God patterned from ancient kings, emperors, and lords who fit the characterization tyrant. This undermining of freedom in the name of freedom is carried out quite effectively by the quintessential reformer, Martin Luther, as he wrestles with the Catholic humanist Desiderius Erasmus—a struggle that in important ways mirrored the contrast between the positions of Augustine and Pelagius. Luther is explicit in his intention to shatter free-will in order to establish the idea of a God who foresees, purposes, and does all things according to his own immutable, eternal, and infallible will. This position not only devastates human agency but suggests that God should then be factored as the principal causal agent in what is classified as "the fall." Further, it undermines the foundation for ethical evaluations by Christians, especially when we hear from Luther that even though being good God cannot do evil, God uses the devil to do evil deeds. Erasmus, in his response to Luther, reinforces the validity of the synergistic view that human freedom is both a gift and a task, through which we exercise the power of the will to embrace or turn away from that which God desires of us. Calvin's predestinationism, which has a strong family resemblance to Luther's position, only makes more explicit the problem the orthodox position poses for a doctrine of sin and for ethical evaluation already present in Luther's attempted demolition of free-will. This predestinationism strengthens the image of God as tyrant, and this is not mitigated by the associated compatibilist approach to freedom. Without doubt twentieth-century Reformed giant Karl Barth is to be commended for his modification of Calvin's double predestination by his development of the concept of the humanity of God, and his use of the language of partnership to talk about God-human relations. However, the God Barth portrays is still the eternal sovereign-free-absolute who surrounds humanity from all sides. This being so, even with the claim that each human must embrace God's choice of them to be God's partners, there is not enough "room" for us to have free-choice in the realistically libertarian sense.

## LUTHER AND ERASMUS—DELVING BENEATH THE RHETORIC OF GRACE

Augustinian thought is clearly the foundation for Luther's view that all human perceptions are disfigured and our judgments are tainted. In Luther's view, trust in reason is reflective of a false estimation of human ability and reliance of human effort. It is linked to the folly of "works-religion" that "panders to man's cardinal sin, his pride in his own achievements and his desire to be self-sufficient." While this inclination heightens human pride regarding our own achievements and our desire to be self-sufficient, it tyrannizes the conscience, leading to perpetual fear of falling short of a required standard. Yet, it seems our sinful nature demands that we must proceed by the route of "will-works."[1]

Luther's view of the extent of the human dilemma is evidenced in his claim that on the path of will-works our reasoning does enable us to see clearly that good is to be promoted and evil avoided. However, Luther also reminds us that reason alone cannot tell what is good or what is evil. Natural reason, he suggests, "is like a man who wants to go to Rome, knows that there is a right road to get there, but cannot decide which direction it is." In other words, reason is only aware of a purely formal sense of moral obligation but it cannot attach this sense of obligation to specific duties or concrete policies of conduct.[2] Regarding the solution to this dilemma, Luther, like Augustine, holds that God's grace has made provision for us to be directed to the right path. It is this orientation that is usually lifted up in popular discussions of Lutheran theology under the caption "justification by grace through faith."

Luther argues that the righteousness fundamental for salvation is "alien righteousness" that is "instilled in us without our works by grace alone—while the Father, to be sure, inwardly draws us to Christ—is set opposite original sin, likewise alien, which we acquire without our works by birth alone."[3] Luther's treatise on "The Freedom of a Christian," sent to Pope Leo X in 1519, gives an idea of the scenario set up by God to point human beings toward the correct path of salvation. In this work, Luther claims, among other things, that Scripture is divided into commandments and promises. The former teach things that are good, but the things taught are not done as soon as they are taught, for the commandments show us what we ought to do but do not give us the power to do it. "They are intended to teach man to know himself, that through them he may recognize his inability to do good and may despair of his own ability."[4] It is this despair that makes us open up to the power of the gospel preeminently reflected in the fact that it was the devastation of the cross which set the stage for the resurrection of Jesus the Christ.

Living in the resurrected life of Christ through faith "Christ's righteousness becomes our righteousness and all that he has becomes ours; rather, he himself becomes ours." This first and alien righteousness, Luther suggests, "is an infinite righteousness, and one that swallows up all sin in a moment, for it is impossible that sin should exist in Christ." While the sin is taken up in Christ all at once, the alien righteousness continues in one's life until it is made perfect at the end through death. It is living in the resurrected life of Christ that human beings express the second kind of righteousness, their "proper righteousness" which is dependent on the first kind. It "is that manner of life spent profitably in good works, in the first place, in slaying the flesh and crucifying the desires with respect to the self, of which we read in Gal. 5:24." This righteousness also involves "love to one's neighbor" and "meekness and fear toward God." In the process the Christian is transformed into Christ's likeness.[5]

As we proceed, it will become evident that despite the suggestion of some degree of human freedom in the exercise of faith, there was beneath these declarations a theological substructure that had been thoroughly infected by Augustine's most extreme ideas that undermines any contemporary attempt to base a doctrine of human freedom on Luther's doctrine of salvation by grace through faith.

Erasmus was not enthusiastic about entering into a debate with Luther. He had to be cajoled by associates into making a response to Luther's teachings on free-will, the result being his small treatise of 1524 setting out his difficulty with the latter's position. This Erasmus did with due recognition that Luther's teachings constituted the primary voice of the Reformation movement. Exactly because of this recognition, it is quite disappointing that in his treatise Erasmus only makes reference to second hand opinions of Luther's ideas. It seems that to appease his fellow Catholics, he had never actually read Luther. He had spent much time identifying challenges associated with the process of interpreting the scriptures, these ranging from the limited capacity of human beings to know to the fact that there are some things God does not wish for us to know. Given his basic convictions, Erasmus was actually not enamored by many customary religious claims, and at times he leaned toward skepticism. His struggle in these matters resulted in the declaration that, although he held that scripture cannot contradict itself, there are some passages that obviously support freedom of the will and some seeming to deny it. With this background, his basic definition of free choice was "the power of the human will by which a man can apply to or turn away from that which leads unto eternal salvation,"[6] and based on what he had heard about Luther's doctrine, he concluded that it violated this basic definition.

As part of the general foundation for his argument against Luther, Erasmus expresses the view that although as Adam's progeny the human being possesses free-will that has been wounded, it is not extinct. Although the will has contracted a paralysis making it susceptible to sin, free-will has not been destroyed.[7] Having said this, he hastens to state his difficulty with the Pelagian position, which, in his view, ascribes too much free choice to human beings. In what I consider a misrepresentation of Pelagius's position, Erasmus claims that he held the view that once through the death and resurrection of Jesus Christ liberating and healing grace was received, no new grace was needed to enable human beings to exercise free-will toward salvation. Erasmus then differentiates his position by declaring: "But we owe salvation solely to God without whose grace the will of man could not be effectively free to achieve good." He continues: "The strength of soul, with which man can pursue the good he knows and avoid all evil, is in itself a gift of the creator." There is no doubt that, being a Christian humanist, Erasmus, not unlike both Pelagius and the early Augustine, wished to protect the idea that the goodness that characterizes the human being by virtue of being God's creation could not be eclipsed by human action. Also, while expressing leanings that are consistent with Pelagius's explicit declarations, he is again not out of step with the spirit of Augustine's early declarations, when he suggests that there had been non-Christian philosophers who possessed some knowledge of God, and hence also some trust and love of God. As a result these philosophers "did not act solely out of vainglory's sake, but rather out of love of virtue and goodness, which, they taught, was to be loved for no other reason but that it is good."[8]

Erasmus's position was that what was evident in these non-Christian philosophers reflected a capacity with which all human beings start out because of a natural grace given by God. In his view, Luther's position that the human will on its own had no capacity for good served to minimize God's mercy in one place in order to enlarge it elsewhere. Thus God visited the consequences of one person's sin unto all in order that the death and resurrection of one person would enable justification through faith, even though the justified can still do nothing else but be sinners.[9] Erasmus suggests that, by denying any freedom to the human will, Luther's position affirms absolute necessity, and is tantamount to the admission that God works in human beings not only the good works, but also evil ones.[10] He suggests that the "conditional promises" found in the Scriptures make no sense if, in the end, it all depends on God.[11] There is agreement with the Lutheran position that God's grace is associated with every exercise of will that leads to salvation, but the Lutheran standard is contravened with the claim that there is cooperation between grace and free-will. This position Luther might have perceived as somewhat acceptable when addressing certain mundane matters of everyday life. However, it was for him completely unacceptable to suggest that any good effort, on the part of human beings, had any merit where salvation was concerned—this being so, even if, as I suggest, there appeared to be some degree of human freedom in the response of faith. At first glance, this would also not be inconsistent with Luther's declaration that "salvation belongs to the eternal order and is incomprehensible to human capacity."[12]

In articulating his moderate synergistic stance on free-will, Erasmus spent much effort struggling with the concept of grace, from which emerged his own multilevel explication. Beyond "natural grace" with which everyone was born, was "extraordinary grace," which moved the undeserving sinner to contrition and "offers everyone favorable opportunities for repentance." Yet, even when one has not abandoned the inclination to sin, that person is capable of "giving alms, can pray, practice pious exercises, listen to sermons, request pious people to intercede for him with God, and thus by means of these and other ethically good works, apply in a way for obtaining the ultimate grace." No one is refused this grace. "One needs only to attach the rest of one's own will to God's help, which merely invites to, but does not compel to betterment."[13] Lured by God's grace we must turn our wills, which in the first place God has made capable of turning one way or another, toward the way that leads to salvation. Then "efficient (cooperative) grace" and "final grace" leads to the final goal.[14]

Erasmus was clear that at all times God should receive glory. He writes: "We should not arrogate anything to ourselves but attribute all things we have received to the divine grace, which called us when we were turned away, which purified us by faith, which gave us this gift, that our will might be synergos (a 'fellow-worker') with grace, although grace is itself sufficient for all things and has no need of the assistance of human will." Commenting on Philippians 2:13, he suggests that "a good will cooperates with the action of grace." He is explicit that grace is the principal cause and the will secondary; the latter can do nothing apart from the principal cause, since the principal cause is sufficient in itself. By way of analogy, he indicates: "Just as fire burns by its natural strength, and yet the principal cause is God who acts through the fire, and this cause would of itself be sufficient, without which the fire could do nothing if he withdrew from it." He also points us to the experience of a child who could not have stood up if the father had not helped him to his feet. This child could not have grasped the apple if the father had not assisted his feeble legs. Indeed, there would have been no apple for the child if the father had not shown one to him. Then in wonderful dialectical mode Erasmus first asks: "What then can the infant claim for itself?" Then he adds: "Yet he did do something."[15]

In his scathing response, Luther indicates that it is Erasmus's claim regarding the will's contribution to salvation that is the hinge upon which their disputation turns. Luther suggests that Erasmus's lack of clarity on this matter is quite disastrous, "for you cannot know what 'freewill' is without knowing what ability man's will has, and what God does, and whether he foreknows of necessity."[16] Here that which lies behind the notion of salvation by grace through faith becomes quite explicit as Luther states unequivocally that "it is fundamentally necessary and wholesome for Christians to know that God foreknows nothing contingently, but that He foresees, purposes, and does all things according to His own immutable, eternal, and infallible will." This "bombshell," he says, "knocks 'freewill' flat, and utterly shatters it."[17]

Erasmus's discussion is not nearly as elaborate and explicative as is Luther's. Still it is interesting that, in his response, Luther does not refer to important elements of Erasmus's discussion, like that on the operation of the levels of grace listed above. I also find noteworthy that in the process of his attack on Erasmus, he turns what I think is a clear indication of Erasmus's recognition of human limitation beyond that associated with finitude *per se* (which is the result of sin) into an occasion to label him a semi-Pelagian. Luther claims that, while Pelagius had argued that free-will included both the power of discernment and choice, Erasmus ascribes to free-will only the power of choice. On the basis of his view that to locate in free-will any capacity that contributes to salvation would be to ascribe divinity to it, Luther suggests that Erasmus's "restraint" was tantamount to making "a lame 'half-freewill' into a God."[18]

Given my reading of Erasmus, Luther's accusation seems mostly an attempt to slander him. Erasmus's claim concerning the will's limitation seems quite consistent with his position that, as a result of the fall, the human will has subsisted in a weakened state, but is not totally depraved and corrupted. Neither does it contradict the view that, while the will is now obscured by sin, it is not altogether extinguished in its capacity for willing—it remains free in that it continues to do what it was designed to do, and that is to will (make judgments and take decisions). Being God's creation and made in the image of God, which human beings can do nothing about or change by virtue of our actions, human beings remain rational and never lose completely the inclination to will that which is of God.[19] However, being now diminished in its capacity to appreciate the meaning of God's laws and other signs pointing to what God wills, the will is much more prone to choose inconsistently with what God desires.[20] And whatever good results from our pursuits and merits gained as a result, it is not sufficient for salvation.

In striking contrast to Erasmus's understanding, Luther's reading of the Scriptures led him at one point in his response to portray human beings as hapless, helpless "beasts of burden" caught in a struggle between God and Satan. In what seems a dramatic rendition of Augustine's position, he asserts that the human will has no power "to choose to which rider it will run, or which it will seek; but the riders themselves fight to decide who shall have and hold it. If God rides, it wills and goes where God wills . . . If Satan rides, it wills and goes where Satan wills."[21] Luther does acknowledge that, where it concerns our use of money and possessions, there is a kind of free-will, but this has no application to matters of salvation and damnation.[22] In the process of argument Luther attempts to show that Erasmus unwittingly denies what he strove to affirm. So he makes a case which has at its center the claim that Erasmus's position was "that freewill exists and has power, though ineffective without God's grace." In Luther's thinking, this is like saying "freewill is something which is not free,"[23] and this is a contradiction in terms.

Erasmus does accord to human will more effective capacity than Luther acknowledges. While free-will is not the sufficient cause of salvation, it is of such necessity that without its exercise by human beings they will have no salvation.[24] On the other hand, my recognition that Erasmus believed that it is only through grace that the will is enabled to lay hold unto salvation, makes me resistant to Luther's claim that, by Erasmus's stance, only the least valuable part of human beings (the flesh) was redeemed while the most excellent part (the will) was self-sufficient and not needing Christ.[25]

Luther's leaning toward the negation of human freedom in the matter of salvation should be clear by now. At the same time, it might be pointed out by some that in Luther's scheme God's sovereignty does not give God absolute control over human redemption—the human may will as Satan wills. This is an interesting point because, according to Luther, the human condition is such that we sin by necessity; that is, we sin "not of compulsion, but of what they call immutability." In this condition, the human "without the Spirit of God does not do evil against his will . . . but he does it spontaneously and voluntarily." This, Luther says, "is what we mean by necessity of immutability: that will cannot change itself, nor give itself another bent, but, rather, is the more provoked to crave the more it is opposed, as its chafing proves."[26] It is exactly this thinking that further elevates Luther's perspective on God's gracious work through Christ in the minds of many contemporary admirers.

These persons would certainly appreciate Walter Altmann's representation of Luther's quite combative Christology. He portrays Jesus' self-emptying as occurring within the context of a battle against tyrannical powers. Not only does Jesus enter in the situation of captive humanity in a battle of historic and cosmic dimensions, but he goes into the depths of hell in order to free the imprisoned. Christ, who is eternal and insuperably righteousness, makes himself the supreme—the only sinner. All the fury and violence of the world's sin is arrayed against his righteousness, damnation against blessing. Jesus becomes "at the same time cursed and blessed, at the same time alive and dead, at the same time grieving and rejoicing, so that he might absorb all evils in Himself and bestow all blessings from himself." The result is that Satan and his associates are routed and human beings are freed, restored to God's favor, taken as God's own and under God's protection.[27]

According to popular ways of interpreting Luther, it is operating under this protection that the Christian "is a perfectly free lord of all, subject to none," and it is living by God's grace as a justified sinner that one is able to be "a perfectly dutiful servant of all, subject to all."[28] The Christian who truly appreciates this condition lives her life constantly reminding herself that "although I am an unworthy and condemned [person], my God has given me in Christ all the riches of righteousness and salvation without any merit on my part, out of pure, free mercy, so that from now on I need nothing except faith which believes that this is true."[29]

That just described can certainly be exhilarating for some. However, as one who promotes human freedom that is finite, realistically libertarian, and relational, I cannot avoid receiving its portrayal of Christ's work and its consequences in light of Luther's strident assertion quoted earlier that "it is fundamentally necessary and wholesome for Christians to know that God foreknows nothing contingently, but that He foresees, purposes, and does all things according to His own immutable, eternal, and infallible will."[30] I, therefore, suggest that those who wish to protect human freedom by arguing that God eternally foreknows what human beings would do contingently should appreciate that this is not Luther's position. Luther's position is that "being done contingently" does not, in Latin, signify that the thing done is itself contingent, only that it is done by a will that is contingent and changeable. A deed, he suggests, cannot be said to be contingent unless it is done contingently. Here he proposes what seems a conveniently extreme understanding of contingent action, beginning with the claim that it would be "by chance (as it were) and without premeditation."[31]

My assessment of this understanding is reinforced by his further explanation that contingency occurs "when our will or hand fastens on something presented to us as if by chance, without our having previously thought or planned anything about it."[32] I argue that the more customary understanding of contingency can be explicated in terms of: (a) contingent truths, that is, propositions that while true can be denied without self-contradiction; (b) contingent events, that is, possible occurrences that may or may not happen, or an actual occurrence the non-occurrence of which can be envisaged without self-contradiction. None of these preclude previous thought or planning by one who articulates propositions or takes decisions that lead to one or other kind of occurrence internal or external to one's self. Contingent actions and events would be linked to contra-causal freedom because, under conditions such as those I set out in chapter 1, antecedent causal conditions would allow for more than one possible outcome, and any actual outcome would depend on the choice of the personal agent, with the agent being the relevant cause for determining the outcome. In this scenario of contingent action "antecedent conditions do not have a deterministic causal control over the process of human choice and action . . . although they present the causal materials that the person mixes in decisive ways."[33]

Nevertheless, it was a process of argument which seems to presuppose commitment to God's eternity and simplicity that led to Luther's explication of contingency. He argues that if Erasmus claims that "God is by nature just, and kindness itself," which connote immutability, he must say the same for God's knowledge, wisdom, goodness, will, and other divine attributes. He suggests that it is therefore inappropriate to claim that God's will is immutable and yet prohibit claims regarding God's foreknowledge. Therefore, Luther suggests by a rhetorical question that God wills what God foreknows and foreknows what is willed. Soon after he makes a claim which challenges any thought one might harbor that his recognition of contingency in human action might be taken to suggest that there is any aspect of human life over which God does not have deterministic causal control. He insists that "all we do, however it might appear to us to be done mutably and contingently, is in reality done necessarily and immutably in respect of God's will."[34] Where the mundane matters in which human beings have a kind of free-will are concerned, he insists that even these decisions are "overruled" by God's free-will, which God exercises according to God's own pleasure.[35] This follows from his clear conviction that, in the final analysis, power belongs to God, and so God's "changeless and sure" will rules over the mutable (and corrupted) will of human beings.[36]

The extent of Luther's conviction on the dominating power of a sovereign God is expressed as he identifies "the God of this world" on one hand, "the true God" (Satan), on the other, and discusses the relation between them. He takes the position that even though Satan works against God and seeks to destroy human beings, Satan ultimately serves God's will in the world. Luther declares: "So that which we call the remnant of nature in the unGodly and in Satan, as being a creature and a work of God, is no less subject to Divine omnipotence and action than all the rest of God's creatures and works. Since God moves and works all in all, He moves and works of necessity even in Satan and the unGodly."[37] So important is the defense of God's absolute rule that Luther proceeds to claim that God works in Satan and the unGodly "according to what they are, and what he finds them to be"; that is, God works through their evil and perversion. The convoluted ethics that results from this defense of God's omnipotence and sovereignty is evident in the following declaration, which suggests that God does God's "dirty work" through evil agents God created and who have no choice in the matter—yet they alone are culpable. Here you see that when God works in and through evil people, evil deeds result; yet God, though He does evil by means of evil men, cannot act evilly Himself, for He is good and cannot do evil; but He uses evil instruments, which cannot escape the impulse and movement of His power. The fault which accounts from evil being done when God moves to action lies in these instruments, which God does not allow to be idle.[38]

With this in mind, how can one reasonably discount the complaints raised by Erasmus in reaction to "conditional promises" in the Scriptures which imply free-will? As if speaking to God, Erasmus asks:

Why do you [God] make conditional promises, when it depends solely on your will? Why do you blame me, when all my works, good or bad, are accomplished by you, and I am only your tool? Why blame me, when it is neither in my power to preserve what you gave me, nor to keep away the evil you implant in me? Why do you implore me, when everything depends on you anyhow and can be carried out only by your will? Why bless me, as if I had done my duty, when everything is your achievement? Why do you curse me, when I have merely sinned through necessity? What is the purpose of many commandments, if it is impossible for anybody to keep them?[39]

My reading of Luther demands that I now push beyond Erasmus's complaints with my own questions concerning the foundation of Luther's doctrines of sin and salvation. First I ask: On the basis of what has been said so far, might we be justified in declaring that from our parents Adam and Eve till now, as helpless beasts of burden, human beings have been caught up in a titanic struggle about which they have had little to no say?[40] When I consider this matter in light of Luther's earlier-quoted declarations, which suggested that human beings will according to who rides them, God or Satan, I am also led to ask: Is not that which we will, at any particular time, attributable to either God or to Satan? Might it not be that Adam and Eve had little chance, being caught between "the powers," and we most definitely have little responsibility for our basic condition? Even if Luther is convinced that the carnal mind is "death itself and enmity itself,"[41] might it not be that the carnal mind is, in the final analysis, God's responsibility? And while some might take joy in Luther's view that the ability of human beings to be what God wants us to be must be given by God, is this necessarily an expression of grace? In the scenario, which involves the struggle between riders, is it not reasonable to view the work of redemption as having very little to do with human benefit, but as simply the result of a power-play in which God repossesses God's hapless, helpless human creatures who had been taken captive by God's opponent through the seduction of our first parents?

## Is This What God's Grace and Christian Freedom Look Like?!

In answering this question I begin with Jürgen Moltmann's declaration that "Luther proceeded from the 'unfree will' in order to find the freedom of faith."[42] I suggest that Luther develops the notion of the unfree will for the sake of his God-concept, which is that of a tyrant God who actually rules with an iron fist, but is made to seem benevolent when the human is made to seem incompetent and most needy and every appearance of intrinsic goodness and worth in her is discredited. Much like the experience of my slave ancestors in the Caribbean who were systematically stripped of any sense of native worth so that they would perceive as noble and humanizing their enslavement by European Christians, there is the attempt to make the absolute rule of the all-controlling tyrant God of Christian orthodoxy seem like ultimate benevolence. We hear then in Luther's commentary on chapter 3 of Romans that the expression "all under sin" must be taken in a spiritual sense, which means that it does not deal with human beings as they appear in their own eyes and before other human beings, but as they are before God. There "they are all under sin, both those that are obviously evil even in the sight of men and those who appear to be good to themselves as well as other men."[43]

Human beings may indeed be all under sin in that our existence as finite creatures alienates us from that which is our ultimate ground, and, being finite works in progress, we certainly will miss the mark where the good is concerned. Nevertheless, we operate in this general condition in different ways. I contend that one who has grown up with abuse and has had their psyches twisted for life is not under sin in the same as the violator. The oppressed slave, poor, woman, minority are not under sin in the same way as the slave owner, exploiter, oppressive-abusive male, racist, etc. The animist Taino encountered by Christopher Columbus in the Caribbean, and who Bartolome de Las Casas describes as "a docile and good-natured people, accustomed to the practice of moral virtue more than any other nation,"[44] were not under sin in the same way as the Spanish Christians who set upon them in the name of God and Crown, enslaving them, brutalizing them, forcing them to be Christians, and wiping them out as a viable culture. To be able to say they were so, one would have to become as cynical as Luther sounds in further commentary on Romans 3: "Even though they do good works outwardly, they do them either because they fear punishment or because they love riches or glory or some other creature good, but not because they want to do them gladly; so the outer man, it is true, applies himself diligently to good works, but the inner man is filled to overflowing with opposite lusts and desires."[45] Luther and his spiritual mentors Augustine and Paul were very aware of their own lives and the lives of some members of the communities of which they were a part, but neither the fact that Paul's assessment is classified as Scripture or Augustine's and Luther's classified as

Christian classics justifies the obscuring of different ways in which persons have exercised their wills in judgment and decision-making as they operate in the world.

I proceed to the close of my discussion on Luther by stating my difficulty with Paul Tillich's alignment with Luther's position on free-will over that of Erasmus's (and Pelagius's), in which he insists that Luther's position does not lead to philosophical determinism. The doctrine of the bondage of the will, he suggests, presupposes the freedom of the will—that is, "Only what is essentially free can come under existential bondage." Characterizing existential bondage as "sin" refers to the freedom human beings have to contradict our essential nature. Tillich suggests that grace, as emphasized by Luther, "does not destroy essential freedom"; but grace "does what freedom under the conditions of existence cannot do, namely, it reunites the estranged." He asserts that in the realm of finite relations, all decisions are expressions of humanity's essential freedom, "but they do not bring reunion with God."[46] "Attempts to overcome estrangement within the power of one's estranged existence lead to hard toil and tragic failure. . . . Only a New Being can produce a new action."[47] In response I say, if Tillich's representation, along with the conceptual justification expounded throughout his *Systematics*, portrayed Luther in all the most decisive facets of his theology, there would hardly be a problem. But as we have seen, this is not the case. Luther's despair over the human condition, on one hand, and, on the other hand, his views regarding God as sovereign ruler, effectively undermines the viability of any theological anthropology that includes the presupposition of essential freedom. Essential freedom may be a necessary presupposition to existential bondage in abstract "dialectical" analysis, but it means very little where human welfare is concerned when considered in Luther's theological scheme as it became explicit in *Bondage of the Will*.

I am now ready to declare that Luther's God—who does all things according to "his own immutable, eternal, and infallible will" such that "free-will is shattered," and as the one who uses evil instruments, even Satan, for his purposes—has to be seen as the one who orchestrated the scenario of temptation, fall, and redemption to satisfy "his" own purposes. Those who would refute this claim need to listen carefully to Luther in the concluding section of his reply to Erasmus. There, along with other proposed justifications for his rejection of free-will, he makes his predestinationist inclination quite obvious once again. He declares: "For if we believe it to be true that God foreknows and foreordains all things; that He cannot be deceived or obstructed in His foreknowledge and predestination; and that nothing happens but at His will (which reason itself is compelled to grant); then, on reason's own testimony, there can be no 'free-will' in man, or angel, or any creature."[48]

Being shocked some might suggest that this position was not central to Luther's theological system or claim that it was not his last word on the matter. Such persons should read his 1537 letter to Wolfgang Capito, in which he indicates that he would not mind if all his works except two were destroyed. As he put it: "I acknowledge none of them to be really a book of mine, except perhaps the one on The Bound Will and the Catechism."[49]

I suggest then, that any who argue for Christian freedom on the basis of Luther's theology should, in the final analysis, be able to embrace the following: They have been predestined to be God's and thus reclaimed by God from Satan who in all "his" evil against human beings has all along been doing God's work. These Christians should be joyful that, from the vast numbers of persons who have ever inhabited the earth, God in God's inscrutable wisdom and unfathomable justice has graciously predestined them and other Christians for that state of freedom in which God rules (rides) them for the sake of God's sovereign purposes in and through them. They should also give thanks for the wonderful drama of fall and redemption orchestrated by God to make their predestined status evident. Finally, in the midst of the horrors of the world, they should be consoled by the awareness that it is God who is working through evildoers according to what they also were predestined to be, and, consequently, what God finds them to be, as they are impelled to action by the movement of divine omnipotence. What an amazing sense of freedom this must engender! And why should this kind of freedom not be defended when Luther has assured us that what in our experience of the world cannot be explained by the lights of nature and grace, will be explained one day when the light of glory reveals "God, to whom alone belongs a judgment whose justice is incomprehensible, as a God whose justice is most righteous and evident—provided only that in the meanwhile we believe it, as we are instructed and encouraged to do by the example of the light of grace explaining what was a puzzle of the same order to the light of nature."[50]


## CAN CALVIN BE REDEEMED?


Turning to John Calvin's discussion on free-will in *Institutes of the Christian Religion*, we find him acknowledging that the notion is used in a variety of ways. His general approach to the term is influenced by the view that the characteristics with which the term is associated are too insignificant to warrant such noble classification. He focuses on what he perceives to be the most significant connotation of the term, which is that free-will refers not merely to the recognition that the will is not externally compelled, but it also includes the idea that human beings can freely determine their own path and the direction of their whole life in autonomy. This, he says, pretends that "man" who wills is not a fallen and falling "man," whose life's direction is already decided because of the fall. Calvin, therefore, cannot understand any profound declarations regarding free-will, when human beings are actually slaves to sin.

This, however, is not an argument against free-will *per se*. The key to appreciating Calvin's approach is his view that the soul is divided into two parts: understanding and will. The office of understanding is "to distinguish between objects, as each seems worthy of approval or disapproval; while that of the will, to choose and follow what the understanding pronounces good, but to reject and flee what it disapproves."[51] The seat of understanding is the mind, and from its considerations come governance for the will. Before the fall the harmonious working of these agents enabled the latter to make choices that gave appropriate direction to human appetites.[52] Before the fall human beings had freedom of will in the sense that, while it had the ability to choose both good and evil, it was inclined and had the ability to choose the good for which it was formed. But now, all the progeny of the first human beings (Adam) "deriving their origin from him in his corrupted state, have contracted from him a hereditary taint." The will remains free in a sense somewhat similar to that promoted by the earlier Augustine (as against Augustine in struggle against Pelagius) and also to that promoted by Descartes. Thus, at a basic level, the progeny of Adam continues to have a will that persists in its ability to do that which God designed it to do, which is to will. For Calvin, this is limited to choosing (not also judging as in Descartes). The will is moved by necessity because that which it chooses is governed by an understanding that is weakened and corrupted, and in its operation it testifies to the gospel of John's declaration that "the light still shines in the darkness, but the darkness comprehends it not."[53]

As such, human willing always reflects the state of the understanding which, having wandered through various errors, stumbling repeatedly as it gropes in darkness and strays away, becomes incapable of seeking and finding truth.[54] At the same time, it cannot be said that human beings are compelled in their choosing, because their will *qua* will retains its original capacity to will. It is for this reason that Calvin can adjudge each individual as responsible for the sinful paths she/he takes. As he says at one point: "If the fact that he must do good does not hinder God's freewill in doing good; if the devil who can do only evil, yet sins with his will—who shall say that man therefore sins less willingly because he is subject to the necessity of sinning?"[55] Yet, there is more to Calvin's doctrinal framework with implications for our discussion on freedom, and which serves to make me question the benefit of his teaching for those who have been constantly beaten down and made increasingly unfree by the powers of this world.

Calvin is as concerned with protecting the sovereignty of God as he is with establishing the wretchedness of human beings. As such, he makes it clear that any doctrine of free-will is always in danger of robbing God of honor. The first element of the foundation for this position emerges in his discussion of God's providence in relation to God's omnipotence—this captured succinctly in a declaration for which he calls on Augustine for support. It is that: "God's will is the highest and first cause of all things because nothing happens except from his command or permission."[56] Calvin does not deny that some things might appear to be fortuitous, and he appreciates that the term "fate" is often repeated in Ecclesiastes. But he is of the mind that these explanations for global events only appear reasonable because "the order, reason, end, and necessity of those things which happen for the most part lie hidden in God's purpose, and are not apprehended by human opinion." God's providence must be considered with regard to the future as well as the past and we must "not try to make God render account to us, but so reverence his secret judgments as to consider his will the truly just cause of all things."[57]

Calvin addresses the most obvious objection to his position—this framed in terms of what might be considered by a detractor to be the absurd and horrendous consequence of following Calvin's position to its logical end. Calvin sounds somewhat like Luther as he responds to the possible suggestion that if "meticulous providence" is the case, then people such as murderers and adulterers. should not to be held responsible for their actions. As Calvin must, he acknowledges that "unless he [God] willed it, they could not do it." But he hastens to claim that the actions of these persons are not pursued because they wish to serve God; "unbridled lust" and "obstinacy" cause them "to strive against God." He also claims that human beings "serve his just ordinance by doing evil, for so great and boundless is his wisdom that he knows well how to use evil instruments to his good." This claim is not meant in any sense resembling that suggested by Paul's indication in Romans 8:28 that God works in all things that happen to bring forth good for the sake of those God loves. The clear suggestion is that what God permits to take place is connected with what God wills to take place. So then, "thieves and murderers and other evildoers are the instruments of divine providence, and the Lord himself uses these to carry out the judgments that he has determined with himself."[58] There is, therefore, no way to separate anything that happens on the earth, good or bad, from God's meticulous providence, that is, God's perfect will.

A concrete example of how a Calvin-like theological disposition works out for the weak and oppressed is seen in elements of a discussion by highly regarded Caribbean biblical theologian and church leader Bill Watty, in particular his evaluation of the violent and oppressive history of that region. In developing his conception of "God who is God" (as against the God who is the product of our limited and limiting theological constructions) he suggests that "God wanted the Caribbean to be discovered by Europe." He proceeds to declare that it boggles his "imagination to contemplate what would have been the consequence for modern history if Columbus had not ventured into the Caribbean." Pointing to the introduction of Christianity into that region, he claims that Columbus was not so much the one who carried Christ "but who was carried by Him who rides upon the wings of the winds (Ps. 104:3)."[59] In another writing project, I indicated my suspicion that Watty "does not see a direct and necessary causal connection between God's intentions and the specific attitudes and activities of European colonizers." However, I continued to say that "a detractor could quite legitimately suggest that nothing in Watty's conceptions precludes the position that the atrocities of colonizers were also orchestrated by this 'God who is God,' in order to satisfy some inscrutable purpose for both victims and victimizers." In that writing, I classified the God of Watty's construct as "the arch-imperialist who stands above all criteria and frameworks by which good and evil, justice and injustice, can be evaluated." As such, I suggested, "that which has occurred in the Caribbean is right because God has willed it, even if this constantly involves the elevation of the violent and oppressive at the expense of those who are weak and vulnerable."[60] It would be equally so in other similar situations.

I now assert that it can only be from a position of privilege that one could declare to slaves and their progeny, in the Caribbean and those all over the world who continue to inherit the legacies of poverty and oppression, that while attention is to be given to secondary causes "in their proper place," they should find solace because they know "that their plans, wills, efforts, and abilities are under God's hand." The moral plausibility of a theological system should be questioned when it includes the proposal to those pressed down under the savage lashes of life's woes that they should rest in the recognition "that it is within his [God's] choice to bend them whither he pleases and to constrain them whenever he pleases."[61] Calvin admonishes his audience to overlook injustice and wickedness so as not to encourage the desire for revenge, and immediately the prophet Amos comes to mind. I also wonder if it is only in modern and contemporary times that men and women have been raised up who have been able to stand up for themselves and for others without being driven to revenge. Calvin continues to suggest that the Christian should "remember to mount up to God, and learn to believe for certain that whatever our enemy has wickedly committed against us was permitted and sent by God's just dispensation."[62] Immediately, I remember those who have suffered at the hands of men like Adolf Hitler of Germany, Benito Mussolini of Italy, Augusto Pinochet of Chile, Francois "Papa Doc" Duvalier of Haiti, Joseph Stalin of Russia, and Idi Amin of Uganda, among others.

My estimation of the capacity of Calvin's doctrine to foster freedom is diminished further with direct engagement of his doctrine of predestination.

In his most explicit definition this has to do with "God's eternal decree by which he compacted with himself what he willed to become of each man. For all are not created in equal condition; rather, eternal life is foreordained for some, eternal damnation for others."[63] In his discussion of scriptural scenarios, including the dynamics of Israelite existence, which dramatize the meaning of predestination,[64] it becomes clear that this doctrine is not merely about eternal destiny, but about the roles God chooses for an individual or group as they participate in God's earthly purposes. It is also clear that effectiveness in the earthly calling has nothing to do with one's eternal destiny.

I do not ignore Calvin's claim that holding the position he does was demanded of him by the Scriptures. He can also be perceived as expressing humility when he reminds his reader "that when they inquire into predestination they are penetrating the sacred precincts of divine wisdom."[65] There are indeed some in this world who need help in appreciating that there are things to which they cannot simply lay claim, as they have done with numerous people and with the possessions of others. Adopting Patterson's language, there are restraints to their inclinations to sovereignal freedom. Yet, I am greatly troubled by the strong impression that of greatest emphasis in Calvin's scheme is God's sovereign freedom. Speaking about God's election of Israel, he says: "God has already shown that in his mere generosity he has not been bound by laws but is free, so that equal apportionment of grace is not required of him." And in the exercise of this freedom, God "seals his elect by call and justification, so, by shutting off the reprobate from knowledge of his name or from the sanctification of his Spirit, he, as it were, reveals by these marks what sort of judgment awaits them."[66] Here I simply point the reader back to my evaluation of Watty's interpretation of Caribbean history, in light of the intentions of "God who is God," and I proceed to indicate an even more disturbing position. It begins with the indication that while a general discussion of free-will allows some space for one to argue for a different kind of responsibility for Adam over that of human beings born with a corrupted understanding, this is not permitted by Calvin's discussion of God's meticulous providence. Even more than was the case with Luther's pronouncements about the status of human beings, this insight enables me to suggest, quite reasonably, that maybe Adam and Eve might not have been as free before the fall as is argued by Calvin and other orthodox thinkers.

I invite an argument to dissuade me from the position that neither an uncorrupted understanding nor a properly guided will makes a difference for a decision made or the outcome from that decision, if nothing happens except from God's command or permission. This is so especially if God's permission is actually an expression of God's perfect will. Actually, it seems that in this framework the notions "will" and "permission" are better represented as "will exercised directly and explicitly" and "will exercised indirectly and subtly."

The notions of God's will exercised directly and that will exercised indirectly have special relevance for the use of the concept of "compatibilist freedom" by members of the Reformed community to explain discrepancies such as that which is glaring in the *Westminster Confession*. On one hand, it declares that "God from all eternity . . . freely and unchangeably ordains whatsoever comes to pass," and almost immediately after, "nor is violence offered to the will of the creatures, nor is the liberty or contingency of second causes taken away."[67] Applied to my decision as a youngster to commit myself to Christ, it can be said that this was a free decision because there came a point at which this is what I wished to do, and I chose to do what I wished. At the same time, demanded by the doctrine of predestination, it has to be said that what I desired resulted from the secret work of the Holy Spirit guiding my desire and thereby effecting that which was God's sovereign decision in the beginning. The status of this scenario is dramatized when contrasted with the example of a man in a locked room utilized by John Locke in his discussion of freedom in his *Essay Concerning Human Understanding*. In that situation the sleeping man was taken by others into a locked room with internal dynamics that made him desire to stay there when he came awake, not knowing that even if he wanted he could not leave.[68] According to the Calvinist scheme, in the case of one who decides for Christ, it is not simply that choosing Christ is presented as overwhelmingly appealing; it is that the will was locked into this one option, making its choice unavoidable. Still, it was a choice.

I acknowledge that Locke's example was used to support his position that freedom is not solely about volition or preferring, but about the person having the power to do, or choose not to do, as the mind inclines one to do.[69] However, my approach to freedom in terms of dimensions and categories enables me to claim that the man in Lock's locked room still had the space to find the situation in the room unappealing and attempt to get out. Even if at that point he found that the choice to leave was not available, he would still have the option to accept his situation or to act out his displeasure through various expressions of rebellion that might have convinced those who locked him in to open the door. None of these options are available to one who exercises her/his will in the framework of predestination as understood by Calvin. Considered in light of predestination linked with meticulous providence, we are required to embrace the position that every detail of the process by which the man got into the locked room (as it was with my decision for Christ) and his behavior in the room is governed by the secret counsel and directed by the present hand of God. This is because God's omnipotence is not the mere possession of a capacity, but power that is a "watchful, effective, active sort, engaged in ceaseless activity," a power "directed toward individual and particular motions."[70] So then, "not only heaven and earth and the inanimate creatures, but also the plans and intentions of men, are so governed by his providence that they are borne by it straight to their appointed end."[71]

Nevertheless, human beings are drawn into a mire of self-condemnation by Calvin, Luther and others. In the mire, as progenies of Adam (and Eve), we accepted blame for our condition and adopt a disposition of beholdeness for God's orchestration of salvation. We may, like Calvinists, extol God's sovereign freedom and look to that day when we will know for certain if God had predestined that we would be among the redeemed; or like Lutherans we may give thanks that, having been found guilty for that which God was in charge of from the beginning, the righteousness that properly belongs to Jesus Christ has been graciously imputed to us.

In the very process of denying effective finite-freedom (which works for human good) as a natural quality of human character, Augustinian and classical Reformed thinkers have, at least, affirmed that if one wishes to espouse human freedom that is meaningful, there is a minimum level of personal autonomy that must be enjoyed. This means that the causal influence that any other actuality contributes to a person's life-processes cannot be so significant that the person's own decisions about herself have no discernible causal consequences on her internal life, if nothing else. On this matter, Neville suggests that theories of causation in the modern period of European philosophy have not been helpful for understanding the combination of intentional action and free choice in responsible behavior. Deterministic theories, he says, "have given a good account of how agents control action, and hence have been favored by thinkers such as Calvin, Spinoza, and Jonathan Edwards." But he is clear that "determinism cannot stop responsibility with the agent; the antecedents are just as responsible as the person, and hence there is no real responsibility." As we have seen, "when this is the causal theory behind predestination, it always turns out that God and God alone is really responsible for everything because the divine creation is the only true initiating force."[72]

Surely, this is the risk that arises when contemporary theologians like Kortright Davis suggests that "Ultimate Reality has not always been translated into terms of ultimate and unconditional freedom for God."[73] In light of a history of external domination in the region Davis is from (the Caribbean), it is apparent that his approach to God-talk is intended to constitute the conceptual foundation of resistance to attempts by representatives of any power (economic, cultural, or theological) external to the region, to constrain the experience and exercise of freedom by that region's peoples. In other words, Caribbean freedom must be exercised in light of Caribbean priorities, as these are illuminated by the spirit of God in the midst of Caribbean peoples. While this intention is laudable, Davis' theological anchor, which suggests that there is nothing outside of God which has any influence of who God is and what God does, effectively eliminates any authentic space for ventures in freedom as expressions of the humanity of Caribbean peoples, and other peoples who have been subject to similar oppression. These communities will have simply moved from being people whose desires did not matter when human imperialists took decisions for them, to people whose desires do not matter when God the absolute imperialist takes decisions for them.

## Barth—Some Progress, But Not Enough

At this point, it must be acknowledged that twentieth-century Reformed giant Karl Barth worked masterfully to redeem Calvin's hard-nosed form of pre-destinationism. While the complexity of his theological scheme is evidenced in the fourteen-volume *Church Dogmatics*, the basic elements of his theological revisions are chronicled in the small text *The Humanity of God*.[74] Barth is clear that it is only in Jesus Christ that one can have any meaningful knowledge of who God is, how God acts toward humanity, and the consequence for human beings. In light of this basic position, he reconstructs Calvin's notion of double predestination to now refer to the conviction that Jesus is the representative elected-rejected so that humanity becomes the rejected-elected. As the humanity of God, Jesus represents the fact that God decided in eternity that God would not be God without human beings and human beings would be human in relation to God.[75]

Having elaborated on the benefits of his view for the dignity of each human being no matter how vile,[76] Barth makes it clear that it is only through Jesus Christ that we realize humanity freed from slavery to sin. In the process he points us beyond the master-slave imagery, about which I will say more in the upcoming chapter, when he emphasizes that God in Christ chooses human beings to be God's partners, even as God remains the superior partner. Indeed, he declares: "God's high freedom in Jesus Christ is his freedom for love. The divine capacity which operates and exhibits itself in that superiority and subordination is manifestly also God's capacity to bend downwards, to attach Himself to another and this other Himself, to be together with him."[77] This shift of imagery is surely linked to the very major shift he made from the conception of sovereignty he held as a young theologian. His mature position is best put in his declaration that "the concept of God without man is indeed as anomalous as wooden iron."[78]

Barth certainly resists the idea that human beings have natural or neutral freedom, but there is a definite, if restrained, recognition of free-will and free choice. This is evidenced by the position that while God is the source and measure of freedom, the freedom of human beings is to respond to the gift offered by God. Thus "human freedom is the joy whereby man appropriates for himself God's election." Central to this election is God's election of Godself in Jesus Christ to be humanity's Lord and partner. Each individual is, therefore, called, in the midst of the community of elected humanity, to acknowledge and confess "this divine election by willing, deciding, and determining himself to be the echo and mirror of the divine act." As such, "each one is responsible for his relationship with God and his fellow men."[79] Presbyterian theologian and one-time student of Barth Shirley Guthrie represents well the Barthian perspective on freedom as he talks about God's plan (effected through Christ) "to free us from slavery to all the internal and external, psychological and social powers that enslave and dehumanize us in order that we might be genuinely free people—people who discover and fulfill their own true humanity as they freely love God and their fellow human beings (all of them)."[80]

My speculation is that it is because Barth could not let go of the view that some exercise of contra-causal freedom needs to be involved in any authentic human response to God's prior decision regarding commitment to us that, despite his fascination with the passage from Colossians 1:19-20[81] and his listing of commendable qualities found in traditional universalists, he would not declare himself to be one. I agree that the idea that God's first and final word is "Yes" rules out any theological justification for setting "any sort of limits to the loving-kindness of God which appeared in Jesus Christ,"[82] and, as such, precludes any human from being able to justifiably judge anyone to be outside of God's favor and ineligible for salvation. Nevertheless, this "Yes" does not itself compel any and every human to also say "yes" to God. Nor does it determine that the human beings saying "yes" is not important for a personally transforming appropriation of God's "Yes."

An interesting position I ask the reader to consider is that while God does not determine that human beings will say "yes" to God because God has said "Yes" to us, God's self-determination not to be God without humanity obligates God to do as much as can be done by one with a nature and commitment such as God's to lure human beings to say "yes" without eclipsing our freedom. God, having decided not to be God without human beings, is obligated to Godself to work at this as long as there are human beings who have not embraced their communion with God, and as long as God remains God. This position contrasts with interpretations of Philippians 2:10-11 like that which informs Barth-influenced Disciples of Christ theologian Joe Jones' soteriological universalism. Jones posits that there is a point of ultimate transition in dying in which "one encounters face to face the almighty reality of the triune God. At this point of ultimate transition, God's gracious love 'irresistibly' confronts and empowers all persons—even the most horrendously evil—to say an authentic and grateful yes to God."[83] In keeping with my position on human freedom, I embrace Philippians 2:10-11 in light of the hope that the "day" will come when God's patient wooing will result in the state where all people choose to embrace God's primordial decision to be for human beings and fulfill God's desire that all human beings will be for God. This is the kind of universalism to which I subscribe.

It needs to be said that, while Barth glances furtively in the direction I wish the reader to go, he is not able to travel with us. This seems the result of two factors. Firstly, he is committed to the traditional doctrine of a fall, and so understands human life as such to be one of alienation. This being so, he does not value in the same way I do the complex of elements that make up human life, and, in fact, classifies human existence as such using terms like "false," "appearance," and "enslavement."[84] What this means is that the struggles and outcomes (good and bad) of ordinary decision making in the ambiguities of life that I consider unavoidable in the pursuit and exercise of human freedom are disvalued. Indeed, rather than being expressions of our humanity, they are seen as expressions of our alienation from God and from our true [human] nature.[85] In the final analysis, therefore, even though Barth might acknowledge that human beings can say "no" to God, it does not actually constitute contra-causal freedom, because in his scheme *real* human freedom is reduced to deciding for God through Jesus Christ. Any choice of its contrary is a sign of unfreedom, that is, slavery to sin. Secondly, Barth's God is still the omni-qualitied sovereign of Augustine, Luther, and Calvin, who predestinates, even if his understanding of the structure of predestination is different from that of his theological predecessors.

That discussed so far makes me anxious when I hear from Barth that God "surrounds man from all sides. He is man's Lord who is before him, above him, after him, and also with him in history, the locus of man's existence."[86] It makes me wonder: even though in Barth's scheme we human beings must choose our closeness, is there enough "room" for this to be a real choice, or are we simply overpowered, sooner or later, by God's predestination and presence? I am certainly not encouraged when he declares: "Human freedom as a gift of God does not allow for any vague choices between various possibilities. The reign of chance and ambiguity is excluded."[87] Soon I will expound on my view that what Barth sees as contradictory to Christian freedom is simply a function of finitude, which is as fundamental to the definition of "human" as freedom is. This being the case, vagueness and ambiguity will not be eliminated by God's immanence. Finally, growing in understanding is also an important gift of humanity, and the contemporary struggle with what it means to be a free individual in community is an expression of this process. Indeed, it represents an evolution in the definition of "human," and ought to signify human beings coming to learn more about ourselves as members of a species, not further alienation from our true selves. This is the emerging reality of human existence, which needs to be guided by considerations like the ones with which I am struggling in this text. To see this as an expression of unreality when it does not include a "yes" to a God, understood to be omni-qualitied and predestinating, is a travesty.

## DISSATISFIED, AND LOOKING AHEAD

It is worth repeating that I reject indeterminism as the appropriate alternative to the determinism I resist. Robert Neville acknowledges that indeterministic theories do allow enough play for agents to intervene and put their stamp on the flow of causal processes. "But then the agent's choices, arising out of indeterminism, are arbitrary; for the choices to be truly responsible, they ought to arise out of the real character of the agent." Furthermore, if the causal processes of nature are sufficiently indeterminate as to allow a wide range of free actions, then a person's actions also will be compromised by random interventions. Neville's conclusion is that the determinism-indeterminism controversies in modern philosophy are simply not helpful for understanding either ordinary human responsibility or the relation of human causation to divine causation.[88]

Like me, Neville's own approach to the dynamics of causation is influenced significantly by engagement with Process-Relational thought—he refers specifically to Alfred North Whitehead and John Cobb, who are pioneers, in different ways, of this conceptual framework. This conceptual orientation will figure more prominently in my considerations as I progress through this project. At this moment I convey Neville's suggestion that the older modern conceptions assumed that the actualized past, the set of antecedent conditions, contains the power for actualizing possibilities in the present.[89] Process philosophy, he says, reverses the locus of power so that the present moment contains the creative power that actualizes possibilities. The past consists of actualized "things" that enter the present as potentialities for integration into the emergent new actuality; the past thus provides the "raw material" for creative integration into the present, with the future consisting of the logical structures or possibilities for integration.[90]

Clark Pinnock shares some similarities with Neville's position and is explicit that the idea of human freedom is central to God's intention. He echoes Erasmus's view when he indicates that the Bible itself suggests this in many ways, and he provides examples that portray God seeking freely chosen and reciprocal relationships with human beings who are capable of doing good and evil. These human activities affect God, and God sometimes reacts in ways God comes to regret. God, he claims, "sovereignly created responsible free beings and wants them to be creative in their own way," making their own unique contributions to history.[91] Pinnock does not endorse autonomy, but supports significant human agency. There is, he says, "a destiny that is given to us from the past with which we work." In the Process-Relational scheme, some call this "destiny" "stubborn facts," which as Pinnock suggests "we bend and reshape in the present to our particular ends. Destiny only becomes fate when its weight overcomes freedom. We all actualize our own being in the present out of a destiny that comes to us from the past, combined with the possibilities that confront us from the future, as God challenges us to go forward."[92]

In preparing to close this chapter, I first point the reader to some common sense talk on freedom from Clark Pinnock and Richard Bauckham. Pinnock indicates that belief in real freedom is something like belief in God; it is difficult but impossible to deny. This is because we intuitively accept freedom as fundamental and necessary. He suggests that belief in freedom is not so much a modern belief as it is a perennial commonsense notion that is very difficult to deny in practice. "It is a form of the experience of voluntary action in which we sense that real alternatives lie before us."[93] He asks: "how many actually believe that their choices are nothing more than the products of previous states of mind?" I re-frame it to read: how many actually believe that any good we will is so totally determined by God, that we dare not say we had some role in it? Pinnock declares confidently that we know that we shape the influences we have received in significant ways, and that we cannot excuse ourselves when they do wrong. "Certainly there are inputs into human behavior from nature and the environment, but as persons we also partly transcend these factors. Human nature essentially emerges and is not pre-determined."[94]

Pinnock would also insist, like Neville does, and other proponents of human freedom probably would, that freedom of choice, undergirded by freedom of will, is valuable not merely in itself but because it is freedom to make right choices. Certainly, in every moment of choice there is always the risk that one will make the wrong choice,[95] and I do not pretend that the basis on which to make correct choices is always clear and that the conditions beneficial to such choosing are always in place. However, the yearning should always be to choose rightly and to choose that which is good, with the expectation that the quality of our choice contributes to the quality of our characters and that of the world in general. Here Bauckham is unequivocal in his declaration that only with choice is human goodness possible. He points us to the Genesis story in which Adam and Eve were free to eat of the tree of knowledge of good and evil but were commanded not to do so. He proceeds to suggest that "without that freedom they could have been innocent. But only by freely choosing to obey God could they become good." This, he suggests, "is ultimately why serious freedom of choice must at all costs be protected and valued."[96] I go beyond Bauckham and suggest that, in the final analysis, the choice is not between innocence and goodness, but between inauthentic and authentic humanity. And having shown that the dominant streams of orthodox Christian thought cannot provide an adequate theological foundation for the freedom that is compatible with authentic humanity, I proceed to struggle with biblical and theological ideas that could open the path to a more adequate foundation.

# NOTES

1. B. A. Gerrish, *Grace and Reason: A Study in the Theology of Luther* (Oxford: Oxford University Press, 1962), 106. Gerrish's reference is the Weimar edition of *Luther's Works*, vol. 40, 325.33ff.

2. Ibid., 13-14. Gerrish's reference is the Weimar edition of *Luther's Works*, vol. 10, 203.10ff.

3. Martin Luther, "Two Kinds of Righteousness," in *Martin Luther's Basic Theological Writings,* ed., Thomas Lull (Memphis, TN, Fortress Press, 1989), 156.

4. Ibid., "The Freedom of a Christian," in *Martin Luther's Basic Theological Writings*, ed., Lull, 600.

5. Luther, "Two Kinds of Righteousness," in *Martin Luther's Basic Theological Writings*, ed. Lull, 156-157.

6. Desiderius Erasmus, "The Free-Will," in *Milestones of Thought,* trans. and ed. Ernst Winter (New York: Frederick Ungar Publishing Co., Inc, 1961), 20. Martin Luther examines this definition in *The Bondage of the Will* .

7. Ibid., 26.

8. Ibid., 28.

9. Ibid., 90.

10. Ibid., 88.

11. Ibid., 35-36.

12. Martin Luther, *The Bondage of the Will,* trans. J. I. Packer and O. R. Johnson (Grand Rapids: Fleming H. Revell Company, 1957), 139.

13. Erasmus, "The Free-Will," 29.

14. Ibid., 30.

15. Ibid., 87.

16. In fact, he makes it clear that the whole work is lacking in quality.

17. Luther, *Bondage of the Will*, 79-80.

18. Ibid., 141-142.

19. This is so, even if, at times, the only evidence is the restlessness about which Augustine speaks.

20. My own view is that, considered in the context of the Genesis story, human understanding was limited from the very outset. This was, in part, the reason why they were vulnerable to the serpent's lures.

21. Luther, *Bondage of the Will*, 103-104.

22. Ibid., 107.

23. Ibid., 104.

24. Here I say, in the sense of establishing one as Christian.

25. Luther, *Bondage of the Will*, 153.

26. Ibid., 102-103.

27. Walter Altmann, *Luther and Liberation—A Latin American Perspective* (Minneapolis: Fortress Press, 1992), 20. Altmann's reference is *Luther's Works*, eds. Jaroslav Pelikan and Helmut T Lehman (St. Louis: Concordia Publishing House and Philadelphia: Fortress Press, 1955), 10:364-364.

28. Luther, "The Freedom of a Christian," in *Luther's Basic Theological Writings*, ed. Lull, 596.

29. Ibid., 619.

30. Luther, *Bondage of the Will*, 79-80.

31. Ibid., 81.

32. Ibid.

33. Robert Neville, *A Theology Primer* (Albany: State University of New York Press, 1991), 78-79.

34. Luther, *Bondage of the Will*, 80.

35. Ibid., 107.

36. Ibid., 80-81.

37. Ibid., 204.

38. Ibid.

39. Erasmus, "The Free-Will," 34-36. Some of the Scripture passages identified are: Joel 2:12; Johan 3:8; Isaiah 46:8; Jeremiah 26:3-4; Exodus 32:9; Ezekiel 20:13; Psalm 80:14; Psalm 33:13-14.

40. The spirit of this question is reflected in Job 1:6-12.

41. Luther, *Bondage of the Will*, 300.

42. Jürgen Moltmann, *The Church in the Power of the Spirit* (Minneapolis: Fortress Press, 1993), 14.

43. Martin Luther, *Lectures on Romans, Library of Christian Classics*, vol. xv, trans. and ed. Wilhelm Pauck (Philadelphia: Westminster Press, 1961), 86.

44. Bartolome de Las Casas, *History of the Indies*, trans. Andree Collard (New York: Harper and Row Publishers, 1971), 66.

45. Luther, *Lectures on Romans, Library of Christian Classics*, vol. xv, 86.

46. Paul Tillich, *Systematic Theology*, vol. II (Chicago: University of Chicago Press, 1957 [1958]), 79.

47. Ibid., 80.

48. Ibid., 317.

49. Gottfried G. Krodel, ed. and trans. *Luther's* Works, vol. 50 *Letters III*, general ed. Helmut T. Lehmann (Philadelphia: Fortress Press, 1975), 172-173.

50. Luther, *Bondage of the Will*, 317.

51. John Calvin, *Institutes of Christian Religion*, ed. John McNeill, trans. and indexed by Ford Lewis Battles (Philadelphia: Westminster Press, 1960), [I.xv.7], 194.

52. Ibid., [I.xv.8], 195.

53. Ibid., [I.ii.12], 270.

54. Ibid., 271.

55. Ibid., [II.iii.5], 295.

56. Ibid., [I.xvi.8ff], 208.

57. Ibid., [I.xvii..1], 211.

58. Ibid., [I.xvii.5], 217.

59. William Watty, *From Shore to Shore: Soundings in Caribbean Theology* (Barbados: Typeset by CEDAR Press, [Printed in Kingston, Jamaica], 1981), 14.

60. Michael Miller, "Mission in Pluralistic Contexts — A Caribbean Perspective," in *Chalice Introduction to Disciples Theology*, ed. Peter Heltzel (St. Louis: Chalice Press, 2008), 279.

61. Calvin, *Institutes*, [I.xvii.6], 218.

62. Ibid., [I.xvii.8], 221.

63. Ibid., [III.xxi.5], 926.

64. Ibid., [I.xviii.1-4]. 228-237.

65. Ibid., [III.xxi.1], 922.

66. Ibid., [III.xxi.7], 931.

67. General Assembly, The Presbyterian Church USA, "The Westminster Confession" in *The Book of Confessions* (Louisville: The Office of the General Assembly, 1991), 6.014, C, III.

68. John Locke, *An Essay Concerning Human Understanding*, vol . I, collated, annotated and with commentary, Alexander Campbell Fraser (New York: Dover Publications, Inc., 1959), 317.

69. Ibid., 325-326.

70. Calvin, *Institutes*, [I.xvi.3], 200.

71. Ibid., [I.xvi.8], 207.

72. Neville, *Primer*, 79.

73. Davis, *Emancipation*, 8.

74. In this work Barth reflects on the movement from his initial extreme reaction to the way Christian theologians of nineteenth-century Germany had conformed to the wider intellectual and social culture of that nation to a more complex position grounded in the idea of the humanity of God. See: Karl Barth, *The Humanity of God* (Richmond, VA: John Knox Press, 1963).

75. Barth, "Humanity of God," in *The Humanity of God*, 45-46. As Barth put it: "The deity of the living God" has "its meaning and its power only in the context of His history and of His

dialogue with man, and thus in His togetherness with man." In other words, "God's deity . . . rightly understood, includes his humanity." Those interested in experiencing Barth at his dialectical best as he explicates this matter might scrutinize the subheading. "The Eternal Will of God in the Election of Jesus Christ," in *Church Dogmatics,* II.2, Karl Barth, eds., G. W. Bromiley and T. F. Torrance (1957; reprint, Edinburgh: T. & T. Clark, 1982), 145-194.

76. Ibid., 53, 58-60.

77. Ibid., 48-49.

78. Ibid., "The Gift of Freedom," in *Humanity of God,* 72.

79. Ibid., 79.

80. Shirley Guthrie, *Christian Doctrine,* rev. ed. (Louisville: Westminster John Knox Press, 1994 ), 133.

81. "For in him all the fullness of God was pleased to dwell, and through him God was pleased to reconcile to himself all things, whether on earth or in heaven, by making peace through the blood of his cross."

82. Barth, *Humanity of God,* 61-62.

83. Joe R. Jones, *A Grammar of Christian Faith: Systematic Explorations in Christian Life and* Doctrine, vol. II (Lanham: Rowman and Littlefield Publishers, Inc., 2002), 723.

84. Barth, "The Gift of Freedom," from *Humanity of God,* 76, 77.

85. Ibid., 80.

86. Ibid., 72.

87. Ibid., 77.

88. Neville, *Primer,* 79.

89. Ibid.

90. Ibid.

91. Pinnock, *Most Moved Mover,* 126-127.

92. Ibid., 127.

93. Ibid., 128.

94. Ibid., 127.

95. Richard Bauckham, *God and the Crisis of Freedom* (Louisville: Westminster John Knox Press, 2002), 47.

96. Ibid., 48.

*Chapter Four*

# The Mixed Message of the Scriptures Regarding Freedom

Whatever is the road a Christian is inclined to take in pursuit of freedom she/ he cannot avoid exploring biblical sources directly to see what is being said about it. When I do so I find a mixed message that poses a real challenge for human development. For example, there is no doubt that the story of the Exodus makes clear that God does not wish Israel to be enslaved to any other nation, but this is because they are God's slaves. In this framework, Israel's entry into covenant relations with God, which to some suggests real freedom of choice, is in effect acceptance of their enslavement to God. From this foundation there emerges an ethos in which Israel is enslaved to the God of Israel, and the vulnerable from within, and others from without, Israel are enslaved to the powerful in Israel. In the New Testament there is evidence of the acceptance of the institution of slavery by Christians, and the spiritual freedom in Christ is also seen as a kind of slavery. While elements of a theology of freedom are evident in Paul's writings, the superior-subordinate schema for various kinds of relations persists with consequences that continue to be evident in our time. Indeed, the use of language carrying the affective power of this schema to define dispositions of faith only served to reinforce a mentality that flowered in most inhumane ways when Christianity became aligned to power. The pernicious character of the legacy of slavery and subordination becomes most evident in situations where ordinary believers, oftentimes already marginalized by social and politics structures, becomes convinced, with the help of biblical injunctions, that their inadequacy as sinful human beings requires that they turn over their lives to others perceived to be the appointed representatives of God. As representatives of God, those in charge are valorized for exercising power in the mode of domination and control.

A strong argument emerging from this chapter is that any proposal for freedom in our era that utilizes Hebrew and Christian Scriptures ought not to overlook the fact that they were developed in epochs generally characterized by acceptance of striking expressions of unfreedom, including slavery, and various forms of oppressive hierarchy. Despite claims made about Jesus as God incarnate, reflection on the idea of God as ultimate and sovereign is mostly governed by embedded conceptions of rulership that are, in many aspects, despotic. Therefore, we need to be judicious in how we appropriate scriptural pronouncements on freedom that informed the thought of both the orthodox and heterodox thinkers discussed in chapters 2 and 3, and more recent defenders of free-will theism.

## EARLY CHRISTIAN CONSIDERATIONS ON FREEDOM AND THEIR GRECO-ROMAN INFLUENCES

Worthy of note as we set out on this journey is Paul Tillich's suggestion that the Stoic notion "that every individual participates in the universal logos" was an important factor in the emancipation from systems of law that did not recognize the personhood of all, and which led to the kind of self-relatedness and individualization associated with personal freedom. More significant is his further claim that appreciation for "the uniqueness of every person was not established until the Christian church acknowledged the universality of salvation and the potentiality of every human being to participate in it."[1] Orlando Patterson provides valuable assistance for our understanding of the Christian contribution, especially through the efforts of the apostle Paul. In the process he identifies ways in which Paul's efforts were informed by the immediate framework influenced by the further development of Greek cultural dynamics in the Roman Empire.

The Roman social structure in which Christianity emerged was as dependent on slavery as the Greek society it superseded, and manumitted slaves continued life with significant social and legal restrains to their external freedom. Yet it also cannot be overlooked that, over time, a significant percentage of the population was made up of freed people who would experience and contemplate the striking contrast between the condition of slavery and that of freedom (as far as they experienced it). This phenomenon had its foundation in the high rate of manumissions that resulted in an emergent class of dependent citizens whose progeny would become full citizens. "It was only a matter of time before the majority of citizens were descendants of freedmen."[2] Focusing on the apostle Paul's theology of freedom, Patterson reminds us that Tarsus, where Paul grew up, had a large-scale slave system.[3] Therefore, I am a little surprised at Patterson's claim that it is the secular experience of slavery-into-freedom which constituted "rebirth into social life" that was *"miraculously transposed* (italics mine)" by Paul "into a doctrine of spiritual freedom from which the Western mind would never be released."[4]

It should be pointed out that Paul's considerations on freedom emerged in the process of ongoing conflict among members of the fledgling Christian community regarding the means by which one properly qualified as a Christian. As Francis Watson put it, this was "an inner-Christian debate about Christian identity."[5] This conflict had led to the general meeting in Jerusalem which is depicted in Acts 15:1-29. Interestingly, Paul does not refer to that meeting, but the issues he raises do reflect its central concerns. The combination of Galatians 1:6-7, 5:1-12, and 6:12-13 suggest that some were insisting that, for Gentiles to be authentic Christians, along with commitment to Jesus, they should be circumcised and also adhere to other tenets of Jewish law. This requirement, Paul views as a sign of regression and a subversion of the freedom that resulted from the death and resurrection of Jesus. The severity of the situation, as Paul understood it, is reflected in Galatians 4:8-11 where he suggests that those who insisted on burdensome requirements were returning to a state of slavery to spiritual forces opposed to the Spirit of Christ.

There is no question that Paul is convinced that members of the new community had come into a unique quality of freedom, whatever was their prior circumstance. This is represented in the famous declaration of Galatians 5:1: "For freedom Christ has set you free; stand firm, therefore, and do not submit again to a yoke of slavery." Patterson is in accord with many biblical commentators in his claim that the radical nature of Paul's vision would have been most evident in Galatians 3:28 when he declared that among those who had put on Christ "there is no longer Jew or Greek, there is no longer slave or fee, there is no longer male or female; for you are one in Christ Jesus."[6] This freedom he intended to defend with great vigor.

Given my purposes, Patterson becomes really interesting when he points out that running parallel to the root categorical antithesis of slaver-freedom is a set of other antitheses: law-grace, death-life, and sin-reconciliation, which can be seen as both correspondences and subcategories of the root antithesis.[7] Further, Patterson understands these other antitheses to be direct analogies to the three constitutive elements of real slavery: powerlessness, social degradation or dishonor, and natal alienation. Applying these features in his theology of freedom, Paul argues that the spiritual slave is completely powerless under law, has no honor before God or other human beings, and reflects the influence of elemental spirits. However, in freedom through Christ she has the power of grace and recognition in the community of God.[8]

Patterson elaborates more extensively on the third antithesis, sin-alienation, which, for him, is the spiritual counterpart to natal alienation. He suggests that, in developing this element, Paul draws heavily on the Roman experience of slavery and redemption, specifically the feature of the Roman law of slavery known as *postliminium*. This notion refers to the fact that a Roman citizen, having been captured and enslaved by an enemy, loses his rights as a citizen; but if he escapes and returns to Roman soil, his free status is restored. We are then provided with a fascinating explication of the soteriological significance of Jesus' death and resurrected life. This begins with the explanation that if the captive Roman was redeemed for money, the right of *postliminium* would not be fully restored until the sum was paid off.[9] Our attention is then drawn to Paul's comment in Romans 5:8-11, especially verse 10: "For if while we were enemies we were reconciled to God through the death of his Son, much more surely, having been reconciled, will we be saved by his life." Patterson asks rhetorically: "If we are reconciled through Jesus' death, why is there need to be reconciled again through his life?" His answer is that, viewed in the framework of *postliminium*, the sinner who is a captive of the kingdom of sin is like his real-world counterpart, and is treated like an enemy, that is, "estranged from God's kingdom and from his mercy and protection." Reconciliation, grounded in Jesus' death, brings the sinner back to the kingdom of God, but the process is not complete. Like the real-world counterpart, the sinner's restored status cannot be fully enjoyed until the ransom is paid off. However, having paid the initial ransom, Jesus relieves the redeemed sinner from having to make repayment. Instead, having "died to the death of slavery through Christ's blood," the reclaimed sinner becomes a believer who lives "in anticipation of being fully reconciled to his former status as a free spirit in God's kingdom with the return of the resurrected Christ in the *parousia*."[10]

Patterson identifies certain emphases utilized by Paul to dramatize his privileging of personal freedom in Galatians, especially the secular model of manumission. The emphasis on "equality in freedom" expressed in the famous declaration of Galatians 3:28 "directly parallels the secular Roman ideal of personal freedom: equality before the law." Paul's metaphorical use of two models of freedom, adoption and restitution, is highlighted; and Patterson acknowledges that manumission by means of adoption was rare in the empire during Paul's time. It is suggested that very likely Paul looked to the more common Jewish practice, "which entailed the most complete emancipation of the slave, making him fully equal with other heirs of the master."[11] The second notion, restitution, is discussed in relation to the allegory of Abraham's two sons, and there is the suggestion that Paul might have had in his mind the popular Roman motif of the wrongfully enslaved free person who was restored to full freedom. The most striking significance for the notion of freedom emerges as we are reminded that Hagar's son was generated by natural means and Sarai's son was generated by an act of grace bestowed on one who was naturally barren. As used by Paul then, in the development of his theology of freedom, this story is "a cunning attack on the principle of inheritance by birth and of membership through descent, laying the foundation for Christian universalism and anti-ethnicity." As portrayed by Patterson, Paul does seem somewhat supersessionist,[12] but it is a radical move to argue that "the non-native, gentile slave is freed and adopted; and the natural children, in the second metaphor, are . . . the real aliens and slaves and are cast out by the son of the barren woman, who bears him only by means of faith." The progeny of former slaves would hear that "the stranger becomes the native and inherits his tradition, as the Gentile, through faith in Christ, inherits the promise of Israel."[13]

According to Patterson, this understanding "directly transposes to the spiritual level what was the single most important sociological transformation of Paul's time—the freedman's appropriation of the native Roman, and Corinthian, political, demographic, and social heritage."[14] Given Patterson's understanding of Paul's intention in Galatians, this interpretation is quite plausible. Against the background of the features of slavery earlier described, Paul's appropriation of the story of Abraham's two sons does establish the "somebodyness" of persons who had been either socially dead or severely marginalized. Among other things, this "somebodyness" involves belonging, in the sense of having lineage (with Jesus Christ as the common ancestor) and also in having a claim to benefits (joint heirs of a common heritage) and resources (a community that shares burdens). I now hasten to say that, while Paul utilized concepts from Roman law to revolutionize the Hebrew story of the sons, it was as the story was told within the Hebrew context that elements were available for radical application. I also have the sense that it is when embraced in relation to the Hebrew understanding of manumission as adoption that its powerful significance for the new life of freedom in Christ would have been appreciated. These features, along with others, suggest that, in developing his theology of freedom, Paul was in direct conversation with the tradition he claimed as his own, even when for rhetorical purposes he sometimes minimized its significance. In making this claim I am also suggesting that, while the immediate circumstance of Roman slavery might have provided images and concepts for Paul's articulations on freedom, his valuation of freedom would have been heavily influenced by his Jewish ancestry with its dramatic stories about slavery and freedom, exile and restoration.

## THE HEBREW BACKGROUND FOR CHRISTIAN UNDERSTANDINGS OF FREEDOM

Jamaican church leader and theologian Ashley Smith is just one of many Christian thinkers who testify to the ongoing power of the religio-theological tradition on which Paul called as he developed his reflections on Christian freedom. Smith is quite clear that "for the Christian concept of liberation is a direct derivation from the biblical record of the emancipation of the people of

Israel from Egyptian bondage." The context of Egyptian slavery is the framework in which the need for freedom is felt. From his analysis of this scenario, as it is depicted in Hebrew Scriptures, Smith suggests that the process of liberation begins with the dawning of awareness that the condition of bondage is not only unbearable but terminable, that is, the existence presently known is not the only possible existence—there are alternatives. Adopting the title of a recent work on Liberation Theology, "there is another possible world."[15] Smith goes into a more generalized discussion of the dynamics associated with the new awareness. This includes radical doubting and questioning and an accompanying increase in the awareness of the ability to make choices within the limitations imposed by the constraints of a particular situation.[16]

While Smith's countryman Patterson would be quite supportive of his sentiments in regard to freedom, he would not be so convinced about the eligibility of the Exodus story for the kind of regard in which it is held by Caribbean theologians, as well as others. Among other reasons, Patterson is skeptical of the account as given in Hebrew Scriptures because there is no supporting extra-biblical reference to the flight from Egypt. While he is not resistant to the idea that Israel, like many other groups all over the ancient Near East, was a subject low-status group, he suggests that this does not amount to slavery "as we understand the institution." Thus he makes the strong assertion that Israel's "epic history, in which its Egyptian sojourn was retrospectively reinterpreted as slavery, has no special part in the history of individual freedom."[17]

In his skepticism regarding historical evidence to support the Exodus story in the Bible, Patterson is in company with many biblical scholars, and I have been convinced about this for some time. However, in assessing the story's liberative significance I lean in the direction of Patterson's former academic colleague Michael Walzer, who in his text *Exodus and Revolution* defends the concrete actuality of the event. Walzer claims that while the Exodus account of deliverance is expressed in religious terms, it "is also a secular, that is, a this-worldly and historical account." More importantly, he suggests, "it is a realistic account in which miracles play a part but which is not itself miraculous."[18] Walzer certainly wishes to paint a picture of a cultural ethos being created under the influence of an event when he claims that "the Israelites do not, as is sometimes said, go wandering in the wilderness; the Exodus is a journey forward—not only in time and space. It is a march toward a goal, a moral progress, a transformation." Therefore, "the men and women who reach Canaan are, literally and figuratively, not the same men and women who left Egypt."[19]

Given Patterson's assertion that Israel's retrospective characterization of its sojourn in Egypt as slavery has no place in the history of individual freedom, Walker's claim that "the subject of the march is the people of

Israel" is quite telling. On its face, this claim does not preclude concern for individual freedom, but it suggests that any such concern will occur in light of a foundational commitment to communal welfare. There is certainly a hint of this disposition as Walzer portrays a striking contrast between Genesis, which, he suggests, "is a collection of stories about individual men and women; they are mostly members of one family, a family, moreover, with a singular destiny; but we are focused on individuals," and Exodus, which "is the story of a people."[20] The description of the dramatic process by which freedom is gained, and of the eventful journey that follows, is designed to make clear what is necessary for the emergence of viable community. Thus, where Patterson's analysis of Paul focuses primarily on the bestowal of personal spiritual freedom through Jesus Christ, Walzer's understanding of the significance of the Exodus highlights the view that it is as the experience of freedom from Egypt is appropriated in Israel's life as a community that oppression takes on a moral significance. It is this process, Walzer suggests, that established the grounding for the concept of redemption in Hebrew and English—this meaning "to buy back . . . the freedom of a slave"—and "the Hebrew noun translated as 'deliverance' comes from the verb 'to go out.'"[21] The spiritual power of these concepts is explicitly linked to socio-historical and political processes.

Biblical scholar Richard Bauckham seems allied to Walzer in his disposition toward the Exodus as he reminds us that the Old Testament has no abstract definition of freedom, but conceives of freedom in quite concrete terms. Taking Israel's enslavement in Egypt to be paradigmatic, Bauckham suggests, for example, that "it is not the abstract status of subjection but the concrete evils of oppression—intolerably hard labor, enforced infanticide (Exodus 1:11-16)—that distresses the people and evoke God's concern and redemptive action (Exodus 2:23-25; 3:7-10; 6:5-7)." The value of freedom, he suggests, was experienced "in its concrete benefits: freedom to supply one's basic needs and to enjoy the ordinary pleasures of life without being exploited by others."[22] These concerns were certainly linked to "economic independence and freedom from fear of harm." At the same time, he, like Walzer, insists that the freedom of Israel was not understood primarily as the freedom of an individual (or family) from oppression by others—this being an individualistic understanding of freedom that is easily projected back from modern times. Indeed, the individual Israelite did not have lordship over his/her life; she "was not his or her own master, but God's slave."[23]

In a striking elaboration, Bauckham emphasizes that the Exodus did not simply liberate Israel from any kind of lordship, but Israel was freed from its Egyptian oppressors in order to serve God. God's insistent challenge to the pharaoh was not simply "Let my people go," but "Let my people go that they may serve me" (Exodus 7:16; 8:1, 20; 9:1, 13; 10:3).[24] Jon Levenson comments: "The emphasis, I think, falls on that last word: that they may serve Me and no one else."[25] Thus "the point of the exodus is not freedom in the sense of self-determination, but service, the service of the loving, redeeming, and delivering God of Israel, rather than the state and its proud king."[26]

Walzer and Bauckham are clearly impressed with the orientation toward freedom portrayed by the Scriptures to have been established in the earliest period of Israel's emergence as a people. My attitude to their view is influenced, among other things, by my conviction that a significant enough degree of individual self-determination is important for the experience of authentic freedom. This position will receive further elaboration in the course of the chapter. For now I continue to examine ways in which the post-Egypt experience of the Israelites is analyzed in order to further uncover the background to influences that have affected traditional Christian understandings of freedom. With this in mind, I delve further into Walzer's ideas, which nuances, in a progressive way, insights from Bauckham.

At the heart of Walzer's analysis is the view that the Sinai covenant was the central symbol of Israel's communal character and that freedom was vital to this character. He argues that, while scholarly investigations might have revealed structural and verbal similarities between the Sinai covenant and the ancient suzerainty treaty, "they tell us little about the agents of the covenant or its subject matter." His view is that there is actually "no precedent for a treaty between God and an entire people or for a treaty whose entire conditions are literally the laws of morality."[27] Evidence of this uniqueness, which connects directly with the privileging of freedom, is suggested in his claim that while the same Hebrew word is used for Pharonic slavery and service to God, the latter is radically unlike the former—the former is enforced by coercion; the latter by communal consent. Characterized by Walzer as "radically inclusive," this scenario involves "all the people of Israel" giving consent to the arrangement at hand (Exod. 19:8)." He presses home his point by suggesting that, while Israel was set free from Egyptian bondage through God's unconditional action, that which would actually inform their relationship with God (the Mosaic-Sinai covenant) was radically conditional.[28] A similar contrast is also evident when the Abrahamic covenant is placed alongside the Sinai covenant. There is the interesting suggestion that the biblical narrator wishes for us to appreciate that God had no wish to transact the latter covenant while the people's self-understanding was dominated by the experience in Egypt. We, therefore, hear from Walzer: "The covenant waits until they have savored their freedom—and marched as far as the holy mountain. There they stand between Egypt and the promised land, and they have to choose."[29] As he puts it later regarding Israel's choice to be in covenant: "The people could have chosen differently, though God would presumably have been astonished had they done so. The covenant introduces into the Exodus story a radical voluntarism that sits uneasily with the account of the original deliverance—where God, absolute and almighty, makes all the decisions."[30]

It is in this strident emphasis on freedom of choice that I notice a striking difference between Walzer and Bauckham. Bauckham makes clear that Israel's new status is radically different from what it was in Egypt, with this difference reflected in how God chooses to act and how God's status affects Israel's relation to any earthly ruler. God, he says, "was dedicated to the interests of God's people, and God's lordship was experienced as liberation from all human lordship."[31] However, reflected in Walzer's explicit focus on "voluntarism" and in the recognition that Israel could have chosen against covenant, is his commitment to the position that God did not just desire devotion and service without question or competition. Instead, God desired relationship with a free people. So strong is Walzer's commitment to this position that he claims that "standing at Sinai, they [Israel] embody the excellence of man." He finds supporting insights from tenth-century Rabbi and scholar Saadya Gaon who, citing the account of the covenant in Deuteronomy, indicated that "God . . . gave man the ability to obey Him, placing it as it were in his hands, endowing him with power and freewill, and commanding him to choose that which is good." Walzer continues: "Power and freewill are gifts of God."[32]

My speculation is that Walzer's leaning reflects the fact that as a Jew himself, his sensibilities have been honed not only by the narratives of the Scriptures by intimate awareness of people who were victimized in the German Holocaust. With this in mind, I, as a descendant of slaves and one socialized in a region that still carries the marks of its history, characterized by brutal denial of freedom, have great affinity for what I sense to be Walzer's inclinations. Having said this, I am doubtful whether the rabbinic sources he consulted can give adequate support for his claim that "the general will" emerged from "the wills of independent, noncomunicating individuals."[33] The very fact that many in Israel continued in their inclination to worship other deities suggests that they were not convinced that exclusive commitment to Yahweh was the way to go. Walzer points to Joshua's declaration (Joshua 24:15) regarding his commitment and the commitment of his household to Yahweh, and his challenge to the people to choose. What Walzer overlooks is the fact that Joshua is speaking for his household, and that it was typically the case that patriarchs of households spoke for all its members, including adult women and slaves. What does this mean for their independent exercise of will? Along with this factor, it is quite unlikely that individuals (men and women) operating in a context where communal commitments were so highly prized would have easily declared dissenting positions. It was probably in their best interest to keep their real views to themselves. These comments hint at my view that there is more to the story of freedom in Israel than has so far been represented, which raises questions about the degree to which it can support my inclinations regarding freedom.

From Bauckham's discussion, we learn that given its "sense of being a nation of freed slaves, with only one master, Israel acquired an unusual (in the ancient Near Eastern context) sense of the equal right to freedom of all Israelites." Bauckham quotes from Leviticus 25:42: "They are my slaves, whom I brought out of the land of Egypt; they shall not be sold as slaves." And he suggests that Samuel's reaction to the prospect of a king (1Sam. 8:17) seems to be informed by an awareness of the "oppressive despotism" that was characteristic of monarchy at the time, and that "a political relationship of subjection was inappropriate in the nation God had redeemed from slavery (see also Judg. 8:22-23)."[34]

This is a theological disposition into which I was nurtured in my early years of training, supported by analysis from Liberation theology. Therefore, it was not difficult for me to locate reflections by Leonardo Boff that seem supportive of Bauckham's inclination. In the work *When Theology Listens to the Poor*, Boff interprets the dynamic just described in terms of a commitment to the fundamental rights of the poor, developed on the basis of their experience as exploited aliens in the land of Egypt. He suggests that the collective memory of their own experience of poverty and oppression came to be reflected in a refrain throughout the Hebrew Scriptures: "So you must befriend the alien, for you were once aliens yourselves in the land of Egypt (Deut. 10:19). "You shall not do as they do in the land of Egypt, where you once lived (Lev. 18:3)."[35] These acknowledgments and commitments gave each Israelite responsibilities to fellow Israelites. According to Bauckham, the neighbor was not simply a restraint on one's freedom, but one whom one was expected to love as oneself (Lev. 19:18).[36]

Doing theology in a context with a long history of slavery and colonialism attuned me to the legal provisions and prophetic denunciations that expressed concern for inequality and exploitation in Israel. Many could identify with those in Israel who through lack or loss of economic resources were constantly in danger of being exploited by the powerful. With signs of the plantation systems still prominent we would, like Bauckham and others, quote with gusto passages like Isaiah 5:8 in which the prophet railed against those "who join house to house, who add field to field, until there is room for no one but you, and you are left to live alone in the midst of the land." We were also very aware of the associated "concern to protect those who did not have economic independence: resident aliens, orphans, widows," and the declared position that "no one in Israel, not even resident aliens should be exploited, since it was precisely from oppression as landless aliens in Egypt that God redeemed Israel (Exod. 23:9; Lev. 19:33, 34; Deut. 24:18)."[37]

While I continue to be impressed by that just described, I now cannot overlook the fact that the Israelite framework popularly associated with exodus, covenant, laws, and prophets, also included slavery. In this matter Israel's life was quite consistent with other settings in the ancient Near East. These slaves consisted of foreigners captured as prisoners of war, and Israelites who had fallen into debt and had to sell themselves into slavery. It is, therefore, important to note that in light of source criticism, Deuteronomy, usually characterized as reflecting late monarchic reform, is probably addressing abuses which had in fact taken place in Israel. If Leviticus is from a Priestly source and developed after the fall of Jerusalem, the injunction regarding aliens may well represent a later approach or a later modification of an old practice.

Bauckham spends much time trying to present Israel's practice of slavery in its best light. He hastens to point to evidence that Hebrew Scriptures fully recognize the inconsistency of the enslavement of Israelites with the fundamental freedom and equality of all God's people. He proceeds to point out how the practice was limited in significant ways, and indicates that the laws that protected slaves from their masters (Ex. 21: 20-21) were unique in their contemporary context and moved the status of all slaves beyond being mere chattel. "[A]s mere property they could have no rights to protect them from harm by their owners, but as human beings they do." There was even a law commanding Israelites to harbor runaway slaves (Deut. 23:15-16).[38]

I do not doubt that what Bauckham describes was a significant development in the life of Israel that most certainly helped to lay the foundations for what Patterson considers dramatic developments evident in Paul's writings. At the same time, I am disappointed with the stance taken by Bauckham and others like him as they evaluate slavery in Israel. My attitude is based on the view that, exactly because many Christians look to the life of Israel for ethical guidance, we must be careful to be explicit in acknowledging the areas in which it seems problematic. My base-line difficulty is with the very fact that experience as foreign slaves in Egypt even allowed for a morality that sanctioned any kind of slavery at all. This difficulty is compounded by the recognition that, while there were clear regulations regarding how Israelites who sold themselves into slavery should be treated (Lev. 25: 39-43), and provisions established for regaining their freedom (Ex. 21:1-4; Deut. 15:12-18), there were no similar regulations and provisions for the foreigner bought as a slave (Lev. 25:44-46). I take these features to suggest that Israel's preoccupation with freedom as a communal phenomenon did not allow sufficient attention to its significance for each individual on the basis of their humanity *per se*.

It is also worth considering how effective it can be to promote freedom with the use of language that is itself associated with subjugation and coercion. Here I draw attention to the term used for both Israel's relation to God (e.g., Exodus 7:16; Leviticus 25:42) and their status in Egypt (e.g., Leviticus 26:13). In a number of contemporary English versions of the Bible, the same word is translated "servant" for the former and "slave" for the latter. The root word *abad* does mean to "to work" or "to serve." However, I am convinced that, with Israel's landscape of meaning marked by their history of slavery in Egypt, it is very unlikely that the term associated with that master-slave scenario would not affect the character of their relationship with the sovereign lord when used to describe it.

I am unimpressed by Walzer's claim that slavery in Egypt was enforced by coercion, while slavery to God was by communal consent. As early as the introduction to this project I pointed out that continuous life in slavery (and other forms of oppression) can create a "slave mentality" that easily disposes a community to continue operating like slaves, long after their physical shackles are broken. While Walzer does show awareness of this phenomenon, he is too quick to conclude that Israel was free of its debilitating affects when they chose to covenant with God. It may well be evidence of a pathological condition that former slaves concluded that they could not be a viable community without a dominant-directing presence, and thus escaped one master (Pharoah) only to replace him with another (Yahweh).

Bauckham is clearly in sympathy with Walzer when he suggests that "to exchange the lordship of the Egyptians for the lordship of God was not really to move from one slavery to another, since God was dedicated to the interests of God's people, and God's lordship was experienced as liberation from all human lordship."[39] Here again there is the presumption that slavery, if it is to God, is a good thing. Further, it seems to me that whatever might be the quality of God's concern for Israel, textual evidence suggests that there was a significant level of self-interest involved. As I identified above, Bauckham himself reminds us that Yahweh freed Israel from Egypt for no other reason than that they would serve him. Therefore, I will be bold enough to suggest that whatever God did for Israel, it was so that they would be more committed to their role as "his" slaves, that is, a people in total subjection to him. Surely this objective guided how Israel's lord and master would express his "benevolence," and, in turn, condition the people's expressions of "power and freewill" which Walzer claims are gifts from God.[40] These considerations leave me uncertain of his claim that Israel was constituted in the context of a covenant based on radical voluntarism.

Walter Brueggemann points out that Israel signed on for obedience to Yahweh before they had heard any of the commandments. He displays kinship with Bauckham and Walzer in his suggestion that Israel experienced Yahweh as the God of abundance and generosity in contrast to Pharaoh's regime of scarcity and brutality, and "they knew that any commands from God of abundance would be better than the commands of Pharaoh."[41] Having heard this, we must not overlook the fact that Yahweh's abundance is associated with displays of power, and that when this power was unleashed against those who were not favored it was violent and excessive. Thus we hear in Exodus 13:15 that because of Pharaoh's stubbornness all Egyptian firstborns (human and animal) are killed. And Exodus 14: 22-30 describes a scenario in which it was not sufficient to stop the pursuing Egyptians by getting them stuck in the muddy seabed; they also had to be engulfed in water and drowned. What we hear immediately after this portrayal is quite significant as we consider this God of abundance and generosity, and it has clear implications for our assessment of so-called expressions of power and free-will in Israel: "Israel saw the great work that the Lord did against the Egyptians. So the people feared the Lord and believed in the Lord and in his servant Moses (v. 31)."

While there is little doubt that the liberated people would have felt immense gratitude for what was done on their behalf, a decisive factor in their display of allegiance to Yahweh was the effect of his display of overwhelming power. In a world of competing despots, Israel's general response was probably fueled by a desire to be protected by the most powerful of the lot. Yet they would not have failed to notice what can happen when one crosses Yahweh; not even the innocent is safe. Surely this foundational disposition would affect every other interaction between Israel and Yahweh.

Reflecting on life in Israel Brueggemann establishes a stark contrast between Yahweh's governance and that of the rulers of coercive and exploitative socio-political and economic frameworks he calls Empire. As exemplified in Egypt, the latter operated in terms of scarcity and fashioned anxiety systems of exploitation whereas Yahweh led Israel out of its dehumanizing production system.[42] As a result Israel moved from a situation of brutality and paucity in the midst of surplus to one of generosity/grace and adequate provision.[43] Along with this Yahweh put in place the conditions for the creation of community/neighborhood that was guided by a strong social ethic.[44] Later we hear that the active God who freed Israel from exile and despair was also creating a future for them.[45] Brueggemann mentions that the movement from one ethos to another had to be taken repeatedly because of the strong pull of the ways of Empire, which led to resistance to the common good.[46]

Once again we must not blind our eyes to other elements of the narrative stream that are relevant to our characterization of the God of exodus and restoration. Exploring the prophets, Brueggemann shows Yahweh fluctuating between harshness and tender speech (e.g., Isaiah 40:1-2) and providing dramatic descriptions of Israel's grand future.[47] Yet in Isaiah 10:5-6, which refers to an empire known for its extreme brutality, Israel is reminded of what Yahweh's sovereignty involves and the price to be paid for failure to submitted to it. We hear: "Ah, Assyria, the rod of my anger— the club in their hands in my fury! Against the godless nation I send him, against the people of my wrath I command him, to take spoil and seize plunder. And to thread them down like the mire of the streets." Surely it is this side of

Yahweh that is being emulated by Israel's leaders when, in situations like the renewal of covenant portrayed in 2 Chronicles 15, we hear, "whoever would not seek the Lord the God of Israel, should be put to death, whether young or old man or woman (v.13)." Through these and other scenarios in Hebrew Scriptures Yahweh is shown to be not unlike many worldly despots in that he secures the allegiance of his people by both tenderness and tyranny, and Israel is shown to be not unlike many other "claimed" peoples as they relate to God with both deep attachment and great anxiety.

In the final analysis it is the recognition that Israel's collective psychology was informed by the relationship most fundamental to their self-understanding as a people, that is, their relationship with Yahweh that helps me make sense of a contradictory scenario. This involves, on one hand, Walzer's claim that having been given gifts of power and free-will they developed a framework for ongoing relations that depended on the exercise of these gifts, and, on the other hand, the fact that they developed an institution (slavery) that, by its known character in Egypt, is the very antithesis of the character of the gifts and of the governing principle of the framework of relations.

Therefore, I am of the view that it is dialectical engagement between the Israelite framework that privileges communality and the Greco-Roman framework that was the immediate context for Paul's considerations on personal freedom—an engagement that includes critical analysis of both—and the adoption of relevant ideas from other available frameworks, which will prove most helpful for the development of appropriate Christian understandings of freedom in our epoch. I am also disposed to the position that, in this process, it is not sufficient to simply re-construe the meaning of terms traditionally associated with slave systems; but as far as possible new language needs to be developed that symbolizes the understanding of freedom we wish to promote in thought and practice.

## RETURNING TO NEW TESTAMENT WITH THE CALL OF FREEDOM IN MIND

Following from his discussion of freedom in Israel, Bauckham suggests that "the New Testament's understanding of freedom, as not so much from others as for others, is already implicit in the Old Testament sense of social responsibility."[48] Despite the critique just made, I agree with Bauckham, and I suggest that it is unfortunate that Patterson failed to recognize this and other features of Israel's understanding of freedom to be important presuppositions of New Testament articulations on freedom. One striking example of this deficiency is in Patterson's address of the questions asked after his intriguing analysis of the allegory of Abraham's two sons: "What does . . . freedom bring? And how is it prevented from descending into selfishness and chaos?"[49] An important element of Patterson's answer is provided in his focus on Paul's epistle to the Romans, which he suggests entails a shift of emphasis from personal freedom in Galatians to that of sovereignal freedom. As Patterson explicates sovereignal freedom, ideas emerge that are very reminiscent of both Bauckham's and Walker's discussions of Israel's self-understanding as a free people in relationship with a sovereign God. However, Patterson limits himself to the suggestion that Paul approaches sovereignty "from the viewpoint of the master class held by the conservative Roman church dominated by imperial and other wealthy freedmen."[50]

From his observation of Paul's opening salutation in Romans, biblical scholar Stanley Stowers does support the view that the letter characterizes its ostensive audience as unambiguously gentile. At the same time, he acknowledges that the actual church community in Rome would have probably contained "a Jewish-Christian strain in it."[51] Nevertheless, as he points out in his critique of W. K. Kümmel's ideas, this acknowledgment does not permit us to conclude that Paul had Jews in mind as his actual audience, much less to prove that the letter encodes them as readers.[52] Still, I have difficulty believing that Paul's own sensibilities as a Jew, and his awareness of the general characteristics of the Roman context, would not have allowed for ideas on freedom from Jewish experience to influence his considerations; and this does not preclude the dynamic of the Roman master class informing his analysis.

Given his position that the latter was the case, Patterson, in his application to the Christian life, suggests that the first point emphasized by Paul is that freedom is a gift—a notion which he says would have been alien to the ex-slaves who had toiled to pay for their freedom, or had some relative do so. Instead, this free gift was bestowed by the master: that is, the grace of freedom is bestowed, not earned.[53] Thirdly, "there is a clear shift in Romans from the model of freedom as complete and unconditional manumission to the more common model found in real Roman slave society, namely, manumission as a highly conditioned status." As the recipient of the free gift of freedom, the believer is under a strong obligation to God, "his righteous master." As such, faith is obedience and "true freedom exists only in enslavement to God."[54] As Romans 6:18 puts it: "You have been set free from sin and have become slaves to righteousness."

My earlier examination of ideas of freedom from Hebrew Scriptures, with the help of Walzer and Bauckhan, should have made it clear to the reader how consistent Paul's position is with the idea that Israel was set free from Egyptian slavery to be God's slaves. Yet, Patterson attributes Paul's ideas regarding God's sovereignty over the Christian's life to the transposition of the understanding of sovereignal freedom held by the powerful of Rome.[55] While not doubting that ideas from Paul's immediate context had influence on his considerations, the strong probability of influence from his Jewish heritage is difficult to deny. As such, with the recognition that the God of Christianity is the God of Israel, I have great difficulty understanding how Patterson could have overlooked this influence. Suffice it to say at this point, I find the language used in both contexts equally problematic.

After identifying other features of sovereignal freedom, Patterson proceeds in a direction that I find both fascinating and problematic. He claims that there is no real inconsistency between Galatians and Romans on the view that "personal freedom . . . and sovereignal freedom . . . are necessary and complementary elements in a composite, chordal value which expresses the organic union of human beings and God in a single body, a unified spiritual state."[56] Patterson is clear that Christian freedom, as understood by Paul, is personal and a transaction between the Christian and God. So, intriguingly, he indicates that "the personal spiritual freedom celebrated in Galatians is the freedom of mankind, waiting for God; the sovereignal freedom celebrated in Romans is the freedom of God, waiting for mankind." The latter, he suggests, is a superior freedom in which humankind can hope to share at the appropriate time. However, Christ's redemption comes in two parts. Considering the two parts, I am quite comfortable with the view that "we are first reconciled to the country of God, given 'access' to the grace of his presence, but we have yet to meet him, though the believer has a guarantee that he will at the parousia." However, I am uncomfortable with the view that "at such time there will be complete identity with God, basking in his essence. In this perfect slavery, slavery destroys itself, as master and slave become one."[57]

On reading this declaration, many orthodox theologians would immediately ask for a thorough explanation of the idea of "complete identity with God," and especially for the idea of "basking in God's essence"; others would reject the second because they would not be able to make sense of the idea of non-divine beings, even with the spiritual bodies mentioned in 1 Corinthians 15:42, basking in the very essence of the ontologically unique, ultimate, God. At this point I simply question the moral status of framing the described transaction as one which in the final analysis is between slave and master. While bearing in mind probable anthropological, cosmological, and theological presuppositions, it is one thing to imagine believers getting to a place where finite barriers to communion with God are overcome and they enter into the deepest level of communion possible with the one whose grace and self-sacrificing magnanimity was glimpsed in the life and death of Jesus; it is another thing for one's slavery to be overcome only because one has finally lost all of their identity to the slave master, even if the slave master is God.

The nature of the problem is filled out in Patterson's suggestion that, in the *pre-parousia* condition, the Christian would be "exactly what a slave is to his master: a living surrogate, so completely at one with him that he has no separate identity."[58] Reflecting on his life in Galatians 2:20, Paul does seem to support this position when he declares: "I no longer live but Christ lives in me." When I scrutinize this declaration in the chapter in which it is situated, Paul appears to be establishing a contrast between he and those who, along with Peter, were still operating by the strictures of Jewish law and requiring other Christians to do the same. This seems to be a rhetorical device intended to establish the radical antithesis between the way these people were operating and how they ought to be as persons redeemed through the death and resurrection of Jesus the Christ. In other words, while he understands how their prior socialization would have instilled bigoted attitudes in them, they should now embrace fully the new possibilities for their lives in relation to other lives, exemplified in the way Jesus operated, especially his willingness to give up his life for sinners. Paul's lament in Romans 7 may well betray his conviction that, as a "slave to righteousness," he should have no separate identity from God through Christ, which resulted in a conflict between what he desires to do and what he actually does, and that his conflict reflects a "self-contradiction" to which he is "condemned" because he remains "trapped in the flesh."[59] However, given my view that embodiment with its limitations, challenges, and conflictive dynamics is no trap, but is fundamental to human beings who are partially responsible for determining what being human means, I ask: what can surrogacy have to do with human freedom if the living surrogate loses her/his identity in that of the master; this is surely tantamount to the loss of humanity. And what is the character of righteousness, which, rather than making one the best human possible, denies one of it?

Patterson proceeds to suggest that, along with the acceptance that human beings must engage in an inward struggle to the end of our days, there is another profound discovery. It is that "the home [humanity] seeks, the God in identity with whom it hopes to find perfect peace and freedom, resides within the innermost self. Enslavement in sin, it turns out, is self-estrangement, which is the same thing as God estrangement."[60] Surely the realization that God is present in the innermost self would be vital to the development of inner freedom, with the exercise of ontological freedom at its core. And one can only imagine the power of this conviction for Roman Christians who would have had every reason to be anxious over the fact that they still lived within a state that had the power and disposition to re-enslave them or in numerous ways curtail their personal freedom. At the same time, I suggest that the self-estrangement to which Patterson refers may have its roots in the very consideration of relations with God within the context of a master-slave paradigm, with complete submission considered the ideal state of being for human beings.

As should have been clear from the examination of Augustine's struggles in chapter 2, it is my view that an internal struggle is inevitable as one addresses a range of impulses and ideas that emerge legitimately in human beings whose reason is grounded in the very biological structures we attempt to coordinate through its exercise. Further, one's whole life is never separate from the dynamics in contexts in which we are nurtured or operate. Therefore, where the operations of the soul/mind is concerned, it must first be accepted that yearnings of the body are not necessarily in opposition to them, even the so-called highest expressions that have to do with ultimate concerns. We must also expect various levels of personal achievement ranging from moments of correspondence between aspirations and accomplishments to moments when we fail completely at what we think ought to be achievable in our lives. The latter would be the most explicit form of self-contradiction, which could be the result of a variety of causal factors, including those for which an individual is primarily responsible. I suggest then that, as works in progress, our challenge as human beings is to seek after helpful insights from all our experiences such that they can contribute to our betterment and the betterment of others. However, a perpetual impasse, in which self-contradiction turns to self-estrangement, is unavoidable when we disparage that which is fundamental to being human— the body— by perceiving it as a trap, and, on the other hand, seek after a type of relation with God characterized by slave-like submission, for which human beings are not designed.

What Patterson portrays as an inward battle for freedom as Christians operate in the *pre-parousia* sphere seems equivalent to what Stanley Stowers portrays as a quest for self-mastery. Stowers suggests that "self-mastery as a personal, social, and theological problem is the most palpable issue in Romans 1-8," with lack of self-control presented as the audience's problem.[61] Stowers provides us with the Greco-Roman background to this emphasis on self-mastery. Aristotle, he says, identifies two forms of unrestraint (*akrasia*): recklessness and weakness, with the latter seen by Paul as worse than the former. We learn that weakness (*astheneia*) as portrayed in Romans, is also reflected in other places like 1 Corinthians 8 and 1 Corinthians 9:24-27. In 1 Corinthians 8 "the weak . . . know that only one God exists and that idols have no reality (v. 1-6) but succumb to the feelings and beliefs of their pagan past when faced with idol worship."[62] The latter example comes just after what I consider a discussion of freedom as flexibility, which leads to Paul's explicit description of how he adapts himself to the needs of the weak (v.22-23)—this providing a model for his readers. However, such adaptability should be exercised with the recognition that the Christian life is alike a race, and the Christian portrayed as an athlete is encouraged to exercise self-control (*enkrateuetai*) in all things.[63] Stowers points out that only the explicitly communal goals of Paul's exhortation distinguish this text from the typical Greco-Roman uses of such discourse.[64]

The wider Greco-Roman context in which Paul wrote was one in which it was understood that, "just as intense competition characterizes social life, so a violent competition within characterizes those who aspire to moral excellence and self-mastery." Further, "just as a hierarchy that put everyone in the empire except the emperor under the rule of someone and made a small part of the population masters of others, so the soul was to be the master of the body and reason over the passions."[65]

Stowers communicates the idea that Paul's central message to his Roman audience is that Christ is the enabler of the self-mastery he is promoting. He asserts that "the arguments in chapters 5-8 aim to change the reader's understanding of how they have attained mastery over their passions and desires— this not being through the law but through their identification with Jesus Christ." He proceeds: "According to 6:1-7:6, Jesus' death is somehow the cause of the encoded reader's 'death to sin,' which means that the reader can be free from enslavement to their passions and desires." And, in language more appealing than Patterson's notion of "complete identity with God," he claims that "Chapter 8 combines this motif of liberation from passions through the Spirit with the themes of freedom from contamination and a filial relationship with God leading to future reward."[66] Here Patterson might suggest that an important element of the future reward will be full enjoyment of the believer's *postliminium.*

While I appreciate the fact that Stowers says nothing that suggests any expectation of complete identity with God,[67] I am in agreement with Patterson's view that Paul was of the mind that we struggle with ourselves in the *pre-parousia* state with the anticipation of one day enjoying "that higher freedom— the sovereignal freedom of God which is both near and far in time and being."[68] And, bearing in mind the conditioning of linguistic and social context, I also identify with the statement that while Christians await this experience of higher freedom they would carry out functions, within the context of the church as one body under the lordship of Christ, that are reflective of their unique gifts.[69] At the same time, any identification I have with Paul's considerations on freedom is with great concern over Patterson's claim that the sort of language used by Paul "was word-for-word, exactly how a Roman imperialist would view the Roman state and the sovereignal, integrative role of the emperor, whose grace and excellence had brought peace and glory."[70]

Having said the above, I continue to suggest that a greater openness on the part of Patterson to recognize Hebrew influence on the Christian concept of freedom could easily have made his analysis more dynamic, such that he could identify the ways Paul skillfully utilized the socio-political structure of his context for appropriate metaphors and still identify with the best elements of Bauckham's, and especially Walzer's, analysis of the Exodus. If this were so, Patterson would have been able to give more "substance" to the way Christian recognition of the God of Israel as sovereign served to relativize all earthy governments and systems of authority, including that from which Paul took the majority of his metaphors. This recognition could have been associated with the consideration of how relativization limits the degree to which earthly governments can determine the lives of those who have personal spiritual freedom, which in Neville's categorization is ontological freedom. The analysis of Paul's understanding of Christian freedom could then have been broadened. In the first place, Patterson's discussion of the organic metaphor of body in 1 Corinthians 12 could have proceeded beyond the section which reminded him of "the sovereignal, integrative power role of the emperor" and led to his highlighting of the necessary link between the personal freedom emphasized in Galatians and the sovereignal freedom emphasized in Romans. It could have also encouraged an emphasis on the section of 1 Corinthians 12 that emphasizes mutual need of the members of the body, and even more, that which made clear that the members of the body normally seen as less honorable ought to be clothed with greater honor, and less respectable members treated with greater respect. He could have proceeded to explore influential passages like Philippians 2 in which Christians are encouraged by Paul to adopt the mind of Christ (discerned from his immense sacrifice) that fosters a tender, outgoing altruism, negating selfish ambition, vain conceit, and enabling each to consider others better than themselves. It is this mindset, Paul suggests, that would also enable the Christian not only to attend to his/her own interests but the interest of others.

These considerations definitely link the Christian attitude to that which Bauckham identifies as arising from the Israelites' acknowledgment that divine lordship (sovereignty) gave each Israelite responsibilities to fellow Israelites.[71] Actually, he establishes this connection explicitly. Having acknowledged that Jesus freed no slaves in bondage to other human beings, he quickly declares that "the exodus liberation becomes in the New Testament a type of Christ's liberation of those enslaved in sin and death (e.g., Revelation 1:5-6)."[72] This conviction, Bauckham claims, "is precisely an extension and deepening of the Old Testament concept of freedom, not a replacement of it. A liberation from all oppression cannot exclude the political sphere, even while it goes much further than the political." Indeed, there is not only concern with "inward and individual" dimensions of freedom "but concerns for outward, social relationships."[73] Appropriating elements of Walzer's discussion, I add that it is exactly because the Exodus motif had some impact on Christian sensibilities in its earliest emergence that it infiltrated the general Western ethos and influenced radical movements of various kinds long before it was taken up and popularized by Liberation theologians.

Walzer points out that "so common is the Exodus reference in the political history of the West (or, at least, of protest and radical aspiration in the West) that I began to notice when it was missing—as in the years of the French Revolution, whose leading actors were resolutely hostile to Jewish as they were to Christian conceptions of history."[74]

Having spent time exploring biblical conceptions of freedom, I must now make explicit a concern to which I have alluded at various points in the project. This concern has to do with my recognition that it is the degree to which the development of personal interior freedom is associated with active-concrete resistance to forms of external coercion that the robustness and efficacy of the former will be ensured. This resistance, I suggest, should include resistance to structures of unfreedom and a stance against the symbolic reinforcement of coercion through linguistic means. I, therefore, admit great dissatisfaction when I hear Bauckham's reminder that the early church did not attempt to abolish existing structures of political and social subjection in their contemporary societies in the name of freedom. Instead, there was an attempt to transform them from within by turning them into relationships of voluntary and (where possible) mutual subjection.[75] While I have no desire to impugn what was a fledgling community, my discomfort is not relieved by the further indication that "instead of replacing a model of society in which there are masters and slaves with a model in which the notion of slavery was eliminated, Jesus and the early church replaced it with a model in which everyone is the slave of others—with . . . the understanding that this "'slavery' is entirely willing . . . (Luke 22:26-27; John 13:14; Gal. 5:13)"[76]

My discomfort might seem trivial and unjustified to some. However, having grown up in the Caribbean I am acutely aware that as long as the social ethos that emerges from a slave society is able to maintain linguistic keys, including the very term that identifies the oppressive character of that from which it emerged and which open certain associational doors, it will be very difficult for victims and victimizers to change deep-seated conceptions of self and other that inform the psychology and sociology of their relations. The crucial nature of this matter for Caribbean peoples was portrayed by Reggae icon Bob Marley in his song *Redemption Song*.[77] He challenged those who live with the legacy of colonialism to break the chains of mental slavery, and he gave the reminder that no one else could do so for them; they had to do it for themselves. Intellectual and church leader Billy Watty articulated most poignantly some of the debilitating effects "mental slavery" has had on the psyches of many in that region. In *From Shore to Shore*, he comments on the disturbing ambiguities of the Caribbean personality, which is

> at one and the same time brilliant and unstable, free and irresponsible, ostentatious and insecure, promising much and achieving little, shooting to the top like a meteor and then, in the next moment, plunging downwards into disgrace. The Caribbean person does not believe in himself nor does he believe in others like himself, because he knows that in their innermost beings neither he nor they are really themselves.[78]

Those to whom Marley and Watty refer are people who love Jesus dearly and practice impressive hospitality (being good servants/slaves to each other), but are afraid of success and have difficulty with sustained achievement.[79] Over three hundred years of training in self-deprecation, with the use of the explicit language of slavery and the finessed language of servanthood, has convinced many in this region that they are not worthy or capable of progress beyond a certain measure—they would be "passing their place." Generally speaking, Caribbean peoples are good at presenting themselves in ways that appear confident, but it does not take much to expose the insecurity that lies just beneath the surface. For those who are Christians, these features suggest that their practical learning over many generations that, as "free sons and daughters of God (John 8: 32; Galations 4:7; Romans 3:14-17)"[80] they are to give "the glad and willing service of a child" to God and others, has actually undermined their ability to live the kind of freedom that leads to flourishing in both the external and internal spheres of their lives. As these sons and daughters have been abused by their so-called siblings, their "father," the sovereign master, has, at least, chosen not to do anything; and if "he" is the omni-qualitied God they have been taught to believe in, "he" has actually orchestrated the whole thing. Needed, therefore, is an appropriate form of growing-up that enables the abused sons and daughters of God to view biblical injunctions regarding the life of slavery called servanthood with healthy suspicion. This means that, while I embrace and wish to propagate Bauckham's suggestion (guided by Paul's language in Galatians 5:13) that the Christian ideal is that "freedom is the freedom to love," I recommend that, in our time, there should be no quick emulation of the language or attitude associated with the suggestion that the way to avoid this freedom becoming "an opportunity for self-indulgence" is to see ourselves as "slaves to one another" or anyone else.[81]

It might be argued that in the time of Jesus and Paul there would have appeared to be no better term to convey the attitude of total self-giving that was being encouraged among Christians. It could very well be also that, given the range of reasons for which one might become a slave and the mitigating possibilities associated with the life of slavery,[82] many might have perceived the condition as having some redeeming features. Still, I am dismayed by Patterson's claim that "there is no need to be unduly upset by statements from Paul which suggest that the believers "set free from sin become slaves to God."[83] "Personal freedom," he suggests, "is not necessarily threatened by enslavement to this almighty freedom" because slavery to God "exists on an altogether different level." In helping us appreciate this "different level" he first suggests that "the essence of freedom is righteousness, power and glory, and mankind can experience this only by means of enslavement to God. . . ."[84] However, with the benefit of my struggle with some of the giants of Christian orthodoxy in the previous chapters, it should now be clear that, considered theologically, the promised righteousness is achieved at the cost of a key feature of one's humanity, which is the ability to exercise authentic choice-making that makes any real difference to the structure of our lives.

Being sensitive to the ways the more popular language of servanthood has been appropriated for oppressive purposes, Patterson suggests that "it may well be that medieval and later Christianity sanctioned servitude, but the charge cannot be laid on Paul."[85] I suggest that when one abstracts particular conceptions of freedom from the larger corpus of Paul's writings and the wider Pauline tradition, as Patterson does, it might well appear that Paul has nothing to do with later Christian-sanctioned oppression, by which the freedom of many, especially my (and Patterson's) African ancestors, was undermined. The theologian, however, has an obligation to engage these conceptions in the broader framework of the Pauline writings and the Pauline tradition,[86] and in light of the underlying presuppositions that affect the way they are translated into the concrete engagements of every-day life.

In exploring the broader framework of the Pauline tradition, we do not have to search long before we find pronouncements that are prime examples of attempts to use the language of subjection with supposed liberative intent. The first example is found in Ephesians 5:22-28, which is used widely at weddings in the part of the world I am from. In this reading, it is recommended by a disciple of Paul that women submit to their husbands, and men are encouraged to love their wives as Christ loved the church and died for it. Conscientious users of this reading will go to great lengths to remind hearers that it is immediately preceded by a verse on mutual submission, and men are reminded that Christ gave his life for the one he loved, the church. These considerations, however, do not necessarily further the agenda for women's freedom from traditional male oppression. In the first place, the notion of mutual submission, which seems to apply to general relations within the Christian community at large, has somehow been historically expressed in a hierarchical way, giving to women the wonderful "freedom" to expend themselves for the maintenance of our churches and giving to men the great "burden" of exercising dominance over the churches. Surely this is not unconnected to the fact that, while Paul might have commended a number of female leaders of congregations in Romans 16—this seeming to be compatible with his general declaration in Galatians 3:28—he, in 1 Corinthians 11:3, betrays what I consider a competing theological presupposition regarding the status of women in relation to men. As he proceeds to address the issue of propriety in worship in the Corinthians passage, he establishes a clear hierarchy of status and authority, which is God, then Christ, then men, then women.

I assert that, as this hierarchical presupposition helps us make sense of the way many churches have appropriated the suggestion of mutuality in Ephesians 5:21, it contributes to an explanation of the verses that follow. Here the hierarchy of status and authority is applied to what was the primary framework of engagement between men and women, marriage, and this would have laid the groundwork for relations in other spheres of interaction. So then, in keeping with the understanding of the character of the life and death of Jesus—that is, God's condescension for human salvation—men's love for their female spouses is that of a superior operating with the capacity for condescension for the sake of the inferior wife whose state is improved as a result of her husband's magnanimity. Conversely, as the body of Christ is not free to realize itself without its head, so the wife (as woman) is not free to realize herself without her head, the husband (as man). If I now apply Patterson's preferred language to this scenario, it makes for a quite interesting picture. In the general framework in which all Christians are slaves of God, men live out their enslavement through their head, Christ; women live out their enslavement through their head, men.

Some will argue that much has changed in regard to this dynamic. However, as is the case with vocabulary associated with slavery, given the long history of understanding and practice, much good intention continues to be overwhelmed by the lingering effects of traditional attitudes. It will take arduous effort over time to reshape a long-established framework of relations, and this must involve radical address of the language of subordination. It will also take great effort for the debilitating effects of the language of slavery and submission to be corrected, and central to this process has to be efforts by those who have lived with its disempowering consequences to explore new ways of representing the relationship of Christians to God and to other Christians. This general attitude frames my stance on the ongoing debate in some quarters of the African American community regarding the continued use of the "N" word in popular discourse. I will not dismiss the perception in some quarters that one way to free oneself from the power given to this word by racists is to take control of how the word is used and who uses it. However, there is much more to be said for exercising creativity by fashioning words of greeting and affection that reflect the highest aspirations for what it means to be human and what is involved in mutually enhancing interaction, especially when the disfiguring effects of the history of American slavery and apartheid are still evident. So it should also be for the theological language used to talk about crucial relations that inform the perception Christians have of self and others.

I approach this task with the view that, whereas Jesus *might* have had a focused vision in regard to a radical reorientation of the society in which he operated, the gospels make it clear that those around him did not. It seems to me also that while Paul might have been gripped by the spirit of Jesus' vision, such that he could declare that where the spirit of Christ is there is freedom (II Corinthians 3:17), his ability to appropriate and apply this vision in its fullness was quite limited. So, while Patterson is rightly impressed with his development of the concept of freedom, especially in Galatians, Paul's application of this to slaves, former slaves, and women was not very successful. An example of Paul's general limitation is even reflected in his approach to the development and propagation of the Christian message by fellow Christians. While he claimed freedom for himself as an interpreter of the gospel of Jesus Christ, he was not able to allow similar freedom to others. We, therefore, find him in II Corinthians 11:3-4 railing against those who present "another Jesus than the one we proclaim" which is, I suspect, a perspective different from that which he sanctioned. I suggest that another, more radical perspective than that of Paul's on how to conceptualize and promote human freedom might have been quite helpful in the history of Christianity.

Paul's approach, utilizing language associated with slavery, submission, and subordination, reflected and reinforced the basic acceptance of slavery as one feature of the known social structure. Without intending to, Patterson hits the nail on the head when he declares that "all who live in a large-scale slave society are in one way or another influenced by it, be they monarch or beggar, slave or free, rich or poor, male or female. In a large-scale slave society, the slave relation, like a cancer in the blood, pervades all, pollutes all, degrades all."[87] Thus, the theological pronouncements on freedom he analyzes, in the interesting way he does would have made sense against the background of the well-known structures of the well-established social system of Paul's era. As I perceive it, the Christian framework, developed in that era, would have allowed for varying forms of acceptable slavery. In the example of Philemon and Onesimus it would be master-brother and brother-slave; in marriage it would be slave-head and submissive-slave; in general relationships it would be slave-brother and slave-sister. In the final analysis, all members of the community would be slaves to the absolute sovereign-master, God.

I am convinced that it is exactly because this basic framework, with its related forms of subordination and rulership, continued to be embraced at some level of Christian "consciousness" that as soon as the Christian community became socially powerful and Christians became leaders of societies, they could fashion forms of slavery, that in the West, were multiple times more savage than that which was present when Christianity first emerged.

In his representation of this matter, Alfred North Whitehead suggests that "when the Western world accepted Christianity, Caesar conquered." Whitehead honors "the brief Galilean vision of humility" that was evident in Jesus' life and which inspired the earliest Christian community, but he is clear that this "vision . . . flickered through the ages, uncertainly." He suggests that "in the official formulation of the religion it has assumed the trivial form of the mere attribution to the Jews that they cherished a misconception about their

Messiah." However, "the deeper idolatry, of the fashioning of God in the image of the Egyptian, Persian, and Roman imperial rulers, was retained. The Church gave unto God the attributes which belonged exclusively to Caesar."[88] I add that it is the patriarchal God of Hebrew Scriptures that became the Church's Caesar, and the idea of the Church as the Caesar-God's earthly empire was further developed by Western Christendom. It is exactly with this sensibility that members of Western Christendom could use Hebrew and Christian Scriptures as a tool to provide the ideological foundations for modern slavery in the West. With this in mind, I'm not sure that those in contemporary times, who live with the legacy of modern slavery, racism and other forms of oppression, can be enabled into a healthy experience of self and grow into increasing realizations of what it means to be free if their spirituality is governed by Bauckham's claim that "if the Old Testament emphasis is on God's people as freed slaves, the New Testament emphasis is on God's people as free slaves."[89]

The crucial nature of the task ahead is brought home by Ashley Smith as he describes his own memory of a black Jamaican Presbyterian pastor who sought disciplinary action for a Scottish school principal who taught in a class that it was not God who had made black people inferior and condemned them to be servants of whites forever. According to Smith, "The misguided brother was totally confused when told that it was the accused Scotsman who was right."[90] I have the highest regard for the persistent efforts of Smith, among others, to reorient the mentality of the many in the Caribbean who, like this minister, have internalized the language and mentality of slavery along with traditional justifications informed by Hebrew and Christian Scriptures. I, however, look to the day when there will be greater recognition that significant transformation will not take place unless there is a radical reconfiguration of accompanying conceptions of God that move us from the idea that God desires to relate to human beings as free slaves.

This reconfiguration will enable a new level of analysis for Smith's further observation that "there is a tendency among Caribbean people who have been exposed to the influence of the Christianity of the region to be susceptible to the habit of seeking the intervention of the supposedly omnicompetent outsider whenever difficulties are encountered." This, he claims, is due to the internalization by the victim [of slavery, colonialism and neo-colonialism] of the attitude of the 'significant other' toward them."[91] By my analysis, this syndrome is linked directly to the black Presbyterian minister's confusion, and is, in the final analysis, grounded in the commitment to the idea of an omni-qualitied, sovereignly free God who is the first and final decider of what takes place in the world. Those who are viewed as "significant other" are so because of an "ultimate other." As such, why should those who have been placed in subjection not look to those [the significant other] whom God [the ultimate other] directly or proximally determined to dominate them in colonialism and slavery and now control their fortunes by economic and geo-political dominance? Why should this not be so for those who are still in the grip of racist, patriarchal, and other kinds of oppressive social systems?

## NOTES

1. Paul Tillich, *Systematic Theology*, vol. I (Chicago: University of Chicago Press, 1951), 175-176.

2. Orlando Patterson, *Freedom in the Making of Western Culture*, vol. I (New York: Basic Books, 1991), 234-235.

3. Ibid., 319.

4. Ibid., 324.

5. Francis Watson, "Christ, Law and Freedom: A Study in Theological Hermeneutics," in *God and Freedom—Essays in Historical and Systematic Theology*, ed. Colin E. Gunton (Edinburg: T &T Clark, 1995), 96.

6. Patterson, *Freedom and the Making of Western Culture*, 328.

7. Ibid., 328-330.

8. Ibid., 331. To reinforce his point, Patterson imports a declaration from 1 Cor. 15:43: "It is sown in dishonor, it is raised in glory. It is sown in weakness, it is raised in power."

9. Ibid. Patterson's source is W.W. Buckland, *The Roman Law of Slavery* (Cambridge: Cambridge University Press, 1970), 304.

10. Ibid., 332.

11. Ibid., 339.

12. From the Latin *super* and *sedere* (to sit), the term refers to sitting on the seat belonging to another and thus displacing and replacing that other.

13. Ibid. Being aware that this understanding will be quite appealing to Christian supersessionists, I embrace "inheritance" as "participation in" as against "being given." I also take note of biblical scholar J. Gerald Janzen's commentary on the story being addressed. Among his insights is the identification of two valuable lessons to be learnt. The first is that "the very community of promise and hope, of redemption and liberation . . . is itself capable of becoming a community of oppression." The second is that "Israel's story includes within it this episode which Israel tells against itself. In this way, here and elsewhere, Israel's story contains within itself elements that should guard against that story becoming an ideological weapon against other peoples." See J. Gerald Janzen, *Abraham and all the Families of the Earth: A Commentary on the Book of Genesis 12-50* (Grand Rapids: Wm. B. Eerdmans Publishing Co., 1993), 46-47.

14. Ibid.

15. See Marcella Althaus-Reid et al., ed., *Another Possible World* (London: SCM Press, 2007).

16. Ashley Smith, *Real Roots and Potted Plants: Reflections on the Caribbean Church* (Mandeville, Jamaica: Mandeville Publishers, 1984), 19-20.

17. Orlando Patterson, *Freedom and the Making of Western Culture*, 33.

18. Michael Walzer, *Exodus and Revolution* (New York: Basic Books, 1985), 9.

19. Ibid., 12.

20. Ibid.

21. Ibid., 24-25.

22. Richard Bauckham, *God and the Crisis of Freedom — Biblical and Contemporary Perspectives* (Louisville: Westminster John Knox Press, 2002), 9.

23. Ibid., 11.

24. Bauckham uses the Revised Standard Version wording for this declaration, in which the Hebrew expression is translated "may serve." While the New Revised Standard Version translation of the word as "may worship" is quite legitimate, it seems to be an attempt to reframe the reader's image of the nature of the relation between God and the people of Israel.

25. J. D. Levenson, "Exodus and Liberation," *Horizons in Biblical Theology* 13 (1991): 152.

26. Ibid., 9.
27. Walzer, *Exodus and Revolution*, 74.
28. Ibid., 78.
29. Ibid., 75.
30. Ibid., 80.
31. Bauckham, *God and the Crisis of Freedom,* 9.
32. Walzer, *Exodus and Revolution*, 81. Walzer's reference is Saadya Gaon, "Book of Doctrines and Beliefs," in *Three Jewish Philosophers*, eds. Hans Lewy, Isaak Heinemann, and Alexander Altmann (Philadelphia: Jewish Publication Society, 1960), 116.
33. Ibid., 80.
34. Bauckham, *God and the Crisis of Freedom*, 10.
35. Leonardo Boff, *When Theology Listens to the Poor* (San Francisco: Harper and Rowe, 1988), 60.
36. Bauckham, *God and the Crisis of Freedom*, 11.
37. Ibid., 10-11.
38. Ibid., 13.
39. Bauckham, *God and the Crisis of Freedom*, 9.
40. The reader will recall that Walzer made this point in *Exodus and Revolution*, page 81, which is influenced by the ideas of Saadya Gaon.
41. Walter Brueggemann, *Journey to the Common Good* (Louisville: Westminster John Knox Press, 2010), 23.
42. Ibid., 8-15.
43. Ibid., 16-22.
44. Ibid., 23-27, 39.
45. Ibid., 90-91.
46. Ibid., 31, 44-56.
47. Ibid., 80-81.
48. Ibid., 11.
49. Patterson, *Freedom*, 339.
50. Ibid., 340.
51. Stanley K. Stowers, *A Rereading of Romans—Justice, Jews and Gentiles* (New Haven: Yale University Press, 1994), 31.
52. Ibid., 32.
53. Here Patterson reminds us that there is not a single reference to freedom as a free gift in Galatians.
54. Patterson, *Freedom*, 340.
55. Ibid., 340-341. Patterson refers to the language employed by Paul's in discussing God's sovereignal freedom as "the power language of the imperial elite."
56. Ibid., 342.
57. Ibid., 343.
58. Ibid., 341.
59. Ibid., 343. In Romans 7:15 Paul laments, "I do not understand my own actions. For I do not do what I want, but I do the very thing that I hate."
60. Ibid., 343.
61. Stowers, *A Rereading of Romans*, 43.
62. Ibid., 46.
63. Ibid., 45. Interestingly Stowers points out that in 1 Cor. 9:25 the word used for self-mastery is related to *enkrateia* as discussed by Aristotle in his Nicomachean Ethics (7,1150b).
64. Ibid., 48.
65. Ibid.
66. Ibid., 44-45.
67. Ibid., 343. Patterson's sense that Paul envisions that final reward will involve "complete identity" with God, seems the counterpart of the view that sin as "self estrangement, is the same thing as "God estrangement."
68. Patterson, *Freedom*, 343-344.
69. Patterson, *Freedom*, 342.

70. Ibid.

71. Bauckham, *God and the Crisis of Freedom*, 11.

72. Ibid., 14.The perceived connection between the work of Jesus and the Exodus is obvious in references to him as Passover lamb in 1Corinthians 5:7 and other places.

73. Ibid.

74. Walzer, *Exodus and Revolution*, 5-7. He indicates that "the exodus figures prominently in medieval debates over the legitimacy of crusading warfare. It is important to the political argument of the monk Savonarola, who preached twenty two sermons on the Book of Exodus in the months before his fall and execution. It is cited in the pamphlets just before the German peasant's revolt. John Calvin and John Knox justified their most extreme political positions by quoting from Exodus. The text underpins the radical contractualism of the Huguenot's *Vindiciae Contra Tyrannos* and then of the Scottish Presbyterians. It is crucial to the self-understanding of the English Puritans during the 1640s and of the Americans on the 'errand into the wilderness.' It is an important source of both argument and symbolism during the American Revolution and the establishment of the US as 'God's new Israel.' In 1776 Benjamin Franklin proposed that the Great Seal of the US should show Moses with his rod lifted and the Egyptian army drowning in the sea; while Jefferson urged a more pacific design: the column of Israelites marching through the wilderness led by God's pillars of cloud and fire. The Exodus story is important . . . in the writings of Karl Marx. And, of course, the Exodus has always stood at the center of Jewish religious thought, playing a part in each of the reiterated attempts at Jewish politics. . . . Zionism has sometimes been conceived in messianic terms, which both derive from and stand in tension with Exodus thinking; but is also a call for a literal exodus—an escape from oppression and a journey to the promised land—and the biblical narrative has provided much of its imagery. Other nationalisms, too, have found hope in a promise that seems to include, whatever else it includes, the idea of political independence. The Book of Exodus came alive in the hands of Boer nationalists fighting the British, and it is alive in the hands of the black nationalists in South Africa today."

75. This is most evident in Ephesians 5:21-6:9 with regard to marriage, parenthood, and slavery as already noticed and in 1Peter 2: 13-17, with regard to political structures.

76. Bauckham, *God and the Crisis of Freedom*, 15.

77. Robert Nesta Marley, *Redemption Song*, copyright: Lyrics © EMI Music Publishing Company.

78. William Watty, *From Shore to Shore: Soundings in Caribbean Theology* (typeset by CEDAR Press, Barbados; printed in Kingston, Jamaica, 1981), 6.

79. It will be obvious to some that many aspects of the assessment of Caribbean peoples are quite applicable to other communities that carry the direct legacy of colonialism and slavery in the modern era and also to women who have been the subordinated for vastly longer, even within oppressed communities.

80. Bauckham, *God and the Crisis of Freedom*, 15.

81. Ibid., 15.

82. Some like to point to the possibility of a slave becoming a member of the slavers family.

83. Patterson, *Freedom*, 341.

84. Ibid.

85. Given his extensive and celebrated research on the matter, he, much more than many, knows well of the unbelievable brutality and dehumanization of modern slavery sanctioned by Christian scriptures in which Africans were the primary victims, and also the long-standing and ongoing oppression of various communities informed by the same source.

86. Being aware of the debate among Bible scholars regarding the authorship of books like Ephesians and Colossians, I take the position that, while Paul might not have been author of these works, his disciples who wrote them were careful to faithfully reflect his positions on the issues addressed.

87. Patterson, *Freedom*, 319.

88. Alfred North Whitehead, *Process and Reality* (corrected edition), eds. David Ray Griffin and Donald W. Sherburne (New York: The Free Press, 1978), 342.

89. Bauckham, *God and the Crisis of Freedom*, 15.

90. Ashley Smith, *Emerging from Innocence: Religion, Theology and Development* (Mandeville, Jamaica: Eureka Press, 1991), 55.

91. Ibid.

*III*

# The Journey Toward Freedom — Restructuring Theological Foundations

# Chapter Five

# Breaking Away in the Name of Freedom

This chapter signals a turning point toward a theological infrastructure to support freedom that is finite, realistically libertarian, and relational, intended to counter the master-slave, dominant-subordinate schemas in which many have operated for much too long. I recall Michael Walzer's reminder that the Hebrew noun translated "deliverance" comes from the verb "to go out," and that the words "deliverance" and "liberation" are closely related. These terms, he suggests, take their larger meanings from Israel's experience of Egyptian slavery.[1] I add that these meanings are relevant to the claiming of one's own freedom, as opposed to waiting for a time when there might be manumission through the good graces of some benevolent Other. Especially those with a history of direct coercion, and also those who live with the material, psychological, and spiritual consequences of such coercion, need theological images, concepts, and understandings that create internal and external space for meaningful decision making that expresses and fosters freedom.

I will begin the chapter by confronting approaches to biblical authority, biblical content, and theology that privilege a tyrant model of God and portray human beings as sinful and incapable of choosing rightly in regard to good and to God. We need to question sovereign-subject, master-slave schemes for God-human relations and headship-subordination schemes for human-to-human relations. We need to question the tainted language of servanthood and open up to language that promotes partnership. Even free-will theists, who claim to value human choice in God-human relations, often continue to defend crucial features of classical theism, leading them into theological inconsistencies and ethical confusions that undermine their good intentions.

I have contended that, generally speaking, classical God-concepts have been informed by images of sovereignty influenced by the character of ancient kings, Caesars, and lords. We have seen that orthodox giants such as Augustine, Luther, and Calvin have justified such God-concepts so as to place the Christian sovereign beyond the constraining features of earlier Jewish constructions. Thus, while Christians claim that the best image we have of God is Jesus the Christ, whose life was characterized by limitation, vulnerability, and caring concern that led to his death, dominant strands of Christian tradition have still hankered for the absolute sovereign lord who, at the most fundamental level of "his" being, operates outside of the temporal sphere, from which perspective (the only authentic one, according to such theologies) the meaningful facts of human life and all life are eternally settled. The claimed categorical distinction between the temporal sphere in which human beings operate and eternity renders the decisions and actions of the eternal God beyond evaluation by temporal-finite human beings, especially in view of the conviction that human beings are fallen and corrupt.

At the heart of the difficulty in evaluating character and condition of human beings is the continued use of the story of Adam and Eve as the starting point for theological anthropology. It is a sign of our psychological and theological entrapment that many are not able to embrace contemporary insights, from a range of disciplines, that enable us to move from the orthodox Christian view that all human beings carry the legacy of a fall to the idea of an evolving human species that is able to cripple and destroy as well as responsibly exercise freedom for the sake of individual growth and global flourishing.

## A REALISTIC APPROACH TO SCRIPTURE AND THEOLOGICAL REFLECTION

It may very well be that there are limits to the ways any contemporary struggle for freedom can be benefited by biblical narratives, declarations, and images. In some instances they will be quite enlightening, but in some quite inadequate, and in others they might be very inappropriate.[2] I agree with theologians who, like my retired colleague Clark Williamson, recognize that "revelation cannot be separated from interpretation. We cannot say, first there is revelation and then, later, the community interprets it. To name an event as revelatory is already to interpret it."[3] Furthermore, the interpretations that feed theological endeavors are carried out in light of formal conceptual structures and embedded notions[4] associated with a range of latent images. These elements usually reflect the desires, hopes, fears, and anxieties that we harbor within us.

Bill Watty reminds us that failure to recognize the partial and provisional nature of the doctrinal systems that emerge from this dynamic leads to unrealistic claims of universality and finality.[5] This being so, the path toward authentic freedom must resist idolizing any traditional doctrinal system, recognizing that no system is more than a limited and limiting contextual vision, however influential. It is this attitude that has enabled me to step away from elements of the theological frameworks of the church "fathers" whose ideas have been explored in this work, and has permitted critical evaluation of biblical pronouncements. The crucial need to do the same with specific concepts of God is brought home when we appreciate that, whatever might be one's evaluation of the God of Israel, the character of this God seems to be the product of the divinization of an idealized human leader; that is, the best mix of king, judge, seer, priest, and prophet who exercises extraordinary power that is cosmic in scope. However, this God is not omni-qualitied, immutable, or impassable. Thus, while "the God of Israel" is "highly exalted," limits are set on this God's domination and control. This left room for human beings, including God's slaves Israel, to operate with freedom in ways that pleased God, made God jealous, reassured God, incurred God's wrath, even made God wish human beings had not been created. In contrast, the early Christian synthesis of Hebrew and Greek ideas fashioned a God who was a troublesome mix of features from the two streams. In some ways God remained the God just described, and in other ways God became the antithesis of things temporal and finite and also the reification and absolutization of sovereignal freedom.

## CONTENDING WITH GOD AND GOD'S SERVANTS

At the heart of the hybrid conception of God that emerged from the early Christian synthesis of Hebrew and Greek ideas was the attribute of perfection, which was associated with the notions of immutability and impassibility. Together these concepts ensured that the perfect being could never be moved by anything outside of self and indeed was not capable of change of any sort. This God, being perfect, entertained only perfect things, which, in effect, excluded the thoughts and pronouncements of sinful human beings. Here theologian Joe Jones points out that, preoccupied with settling the Christological controversy that had split the church, those who met at the first ecumenical Council at Nicaea in CE 325 did not give adequate recognition to the fact that the idea of an immutable and impassible God conflicted with the doctrine of incarnation that they ratified. "At Chalcedon in 451, the church set up some further rules about the divine and human in Jesus Christ, but it did nothing to examine and cancel the syntax of divine impassibility."[6] Yet, this was a God with whom Christians sought intimacy, and to whom they perceived themselves relating through prayer. That this could and did lead to great confusion is evidenced in the venerable Saint Anselm's struggle with the question of how God can be merciful and at the same time impassible. He suggests that together these characterizations "make God merciful and not merciful." In his attempt at resolution, Anselm suggests that God is only merciful in terms of human experience, but not merciful in terms of God's being. As a requirement of his faith, Anselm cannot but claim that God does "save the sorrowful and pardon sinners." Yet, given his understanding of perfection, which involves impassibility, he also says, "You are not merciful because You do not experience any feeling of compassion for misery."[7]

Many thoughtful Christians before and after Anselm have shared his lament as they have sought to make sense of the God-concept they have been given, because in the final analysis the basic image guiding their pursuit of God-human relations seems to be somewhere in the intersection between absolute king (with Caesar as the Roman equivalent) and servile subject, master and slave. For those who might be considering that the first is a step above the second, I give a reminder of the understanding of sovereignal freedom that informed that pattern. As I indicated earlier in this work, informed by Orlando Patterson's explications, this has to do with the perceived right or privilege of one to act as she/he pleases regardless of the wishes of others, and indeed to dominate others. I also mentioned that, considered in light of its socio-political implications, this form of liberty is really authoritarianism—the right of a slaveholder or political leader, for instance, to operate without restraint. This image of God would have only been slightly modified in the medieval period by the ethos of feudalism, under which the primary image of God-human relations would probably have been lord and serf. Whereas Augustine and Pelagius conducted their struggle in light of the idea of God as sovereign/master, the Luther-Erasmus and Calvinist-Arminian struggles would have taken place in the shadow of the medieval pattern.

Therefore, the orthodox Christian explications of the relation between God and the world could be seen as reinforcing in human beings the relational dispositions that correspond to the God-images just listed. In their times, these orthodox thinkers certainly contributed to the advancement of theological considerations on God in relation to the world and human beings. Yet the basic models for God-human relations in these frameworks would have hindered them from addressing certain levels of the human struggle for freedom, because such struggle would be understood to contravene what was "properly basic" for a life of faith. As such, these models do not support consideration of important expressions of freedom, especially freedom from "God" and the church.

The result is that, while most Christians will very frequently mouth the word "freedom," we do not even want the freedom exemplified in word and deed by Jesus the Christ, as it involves risk-taking and oftentimes leads to great discomfort. We are therefore quite willing to give ourselves over to others who present themselves as carrying the burden of freedom on our behalf. These people become the determiners of guidelines for private and public life and belief. They are lauded for being insightful, brave, and adventurous, and exalted as representatives of God's truth and wisdom. The faithful then submit to them as any grateful subject, slave, or serf should. The Grand Inquisitor (in a short story by the character Ivan in Fyodor Dostoyevsky's *The Brothers Karamazov*) portrays this situation in the following way: "And everyone will be happy, all the millions of creatures, except for the hundred thousand who govern them. For only we, we who keep the mystery, only we shall be unhappy. There will be thousands of millions of happy babes, and a hundred thousand sufferers who have taken upon themselves the curse of the knowledge of good and evil."[8]

It is an interesting combination of arguments that takes us to this declaration. Together they dramatize how easily the powerful manipulate the picture of both the amazing and the awful possibilities that result from ventures in freedom, in order to maintain control. So Ivan's Inquisitor declares:

> Freedom, free reason, and science will lead them into such a maze, and confront them with such miracles and insoluble mysteries, that some of them, unruly and ferocious, will exterminate themselves; others, unruly but feeble will exterminate each other; and the remaining third, feeble and wretched, will crawl to our feet and cry unto us: "Yes, you were right, you alone possess his mystery, and we are going back to you—save us from ourselves."

The primary means of control is exposed in what soon follows: "They will become timid and will look to us and huddle close to us in fear, as chicks to a hen."[9]

The powerful know that as fear in general is one of the most crippling emotions, the fear of self is the quickest way to commit psychic suicide. This being so, Ivan's utilization of the expression "the curse of the knowledge of good and evil" serves as an important key to open the door to a uniquely Christian anxiety. Clearly his expression is linked to Genesis 3:22, where it is suggested that in attaining to "the knowledge of good and evil" the human beings had overstepped their bounds, were trespassing in the divine realm, and could then be tempted to take the ultimate step of seeking equality with the *Elohim*.

This situation is consistent with the oft-repeated position within orthodox Christianity that human beings tend towards *hubris*, and that this tendency is easily fueled by the pursuit of freedom through enlightenment. The recommendation is therefore that, as a general principle, the faithful should play it safe and not go too far. Since human beings do need the benefits from some pursuits of these kinds, a select few will venture on behalf of others, and face the possible consequences. Ivan reminds us that often-times the motive behind encouragement towards the safe (unadventurous) life is domination and control. We can then understand why, given the intellectual and cultural ethos in nineteenth- to mid-twentieth-century Germany, Jürgen Moltmann would suggest that abuse of power is the inevitable outcome of human quests such as those just described, on the assumption that they result from the exercise of freedom. From this follows the position that when liberty is understood as "free choice of the will . . . one imputes an absolute sovereignty to man and provides him with divine attributes."[10] I suggest that this claim would be correct if "free" meant "completely free," but none of those I have examined in this text who defend "free choice of the will" go that far, and the fact of human finitude runs counter to such an understanding. On the other hand, the threat of "curse," as alluded to by Ivan, ensures that many of us will never dare to imagine ourselves free enough to explore life and pursue experiences beyond certain limits determined by those who, because of their so-called risky exercise of freedom to venture into uncharted waters of experience and enlightenment, can, at least, say where the boundary line is not.

I can imagine that a probable argument of justification by those with "unique insight" might take an Irenaean-like path, beginning with the claim that God had intended Adam and Eve to grow into maturity and into the level of insight deemed appropriate by God, but they sought to take things into their own hands rather than submit to God's process. Because of God's gracious work of redemption in Jesus, the church has emerged as the context in which God-oriented maturation now takes place. Within the church God has chosen some for special insight in order that they might guide this process, ensuring that those who constitute the general population of the church do not go off-track again. From this disposition emerges a shepherd-sheep hierarchy, corresponding to the master-slave/lord-serf hierarchy, in which a few lead and the many are led—even if the shepherds are claimed to be *simul iustus et peccator*. Many non-Catholics love to point to the papacy as the ultimate expression of ecclesiastical hierarchicalism. But local pastors in a range of contemporary non-Catholic communions operate as if they are popes. Church leaders who treat members as capable of using their own minds and who encourage them to operate with responsible freedom are often viewed by more "traditional" Christians as lax and unholy. In many contexts, it is congregations in which leaders are spiritual dictators and members operate like obedient children that are growing at phenomenal rates.

Given that, as I mentioned before, historic and contemporary church hierarchies are ultimately grounded in understandings of God, continuous, critical review of the narratives and doctrines utilized in fashioning God-images will unravel the patterns on which church systems and relations are grounded. With this in mind, I return to direct discussion of the picture of God in Genesis 3 that is associated with the idea of "curse." That chapter pictures a God who is thoroughly anxious about what human beings might achieve through ventures beyond eating of the tree of the knowledge of good and evil. I suggest that in the honor-shame context undergirding the narrative world, this God is not only anxious about what might happen next but has been made to look bad (dishonored) by Adam's and Eve's acquiescence to the serpent's lure. Portrayals of God's responses in other parts of Hebrew Scriptures (e.g., Numbers 11:1-3; Deuteronomy 29:25-28) make me think that there was probably a fair degree of anger associated with the sense of dishonor.

This is certainly not incompatible with satisfaction theories that continue to be popular in many churches that are concerned not only with the restoration of God's honor but also the appeasement of God's wrath. My position on this matter is consistent with the dominant disposition in feminist theology. Feminist theology, Elizabeth Johnson asserts, "repudiates an interpretation of the death of Jesus as required by God in repayment for sin. Such a view today is virtually inseparable from an underlying image of God as an angry, bloodthirsty, violent, and sadistic father, reflecting the very worst kind of male behavior."[11] The roots of this disposition are in the doctrine of substitutionary atonement developed in the early centuries of Christian history, inspired by passages like Romans 5:17-18 and Hebrews 9:22, 28. When interlaced with the view of second-century apologist Irenaeus and others that Adam's and Eve's (mis)adventure caused them to fall into the hands of God's enemy, substitutionary atonement resulted in the complications of ransom theory and of the notion of Christus Victor. Eleventh-century Scholastic Anselm of Canterbury is usually associated with the refinement of substitutionary atonement in terms of satisfaction. The basic idea is that, while humanity (present in Adam) was liable for dishonoring God, given who God is, only one of equal status could ensure that adequate satisfaction—this to restore God's honor and/or appease God's wrath. Being categorically unique, only God was eligible to make restitution to God. This was understood to have been addressed through the death of the innocent one Jesus, considered fully God and fully human. John Calvin later emphasized that by taking on the punishment due to human beings, Jesus satisfied the demands of justice.

Given the views that are associated with the atonement theories mentioned, a number of difficulties arise. It seems to me that God's initial grasp on Adam and Eve could not have been secure. Some might claim that God's grasp was adequate enough to establish Adam and Eve as God's, and yet allow them the "space" to exercise freedom. That being the case, it seems God was not very gracious toward "his" "young" children, given that they were learning how to choose rightly when caught in the middle of strong influences. Actually, I have always struggled to understand the standard of justice which required that, because of a particular instance of disobedience under the influence of the serpent, the devil automatically gained rights over God's creatures. Somehow, God's commitment to this strange standard of justice was stronger that the passion for keeping Adam and Eve in God's province and helping them learn through their mistakes. Further, it has never made sense to me that the same God who is said to have poured out "himself" (*kenosis*) in the person of Jesus of Nazareth is that God whose requirement of satisfaction necessitated the death of Jesus. Finally, I point out another troubling option, derived from my earlier engagement of Erasmus's ideas, that maybe God was playing a game with human beings. Might it be that God deliberately limited grace on one level (the immediate address of Adam's and Eve's misadventure) so that the expression of grace might be magnified at another level (in the work of Jesus)? If this were so, the situation would not be very different from the Athenian slave-owners mentioned by Patterson who benefitted doubly from the manumission of slaves. They would have the eternal gratitude of the slave, even as the slave was hemmed in by oppressive social structures that determined their continued subjection to and dependence on the former owners in crucial areas of their lives.

## CHALLENGING SOTERIOLOGICAL FOUNDATIONS

Let us spend a little more time with the notion of "satisfaction," since it still dominates Christian soteriology.[12] I do not think that love means that an offense should be overlooked. Nevertheless, the dispensing of justice, guided by a commitment to fairness, should involve the best understanding of the circumstances surrounding the matter being adjudged, and the character of the offense itself. In the first place then, it seems totally irrational to hold that a wrong exercise of will, even by those considered the earliest progenitors, should so corrupt the will itself as a feature of the human character that the will of every other human being is debilitated, regardless of the status of the one offended by the initial action. Further, it is time that we stop assessing the effect of Adam's (and Eve's) sin by using an outmoded biology in which a lapse in the judgment of a parent corrupts interminably the DNA of all progeny, leaving the very seat of judgment invariably oriented to evil choices. While some Christians have moved away from this position, I am confident in asserting that it is still presupposed by the doctrine of sin and salvation taught and preached in a wide variety of settings in the country in which I reside (USA) and many other contexts around the globe.

I am not shifted from my disposition toward the dominant Christian doctrine of sin by discussions like that of Eastern Orthodox theologian Vladimir Lossky, who claims that human nature itself (not just the relation between particular faculties) was corrupted by Adam's sin. This claim is grounded in the position that "the first man contained in himself the whole of human nature." Indeed, "when first created, the first human had no particular name, but was universal man."[13] Thus, even though because of sin "these first two human beings became two natures; two individuals, with exterior relationships between them,"[14] "God by His providence and power, included all mankind in this first creation."[15] Here Lossky is intent on establishing the case that, with all human beings participating in the nature which characterized this first human being, the separate actions of Adam and Eve reflected the corruption of one nature and determined the character of all who have that nature.

However, if one follows Lossky's reading, one would need to conclude that human nature was established before the emergence of Eve as a particular person and before the acts of disobedience. This means that God's pronouncement in Genesis 1:31 that the created order, with the newly introduced human factor made in God's own image, is now not just "good" but "very good" should be that which guides our characterization of what it means to be human *per se*. This would influence my engagement of Lossky's claim that "the nature is the content of the person, the person the existence of the nature."[16] This being the case, what disobedience could change a nature created in the image of God and whose mere existence determined the characterization of all things as "very good"? Rather, Williamson has it right when he indicates that "the deeper insight of the scriptures is that all human beings are loved by God, that God calls the creation of human beings 'good,' that we are given and called to serve the well-being of each other."[17] I recall Richard Bauckham's suggestion that without freedom Adam and Eve would have been innocent, but only by freely choosing to obey God could they become good.[18] This is consistent with my view that there must be a distinction between ontological goodness and moral goodness—the former being *a given* by virtue of human beings being God's creation, and the latter a possibility associated with choice-making.

In considering moral goodness, it should be recognized that morality constitutes more than a system of particular behaviors, judgments, or observations that people ought to follow. Simple adherence to a code of conduct, informed by a system of beliefs, even well-established religious beliefs, does not make one moral. Instead, it is often an expression of moral irresponsibility in which we expend very little effort struggling with the decisions that we make, the prejudices that we harbor, or the thrust of our reactive thoughts. Morality emerges and moral agency is developed through considerative wrestling with our decisions in light of actionable choices, discernable motivations and ends, and ideals we hold dear. This process involves appreciation for the fact that as finite human beings we operate within a complex network of decision makers and other vulnerable entities in a world that, among other features, is characterized by much ambiguity. It is with these convictions that

I proceed to further explication of the freedom required for choice-making that has integrity, by providing further reflection on the Genesis narrative.

My exploration of the Genesis narrative suggests to me that there needs to be a two-tiered approach to our understanding of the relation between Adam, Eve, and their progeny. Accepting for the moment the notion that the first human beings were brought into existence by God's direct and exceptional activity, it is clear that God's intention is for their further multiplication to take place not by exact replication (as in the production of machines) but a natural (not supernatural) process involving interaction between Adam and Eve or the combination of reproductive elements from them both.[19] Thus even the biblical stories suggest that all human beings after the first-created pair would be products of natural biological reproduction rather than supernatural intervention. This approach, I argue, ought to influence the evaluation of the human capacities to discern God's will, judge things intuited and perceived, and make decisions.

One might then think of Adam and Eve as parents of humanity (in the theological sense) in the same way that we think of the Australopithecans as parents of *Homo sapiens* (in the anthropological sense). The former are the necessary precursors to the latter, and the latter has many features in common with the former, but there are crucial differences that place the latter in a different genus. Adam, having been created by direct supernatural means, should not be treated as the paradigmatic human, since all subsequent generations of human beings have, unlike Adam, been conceived in an interconnected world where God is only one of many determinants of character. It is then the generation of offspring from the cohabitation of Adam and Eve (represented in Gen. 4:1-2) that symbolizes the human beings who actually inhabit the earth now. It is to them, and the typical dynamics associated with their emergence, that we should look as we attempt to characterize human nature as such.

In this complex dynamic, pre-natal and post-natal influences indelibly mark individual personalities and the ethos of families-tribes-ethnicities-cultures. The human connection to a God is not unambiguously clear. Human life is now marked, theologically, by a persistent quest to discern God's will and even to identify what we mean by "God."[20]

The nature of this struggle becomes clearer when we factor in the generally accepted view that human beings are animals with highly developed subjectivity and cognitive capacity. This capacity enables them to be conscious of and evaluate their animal nature, develop ways to live that are not restricted to the most basal of their animal instincts, and even imagine and reach after states of being that are consistent with what is considered ultimate. Focusing on the theological implications that follow from this position, I suggest that, while I do not disagree with Calvin that God placed in human beings "by natural instinct, an awareness of divinity,"[21] and while it is not inconceivable that God constantly "replenishes" this sense,[22] the emergence of self-expressions unacceptable to orthodox piety does not prove that human beings are "hardened in insolent and habitual sinning."[23] And that fact that some do not glorify the personal God with whom Christians claim to have relationship through Jesus the Christ does not necessarily mean that they suffer from "oblivion" in the negative senses of "insolence" and "brute contempt" said to result from humanity having taken leave of its senses.[24]

Instead, our diverse responses might simply be a consequence of the struggle we are born into by virtue of being the offspring of man and woman, as animals with a high level of subjectivity, cognitivity, imagination, and with a connection to God that is not unambiguously clear. This position is closer to what Matthew Myer Boulton identifies as the amoral sense of oblivion, which has to do with human ignorance of God's presence and activity around us and within us. This feature is at root reflective of both human finitude and divine infinitude, and points to an important growing edge for believer and non-believer alike. At the same time, it might well be that some, in the pursuit of wholesome humanity, will portray the effects of God's presence without recognizing that presence. As I embrace it, the story of disobedience is a way to make sense of the tragic element of choice-making that comes with living as human beings in the world and, in the process, learning what being human means in relation to what "God" means. The process toward moral goodness that depends, in part, on effective choice-making is certainly linked to our growth in psychological maturity. And given that this maturity results from the way we deal with our misfortunes and mistakes, among other things, it is highly improbable that it can be achieved without, at some point, going against God's ideals for us.

This being so, I suggest that, while we should not refuse to consider the continuing implications of our earliest precursors' life-choices, we also should not automatically construe the history of human choice-making with its ambiguities, mistakes, and even brutal outcomes, as a history of failure that reflects degradation. Instead, this history ought to be viewed as a process of exploration, struggle, and hopeful yearning that in cooperation with God and others human beings should lead to better choice-making. Human struggles in the midst of ambiguity do often result in quite diabolical outcomes that we should mourn and seek to correct, but human choices have also produced magnificent expressions of creativity and transcendence that suggest a capacity to operate above our fears and our instinct for self-protection, and to be more consistently guided by what is most life-enhancing.[25]

Clearly these stereological and anthropological considerations have significance for our understanding of the type of God with which Christians are related and the character and significance of human freedom in the structure of this relating. The difficulties that have been identified feed the perceived need for new conceptions of God that correspond with freedom that is finite, realistically libertarian, and relational. However, before launching into that enterprise it seems wise to face two distinguished figures within Christian tradition who, in the eras and settings in which they operated, championed the cause of human freedom with their own brand of critical engagement with traditional conceptions of God. There is Scottish-American Restorationist Alexander Campbell, who is the more scholastic of the two persons considered founders of the denomination called the Christian Church (Disciples of Christ), which, along with other off-shoots, grew out of the Second Great Awakening in the United States.[26] There is Jacob Arminius who, in the late sixteenth century, worked assiduously to modify the Calvinist doctrine of predestination so that it might accommodate a meaningful understanding of human freedom. Given that his ideas became influential in the broad Wesleyan tradition and a range of more explicitly evangelical communities, Arminius's contemporary influence is even more pervasive than Campbell's. In recent times Arminius's thought has figured in the theological movement called Open Theism, ideas from which I engage in this project. His utilization of the idea of middle knowledge in his discussion of God's knowledge also establishes an alliance with contemporary Christian apologists who utilize "possible worlds" thinking in their philosophical and theological pursuits.

## WRESTLING WITH FAMOUS FREE-WILL THEISTS: ALEXANDER CAMPBELL AND JACOB ARMINIUS

### Alexander Campbell

In some of his declarations Alexander Campbell nudges Christian orthodoxy closer to the dynamics of freedom I promote. Although his soteriological formulations include ideas like "infection" and "inheritance" he steps away somewhat from the kind of biology that undergirds Augustine's anthropology. In *The Christian System* he states that it is not only physical features that children inherit from parents. "The moral constitution of man is as clearly transmissible as any physical taint, if there be any truth in history, biography, or human observation." This view is consistent with his earlier indication to a reader in *The Christian Baptist* that it is the nature of moral evil to replicate itself. Campbell's leaning towards the traditional positions on human sinfulness seems evident in the declaration: "Your nature, gentle reader, not your person, was in Adam when he put forth his hand to break the precept of Jehovah." At the same time, it also suggests that he is not totally in accord with the position that we are fully identified with Adam—this evidenced by his distinction between "nature" and "person." Therefore, in discussing the character and consequence of Adam's sin he suggests to his reader that while "our nature sinned in Adam" "you did not individually sin." Later he suggests that while, as God warned Adam, all human beings are now born mortal and with "hereditary imbecility to do good," "all are not equally depraved."[27]

Campbell seems to be lifting up the significance of individuality in a way Lossky would find quite difficult, even unacceptable. Lossky operates with the fundamental presupposition that the divine nature in whose likeness human beings were created is Trinity. Thus, he is insistent that, while individuals (as members of the whole community of human beings) express the one human nature, to become fixated on human nature as it has been "divided, split up, broken into many individuals" is to use as our criterion the nature which resulted from the fall and "has lost its likeness to the divine nature."[28] My response to Lossky accords with what I interpret to be Campbell's disposition that seems to be based on observation of human behavior, biblical testimony, and a general understanding of what is entailed by any claim that actual people are moral and as such are subject to judgment for their behavior. Campbell's position is that "although without the knowledge of God and his revealed will—without the interposition of a mediator and without faith in him—'it is impossible to please God,' still there are those who, while destitute of this knowledge and belief, are more noble and more virtuous than others."[29] He alludes to a natural capacity human beings have for clear understanding and righteous willing when he follows up with an example from the writer of Luke-Acts: "The Jews in Berea were more noble than those in Thessalonica, in that they received the word with readiness of mind, and searched the Scriptures daily whether these things were so (Acts 17:11)."[30]

Interestingly, in *The Christian Baptist* Campbell sets his moral argument within a broader assessment of dynamics in the supernatural realm prior to the existence of Adam and Eve. He indicates that God made rational beings of different orders; that is, God made beings capable of obeying and disobeying God's will. Without this capacity, he says, "they would be neither virtuous nor vicious, happy nor miserable." These beings, he asserts, were necessarily created under law that was broken through disobedience by one or more of them—this act of disobedience being the first moral evil.[31] As it pertains to human beings, Campbell claims that "it is essential to moral good that the agent acts freely according to the last dictate or the best dictate, of his understanding." He, in effect, defends contra-causal freedom when he continues to say that "if a rational being was created incapable of disobeying, he must, on that very account, be incapable of obeying. He then acts like a mill wheel, in the motions of which there is no choice; no virtue, no vice, no moral good, no moral evil."[32] Returning to *The Christian System* we find Campbell, some years after the engagements of *The Christian Baptist* , working his way towards his most strident anti-Calvinist position with declarations such as "man, with all his hereditary imbecility, is not under an invincible necessity to sin. Greatly prone to evil, easily seduced into transgression, he may or may not yield to passion and seduction." Campbell also declares: "Because of the interposition of the second Adam, none are punished with everlasting destruction from the presence of the Lord but those who actually and voluntarily sin against a dispensation of mercy under which they are placed . . ." Indeed, the significance of open choice is reinforced with the quotation from John 3:19: "For this is the condemnation of the world, that light has come into the world, and men choose darkness rather than the light, because their deeds are evil."[33]

Unfortunately, while nudging Christian orthodoxy in a freedom-oriented direction, Campbell's theology was still firmly moored to a conception of God's sovereignty that hindered him from heading resolutely in the direction I am going. Indeed, his portrayal of sovereignty was tantamount to a celebration of despotism. In *The Christian Baptist*, Campbell responds to a "skeptic" who suggests that, given that God is first cause and "responsible for all things, especially evil," God should prevent evil. Campbell argues that it is inappropriate to suggest that God is "responsible." To do so would be "to lose sight of the essential attribute of deity. A supreme can neither be responsible nor accountable; for responsibility and accountability imply dependence. To whom can a Supreme be responsible? An independent dependent being is no greater contradiction than a responsible Supreme." Campbell moves to the end of this paragraph, giving details of features of the world created by God and for which God is answerable to no one: "So much sea, so much cold, so much darkness, so many reptiles, so many monsters in the ocean, so many conflicting and jarring elements in this material system . . ."[34]

Campbell continues on this dangerous path when he declares: "If [God is responsible] to his creatures, then he is like them; if not to them, to none."[35] This claim, especially when considered in light of those made before, makes it clear that God is above any framework of assessment by which human beings can make any determination of what is good or evil, just or unjust. Further, if God cannot be identified with any known or knowable framework of ethical assessment, in terms of which good and evil are evaluated, we will not be able to say that what we consider good and evil have anything necessarily to do with God; neither one (good or evil) can properly be applied when considering our relationship with God. We will then be pushed to a number of unappealing consequences. The first is that when used by Christians the terms good and evil lose significance altogether. The second is that we abandon attempts to establish that God is the foundation for moral judgments, and decide that terms like good and evil and related terms like justice or injustice will be useful in ongoing evaluation of human behavior only as grounded in an ethical framework which is throughgoingly humanistic. The third option allows for the continued use of these terms as part of the vocabulary of theological ethics. However, what they mean at different times will be determined by those who have the power, authority, and influence to establish actions-attitudes-situations to be good or evil, just or unjust and attributable to God or not. These determinations would be seen as acceptable because the powerful say so, irrespective of how heinous and inhuman a situation might appear.

With the third option in mind I go to the Bible, in particular the Deuteronomist's fascinating depiction of the brutality inflicted by Israel on the people of the "promised" land. A striking example is Joshua 11, which seems to be a summary description of the elimination of the Northern kings. Here we have tales of plunder, and the indication that Israel's army "destroyed them, and they did not leave any who breathed (v14b)." We learn that in situations where there was resistance, "it was the Lord's doing to harden their hearts so that they would come against Israel in battle, in order that they might be utterly destroyed, and might receive no mercy, but be exterminated" (v. 20). There is 1 Samuel 15:3-5 where Israel is commanded to attack the Amalekites and totally destroy everything that belongs to them. We hear: "Do not spare them, but kill both man and woman, child and infant, ox and sheep, camel and donkey (v.3)." This echoes what, for me, is the most comprehensive statement of this approach in Deuteronomy 20: 16-18a: "But as for the towns of these peoples that the Lord your God is giving you as an inheritance, you must not let anything that breathes remain alive. You shall annihilate them—the Hittites and the Amorites, the Canaanites and the Perizzites, the Hivites and the Jebusites—just as the Lord your God has commanded." The brutal character of the Deuteronomist's God is also on display in 1 Samuel 15:17ff as it depicts a scenario in which Saul, the leader of God's special people, is chastised for not completely destroying everything he encountered. Some will remind me that Deuteronomy 20:18b justifies comprehensive slaughter as necessary to protect Israel from temptation by the local religions, and 1 Samuel 15:2 rationalizes it as "pay-back" for a previous attack on Israel. My quick response is that in our time, informed by various humanistic conventions, we have a classification for actions like these, whatever is the reason for which they are carried out and in whichever name they are pursued; it is genocide.

In Joshua 11 the savaging of the Northern peoples is justified by the explanation that "Joshua took the entire land, according to all that the Lord had spoken to Moses; and Joshua gave it for an inheritance to Israel according to their tribal allotments (v.23)." Deuteronomy 20:16a similarly explains that the Israelites are to take possession of the "towns of the peoples that the Lord your God is giving you as an inheritance." Similar rationales were used by European Christians who in the so-called age of discovery invaded and colonized many lands and peoples in what is now called the Global South, subjugating and decimating local populations, exploiting resources, and instituting the heinous transatlantic slavery trade.

There are no passages in the New Testament that are comparable in their level of violence to those just identified, yet one is left in no doubt regarding what some early Christians thought about those who did not embrace the way they had found to freedom and eternal life. Many have reflected on the accommodating tone of Paul's speech on Mars Hill portrayed in Acts 18. This is so, even as he works his way to verses 30-31 where he makes it clear that since God and he had certainty about who Jesus is, the non-recognition or rejection of this by others would result in harsh judgment. The compellingness of the logic of Jesus as *the* revelation of God seems to be presupposed in Paul's warning that the mere fact of Jesus' existence, and/or the fact of having heard about Jesus, means that all human beings are now without excuse if they do not repent; that is, if they do not commit themselves to the Christian way. In Jude 1:5, the author, using the example of Israel, warns believers against moving to another opinion regarding God and Jesus; that is, becoming unbelievers. The suggestion seems to be that as the consequence was destruction for those in Israel, so it will be for those in the Christian community who choose another path.

## Jacob Arminius

The God Campbell understands to be beyond ethical evaluation is also for many the eternal One who, in one infinite intuition, sees all things in all spheres and times (past, present, and future) and knows completely and infallibly all things necessary and contingent. Quite famous within Reformed circles is Jacob Arminius who, in resisting the Calvinist doctrine of predestination, argued that the eternal God is able to foreknow all things and yet not impinge on human freedom. Given the range of discussions he had on this matter, one cannot avoid doing Arminius some disservice in treating his diverse writings in a few pages. However, by addressing some key points of his thought I will identify elements of classical theism that continue to quietly influence orthodox Christian God-talk and undermine well-thinking attempts to establish the importance of free-will for the integrity of human beings.

Not surprisingly Arminius has a strong interest in matters related to human salvation—this associated with his position regarding the way God created human beings to be. Convinced that, as created by God, the human will is "the work of the highest goodness and wisdom in the universe,"[36] he resists the idea that God's providence should operate in a way that is contrary to it. If there is any predestination, he suggests, it is "the decree of the good pleasure of God in Christ, by which he determined, within himself from all eternity, to justify believers, to adopt them, and to endow them with eternal life."[37] What God knows eternally are those who would, in time, "through his prevenient grace, believe, and, through his subsequent grace would persevere."[38] Of course, God also knows those who would do otherwise. This is the kind of knowledge presumed in Arminius's claim that "no one is chosen by God to adoption and the communication of the gift of righteousness, unless he is considered by Him as a believer."[39] And the graciousness of God's decree regarding the believer is fuelled by "the love with which God loves men absolutely to salvation, and according to which he absolutely intends to bestow on them eternal life." At the same time, the reminder is given that "this love . . . has no existence except in Jesus Christ, the Son of his love."[40]

For many, Arminius's position sounds quite wonderful. Indeed, in important ways it represents significant progress from the Calvinist and Lutheran positions on freedom of the will. The first step toward making rational sense of it is by way of his discussion of God's knowledge in the context of his public disputation on the nature of God. [41]

In analyzing Arminius's declarations it should be appreciated that he embraces the "schoolmen's" distinction between three types of knowledge that God possesses. The first type of knowledge identified is natural or necessary knowledge by which God understands Godself and all things possible. The second is free knowledge by which God knows all other beings, that is, what actually exists. The third type, middle knowledge, is that by which God knows that "if this thing happens, that will take place." The first precedes every free act of God's will; the second follows the free act of God's will; the last precedes the free act of God's will but hypothetically. [42]

It is middle knowledge, understood to be pre-volitional, hypothetical, and not associated with any actual world, creature, or situation that seems to do best at allowing for the knowledge God is said to have about believers in general and yet protect the libertarian freedom of the individual believer. If taken to pertain to general classes and scenarios, middle knowledge would translate to the proposition: If such and such a class of creatures, in such and such world (e.g., one in which persons have libertarian freedom), under such and such conditions of life, makes such and such choices, then such and such will result. That which God knows about these scenarios is classified as counterfactuals of freedom. Where the salvation of human beings is concerned, this should result in the simple conditional: If human beings exercise faith in Christ then they will belong to the class of persons to receive adoption, justification, and eternal life. In other words, God from eternity established certain conditions such that those who embrace God's gracious enablement (prevenient grace) toward faith in Christ, will, through the work of the Holy Spirit, be recipients of the status of believer that God eternally established for those who do this.

However, having read a range of Arminius's pronouncements, I lean to the position that he had individuals in mind when he claimed that "no one is chosen by God to adoption and the communication of the gift of righteousness, unless he is considered by Him as a believer."[43] This being so, middle knowledge (as he employed it) appears to have a family resemblance to conventional understandings of foreknowledge. The recognition that these individuals to which Arminius refers can only legitimately choose God through Jesus Christ encourages the question: What about the majority of the world's population who by virtue of birth and socialization has in faith chosen relationship with God through other means? Surely, this detail should matter to God's evaluation of contingencies. The scenario becomes more distressing with the recognition that God's election necessarily includes reprobation.[44]

William Lain Craig, informed by his reading of Luis Molina, who he identifies as the chief architect of the theory of middle knowledge, claims that the issue is not whether "the notion of hell [the destination of the reprobate] is incompatible with a just and loving God" or "the inconsistency of a loving and just God's condemning persons who are either un- , ill-, or misinformed concerning Christ and who therefore lack the opportunity to receive Him."[45] Instead, it is simply that an eternal God knows "what any free creature *would* do in any set of circumstances. This is not because the circumstances causally determine the creature's choice, but simply because this is how the creature would freely choose."[46] Thus, as John Milton claimed in regard to Adam's fall, reprobation is certain, but not necessary, since it proceeds from their own free will.[47] Craig faces the questions: "Why did God create this world when He knew that so many persons would not receive Christ and would therefore be lost?" Even more radical is the question: "Why did God not create a world in which everyone freely receives Christ and so is saved?"[48]

Employing possible worlds thinking, Craig answers these questions with the suggestion that, while "by natural knowledge God knows what is the entire range of logically possible worlds," by means of middle knowledge God "knows, in effect, what is the proper subset of those worlds which it is feasible for God to actualize." In God's sovereignal freedom God decides "to actualize one of those worlds known to Him through His middle knowledge." Craig suggests that God's decision "is the result of a complete and unlimited deliberation by means of which God considers and weighs every possible circumstance and its ramifications and decides to settle on the particular world He desires."[49] Kenny adds to our understanding as he represents the theory of middle knowledge to mean that by knowing "what any possible creature would freely do in any possible circumstances . . . and by knowing which creatures he will create and which circumstances he will bring about, he [God] knows what actual creatures will in fact do."[50] In this framework it is not only that God knows to be reprobate persons that would freely reject God in every possible world God could have actualized in which the person existed. God also knows which persons will freely reject God in this actual world. This being the case, it seems not to matter whether or not those God knows as reprobate are exposed to the "gospel" in this actual world and given adequate opportunity to make a choice for Jesus the Christ (the only route to God). They would still choose against him.

With high regard for Arminius and other free-will theists who, over the years, have exercised great effort in refining the theory of middle knowledge, I continue my expressions of concern. It is difficult to imagine what elements of "a complete and unlimited deliberation" by God would lead to the conclusion that it was only feasible to actualize a world in which there is *one* "true" path to God, and yet in the feasible world there are a number of apparently credible paths. Further, the moral plausibility of this scenario is suspect when it is considered that all persons in the actual world have no choice about the religious situations into which they are born—a fact that has significant influence on understandings of God and the kind of relationships developed with God. This being so, it seems reasonable to assert that, even if God in deciding to create this world saw those who would not choose Jesus the Christ, it should not be inevitable that they are culpable and reprobate.

Here the reader should take note that the decision for Christ that Arminius (and Craig) think is fundamental for salvation is linked directly to the doctrine of sin and the soteriology I have already critiqued and reframed. I now suggest that even those who disagree with my stance on these doctrines should have some appreciation for the view that the creator of a world with only one acceptable route to salvation should, at the very least, be in mourning that in this best possible world a vital need of many (salvation) cannot be met because the course of their lives has been conditioned by religious frameworks into which they were born. Instead, what we hear from Arminius is that reprobation "is the decree of God's anger or of his severe will, by which, from all eternity, he determined to condemn to eternal death, all unbelievers and impertinent people, for the declaration of his power and his anger." We hear that these people will also be condemned for other sins they might have avoided in Christ, but clearly unbelief and impertinence are fundamental reasons.[51]

With the words "impertinence," "anger," and "declaration of his power" we are again face-to-face with a God image that is much like the stereotypical king, Caesar, and feudal lord identified previously, who is quite conscious of his status in relation to his subjects, and, therefore, is very touchy about the way the latter ought to act in relation to his wishes. This attitude to status and power seems to condition God's expressions of love and grace. Arminius does declare that God's predestination is purely gracious, and that it is connected to "the love with which God loves men absolutely to salvation, and according to which he absolutely intends to bestow on them eternal life."[52] And pointing to Molina's distinction between God's absolute and conditional intentions for creatures Craig does claim that, despite "God's absolute intention that no creature should sin and that all should reach beatitude," it is not "within the scope of God's power to control what free creatures would do if placed in any set of circumstances."[53] However, Craig also asserts that "should God then choose to actualize precisely those circumstances, He has no choice but to allow the creature to sin." Indeed, it is possible "that in order to achieve a multitude of saints, God had to accept an even greater multitude of sinners."[54]

Bearing these considerations in mind, it seems difficult to avoid the position that it is God who, from the totality of possible worlds, chose to actualize one possible world, the feasibility of which was linked to a scenario in which the salvation of some implies the damnation of others. This being so, might it be that those who seem, from one perspective, to be reprobate are, from another perspective, casualties of God's desire?

At this point it might be suggested that Arminius's most sophisticated God-talk does not reveal an entity that looks anything like the human figures to which I have likened his God-concept. It is the case, however, that, like his Scholastic mentors, his abstract analysis is designed to support a foundational belief in a personal God, and this is why he could characterize God's attitude in the way just depicted. Among the many places he addresses God as a particular personal being is in his discussion of "the Object of Theology." There he claims that "it is not sufficient to know that there is some kind of nature, simple, infinite, wise, good . . . omnipotent, happy in itself, the Maker and Governor of all things." He suggests that "to this general kind of knowledge there ought to be added, a sure and settled conception, fixed on that Deity, and strictly bound to the single object of religious worship."[55]

When, in this framework, Arminius discusses the human condition in relation to God's character, it is quite antithetical to the anthropological scenario I proposed earlier that is characterized by a process of self-discovery and development (humanization), involving experimentation, choices that are good and bad, with diabolic and majestic outcomes, in the midst of ambiguity. Instead of a relationship that privileges the evolution of the human being through our capacity for partial self-creation and a God that works creatively with the ongoing dynamic, Arminius portrays the most primal relation between God and humanity (before the fall) as one in which the human was legally required (legal righteousness) to give the sovereign his due. What was due is consistent with what we know of the stereotypical sovereign of antiquity, that is, conformity and adoration (worship). With God being the eternal sovereign and creator, "preserving and governing providence" along with "eternal life" was the repayment for obedience.[56] In this legal framework, we have, on one hand, a situation in which, by disobedience to the law (what I call experimentation), the human renders herself a child of wrath.[57] On the other hand, "God, the punisher and most righteous avenger of sinners,"[58] is seen as either unwilling or unable (by the demands of the law) to repair the situation, except through a mediator. That Jesus Christ was appointed as mediator and reconciler is understood by Arminius to be an expression of the justice and mercy derived from the primitive goodness of God. And so, "every saving communication which God has with us, or which we have with God, is performed by means of the intervention of Christ."[59]

Arminius does address my query about the radical disequilibrium between what is said to be God's desire for human salvation and the opportunities all human beings have to make a legitimate choice for relationship with God through Christ, the only way to God. As he represents the concern, Arminius speaks of the "particular and restricted" means agreeing "neither with the amplitude of God's mercy, nor with the conditions of his justice, since many thousands of men depart out of this life, before even the sound of the gospel of Christ has reached their ears."[60] In this answer Arminius shows his kinship with many orthodox Christians who, in their commitment to defend the status and rights or the eternal sovereign, reveal their lack of concern for humanity as a whole, even though we are claimed to be created in the image of God. Sounding very much like Alexander Campbell, Arminius asserts that "the reasons and terms of Divine Justice and Mercy are not to be determined by the limited and shallow measure of our [human] capacities or feelings; but must leave with God the administration and just deference of these his own attributes." He then resorts to passages from the Scriptures to show that the final justification for the limited means of salvation is God's sovereign decree and the Father's covenant promise to Christ.[61]

Once again we encounter an understanding of power that is in the mode of domination and control that, in effect, endorses the attitude that "might makes right." Despite what might appear to many well-thinking humanitarians as both reasonable and gracious, the opposite approach is still claimed as justified by Christian orthodoxy, on the basis that it is the will and decision of the divine and sovereignly free monarch. If the more sensitive souls among humanity should protest this understanding of power their judgment is quickly maligned, supported by the claim that a naive concern that all be saved reflects the distortion of thought and arrogance that are the result of human fallenness. Indeed, it represents not only a failure to appreciate divine justice but a lack of respect for the sovereign freedom of God. Like Arminius (and Craig), the Scriptures are usually called on for support in a way that suggests that the Bible contains self-evident truths rather than being, at least, in part, the outcome of existential wrestling by finite human beings in the midst of the ambiguities of life.

What then, do we make of Arminius's more abstract analysis by which he seeks to establish what is most fundamental to God's character as the ultimate, in the process of which he provides rational grounding for the claim that the promotion of God's exhaustive knowledge is compossible with a vigorous defense of human freedom? In his embrace of Scholastic wisdom on these matters, Arminius opens up to strong influence from the Hellenistic search for the first principles that ground the contingent character of the world with its causal processes.[62] This being so, he embraces the idea of a simple uncaused and necessary ultimate "void of all composition, and of component parts." As simple, the ultimate "neither consists of material, integral and quantitative parts, of matter and form, of kind and difference, of subject and accident, nor of form and the thing formed, (for it is to itself a form, existing by itself and its own individuality)." Indeed, the ultimate is "his own Essence and his own Being, and is the same as that which is, and that by which it is."[63] With these descriptions in mind, including the reminder that the last is a way of saying that the ultimate's essence is its existence, some questions need to be asked. While Arminius uses personalist language to refer to the ultimate, in what way is this ultimate equivalent to the relational God of Christian piety? In what way is this a God who desires relationship with human beings, hears and responds to prayers? Can this even be the One Arminius represents as offended by those who choose not to enter into relationship? And most important at this point, in what way is this the actual being that Arminius claims foreknows infallibly what human beings will decide by their own free-will?

In attempting to determine what Arminius's claims about God's fundamental character might mean, it seems wise to start with his view on how we come to be able to say anything about God. While immediate (face to face) knowledge is reserved for the blessed in heaven, we on earth arrive at knowledge mediated by images and signs, with the two modes being affirmation and negation. In the first, simple perfections in the creature, understood to be productions of God, are attributed analogically to God, and "understood [to be] infinitely more perfect in God." In the second, "relative perfections and all the imperfections which appertain to creatures, as have been produced out of nothing, are removed from God."[64] Since it is only by analogy that features like knowledge and foreknowledge can be attributed to God, it seems reasonable to ask: what makes this a meaningful attribution? I suggest that, whatever else is involved, the attribution needs to be made with a mode of speech that is neither univocal nor equivocal. This means, on one hand, that we should not speak about God in a way that suggests that God and human beings are categorically the same. On the other hand, God and human beings cannot be portrayed as so radically different (in being, capacity, and action) that words like "knowledge" that have developed a particular range of meaning when associated with human experience lose their capacity to communicate meaningfully when used in regard to God. This is also true if one wishes to argue that a personal God that is capable of intimate involvement in human affairs with desires and feelings is also the simple ground of existence.

With these considerations in mind, I give the reminder that we only have a sense of what it means to be personal through observation of human persons. I assert, therefore, that when we claim the ultimate to be thoroughly simple, as Arminius has done, it is not possible to establish sufficient connection between the being and life of human beings and the ultimate to determine what constitutes a justifiable claim that the ultimate knows all things necessary, actual, and contingent by its own essence through one infinite intuition. The situation should become even more challenging for those who identify with Arminius's more personalist language when we hear from him that "from Simplicity and Infinity" which are the preeminent modes of "the Divine Essence;" that is, that by which God exists, "arise Infinity with regard to time, which is called 'Eternity;' and with regard to place, which is called 'Immensity;' Impassability, Immutability, and Incorruptibility." Further, he declares that "as simple being God is never in [*potentia*] capability, but is always in act."[65] In other words, the ultimate ("God") with existence identical with essence is incapable of change and cannot be influenced by anything that occurs outside of itself.

Arminius exerts much effort in a variety of contexts to explain the elements of God's knowledge, and in his discussion with Francis Junius delineates the kinds of knowledge in a way that is generally consistent with his categories of natural, free, and middle knowledge. He claims that "the knowledge of God is called eternal, but not equally so in reference to all objects of knowledge." He explains that the knowledge by which God knows Godself and in-self all possible things is absolutely eternal. However, that by which God "knows beings which will exist, is eternal indeed as to duration, but, in nature, subsequent to some act of the divine will concerning them, and, in some cases, even subsequent to some foreseen act of the human will." He proceeds to lay out a simple schema depicting "the order of the God's knowledge, in reference to its various objects." (1) God knows what God of self is able to do; (2) God knows all things possible, that is, what can be done by those beings which God can make; (3) God knows all things that shall exist by the act of creation; (4) God knows all things that will exist by the act of creatures and especially of rational creatures, even if these things result from the actions of God's creatures and especially of rational creatures; (5) God knows what God will do through the actions of creatures and especially those that are rational, or at least receiving occasion from them.[66]

These are interesting formulations that in theory support the idea of exhaustive, infallible knowledge of things necessary, actual, and contingent. However, the challenge still persists to determine how these features of knowledge can be properly characteristic of a simple ultimate, the essence of which is its existence. Clark Williamson is of the view that immutability/ impassibility is an important emphasis in articulating God's faithfulness and constancy: that God is (God's existence) and who God is (God's character) are necessary. "If God were in all respects mutable, God might cease to be or cease to be God. But to assert that God is in all respects immutable/impassible is to exempt God from involvement in time, history, and relationships."[67] This claim only highlights the fact that if God is simple being, God's essence is God's existence. Therefore, it would not be justified to apply Williamson's distinction to God, that is, it would not be legitimate to say that in some respects God is involved in time and is affected by external relations and in some ways not.

The complex of impressive attributions that follow from simplicity and infinity do enable the claim that God, as conceived by Arminius through philosophical analysis, is present to all times and places simultaneously. One could even appropriate Vladimir Lossky's distinction between "the essence of God . . . which is inaccessible, unknowable and incommunicable; and the energies or divine operations . . . in which He goes forth from Himself, manifests, communicates, and gives Himself."[68] However, it would still not be justified to say a simple God is intentionally involved in temporal processes. Therefore, by my calculations this means that exactly that which is used to support the idea of God's presence to all time simultaneously, excludes God from the kind of intimate involvement in the actual details of life that orthodox Christians usually have in mind when they speak of a God who is both transcendent and immanent.

It is quite telling that, while expressing sympathy with the philosopher Boethius' definition of eternity, Arminius feels compelled to modify it so that it shifts from "an interminable, entire and at the same time, a perfect possession of life" to "an interminable, entire and at the same time, a perfect possession of Essence." In explaining this, Arminius suggests that essence is "the first moving cause of the Divine Nature, before Life; and because Eternity does not belong to Essence through Life, but to Life through Essence."[69] It makes sense that he would adopt this position since, as he put it elsewhere, "the life of God is his essence itself, and his very being; because the Divine Essence is in every respect simple, as well as infinite, and therefore, eternal and immutable."[70] I add, from his previous explications: impassible, and fully actual. But what does this have to do with life as human beings live it? William Placher provides some assistance toward an answer through his exploration of Boethius' definition, which he translates as "a perfect possession all at once of limitless life." Claiming to take Boethius' actual words seriously, Placher indicates that "life seems to be an obviously temporal category, for living things have properties that can exist only temporally." Therefore the possession of life cannot be timeless. "Life must at least involve some incidents in time and if, like Boethius, we suppose the life in question to be intelligent, then it must involve also awareness of the passage of time."[71]

Placher is very correct in trying to explicate Boethius' definition by establishing an analogous relation between life as it pertains to God and life as we understand it from a human point of view. I, therefore, add to his discussion the view that association of any type or degree with life is more than involvement in "incidents in time" or "awareness of the passage of time." As I will later explore in detail, time is not some container in which life occurs or an ontological reality or "thing" that can be known or engaged in terms of its component elements or divisions. Instead, life is constituted by events and processes in which living beings are involved, with present events and processes carried out in light of past events and process and in anticipation of future events and process. What we call time is a way of marking the duration of events and processes that are actually occurring and of structuring their relation with what has gone before and with that for which we anticipate or hope.

Placher asserts that, for Boethius, eternity "is neither simply time like that of creatures indefinitely extended nor a timelessness altogether unrelated to temporal duration. It is 'life.' But 'limitless life' possessed 'all at once.'"[72] Placher works his way to the claim that Jesus (presumed to be God incarnate) demonstrates what divine temporality is and the revelation of what human temporality could be.[73] However, if this idea is to be embraced in tandem with the idea of a simple, immutable, impassible God, it requires further explanation of how Jesus can be the incarnation of a thoroughly simple God. In other words, how can a God that is void of composition (physical or metaphysical), the essence of which is "its" existence, be also understood to exist eternally as a Trinity in which the constituent members share the same essence but are also their own distinct hypostases? Surely it is the latter claim that protects orthodox Christians from falling into what is considered the heresy of modalism, which denies that the economic Trinity is grounded in the immanent-ontological Trinity. However, as explicated by Arminius, this matter seems to challenge the idea of a simple God that is void of all composition.

In discussing certain difficult issues, Arminius claims that, while having common essence, "the divine persons are distinguished by a real distinction, not by the degree and mode of the thing." He reinforces this position with the claim that "a person is an individual subsistence itself, not a characteristic property, nor is it an individual principle."[74] This analysis does provide foundation for the position that Jesus was appointed as mediator and reconciler between God and human beings. However, it seems to undermine an important element of the justification for Arminius's claim regarding the character of God's knowledge on the basis of God's simplicity.

I well appreciate how the desire to establish a necessary ground for existence, through a process of abstraction from features of life as we know it, leads to the idea of a simple ultimate that is immutable, impassible, and always in act (having no potentiality). It is not unreasonable to claim that the ultimate is not, in any way, subject to the structure of life because it is the ground of that structure. This claim does enable the ultimate to be understood as the governing principle in all expressions of life, even as it places the ultimate beyond the limitations of life. Indeed, with the recognition that the concept of an ultimate is an abstraction from the actual dynamics of life as human beings experience it, I am quite able to embrace a modified version (including the replacement of God with ultimate) of an important claim by Arminius. It would read: *"With* eternity as a pre-eminent mode of the essence of *the ultimate, the ultimate* as infinite . . . is . . . devoid of time with regard to the succession of former and latter, of past and future."[75] I could then claim that the ultimate possesses limitless life because all that is characterized as expressing or giving life gains its character from its grounding in the ultimate. However, these moves would presuppose the recognition that the radical categorical distinction between the notion of "ultimacy" and "human life" as we know it does not allow me to confidently claim much more. This would constitute a theological apophatism that excludes the claim that the ultimate has exhaustive knowledge of the details of human life and the decisions taken by human beings in freedom. There would also be no reasonable ground on which to conclude that this ultimate is equivalent to God as an actual entity, and more so a personal being that feels human pains and has meaningful appreciation for our yearnings, fears, changes of heart, and hopes.

It is only because Arminius, like many others, superimposes the personal God of his religious beliefs onto the idea of a simple ultimate generated by philosophical analysis that he is able to claim that God as the simple ultimate has infallible knowledge of all things necessary and contingent through one infinite intuition. I suggest that, given the established entailments from the idea of simplicity, those who follow the Arminian concept should listen to Saint Anselm's own words[76] as he wrestled with the question: how can God respond compassionately to human suffering yet remain absolute and impassible?

> But how are you both merciful and impassible? For if You are impassible, You do not have any compassion; and if You have no compassion, Your heart is not sorrowful from compassion with the sorrowful, which is what being merciful is. But if You are not merciful whence comes so much consolation for the sorrowful? How, then, are You merciful and not merciful, O Lord, unless it be that You are [merciful] according to our way of looking at things and not according to Your way. For when You look upon us in our misery it is we who feel the effect of Your mercy, but You do not experience the feeling. Therefore

> You are both merciful because You save the sorrowful and pardon sinners against You; and You are not merciful because You do not experience any feeling of compassion for misery.[77]

Having said all that, I return to the fact that Arminius was intent, in his wide-ranging discussion of God and related matters, on protecting human freedom. One such point is his discourse with Francis Junius, in the process of which he tackles the Calvinist approach to the character of God's knowledge. Here he explicitly presumes that the ultimate is the personal God of the Bible. In one telling episode Arminius again alludes to natural, free, and middle knowledge as he reiterates his conviction that God's knowledge "is eternal, immutable and infinite, and that it extends to all things both necessary and contingent, to all things which He does of Himself either mediately or immediately, and which He permits to be done by others." Arminius admits to understanding differently than others might "the mode in which He [God] knows future contingencies and especially those things that belong to the free-will of persons, and which God decreed to permit, but not to do of Himself." He refers to those (Calvinists, I presume) who claim that God infallibly knows contingencies because they are present to God in the infinite Now of eternity. This position is not very convincing to Arminius, and he seems to have middle knowledge in mind, in which knowledge depends on contingent causes, when he points to I Samuel 23:12 as support for his assertion that "God knows, also, those things which may happen, but never do happen, and consequently do not co-exist with God in the Now of eternity, which would be events unless they should be hindered."[78] Addressing the kind of situations his reference to the passage is designed to dramatize, Arminius asks: "But how shall the causes of those event, which depend on the freedom of the will, be complete, among which, even at the very moment in which it chose one, it was free not to choose it, or to choose in preference to it?"[79]

Taken at face value, the passage from Samuel could actually be said to depict a situation in which those things God said would happen did not happen. However, I do not need to go that far in order to justifiably assert that, as depicted, the scenario seems to challenge Arminius's claim that God "sees certainly and infallibly, even, things future and contingent, whether he sees them in their causes, or in themselves."[80] In contrast to the Arminian claim that God's "infallibility depends on the infinity of the essence of God, and not on his unchangeable will,"[81] the scenario in I Samuel 23:12 highlights the significance of contra-causal freedom in human affairs and for God's life.

In the Scriptures we actually find a number of examples that suggest limitation in God's knowledge and contextual variability in God's interactions with human beings. Not long after the story of beginnings, there is a scenario in Genesis 6, which depicts the extreme degree to which human beings had become ensnared by evil. The level of regret attributed to God seems to suggest that human beings had turned out far different from God had expected. Indeed, the corrective God employed (the Flood) suggests that God wanted to start things over again. In Genesis 18 we find Abraham in discussion with God over the fate of Sodom, with God willing to change the fate of the city if the conditions worked out with Abraham were met, to find a certain number of righteous people. Exodus 32:11-14 depicts God in another exasperated state because Israel was not behaving as God wished. It is Moses' intercession that stops God from giving up on Israel. In Genesis 22:12 the angel's declaration suggests that it was probably only after Abraham was willing to sacrifice his son that God knew for sure that Abraham was willing to be obedient to divine command. There are other situations in which prophets, portrayed as representing the voice of God, used terms that suggest some degree of uncertainty in God. So we hear in Ezekiel 12:3, "Perhaps they will understand, though they are a rebellious house." In Jeremiah 3:7 there is commentary on Israel's unfaithfulness, with God portrayed as saying, "I thought, 'After she has done all this she will return to me'; but she did not return." Later on in 26:3, Jeremiah is ordered to proclaim God's word to the people, and we hear God saying, "It may be that they will listen."

Biblical narratives are sometimes excessive in their anthropomorphisms. At times, portrayals of God lean so heavily in the direction of univocality that God ends up looking like a supernaturalized human. However, even in their excesses, biblical depictions remind us that appropriate God-talk, which cannot avoid analogizing from human experience, should not so focus on the uniqueness of God that it results in characterizations that have no meaningful connection with the human analogue. At the same time, these narratives assure us that it is not out of bounds for Christians to explore understandings of divine perfection that are different from those developed with the help of Hellenistic conceptualities. God's perfection does not have to be tied to simplicity, immutability impassibility, and pure act. A loving God that desires and pursues communion with human beings is not made deficient if that God does not have the kind of exhaustive knowledge portrayed in Arminius's claim that "no one is chosen by God to adoption and the communication of the gift of righteousness, unless he is considered by Him as a believer."[82]

Soon I will explicate the foundation for the position that God's involvement in life has to do with participation in the events and processes of each life in relation to participation in all life. Indeed, God has the ability to do this as long as there are events and processes in which to be involved. I will show how it is that God does all this as part of a dynamic in which we human beings actualize ourselves in the present out of a destiny that comes to us from the past, combined with the possibilities that confront us from the future, as God challenges us to go forward.[83] Clark Williamson asserts that human beings are created by God to be "free, partially self-creating, self-determining creatures."[84] I reiterate the position that an important feature of human freedom is that the integration of causal factors associated with events and processes and the very act of decision-making itself result in outcomes that are never fully explainable by the sum of these factors. This creates an element of novelty that can never be fully predetermined and which is an expression of creativity that is at the heart of existence. While I depart from Clark Pinnock on important aspects of his doctrine of God and God's relation to the world, my position corresponds with his general view that, although God knows all there needs to be known about the world, there are aspects of the future that even God does not know.[85]

In the upcoming chapter I will follow the leads that emerge when Arminius takes contra-causal freedom seriously, in light of a focus on God as an actual entity that is in intentional relationship with human beings and the world of which they are a part. In such a framework, analogical thinking can be used appropriately to establish God's similarities to and difference from human beings, providing a counter to the thoroughly simple ultimate that is immutable and impassible in all respects, and thus without potential. Instead we will find a God who is di-polar, operates at the heart of the temporal sphere, and is available for authentic communion that contributes to the ongoing formation of humanity.

## NOTES

1. Michael Walzer, *Exodus and Revolution* (New York: Basic Books, 1985), 25.

2. This position does not represent an attempt to discredit the Scriptures, but it reflects an epistemological orientation that I explained in great detail in a previously published text. See Michael St. A. Miller, *Reshaping the Contextual Vision in Caribbean Theology: Theoretical Foundations for Theology Which is Contextual, Pluralistic, and Dialectical* (Lanham: University Press of America, 2007).

3. Clark Williamson, *Way of Blessing Way of Life: A Christian Theology* (St. Louis: Chalice Press, 1999), 63.

4. In the setting where I teach we talk a lot about "embedded theology" that seeps into us by way of expressions, practices, and attitudes that are prevalent in the communities, homes, and churches in which one is nurtured.

5. William Watty, *From Shore to Shore: Soundings in Caribbean Theology* (typeset by CEDAR Press, Barbados; printed in Kingston, Jamaica, 1981), 3 .

6. Joe R. Jones, *Grammar of Christian Faith: Systematic Explorations in Christian Life and Doctrine,* vol. II (Lanham: Rowman and Littlefield Publishers Inc., 2002), 396.

7. M. J. Charlesworth, ed. *St. Anselm's Proslogion with a Reply on Behalf of the Fool by Gaunilo and the Author's Reply to Guanaco* (South Bend, IN: University of Notre Dame Press, 1979), 125.

8. Fyodor Dostoyevsky, *The Brothers Karamazov,* trans. and annotated by Richard Pevear and Larissa Volokhonsky (San Francisco: North Point Press, 1990), 259.

9. Ibid., 258-259.

10. Jürgen Moltmann, "Hope of Resurrection and the Practice of Freedom," in *The Future of Creation — Collected Essays* (Philadelphia: Fortress Press, 1979), 103.

11. Elizabeth A. Johnson, *She Who Is: The Mystery of God in Feminist Theological Discourse,* Tenth Anniversary Ed. (New York: The Crossroad Publishing Company, 2002), 159. Johnson named a number of feminist theologians and biblical scholars who had taken this stance before she wrote her prize-winning book. However, mainstream Christianity has either not paid them any mind or has sought to vilify them.

12. Actually, it seems to me that those who support a Calvin-like understanding of God should, at least, be willing to acknowledge that if the customary ways that human beings attempt to establish what constitutes justice does not apply to God, it requires consideration of the possibility that God might very well follow an all-together different path than the one human beings customarily take in assessing sin and its consequences.

13. Vladimir Lossky, *The Mystical Theology of the Eastern Church* (Crestwood, NY: St. Vladimir's Seminary Press, 2002), 120.

14. Ibid., 123.

15. Ibid., 120. Lossky's reference is *De hominis opificio,* XVI P.G., t. 44, 184 AC. Cf. de Lubac, Catholicism (Eng. trans.), 209.

16. Ibid., 123.

17. Williamson, *Way of Blessing Way of Life,* 169.

18. Richard Bauckham, *God and the Crisis of Freedom* (Louisville: Westminster John Knox Press, 2002), 48.

19. This seems to be suggested in Genesis 1:28 when together they are commanded to be fruitful and multiply in association to chapter 2:24 which refers to the inclination of each to the other such that they would become one flesh—all this pointing to 3:20 where Adam names his companion Eve "because she would become the mother of all the living." Those who would point to Genesis 3:16, which on the surface suggests that as a consequence of "the fall" Eve would experience pain in child-birth and be subordinated to Adam, should read Carol Meyers's *Discovering Eve: Ancient Israelite Women in Context.* Returning to the main point, I suggest that, while there might be some like Augustine who still hold that if there had not been a fall, male-female cohabitation from which offspring emerges would have been without sexual desire, I can't recall Augustine or any other credible scholar suggesting that this reproduction would not involve the engagement of a man and woman or at least male and female reproductive elements.

20. Theologians like Paul Tillich might suggest that the story of Adam (and Eve) is a mythological representation of the intuition of our ultimate grounding in Being itself for which God has become the popular symbol. This being the case, human life will always be affected by what are called spiritual concerns. Maybe the supernaturalizing of Jesus through connection with the logos and the attempt to establish him as a member of the Trinity is born of a strong desire to lay hold on that which is intuited.

21. John Calvin, *Institutes of Christian Religion,* vol. I, ed. John McNeill, trans. and indexed by Ford Lewis Battles (Philadelphia, Westminster Press, 1960), [I.iii.1], 43.

22. Ibid.

23. Ibid., [I.iv.2], 48.

24. Matthew Myer Boulton, *Life in God: John Calvin, Practical Formation, and the Future of Protestant Theology* (Grand Rapids, MI: Wm. B. Eerdmans Publishing Company, 2011), 84-85. Boulton argues that oblivio, not depravity, is the organizing figure in book one of *The Institutes.*

25. For some persons this approach, if embraced, would undermine the significance of the much cherished notion of *Imago Dei* in the definition of what it means to be human—a notion that has been used to both separate and unify, uplift and demean human beings. The history of discussion of its specific meaning paints a picture of great uncertainty. The reader might be interested in my description of some of these approaches in my text *Reshaping the Contextual Vision in Caribbean Theology.* I am of the view that the most helpful interpretation of *Imago Dei* should be in terms of the human capacity for communion with God and also to reflect the character of God in our lives, that is, as far as this is possible in the context of finitude. This entails the challenge to honor and enhance these qualities in all others who bear the *Imago Dei.* It is the case, however, that *Imago Dei* is not the only meaningful way to represent the human capacity for communion with and representation of God. In fact, the history of relations be-

tween Christians and with others has not established that the embrace of this notion is the best incentive for respect for and collaboration among human beings. Later in this work the reader will see that the conception of a di-polar God who is all inclusive and relates internally to the world, including human beings, might well serve as a more appropriate and effective incentive for what many have hoped to achieve with the guidance of *Imago Dei*.

26.  The other founder was Barton Stone, who, like Campbell, started out as a Presbyterian minister and was a notable presence in the Second Great Awakening.

27.  Alexander Campbell, *The Christian System* (Cincinnati, OH: Standard Publishing Company, 1839 ), 14-15.

28.  Lossky, *Mystical Theology*, 123.

29.  Campbell, *The Christian System*, 16.

30.  Ibid.

31.  Alexander Campbell, ed. "Response to Mr. D. A. Skeptic," in *The Christian Baptist*, vol. IV (Bethany, VA: Bethany Printing Office, 1827), 71.

32.  Ibid., 70.

33.  Campbell, *The Christian System*, 15-16.

34.  Campbell, "Response to Mr. D. A. Skeptic," in *The Christian Baptist*, 70.

35.  Ibid.

36.  James Arminius, "A Discussion on the Subject of Predestination," in *The Writings of James Arminius*, vol. III, trans. W. R. Bagnall (Grand Rapids, MI: Baker Books, 1956), 61.

37.  Arminius, "Private Disputations," in *The Writings of James Arminius*, vol. II, ed. James Nichols (Grand Rapids, MI: Baker Books, 1956), 99-100.

38.  Arminius, "Declaration of Sentiment," in *The Writings of James Arminius*, vol. I, ed. James Nichols (Grand Rapids, MI: Baker Books, 1956), 248.

39.  Arminius, "An Examination of the Treatise of William Perkins," in *The Writings of James Arminius*, vol. III, 316.

40.  Arminius, "Private Disputations," in *The Writings of James Arminius*, vol. II, 100.

41.  These ideas were part of Arminius's doctoral examination in 1603, which followed his disputation with Perkins, and at which time he was also made a professor of theology at the University of Leiden, Holland.

42.  Arminius, "Public Disputations," in *The Writings of James Arminius*, vol. I, ed. James Nichols., 448.

43.  Arminius, "An Examination of the Treatise of William Perkins," in *The Writings of James Arminius*, vol. III, 316.

44.  Arminius, "Public Disputations," in *The Writings of James Arminius* vol. I, ed. James Nichols, 101.

45.  William Lane Craig, "No Other Name," in *The Philosophical Challenge of Religious Diversity*, eds. Philip Quinn and Kevin Meeker (Oxford: Oxford University Press, 2000), 41-42.

46.  Ibid., 43.

47.  Anthony Kenny, *The God of the Philosophers* (Oxford: Clarendon Press, 1979), 81. Kenny's source is John Milton, *De Doctrina Christiana* (New Haven: Yale University Press, 1933), 87.

48.  Craig, "No Other Name," in *The Philosophical Challenge of Religious Diversity*, eds. Philip Quinn and Kevin Meeker, 43.

49.  Ibid., 44.

50.  Kenny, *The God of the Philosophers*, 62.

51.  Arminius, "Public Disputations," in *The Writings of James Arminius*, vol. I, ed. James Nichols, 101.

52.  Ibid., 100.

53.  Craig, "No Other Name," in *The Philosophical Challenge of Religious Diversity*, eds. Philip Quinn and Kevin Meeker, 44.

54.  Ibid., 49-50.

55.  Arminius, "The Object of Theology," in *The Writings of James Arminius*, vol. I, 62.

56.  Ibid., 66.

57.  Ibid.

58. Ibid., 67.

59. Ibid., 72.

60. Ibid., 76.

61. Ibid.

62. The most famous attempt was Thomas Aquinas's "five ways" discussed in his *Summa Theologiae* (especially the second and third ways) in support of his argument for the existence of God.

63. Arminius, "Public Disputations," *The Writings of James Arminius*, vol. I, 438. Translated into non-technical language, the classical understanding of essence that dominated Scholastic thought was that on account of which an entity is what it is apart from diversities within its genus and species and despite its own experience of material changes.

64. Ibid., 435.

65. Ibid., 439.

66. Arminius, "Discussion with F. Junius," in *The Writings of James Arminius*, vol. III, 67.

67. Clark Williamson, *Way of Blessing Way of Life: A Christian Theology* (St. Louis: Chalice Press, 1999), 100-101.

68. Vladimir Lossky, *The Mystical Theology of the Eastern Church*, 70.

69. Arminius, "Public Disputations," *The Writings of James Arminius*, vol. I, 439-440.

70. Ibid., 443.

71. William C. Placher, *Narratives of a Vulnerable God: Christ, Theology, and Scripture* (Louisville: Westminster John Knox Press, 1994), 31. Placher's reference is William Kneale, "Time and Eternity in Theology," in *Proceedings of the Aristotelian Society* 61 (1961), 99.

72. Ibid.

73. Ibid., 37-38. Among other things, Placher suggests that Jesus' life does not extinguish but integrates time and to that extent overcomes the difficulties between what we call past, present, and future. "There is in Him no opposition or competition or conflict, but peace between origin, movement and goal, between present, past and future."

74. Arminius, "Certain Articles to Be Diligently Examined and Weighed," in *The Writings of James Arminius,* vol. II, 481-482.

75. For the original see: Arminius, "Public Disputations," in *The Writings of James Arminius*, vol. I, 439.

76. I referred to Anselm's dilemma earlier in this chapter.

77. Charlesworth, ed. *St. Anselm's Proslogion*, 125.

78. Arminius, "Discussion on Predestination," in *The Writings of Arminius*, vol. III, 66. The Samuel passage refers to a situation in which David enquires of God whether the citizens of Keilah would deliver him and his men to Saul. The answer is "yes," but since David then leaves Keilah, the handover does not in fact occur.

79. Ibid.

80. Arminius, "Private Disputations," in *The Writings of James Arminius*, vol. II, 37.

81. Ibid.

82. Arminius, "An Examination of the Treatise of William Perkins," in *The Writings of James Arminius*, vol. III, 316.

83. Pinnock, *Most Moved Mover* , 127.

84. Williamson, *Way of Blessing Way of Life: A Christian Theology*, 107.

85. Pinnock, *Most Moved Mover*, 47-48.

*Chapter Six*

# God-Talk and Human Freedom

I have been intimating throughout this text that the traditional Christian conception of God as omnipotent, omniscient sovereign has been informed by images of power and governance infused with the character of ancient kings, Caesars, and lords. As evident in some of Jacob Arminius's formulations, since the early centuries of the Common Era Christian intellectuals have employed Hellenistic concepts to provide layers of theological justification for these images, and these placed the Christian sovereign beyond the constraining features of the Jewish constructions inherited by the Christian community. The result is that, while Christians might claim that the best image we have of the personal God we worship is Jesus of Nazareth the Christ whose life was characterized by limitation, vulnerability, and caring, when many Christians think of God *per se*, "he" is still the absolute sovereign lord who, at the most fundamental level of "his" being, operates in an infinite non-temporal sphere called eternity. From the perspective of eternity, the meaningful facts of human life, and all life in all times, are settled, whether this is considered in terms of predestination or in terms of exhaustive knowledge or foreknowledge. Given the categorical distinction between the temporal sphere in which human beings operate and the construct classified as eternity, it is difficult to comprehend what characterizations taken from human life lived in the temporal sphere mean when applied to the simple, eternal God. Further, the actions of this God, considered sovereignly free, can never be evaluated on the basis of any standard that makes sense to temporal-finite-sinful human beings.

Open Theist Clark Pinnock, along with others, has attempted to radicalize the Arminian position by developing the view that God self-limits to create space for the loving relationship God desires with human beings. However, this does not go far enough. While God might self-limit for the sake of what

God wants, God, as conceived by Open Theists, still has the right, freedom, and capacity to trump human freedom, if it serves God's purposes.[1] Those who argue that God's actions are governed by love and fidelity, while holding to a Campbell-like view that God can never be evaluated on the basis of any human standard, must admit that, despite decisions arrived at as a result of reading the Scriptures and especially conclusions about Jesus, they have no assurance regarding how God will express God's "love" from one moment to the next. In order to justify this God, in the midst of horrendous and dehumanizing situations of life, some have been able to declare with ease that God disciplines those whom God loves and punishes those accepted as God's children (Hebrews 1:6). I assert that with finite, realistically libertarian, and relational freedom at stake, the fundamental characterization of God needs to be modified. This I will pursue by critiquing traditional God-talk that, among other influences, is informed by the distinction between time and eternity, and, instead, embrace the idea of an infinitely temporal God in association with the Process-Relational idea of God as the self-surpassing surpasser of all to whom the cosmos is linked in its emergence and continued life.

## TIME AND ETERNITY

My experience suggests that most orthodox Christians would be more supportive of Arminius's approach to what God knows than they would be of Clark Pinnock's more recent attempt to radicalize Arminius' position by challenging the idea of God's exhaustive knowledge of things necessary and contingent. Those aware of the history of Christian thought might well insist that Pinnock's venture violates the most popular Christian understanding of the relation of eternity to time that has its beginning with Augustine's fascinating struggle in book eleven of his *Confessions*. With book ten serving as the transition from the more strictly confessional to the more analytic, Augustine signals his position on eternity in the very first sentence of book eleven. Having just been involved in a series of declarations about God and about himself to God, especially on the issue of memory, Augustine asks: "O Lord, since you are outside time in eternity, are you unaware of the things I tell you? Or do you see in time the things that occur in it?"[2]

Augustine proceeds to other declarations in which he extols the greatness of God as creator *ex nihilo*, and this serves as the launching board for the discussion of eternity and time. That eternity is the primary issue on his mind is suggested by the questions he associates with a hypothetical detractor, which is the first of a number of problematics that create space for explanatory answers. There is the general question: "What was God doing before he created heaven and earth?"[3] And further: "If the will to create something which he had never created before was new to him—if it was some new motion stirring in him—how can we say that his is true eternity, when a new will, which had never been before, could arise in it?"[4] The point is, the claim that God willed to create implies a change, and this would not be consistent with the presumed definition of eternity. More explicitly, any argument that God moved from being without a world to creating one brings into play the notion of "'before," "after," and "then," which clearly applies in the world we inhabit but not to the eternal realm to which Augustine had been referring. The eternal realm, as we have been reminded by Arminius (as discussed in chapter 5), is devoid of time with regard to the succession of former and latter, of past and future.

With opportunity created by this problematic, Augustine proceeds to explicate his view of eternity in relation to time. It should be noticed that, with all his struggles with time, the understanding of eternity that is the antithesis of time is never questioned. And, as the character of time as moving instants is progressively shown to be a function of human subjectivity, eternity as the stationary now outside of the sphere of change grows in its significance for human affairs. It is this conviction about eternity that would become the foundation for the explicit espousal of predestinationism that emerged in his struggle with Plagianism. We hear then, as part of Augustine's immediate response to the detractor, that eternity "is forever still"; that is, "nothing moves into the past: all is present," and time, on the other hand, "is never still," and "is never all present at once. The past is always driven by the future, the future always follows on the heels of the past, and both the past and the future have their beginning and their end in the eternal present."[5] By my reading, Augustine, in this closing declaration, is signaling what will be seen more clearly as central to the solution to the puzzles that result from his analysis of time. At this point in the text he continues his steady march to his final solution by declaring, as if speaking to God, that: "It is in eternity, which is supreme over time because it is never-ending present, that you are at once before all past time and after all future time. . . . Your years are completely present to you all at once, because they are at a permanent standstill."[6]

It is with Augustine's view of eternity in mind that I enter into his intriguing exploration of the challenges involved in conceptualizing and measuring time.[7] In this process he progressively narrows down that which can be called "present," the dynamics of which give insight into what is called past and future. Having taken us through important considerations relevant to periods of time we classify as years, months, days, and hours, he addresses what probably appeared to many the best proposal for measuring time. Thus, reflecting, it seems, influence from the image of a moving dial or ticking clock, there is the claim that "the only time that can be called present is an instant, if we can conceive of such, that cannot be divided into the most minute fractions."[8] Augustine is encouraging us to imagine "instants" as extentionless and in constant succession, that is, a succession of "nows." When the present instant is ended it is the past, and the instant to come will be the future. Earlier he had indicated that time derives its length "from a great number of movements constantly following one another into the past."[9] This seems consistent with Schubert Ogden's representation of the popular view of time as "the endless continuum of such instants in which the now is, so to speak, constantly moving as one instant follows upon another."[10]

Referring to the earth and heavens that constitute the created order, Augustine suggests that "the very fact that they are there proclaims that they were created, for they are subject to change and variation; whereas if anything exists that was not created, there is nothing in it that was not there before; and the meaning of change and variation is that something is there which was not there before."[11] In section fourteen he fashions a problematic for a new round of investigation when he observes that maybe all we ever have in the finite realm is the present instant. There is the question: "Of these three divisions of time, then, how can two, the past and the future, be, when the past no longer is and the future is not yet?" After reminding us once again of the contrast with eternity, the status of which is taken for granted, he moves to a quite telling point: "If, therefore, the present is time only by reason of the past that it moves on to become the past, how can we say that even the present is, when the reason why it is is that it is not to be? In other words, we cannot rightly say that time is, except by reason of its impending state of not being."[12] Augustine recognizes that with prolonged duration the present could be divided into past and future and so could not be considered the present. Thus it cannot be considered as having duration. Likewise, any future considered is not actual future because it does not yet exist and it comes into being only by becoming the present, which will be past as soon as it is recognized as present. So "we can become aware of time and measure it only while it is passing. Once it has passed it no longer is, and therefore cannot be measured."[13]

In the sections that follow, Augustine engages in nuanced argument as he drives toward his conclusion in regard to the measuring of time, which consists of a present only perceived in its passing (instant to instant), a future that is not yet, and a past that is no longer. "We cannot measure it [time] if it is not yet in being, or if it is no longer in being, or if it has no duration, or if it has no beginning and no end . . . Yet we do measure time."[14] He eliminates the option of time being constituted by the movement of heavenly or material bodies; that is, its measurement is determined by their movement. And it seems to be his analysis of the sounding of different syllables (e.g., the eight syllabled *Deus Creator omnium*), which, in comparison to each other, are heard as having different durations, that serves as the clincher for his conclusion that time is actually an extension of the mind.[15] The very idea of comparing for the purpose of measurement sounds that are heard after each other but must be retained together for adequate comparison resurrects the problem of the relation between present, past, and future wrestled with in book 11.15,16. Therefore, he concludes that the dynamics of measurement are occurring by means of three functions of the mind, "those of expectation, attention, and memory. The future, which it expects, passes through the present, to which it attends, into the past, which it remembers." Regarding the present, we are reminded that its lack of duration is due to the fact that "it exists only for the instant of its passage," although the mind's attention to it persists, "and through it that which is to be passes toward the state in which it is to be no more."[16] In other words, what we measure are impressions left on the soul/mind by what has already happened and that to which one is presently paying attention (even when objectively past), and by what one expects to take place.

Here it should be noted that, while for Augustine measurement is a function of the mind, time is not reduced to its measurement, that is, the numbers and systems of numbers we use to represent movement. The basic character of time is still understood in terms of instants, even if Augustine claims they have no extension or duration. They constitute every present in which the mind pays attention, anticipates, and remembers, and it is their ordered succession that leaves impressions on the mind and elicits attempts at measurement. In the final analysis, it is the defined character of instants that enables Augustine to establish the radical contrast between the fleeting and ephemeral nature of that which is in motion and constitutes the temporal with the absoluteness of that which is a never ending present, that is, eternity.

A hint of a link with what tradition usually labels foreknowledge comes in Augustine's address of prophesy as foretelling in section nineteen of chapter 11. Although surrounded by discussion questioning the existence of the future, he still is able to make the unequivocal assertion: "You have revealed it [the future] to your prophets."[17] If, as this suggests, eternity is God's vantage point outside of temporal distinctions between present, past, and future, from which to reveal the future to God's prophets, this would imply that though nonexistent when evaluated in terms of the temporal, the dimension of existence to which future refers is objectively real to the eternal God. Augustine must struggle with the paradox—this being the mystery to which he refers at the end of this short section. What is no mystery is that this paradox was the foundation for a link between predestination, foreknowledge, and meticulous providence. That which God determines to happen or foresees is present to God as accomplished, in all the details of its occurrence. Clearly this would involve all causal factors from every time and sphere that have been, and is in any way contributory to that which will play out in a particular way in a temporal present, regardless of how human beings choose to classify a present in relation to other presents.

Ogden is correct when, in the process of evaluating traditional God-talk, he claims, with insights from Martin Heidegger, that the conception of time like that explicated above, and in contrast to which the character of eternity in the sense of "the stationary now" is established, is from "the vulgar understanding of time." Ogden suggests that this understanding is informed by an orientation to the idea of "constant presence-at-hand," "derived from our ordinary perception of objects as located within the field of our phenomenal world." "On this understanding, the present is an extentionless instant or 'now,' . . . and time as a whole is the endless continuum of discrete instants in which the now is, so to speak, constantly moving as one instant follows upon another." He points out that it is "by reference, then, to this conception of time as its 'moving image,' eternity is defined as the 'stationary now,' or as sheer nontemporality or timelessness."[18] This, I suggest, is indeed the case, even with Augustine's sophisticated explication of the challenges associated with measuring and categorizing time. As mentioned above, even as Augustine went as far as to question the very reality of time and concluded that, in the final analysis, the dynamics of measurement are occurring by means of three functions of the mind: expectation, attention, and memory. He still presumed the reality of "instants" in his analysis of the "impressions" of mind that lead to the range of time classifications we have and the number calculations associated with them. And when most traditional theologians speak of God's eternity, it is this utter timelessness (in contrast to the realm of "moving instants"), characterized by complete absence of temporal distinctions, to which they are referring.

It is to speak to these traditional theologians that I employ ideas from Delwin Brown, who poses conceptual challenges to those who would claim that maintenance of the notion of God's eternity, understood as timelessness, can be held in concert with an affirmative position on human freedom. Brown reminds us that, strictly speaking, the understanding that God's timelessness entails God's knowing of past, present, and future all at once, means that God really has no foreknowledge, since foreknowledge implies that something is actually future for God. Augustine and Arminius would probably be in full agreement with him on this point, suggesting that "foreknowledge" is a human category reflecting our perception within the limitations of temporality. Yet they might also suggest that what God knows eternally still must unfold in the process of time. More significant for my purpose is Brown's further claim that the position that God has all knowledge or omniscience, which includes that which human beings will do freely, actually makes human freedom worthless. Our freedom would make no actual difference to what occurs in the future, because that future *really* (i.e., for God) already is. Our freedom would then be ineffectual. Secondly, though some notion of human freedom appears to be saved, it is relatively unreal. Brown goes as far as to suggest that as a result "a chimera of unreality would be cast over the whole plane of temporal existence." He continues:

> All that is part and parcel of a freedom experienced amidst the passage of time, e.g. the perplexing alternatives we face, the troubling prospect of failure or the hope of success, the agony of choosing, the unsettled consequences—all of these elements essential to our temporal freedom are unreal from God's, and thus from the true, vantage point. Thirdly, although one can say "God is timeless, yet knows the temporal world," it is difficult to know what that statement can mean. If, on the one hand, the "timefullness" of human reality is taken into God's timeless knowledge, is temporality not thereby introduced into divine awareness? If, on the other hand, the temporality of our lives is said to be absent in God's knowledge, is the static replica of our lives that is known to God really *us* ?[19]

While Clark Pinnock also has problems with the customary representation of God's relation to time, he does not seem ready to jettison the traditional notion of eternity seen as necessary to any description of the essential character of God. Pinnock's way of addressing the challenges its link to foreknowledge poses for human freedom is to suggest that, although existing "before creation and before creaturely time" and not in any way dependent on human beings, God has since the creation "related to the world within the structures of time."[20] In order to fulfill a desire for a relationship with human beings, which necessarily involves genuinely free choice by us, God has "stooped down" to share the context in which we operate; that is, "God has chosen to become bound up with time and history." Pinnock sounds somewhat like Clark Williamson when he suggests that, "though unchangeable with respect to character and the steadfastness of his purpose, God changes in the light of what happens by interacting with the world." Thus "there is temporal succession in God's thinking." Supported by passages like Jeremiah 18:7-11 and 29:11, Pinnock claims that God makes plans and carries them out, and is willing to change course based on human decision, this implying "a temporal gap between plan and fulfillment. God also remembers the past, interacts with the present, and anticipates the future."[21] Succinctly put: "Scripture presents God as temporally everlasting, not timelessly eternal. It depicts God planning and deliberating, acting and reacting within the temporal. God is presented as experiencing past, present, and future successively not timelessly." [22] For Pinnock this is by choice, not by necessity.

Without doubt Pinnock has helped with biblical and other considerations that support my position that the structure of God's relation to the human beings, which involves foreordination or exhaustive foreknowledge, is not consistent with a credible understanding of human freedom. At the same time, I fear that his claim that this structure is the result of God's choice, in order that human beings might be free to relate to God in a certain way, is not

sufficient to address the threat to human freedom posed by the more dominant view of God's sovereignty in orthodox Christianity. Thus, even if the
dominant characterization of God in the Scriptures is as temporally everlasting, it only reflects the way God has chosen to operate not an abiding feature
of God's character.

Supporters of Pinnock's position would quickly remind me that for Pinnock love is God's primary perfection,[23] and that, in his understanding, "love
woos, it does not compel"; "it is love's way not to overpower but to be gentle
and persuasive"; further, "grace works mightily but does not override."[24]
This view of love and grace is compatible with the claim that God's power
"is not the kind of power spoken of in deterministic theologies, namely raw
power, the power of the puppeteer, the power to make everything else surrender." Instead, God's greater and awesome power is such that God "makes
free agents as creators and movers in their own right."[25] Yet it must not be
overlooked that Pinnock insists that "the future is settled to whatever extent
the Lord decides to settle it. God can predetermine, and foreknow, whatever
he wants to about the future."[26] He also is clear that God is not bound to
persuasion alone. God is able to, and sometimes acts coercively; that is, God
is free to act in ways that are completely contrary to his understanding of
what characterizes love's way.[27]

Pinnock's position is generally consistent with the free-will theists highlighted in chapter 5. In his response to the Skeptic in *The Christian Baptist*
Alexander Campbell did insist that God was not responsible to anyone for
God's choices.[28] It should also be recalled that the One who Arminius claims
"loves men absolutely to salvation,"[29] might well have determined "that in
order to achieve a multitude of saints" in the most feasible actual world there
had to be "an even greater multitude of sinners."[30] Along with these, it must
also be admitted that there are passages in the Bible that appear to support the
view that, in the final analysis, God is neither answerable to human beings
nor conforms to any human understanding or calculation. Quite striking is
Paul's declaration in Romans 9:18-24: "God has mercy on whom God will
have mercy, and hardens whom God wants to harden (v.18)." It should be
noted that even Paul speculates that God might well do this to dramatize both
power and mercy, and in the particular situation being discussed, do so for
the sake of the "new" elect "whom he prepared in advance for glory (v.23)."
Therefore, claiming that God is love, and that God wishes human beings to
relate to God in love, does not seem to hinder the eternal free-sovereign (who
is not subject to standards that sinful human beings value) from shifting the
entailments of love from what they appear to be at any particular time so that
what is "graciously" given to human beings is taken away.

Again, it might be argued that we come to know what God is like in Jesus
Christ, and that we can be confident that God will not act in ways that
contravene Jesus' representation of God through his person and work. To this

I respond that there is nothing in the portrayals of Jesus in the Gospels that limits the free sovereign of Christian orthodoxy from choosing, if deemed necessary according to "his" inscrutable intentions, to limit human freedom in ways that fall short of that required for libertarian freedom as privileged in Pinnock's framework. After all, if one followed the arguments of the typical supersessionist Christian,[31] that which the most pious and discerning minds of Israel understood to be vital features of their covenant relationship with God that would lead to their salvation, were transferred to Jesus and the Church. As a consequence, Israel's salvation now comes through recognition of the lordship of Jesus Christ and in Israel's sublation in the church. As it is addressed in a number of New Testament pronouncements, this shift by God seems quite arbitrary despite how orthodox Christians might choose to represent it. The result is that, while the demand for submission to the will of the sovereign is quite clear, the idea of faith as confidence in the consistency of such a God becomes obscured.

I value highly the suggestion in Genesis 2 that the capacity for exercising contra-causal freedom is intrinsic to the stock from which human beings who inhabit the world derive, and is still fundamental to what it means to be human. Therefore, I wish to encourage frameworks in which it might be practiced at its highest level without ignoring constraints that inform realistic libertarianism. This agenda contributes to my attraction to Schubert Ogden's approach to the conceptualization of time and eternity. Developed in conversation with ideas from Martin Heidegger, this conceptualization protects contra-causal freedom through God-talk that establishes temporality as a necessary element in the structure of God's life, and not merely one feature of strategic self-limitation by God for the sake of relational objectives. Thus there seems to be a guard against the arbitrariness that is still possible within Pinnock's framework, and the groundwork is laid for linkage with Process-Relational ideas of God that, of all the theological schools I am aware of, reflects most impressively a valorization of human freedom.

It might be suggested, at this point, that Pinnock has pressed the issue of God's temporality and human freedom as far as one can go without undermining the necessary link between the doctrine of creation and that of God's sovereign freedom. This link results in an understanding of *creatio ex nihilo*, which is that the self-existent eternal God, out of nothing that was pre-existent, brought into being "the whole universe, in the totality of its spatio-temporal existence, in one act, which is directly rooted in the necessity of the Divine being itself."[32] Usually associated with the very first verse of Genesis, this understanding received direct support from declarations in Maccabees 7:28. However, many are now willing to acknowledge that what follows immediately from Genesis 1:1 not only describes creation as "a continuous series of Divine acts" but also shows that this was a process in which order was fashioned out of the unformed or chaotic. We may attempt to protect the doctrine of *creatio ex nihilo* by adopting Augustine's view that God first fashioned formless matter then gave particular form to it,[33] but there would need to be the recognition that this is a proposal governed by a particular theological commitment. Clark Williamson would add that, along with other considerations that establish its necessity, *creatio ex nihilo* is to be embraced as a "limiting concept," made clear by what it denies. For example, "that the world is God, that it somehow 'emanates' (issues, flows) from God." or "that the world is evil because it was fashioned by God out of recalcitrant matter."[34] Addressing its affirmative quality, he would suggest that it not only sets the stage for a love relationship between God and human beings, but that it makes clear that the world as a whole matters to God.[35]

Keith Ward would suggest that an important expression of God's care for the whole world is that it is a setting for the realization of unique values that are necessarily linked to the finite nature of its inhabitants. Ward gives as one example the very basic endeavor of "going for a brisk, tiring walk that is only possible with a physical body of a certain type."[36] Clark Williamson might add that this particular endeavor is but one element of beings designed to be "partially self-creating, self-determining creatures."[37] In my scheme, that to which both men refer would be linked to realistic libertarian freedom. In this light, one could mention many other examples of value-laden scenarios from the human sphere, and also add examples from the non-human sphere like the very change of seasons that has brought us to late autumn, the time of year that I am writing these thoughts. As such, I identify with Ward's suggestion that the universe in which human beings are situated can be seen "as a particular contingent expression of the imaginative creativity of God."[38] It is this notion of creativity that fuels my proposal of a way to point the concept of *creatio ex nihilo* in the direction of my upcoming argument in support of a God who is characteristically (not strategically) linked to the temporal.

I begin with the suggestion made in a previous work, that whatever else one might struggle over in regard to the character of the self-existing perfect God of classical Christianity, the traditional claim that this God was moved to create without external persuasion implies that, if there can be no other incontestable presupposition when we contemplate "God," we must presuppose a creative drive that further presupposes that to which some refer as the metaphysical principle of creativity.[39] I now add that if creativity is essential to God's being, it is not illogical to consider that as long as God has been God, God has been expressing Godself creatively. And if God is the self-existent one of orthodox theism, God would not have been creating Godself, but something other than self. As such, it is theologically superfluous to argue for a distinction between God before and after the creation of that which is other than God, and it renders moot Augustine's question: "What was God doing before creation?" Indeed, the traditional claim that God's perfection means that God does not need anything outside of Godself, is replaced by the recognition that a God with creativity as a central characteristic finds fulfillment in creating, desires to see creative processes unfold, is committed to being as close as possible to the dynamic outworking of these processes, and contributes the best possible influences to encourage the highest quality of experience and achievement. This for me is the divine disposition that we usually speak of analogously as God's love for the world. It is in terms of this understanding that I find Pinnock's claim that "love is God's primary perfection"[40] most meaningful.

If one proceeds to imagine the constitution of that which was other than God only with guidance from Pinnock's position that God desired a love relationship with human beings, we would need to conclude that the actualities created by God, at least, included some form of the human exercising the kind of freedom that could lead to the choice of a relationship with God. If we broadened the scope of that which informs our imagination to include the complex dynamics of a world which, as Williamson suggests, matters to God, then we would need to include the natural processes that impinge on human decisions and are also valuable in their own right. If one went even further and embraced the view, as I do (and I suspect Williamson would), that the particular planet called earth had billions of years of evolutionary life before human beings appeared, it becomes all the more fascinating to imagine the intricacies of God's ongoing involvement in the processes of emergence, adaptation, transition, and complexification by which the earth emerged. One important result of this dynamic was the emergence of human beings with self-awareness, religious sensibility, the capacity to engage multiple factors in the process of decision-making, and the capacity to link the dynamics of existence in the world to a particular actuality considered ultimate and with whom one can choose to have intimacy.[41]

Of significant import at this point is the recognition that all of the listed scenarios suggest that God has never not been associated with a framework of movement and change, which is, in Pinnock's language, to be "bound up with time and history,"[42] whatever might be the challenges involved in the measurement and categorization of time. This also means that it has always been the case that the fulfillment of God's desire for human beings to love God has been contingent on dynamics in some world. One would be able to make all these assertions that link God inextricably with processes of movement and change, and also unreservedly identify with Charles Hartshorne's claim that, among the ways in which God is distinctive, is that God, "unlike us, is never confronted by a world whose coming to be antedates his own entire existence . . . everything that influences God has already been influenced by him." On the other hand, human beings and other creatures in the world "are influenced by events of the past with which we have had nothing to do."[43] And it is with this vision of the link, between God's life and the life of some world that I proceed to an engagement with Schubert Ogden's appropriation of Martin Heidegger's ideas in his promotion of an understanding of eternity that takes us even further beyond Augustine's construction by way of contrast with time, and Pinnock's understanding of any link between time and eternity as the result of divine strategy. The alternative route involves exploration of the concept of time in terms of the deep-structure of existence, which human beings participate in and express in a unique way, and also with consideration of the most appropriate way to formulate concepts of God in light of our understanding of the dynamics of existence.

## GOD: INFINITELY TEMPORAL AND IMAGINATIVELY CREATIVE

### Reorienting Time and Reconfiguring Eternity

Ogden suggests that the path toward an alternative conception of God which challenges Augustine's dominant position on God's eternity begins with Heidegger's recognition of "the irreconcilable opposition between the conceptuality of [the Greek] metaphysical tradition and the understanding of existence Augustine and others have sought to explicate theologically by means of it."[44] The Greek metaphysical tradition, it is suggested, "is not oriented to the primal phenomenon of our own existence as experiencing selves, but to the derived phenomenon of the objective world as the field of our ordinary sense perception." As such, "temporality can mean only the succession of wholly externally related instants, and relatedness to others, merely simple location in relation to an external environment."[45] By means of his engagement with Heideggerian conceptions, Ogden invites us to embrace the view that our everyday experience of time, in which the "vulgar" concept of time has its basis, is not original but derived, itself grounded in more primal temporality. In Ogden's representation of Heidegger's viewpoint, "the truly primary time of our experience is not the 'within-timeness' in which we order the objects of our ordinary external perceptions, but the time constituted by our experiencing itself, as actual occurrence."[46]

The background to this position is Heidegger's attempt to move the intellectual exploration of Being beyond the limited approach of his era. He identifies with the claim that "whenever one cognizes anything or makes an assertion, whenever one comports oneself toward entities, even towards oneself, some use is made of 'Being',"[47] that is, the notion "is already included in conceiving anything which one apprehends as an entity."[48] Indeed, it "lies in the fact that something is."[49] However, Heidegger is not satisfied with the usual rejoinder that, while self-evident and universal, Being is indefinable, and the complex analysis of *Being and Time* reflects the conviction that if the question of Being is fundamental, it must be explicated and made clear.[50]

It is not the task of this project to delve into the complex details of Heidegger's attempt to set out a formal structure for exploring the question of Being as such. Nevertheless, I must say enough about his explication to frame Odgen's appropriation of the associated notion of time for the development of a position on God's eternity that is an alternative to that of Augustine. Even though Heidegger was not engaged in a direct exploration of God *per se*, I am able to embrace Ogden's utilization of his ideas because I identify enough with Paul Tillich's method of correlation to hold that Christian theology must move back and forth between the eternal truth of its foundation and the temporal situations in which the eternal truth must be received as persons seek answers to questions that emerge in these situations.[51] There is the related conviction that central to the creative interpretations of existence that characterize these situations is humanity's pursuit of creative self-interpretation in which we address puzzles such as: Who am I? What is the structure of my existence? In what is my existence grounded?

It is from the dialectic engagement of the general struggle with the broad questions of existence and the struggle involved in the self-interpretation of particular beings that conceptions relevant to ultimacy and God emerge. This is certainly exemplified in Ogden's engagement of Heidegger's attempt at an existential phenomenology of Being for the sake of his theological project. Given the considerations of the relation between God and the world that I have already provided by way of a development on the orthodox tenet of *creatio ex nihilo*, I engage Ogden's project with the presupposition that God is the ultimate ground of Being and/or existence in the Hartshornian sense mentioned above.

The central concept utilized by Heidegger in his exploration of the relation between Being and time is the German term *Dasein*, which ordinarily means "existence," and he breaks it up into its components *Da* "there" and *Sein* "being" to refer to humanity's conscious, historical existence in the world; that is, our "being there" as particular existents.[52] The interplay of these understandings of *Dasein* reflects the recognition that "everything we talk about, everything we have in view, everything toward which we comport ourselves in any way, is being; what we are is being, and so is how we are."[53] And there is also the challenge to recognize that it is we human beings who experience ourselves thrown into a world and who, aware of our own being as particular existents (more correctly, our possible ways of being in the world), pose questions about what it means to be, leading to considerations of Being as such. Without doubt, the intention is to call attention to the formal concept of existence. However, there is the clear recognition that there is no coming to terms with Being as such except in the lives of actual existents. Therefore, it is in the analysis of the dynamics of the human life (i.e., our state of being as "Being-in-the-world") that we gain the best insights into the structure and dynamics of existence.[54]

It is as we come to terms with what it means to say that the inquiring, self-interpreting human exists most fundamentally in terms of a dynamic interplay between dimensions of time in the deep-structure of her/his existence, from which results attempts to organize, categorize, and measure, that we best discern the significance of time for our understanding of God's eternity.

As human beings, we are concerned with our own being, which, among other features, has potentiality as an important characteristic. In other words, at any point in our lives there are potentialities that are yet to be actualized,[55] pointing to an anticipatory element of our lives. As such, there is a sense in which we are always ahead of ourselves and, in the final analysis, this anticipatory element points to our death.[56] It is our embrace of this future, which represents finitude, and our reaching after the realization of what seems outstanding in our lives, which highlights "historicality" as an element in the structure of existence.[57] It seems then that, even as many harbor hopes regarding what lies beyond death, the fact of death constitutes human beings as Being-unto-death. Thus death, as a kind of boundary line, throws existence, as it is structured in human life, back upon itself. And it is as we live within the boundary lines characterized, on one side, by the fact that we had no choice about being in the world or prior knowledge about getting here ("throwness"), and, on the other side, our impending death, that existence gains specificity and we reckon with "factical possibilities of existing" from among "the endless multiplicity of possibilities that offer themselves."[58] So, intrinsic to any impetus forward is a backward turn in which factical possibilities are disclosed in light of our existential heritage that includes the entailments of Being-thrown-into-a-world with givens. This movement is not avoided by the imagination of post-mortem existence because we can never know if there is actually a way across the boundary line of death until we get there. Therefore, it is as human beings resolutely embrace the fundamental tension at the heart of our lives in the present and, in light of this, pursue meaningful possibilities for authentic existence that the power of finite freedom is realized.[59]

Here, then, is a glimpse of the grounding-structure of experience as such in which future, past, and present are constituent elements of authentic existence, which in its expression in human life in the world (*Da-sein*) has choice-making at its center. That the terms future, past, and present are not, at this level of analysis, referring to the mechanical linear movement of vulgar/public time, measurable in terms of instants, is made clear by Heidegger's categorization of them as "ecstases." For him, temporalizing does not signify that ecstases come in succession. "The future is not later than having been, and having been is not earlier than the Present."[60] As decision-making is pursued for the sake of authentic existence, each of these dimensions (future as anticipation, past as heritage/givens, present as decision-making) implies and is implied by the others. Thus in portraying the deep-structure of existence, which both grounds and is unfolded in the existence of particular beings, Heidegger is able to declare: "Temporality temporalizes itself as a future which makes present in the process of having been."[61] This is why, in the final analysis, Being (the deep-structure and power of existence manifested in the life of actual beings) with its multifaceted dynamics, is at root *Time*[62] in its most fundamental meaning. As such, anything that can be said to-be is necessarily temporal, and we come to know a human be-ing (as she/he discloses Being) in her/his ongoing decision-making in light of the anticipated future, the heritage carried as decisions are being made, and how she/he handles this legacy in light of the anticipated future.

Here it must be acknowledged that each human as Being-in-the-world must necessarily work out her/his potentialities in relation to other existents. As such, Being-in-the-world is also Being-with-others.[63] And, as the dynamics of actual human life (*Da-sein)* unfold, the deep-structure of existence that constitutes the power of our particular being (*Dasein*) is revealed as "Being-alongside-beings-encountered-in-the-world."[64]

Hopefully it has been made clear that it is in the context of very human activities associated with "being there" (*Da-sein*) as Being-in-the-world that *Dasein*, as the deep-structure and power of existence, becomes visible, and the character of primal temporality is discerned. At the same time, our regular involvement with what is present-at-hand or ready-to-hand,[65] in the course of pursuing tasks for the sake of desired ends, easily results in a superficial understanding of time that obscures the underlying dynamics of primal temporality. There emerges a preoccupation with vulgar/public time with its measurements, which, by negation, informs the understanding of what God's eternity means.[66]

## TIME, CARE, AND GOD

A decisive step toward a corrective is enabled by Heidegger's use of the term "Care"[67] in relation to the concept of primordial time to characterize the disposition associated with the human being as Being-in-the-world. This term Care is linked to the German verb *sorgen*, which in its negative expression refers to "being worried about," and in its positive expression refers to "taking care of."[68] Along with other factors, the stubborn facts of "throwness" and "death," along with the anxiety they produce, make the negative expression unavoidable as human beings wrestle with their existence, and this affects every attempt at "taking care of." It is with both senses of the word in mind that Heidegger claims that "the totality of Being-in-the-world as a structural whole has revealed itself as care."[69] Characterized by Ogden, Care as the central feature of human life is expressed in the fact that the human being's relation to her world "is not primarily the disinterested registration of bare data in consciousness, but an active participation in others of an essentially practical and emotional kind."[70] "And it is just this care, this real affective relation to others that constitutes the existentiality or essential structure of human existence."[71] Indeed, it is the human being occupied with the world of her Care and taking time with it, that is the primary and genuine mode in which Time is experienced. The concrete relation of Care to both primordial time, on one hand, and vulgar time, on the other hand, can be easily detected in the following declaration from the text *Existence and Being*:

> All planning, taking of precautions, preventing or calculating of Dasein in its care, says, audibly or inaudibly: "then" this is to be done, "before" that work has to be finished; "now" this has to be tried once more; after I have failed in it "at that time." In the "then" the Care speaks in "anticipation," relating to the future; in the "now" in the mode of "rendering present"; in the "at that time" in the mode of "bearing in mind," relating to the past. The horizon of these three modes of everyday Care is the "later" . . . the "today" . . . and the "earlier."[72]

This declaration reinforces what has been emerging with clarity in our discussion, that the most meaningful framework that should inform theological considerations of time (and by consequence, eternity) is that having to do with decision-making regarding how Care is to be structured and pursued for the sake of authentic existence for self and others. As such, the understanding of "the present" that is most existentially and theologically meaningful is not as "an instant" among "a succession of instants," but as decision-making and action that gives to "a moment" the fullest significance,[73] in that it expresses and enables Care in the deepest, most comprehensive ways possible.

Ogden's representation of Heidegger on this matter helps to clarify the connection between personal selfhood, time as Care, and finite freedom. He indicates that "precisely as Care, human existence has a relation not only to the being of others, but also to itself: to its past through memory, and, even more important, to its own future possibilities by anticipation." This dynamic relation between anticipated future and inherited past with contemporary processes enables the phenomenal world to have significance for us.[74] "Hence, when the present is understood in its primal meaning, it is the decisive 'moment' (*Audugenblick*) in which our experience itself occurs and is constituted."[75] It extends into both future and past and unifies them, fashioning life into a significant whole which is understood and evaluated in terms of what is seen as the central human concern, Care.

With Care understood to be the governing principle of temporality, public or vulgar time is significant only in service of primordial time; that is, as a mechanism for facilitating the effective organization of the decisions and processes that express Care. However, it is in this very process that primordial time is overshadowed by "the 'within-timeness' in which we order the objects of our ordinary external perception"[76] and which is characterized by instants in ordered succession. Without doubt, that which Heidegger calls "datability" is implied by considerations necessarily associated with concrete expressions of Care. Among the examples that dramatize this point is Heidegger's indication that "every 'then,' however, is, as such, a 'then, when . . .'; every 'on that former occasion' is an 'on that former occasion, when . . .'; every 'now' is a 'now that.'" Datability, he asserts, represents "a seemingly obvious relational structure . . . that links . . . the 'now, the 'then,' and the 'on that former occasion'."[77]

I agree with Heidegger that the sun and its light as it moved through the course of a day would have been the first, most natural measure and "dating" of time, around which the activities of a wide range of persons could be organized and coordinated. This public-common-vulgar time would have gained significance and become "clock time," and constant attempts made to refine its measurements to support ever more complex and precise ordering of events and collaboration between people in diverse places.[78] At the same time, it is not difficult to see how preoccupation with more precise calculations in terms of an ongoing multitude of "nows," or "instants" would cause us to forget that this endeavor should serve a greater purpose. This greater purpose, manifested concretely as Care, is primordial time that itself is *Dasein* in the processes of its dynamic self-realization as authentic existence.

## God as Infinitely Temporal

Given the reframing of the concept of time, I now proceed to God-talk that privileges temporality and defines eternity as a form of temporality. Important to this perspective is the recognition that if the God of Christianity is to be seen as personal in any way, especially as the being referred to in the Bible and presupposed by worship and prayer, this God cannot be the antithesis of primordial time expressed in Care for the sake of authentic existence. Instead of antithesis it is analogy that is central to constructing what it means to say this personal God is also infinite and eternal. Those who are inclined to suggest that proceeding by analogy (even *eminentia*) threatens the majesty of God would do well to consider Ogden's claim that the path which involves "the absolute negation of a basic concept with reference to God is more or less ambiguous" and troubling. As he suggests, even when antithesis is emphasized analogy cannot be avoided whenever God is "conceived as having will or purpose and still other perfections that imply temporal distinctions." The continued inclination toward antithesis in some quarters ensures that those who engage in "analogical speaking" must then recoil and empty their declarations "of meaning by the non-analogical denial that the being of God is in any sense temporal."[79] This, I suggest, will be the case, even if, like Pinnock does, it is claimed that God has chosen to operate temporally.

This inclination, Ogden suggests, is even evident in those who allow for the predication of relational concepts to God and rightly insist that these concepts should be understood analogically instead of literally. While not denying the appropriateness of such a stance, Ogden echoes claims already made in this text as he astutely points out that "on conventional metaphysical premises, to say that God is not literally related to the world could only mean that God is literally not related to it; and so the classical *analogia entis*, like traditional theism in general, has been continually caught up in incoherence and self-contradiction."[80] Many traditionalists will probably balk at the view that the being of God should be constructed in terms of the primal temporality Heidegger describes. Nevertheless, in keeping with my resistance to traditional constructions of time and eternity, I am convinced by the position that a personal God—with "personal" understood analogously to the human person—essentially exists as Being-in-the-world.[81] This implies, at minimum, that God and the world are not separable entities such that it is possible to claim any awareness of God outside of the dynamics of life in the world or that there can be any speaking about God using terms that are not in some way reflective of world-dynamics, especially that evident in the highest expression of the personal, that is, human beings.

Considered as personal being, it is most legitimate to hold "that God, like human beings, essentially exists with real internal relations to others," and God's ongoing experiences involve a similar kind of relation to the future and the past as that reflected in our experiences as human beings.[82] For those already familiar with the terminology of Process-Relational theology (which I will say more about later) it should not be difficult to recognize the family resemblance between that just said and the notion of God's consequent nature. In fact, Ogden's language seems most compatible with Process-Relational thinker Charles Hartshorne's insistence that the other aspect of God, that is, God's primordial nature, is an abstraction from God's consequent nature. At the same time it must be said that Alfred North Whitehead, who first developed the notion of primordiality utilized by Process-Relational thinkers, understood it in a way that, in the final analysis, did not undermine temporality. Whitehead did argue that "viewed as primordial, he [God] is the unlimited conceptual realization of the absolute wealth of potentiality." But having said this, he proceeded to indicate that it is also the case that, "as primordial, so far is he [God] from 'eminent reality' that in this abstraction he [God] is 'deficiently actual.'"[83] For Whitehead then, as it is for Ogden (supported by Heidegger's analysis), God can only be understood as fully actual when considered in relation to other actualities by means of God's consequent nature that is subject to the conditions that govern temporal becoming. And I assert that the most plausible account of temporality has to be that which effectively points us to the structure of human experience itself, as Heidegger's explication does.

In preparing for direct consideration of the means by which we best develop a concept of eternity in light of our understanding of temporality, it is important to point to Ogden's reminder that Heidegger, and others who take analogy seriously recognizes that it "implies a difference as well as a similarity between the analogues it serves to relate." As such, when constructed analogically, "God's essential structure is not only the same as [that of human beings] but also, in some significant respect, different from it."[84]

With the recognition that analogy involves both similarity and difference, I embrace the view that God must be understood as essentially related to a world of others in whose being God actively and creatively participates by reason of a similar basic structure of Care. This is in contrast to a structure that privileges perfection, timelessness, and sovereignty. At the same time "God's eternity [will] be constructed not simply as temporality, but as a temporality which is infinite." For Ogden, this position emerges as the appropriate contrast between humanity and God when it is recognized that "the distinctive thing about [human beings] is not [their] temporality but [their] 'finitude.'"[85]

Finitude has to do with the fact that the lives of human beings are characterized by certain limits. We are localized selves that are bounded by an external environment, which includes a world that is a limited space, and we are encompassed by what we ourselves are not.[86] This means that the life of a human being is "confined to some specific range of possibilities inherited from his finite past and projected into his finite future." Indeed, our "relatedness to others is itself relative." We do "not participate in them fully as they are in themselves," but we are "in principle required to encounter them under the perspective imposed" by our "own particular projects of self-understanding."[87] Beneath these features is our "throwness," as Heidegger put it, which, in association with the classical notion of contingency, refers to the fact that we are dependent on a source beyond ourselves for our existence. Then there is the recognition that our lives in the configuration of which we are consciously aware progress toward inevitable death.[88]

By contrast, while God's being, like that of humanity, is Being-in-the-world,[89] God's relatedness to others is radically unlike humanity's in being itself not merely relative, but wholly absolute. What "absolute" means here is radically different from its meaning among Scholastics and also from their thought as utilized by Arminius and others. While the world which includes human beings is genuinely other to God, God is recognized as present at the very heart of cosmic life in the most intimate way possible for one being to be present to others and related to the whole universe of non-divine entities (human and non-human). And God's relation with each and all "is unsurpassably immediate and direct." In the final analysis, it means that God "being related to all others is itself relative to nothing, but is the absolute ground of any and all real relationships."[90]

With this explication as background, I am able to associate Heidegger's concept of Care directly with Pinnock's talk of God's love for humanity,

Williamson's claim that the world matters to God, and Ward's indication that the world is the product of God's imaginative creativity. All these dispositions entail risk-taking as God Cares for the cosmos through ongoing creative involvement in its life in every dimension and sphere, but given that which characterizes God's infinity God can experience a vast range of emotions, in action or reaction, without being overcome by the negative expression of Care, that is, "being worried about."

I close this section with the acknowledgment that, despite the differences between the relatedness of God and human relatedness just enumerated, it might still be suggested by orthodox thinkers that the reason Ogden finds it necessary for the notion of God as "Care" to be linked to the notion of God as "Being-in-the-world" is because he does not take seriously enough the traditional Christian doctrine of Trinity that characterizes a God who in God's own being exercises care in the context of the dynamic immanent relationship between Father, Son, and Spirit. This Trinitarian character enables God to be in a caring relationship independent of the world. As such, it reinforces the position that the world characterized by temporality and finitude is in no way necessary to who God is. While I have no intention in this project to engage in in-depth scrutiny of the Trinity, I will remind proponents of this position that the only legitimate route we have to the immanent Trinity is the so-called economic Trinity; that is, the only way we have insight into the immanent Trinity is through human discernments of God's self-expression in the world. There is nothing in these discernments themselves that requires, necessarily, that a God who is Trinity operated priorly in an eternity that is both infinite and non-temporal. Such a claim is, instead, based on non-necessary cosmological and soteriological commitments that derive from the susceptibility of Christians, like all other human beings, to the negative expression of Care, that is, "bring worried about." For my own purposes, I find quite instructive Paul Tillich's view that Trinitarian monotheism is not a matter of the number three. It is, he suggests, "a qualitative and not quantitative characterization of God"; that is, it is "an attempt to speak of the living God in whom the ultimate and the concrete are united."[91] This position corresponds quite well with my proposal, in the context of my short exploration of *creatio ex nihilo,* of a God whose essential creativity links God's existence to the existence of actualities beyond Godself. And if the arguments associated with this proposal are plausible, this could not be denied even if a detractor persisted in a commitment to the position that God is immanently Trinity.

## So What Does God Know?

The characterization of eternity as infinite temporality, and the understanding that the infinite-temporal God as Being-in-the-world, means that whatever might be one's position on the emergence of the world (if one thinks it emerged at all, and not just *is*), we can conceive of God, in important respects, growing with the world and learning from the world, even as God contributes to the world. Concerning what God knows, it is God's complete openness as conditioned by infinite Care that informs God's connection to the future of each and all human beings. And God's eminent relatedness to all will be that to which absoluteness refers. Here I remind the reader that among the "all," which is our primary interest, is the human born of man and woman within the context of logical and metaphysical limitations, and who operates in ambiguity as she explores, struggles, makes disastrous mistakes, deliberately makes repugnant choices, surprises herself, and also transcends self in surprising and magnificent ways. I suggest, then, that discussion of what God knows begins with logical and metaphysically necessary states of affairs; for example, given the law of gravity, certain "facts" are unavoidable as human beings operate within the world. God, however, as temporal will not have the exact details of choices in any situation before they are made. At the same time, being infinite and completely open to the full range of actualities and possibilities suggests that at any moment in the life of a human being, God will be aware of not only the process that led to that place, but the relation of that particular process to the processes pertinent to the present state of all other human beings, and even other actualities in the cosmos. More importantly, God will have awareness of all the possible consequences that flow from each decision in relation to the decisions of all other entities. And, given God's awareness of all past and present decisions in their relation to each and every other decision, God can even be said to have awareness of the path of decision-making each human will most probably move toward, and be aware of the range of possible options that will be open to the individual, in the order of likely relevance and/or appeal.

Being the God of Care, God will have "ideals" for each human in each and every moment of life that God will seek to lure the human toward. This cannot be overlooked. However, bearing in mind the complex of possibilities relevant to any particular moment of choice and the basic ambiguity that comes with being born of man and woman, God's ideal will not necessarily be the most vivid or compelling, and God will not know exactly what each particular human will finally choose at any moment of decision-making. All this means that, while God can never be completely surprised by any decision taken or be unprepared for the range of consequences that follow from such decision, both Calvin's predestinationism and Arminius's exhaustive-infallible knowledge/foreknowledge are ruled out. What becomes more significant is God's ongoing relation to the complex contours of each and every life and the adventurous-painful-hopeful life of engagement as God seeks to have each human do that which is best for self in relation to that which is best for all other creatures, given the vast and intricate web of interconnection in which human beings struggle for discernment and understanding. Along with this scenario is the picture of a God who, in interaction with human beings, is always fascinated to see what will emerge as the novel outgrowth from decision-making processes.

I imagine that for some people it is a quite frightening prospect that the God being portrayed is not the all-powerful being of traditional formulations. Along with the many threatening situations with which one can be faced, the very fact of being one individual in a vast universe can be most overwhelming. Heidegger stated well the significance of human finitude. And this is reminiscent of my earlier mention of expressions from Tillich who, in explicating the position that self-consciousness is tied to world-consciousness, pointed out that even though human beings are, on one hand, "the perspective-center" of the cosmos, we are, on the other hand, "an infinitely small part" of it.[92] There is no question that great comfort and inspiration can result from the conviction that ultimate control is in the hands of one who is not subject to the contingencies of cosmic existence, especially when there is the conviction that the controlling being is on one's side. At the same time, there needs to be the acknowledgment that, as far as we are usually aware, human effort has been central to accomplishments that have made global existence somewhat more tolerable over the centuries, however we explain it. The multitudes that have not had available to them adequate resources from the temporal-finite sphere have usually not had their lives bettered in any obvious way by direct and obvious interventions from an eternal realm.

It seems to me, then, that it is an expression of freedom when one is able to finally acknowledge that we really do not know the extent of influence that a sovereign God has in human affairs, directly or indirectly. On the other hand, there needs to be greater sense of obligation to utilize the faculties we have, which include the ability to struggle for understanding, to assess life's situations on the basis of values that are designed to ensure the most viable-wholesome-authentic existence for self and others. And we need to be committed to actions designed to facilitate the realization of this state of affairs. In so doing, we will be spared the frustration of waiting on an all-powerful and all-knowing God that operates by standards beyond our capacity to assess, to supernaturally execute dramatic changes in our lives. We will also be saved from the inclination to overestimate what we are capable of achieving with God on our side. When we become arrogant and oppressive in our exercise of freedom, it will not be as easy as it seems to be in some cases, to declare that we have been made capable of acting thus because we are doing God's will.

# FURTHER REFINEMENT OF FREEDOM-ORIENTED GOD-TALK

## Gordon Kaufman and Creativity

After all that has been said to reorient the understanding of God's relation to time and the implications for foreknowledge and predestination, there are those who might still insist that Ogden employed an inadequate understanding of analogy in developing his conception of a temporal infinite God. Like Gordon Kaufman they might claim that "correctly understood . . . the theory of analogy does not so much affirm the adequacy of positive affirmations as the imperfection of all language about God."[93] They will support Kaufman's embrace of Thomas Aquinas's distinction between an analogy of attribution and an analogy of proportionality as more appropriate than the simple claim that analogy implies difference as well as similarity between the analogues it serves to relate. "An analogy of attribution is based on the similarity between cause and effect. . . . An analogy of proportionality . . . points only to a proportion between two elements in realities that are to be sharply contrasted with each other." This underscores "dissimilarity rather than similarity."[94] We are told that it is the latter that properly applies when finite human beings attempt to contemplate and speak about an infinite God. This, however, would probably be the last point of commonality between Kaufman and defenders of Christian orthodoxy, because he is not about defining God by means of qualities that are the antithesis of qualities that suggest temporality and finitude.

Pushing beyond leads from Christian thinkers like Gregory of Nyssa, Pseudo-Dionysius, and Meister Eckhart, Kaufman aligns himself with Immanuel Kant's position that there is really no way to theoretically demonstrate the existence of God, because the human mind simply does not have the ability to go beyond our experience in the world so that there can be cognitive engagement of the absolutely necessary being of classical Christian thought.[95] One recalls that, for Kant, an analysis of ordinary cognition required the differentiation between the world *an sich* (as it is in itself), or the *noumenal* world, unperceived by anyone, and the world as it appears to us phenomenally, as it is perceived by us. Here it needs to be recognized that *noumenal* was not used in the positive sense of that which is knowable by some "nonsensible intuition," because human beings have no such faculty. Instead, it was used in the negative sense "of a thing in so far as it is not the object of sensible intuition."[96] If this is the extent of human limitation within the cosmic sphere, it should not be difficult for the reader to appreciate the implication for cognitive awareness of the being who has been claimed to be, in essence, beyond the finite sphere. It makes senses then, that Kaufman, having embraced this insight, would support Ogden's view that the attempt by traditional Christians to embrace *via negativa* while attributing personal qualities to God ends up contributing to incoherence and self-contradiction.

Kaufman is as effective in demonstrating the implications of a rigorous employment of *via negativa* as Ogden is in demonstrating the implications of analogy for a concept of God. Kaufman acknowledges that the radicalization of negative theology, which results from the positions of more recent thinkers like Emmanuel Levinas and Jacques Derrida, would lead to "utter speechlessness" in matters concerning God.[97] He justifies his continued speaking with the claim that it is only by "speaking about God and through speaking in critique of all such speaking—that we may be led to this conclusion."[98] More importantly, he emphasizes the continued symbolic power of the concept God in Western life. Even if our sensible intuition does not reach beyond the world of phenomena, by means of the name "God" we do posit "an ultimate point of reference in terms of which all realities must be understood, and its claim, therefore, that all aspects of human life (not only religious and moral practices and experiences) should be oriented in terms of this reference point." "God" being the ultimate point of reference "relativizes all human practices, ideologies, and institutions, calling them into question critically—while demanding their transformation in more humanizing and humane directions."[99] Kaufman's intention is, therefore, not to locate God as a Being (who may or may not foreknow and/or predestine), as that is impossible. Instead, it is to find the most appropriate ways to represent the symbolic power of the concept of God for the contemporary era—this having direct implications for how human beings are understood.

Kaufman points us away from any framework in which foreknowledge and/or foreordination might apply by indicating that in the contemporary era the most powerful insight emerging from human experience is that we do not operate under the governance of "a kind of cosmic person standing outside the world, manipulating it from without."[100] Instead we operate within the dynamics of an autonomous nature characterized by "serendipitous creativity" manifested through the evolutionary process. Tellingly, he indicates that this process has produced human beings "with self-consciousness, with great imaginative powers and creativity, with freedom and responsible agency."[101] This is a portrayal of human beings even more on their own and operating with finite-freedom than has been provided by any other Christian thinker considered in this work. It renders moot the discussion on foreknowledge and foreordination, and it magnifies the significance of the recommendations I made, following from my discussion of Ogden's position on how human beings should operate in light of the recognition that God is infinitely temporal. As far as Kaufman is concerned, human action and decision-making ought to be carried out in light of a number of factors. "God," if anything, is "the creativity manifested throughout the universe," and "the creativity manifest in the world now becomes the only appropriate focus for devotion and worship, that which alone can provide overall orientation for our lives."[102] Further, while there is much that is mysterious about the creative process that has caused the "biohistorical beings" called human to emerge "on one of the countless creative trajectories moving through the cosmos," there is awareness that creativity "evidences itself in part through our own creative powers."[103] While we are ignorant of the direction the evolutionary/historical trajectory will move in the future, what it will be is in process as determined in part by human decision-making and action. Thus, whatever future there is, it is contingent on that which is in process, and there is no one external to the process exercising coercive influence on that which is emerging, much more to have certain knowledge of what it will be and where human beings will stand.

Those who take *via negativa* seriously but have difficulty going as far as Kaufman does, might wish to consider a modification I proposed in a previous text. There I suggested that Christians who require a personal God as the foundation of the religious life might have to operate with the acknowledgement that, given our cognitive limitation as finite human beings, we cannot know the degree to which claims we make about God actually correspond to what God is *in se*. In relation to this, I recommended an attitude consistent with Indian Hindu thinker P. B. Vidyarthi's articulation of Sri Ramanujah's philosophy in which he suggests that "there is such a thing as healthy agnosticism."[104] I also identified with distinguished Quaker thinker David Trueblood, who speaks about a "modest and defensible agnosticism that arises from epistemological humility, exercised by 'one who admits that he does not know, and is consequently open to learning.'" Echoing Vidyarthi, Trueblood suggests that this humble person "is genuinely willing to sit down before the fact 'as a little child.'" And he proceeds to suggest that it is even possible, when this line is followed faithfully, to develop what may be truly called a "reverent agnosticism."[105]

## Process-Relational Ideas—Important Insights on God as Actual, Relational, Creative, and Freedom-Enabling

It is with an attitude akin to reverent agnosticism that I present my own view that it is the Process-Relational orientation that facilitates the best combination of ideas from Ogden's and Kaufman's efforts so that the idea of God as an actual entity is maintained, creativity is appropriately privileged, and the finite, realistically libertarian, and relational freedom that human beings have is properly acknowledged and nurtured. Indeed, both men develop their theology in conversation with Process-Relational ideas, and the former is claimed by Process thinkers as a strong ally. Ogden's critical evaluations of traditional God-talk that leads to the conclusion that it "has been continually caught up in incoherence and self-contradiction"[106] is in accord with that of

Process-Relational thinkers of which I am aware. He actually echoes the declaration of Charles Hartshorne that the traditional framework of consideration represents metaphysical false modesty and is illogical and arbitrary. Hartshorne asserts that if the negative theologian is really thinking, she/he must be doing something more than merely refusing to apply human concepts to deity. That theologian must actually be applying human, albeit negative, conceptions. This person is actually asserting that whatever human qualities like "dependence," "potentiality," and "change," may refer to, there is none of it in deity. He declares: "How can he know this unless he understands something positive in deity which is incompatible with such categories?"[107]

Process-Relational theologians pursue analogical thinking in a way more consistent with Heidegger and Ogden than with Kaufman. This is not due primarily to the fact that, while supporting the latter's epistemic position at the level of presentational immediacy, they hold that there is a deeper level of perception in the mode of causal efficacy which is prior to that associated with presentational immediacy. It seems more so because they recognize, on one hand, that to persist in *via negativa* in a way that avoids the incoherence and self-contradiction to which Ogden and Hartshorne point leads inevitably to the place of "utter speechlessness" Kaufman sees as the outcome of the contemporary radicalization of negative theology. This place is unacceptable to Process-Relational theologians, not merely because, as Kaufman suggests, the name "God" continues to have significant symbolic power in Western culture—an approach which leads to the identification of God with creativity. Long before Kaufman privileged creativity, it was one of the foundational metaphysical pillars of Process thought. Alfred North Whitehead actually declared creativity to be "the fundamental energy driving existence," which "is descriptive of the most fundamental relationships participated in by all actualities." As such, creativity "expresses the ultimate fact about actual occasions," and, as such, is "the universal of universals."[108] At the same time, there is Whitehead's ontological principle, which characterizes his conclusion that every condition to which a process of becoming conforms, in any particular instance, must have its ultimate explanation in an actual entity.[109]

The actual entities that make up the world are always involved in creative becoming and/or contributing to the becoming and actualization of other actual entities, with one of these trajectories of becoming producing the human being, described by Kaufman as self-conscious, imaginative and creative, free, and having responsible agency.[110] However, as implied in my earlier discussion of finitude, these entities cannot settle for themselves the logical or cosmological relations to which they must conform for these dynamics to occur. If these logical or cosmological relations are not in place, there is no basis for the creative relationships actual entities have with the past, apart from which they would not emerge in the first place as particular kinds of entities. In his speculative system, Whitehead used the Platonic-like notion of "eternal objects" to represent that which informs the bare structure of logical orders and qualities that are foundational to actual entities in the world. But he was clear that, being prior to any particular actualization, eternal objects constitute pure potentialities. Pure potentialities cannot be seen as existing on their own or as possessing the power of agency.[111] And while creativity is presupposed by any action in which something happens, merely qualifying creativity with "serendipitous" cannot address the issue of what it is that could have brought together creativity and possibility so that there emerged a cosmos, that is, an apparently intelligible framework composed of complex, finely-tuned, and inter-related entities. Among these entities are human beings which, along with Kaufman's characterization, are entities with self-awareness, aesthetic, moral and religious sensibilities, and who have the capacity for self-transcendence. Here it should be noted that, having wrestled with notions like "substantial activity" and "principle of concretion," Whitehead concluded that the function of providing limitation to ensure order and value to give creativity direction can be assigned only to an actual entity—this entity Whitehead called God.[112]

Already going beyond what Kaufman thinks is legitimate by promoting the notion of God as an actual entity, Process-Relational theologians, as theologians, also recognize that the discipline of theology, by definition, requires that the theologian not settle with just basic statements about God such as those just attributed to Whitehead. The theologian must provide explications that are as in-depth as possible to provide guidance for thinking, worshiping, praying, and living authentically in the world (i.e., Christian beliefs that contribute to humane existence). This responsibility must be carried out in a manner that, as far as possible, avoids the incoherence and self-contradiction identified by Ogden. This being so, Process-Relational theologians operate in a way compatible with that of Heidegger, taking our awareness of our own experience as subjects to be the basis for our fundamental God-concepts. This is captured well by Ogden's representation of Whitehead's Reformed Subjectivist Principle, which suggests that we can give an adequate answer to the metaphysical question of the meaning of reality only by imaginatively generalizing elements disclosed in the analysis of experiences of subjects.[113] As we have already glimpsed, this leads to a distinctly different metaphysics from that which was oriented away from the primal phenomenon of selfhood toward the secondary phenomenon of the world constituted by the experience of our senses.

As Ogden already suggested, we know ourselves most immediately as an ever-changing sequence of occasions of experience. And, whereas the focus on external objects led to the imagination that the most fundamental characteristics of actualities were fixed substances or essences, the analysis of the human subject leads to the understanding that, rather than being fixed independent substances, the very being of the self is relational or social. Indeed, it is nothing if not a process of change, involving the distinct modes of present, past, and future.[114] Whitehead's claim that, as a process, an entity "is not describable in terms of the morphology of a 'stuff'"[115] is crucial in appreciating what this insight means for human freedom. The finite, realistically libertarian, and relational nature of this freedom is evidenced in the indication that to be alive, that is, to be in process, has to do with the ongoing address of proposals for diverse modes of "personal" existence—this necessarily having implications for all other existents. And the non-negotiable status of this freedom is evident in Whitehead's reminder that "'decision' cannot be construed as a casual adjunct of an actual entity. It constitutes the very meaning of actuality." Indeed, an actual entity arises from decisions from among relevant possibilities, and by its very existence it contributes to decisions for other actual entities which supersede it.[116] This is reinforced by the later suggestion that "the real constitution of an actual entity progressively constitutes a decision conditioning the creativity which transcends that actuality."[117]

The profundity of the analogical disposition is appreciated as we face the claim that, like other actualities, God, the relational being, is necessarily characterized by process and ongoing interaction with a cosmos of actualities. This interaction involves not only the provision of ideal aims about which these actualities take decisions. It also involves God receiving (prehending), evaluating, and even transmuting the outcomes from human decisions and taking new decisions regarding that which becomes ideal in the new circumstance fashioned by prior decisions. Further insight into what this crucial dynamic teaches us about freedom is added with Whitehead's reflection on the creative synthesis of influences that is associated with decision-making—this captured by his famous aphorism: "the many become one, and are increased by one."[118] This aphorism supports the important claim made elsewhere in this project that every decision-making process, with its outcomes, involves "novelty," being a consequence for self and others that could never occur except for the specific elements being engaged together, the internal and external context in which this is taking place, and the very process of decision-making itself. As such, the outcome can never be fully anticipated on the basis of any prior awareness of contributing elements, contexts, or the person taking the decision.

The ideas being discussed point us away from an understanding of perfection in terms of independence—not needing/being dependent on anything beyond self. This understanding certainly made sense in frameworks governed by substance metaphysics.[119] One also appreciates why, in ancient societies characterized by hierarchical social structures with slaves or serfs at the bottom, independence expressed as sovereignal freedom would be highly prized. Therefore, it is not surprising that it was being privileged in the concept of a simple, immutable, impassible God with no potentiality.

In his opposition to these dispositions, Charles Hartshorne's stance reflects new insights into the structure of existence that is evident in a number of disciplines. He is quite explicit that the idea that total independence is admirable has no foundation in experience and suggests that, since we do not admire this in other human beings, why should this be admired in God? In our experience, sometimes independence is admirable and sometimes dependence is more admirable. His view is that the traditional analysis of God's power in terms of one way causation constitutes the idealization of the tyrant-subject model of relationship.[120] In contrast, Hartshorne recommends that we consider a religious meaning of perfection which designates worshipfulness as the ideal. He suggests that what is deducible from this is a being that is all surpassing and all inclusive. This means that in order to be worthy of worship, God must be unsurpassed by another and exalted beyond all possible rivals—this constituting the difference between absolutely unsurpassed, which was the intent of the traditional understanding, and unsurpassed except by God's self. God's perfection, therefore, would not be assessed in terms of reaching a limited maximum but in seeking unlimited progress—this progress contributed to by the ongoing decision-making that is a necessary part of the human dynamic. The perfect God would then be "'the self-surpassing surpasser of all.'"[121]

While this characteristic constitutes the categorically unique status of God such that God is guaranteed superiority to absolutely every other individual that comes into existence,[122] its actual outworking is, in part, dependent of the novel outcomes from finitely free human beings who are continuously involved in decision-making. So, while God cannot fail to be, or to be God in whatever circumstance (immutability), God is affected by and vulnerable to events in nature and history. While God's supremacy is never questioned, it is understood in a relational framework.

In this framework, informed by the shift from the metaphysics of substance to that of process, relativity is privileged. This principle purports that "to be is to be potential for every becoming"[123] —this helping to explain both the claim that God and other actualities influence each other and that the ongoing process of decision-making involves creative synthesis which produces novelty. Together these ground the conviction that all relations are internal relations—referring to the "fact" that entities everywhere are always taking into themselves (prehending) the products from creative syntheses that have occurred elsewhere, especially those which are more contiguous. This position must be held in tandem with the recognition that creative synthesis is a process that each entity carries out for its own becoming—this constituting the entity's internal life. However, it is in the nature of things (stubborn fact) that, at the most elemental level, individual becoming necessarily begins with external contributions (which are pretended), and leads inevitably to concrescence in which a fully developed entity, as a superjection, contributes to the becoming of another.

In more complex organisms like human beings, the vast network of prehensions-concrescences-superjections in a person's internal life is linked to an array of intentional interactions and unavoidable affects that are integrated to influence personal development and the development of others.[124] In this framework, God the supremely relational being always seeks to influence human decision-making through the offering of ideal aims. These aims constitute a lure for the best actualization of a self in a particular circumstance (characterized by the processes and outcomes of internal and external dynamics) in relation to God's ideals for other lives, and the cosmos as a whole.

Thomas Oord's engagement with Pinnock on the issue of coercion is relevant at this point. He reminds us of the centrality of love in Pinnock's theology. Indeed, Pinnock claims that "love and not sheer power overcomes evil.'"[125] However, Oord also points us to Pinnock's view that God has the freedom to and does act coercively, and he suggests that Pinnock is inconsistent on this issue. He asserts: "If love does not command, does not overpower, does not force, does not compel, and does not override, this means that God does not love when God *does* command, *does* overpower, *does* force, *does* compel, and *does* override." Pinnock, he says, "cannot have it both ways."[126] The primary concern driving Oord's critique is that if God has the capacity Pinnock claims then God has the capacity to overcome evil.[127] Indeed, he points to Pinnock's enthusiastic claim that spirit-filled believers have the confidence "'in the power of God to deliver us from evil here and now,'" and this deliverance sometimes requires coercive power. Oord's immediate response is that "the God that Pinnock envisions has the power to prevent genuine evil and yet fails to do so."[128]

I have much sympathy for Oord's concerns, and I am reminded of Charles Hartshorne's claim that, while "we cannot simply not respond" to the beauty of God's ideal, "our response has to be partly self-determined and it has to be influenced by past creaturely responses in our universe." Persuasion, he declares, "is the ultimate power; not even God can simply coerce."[129] It also means that, whatever is God's intention in a particular situation, God's lure will take on its own novel character as a result of being given and received in relation to the impact of all other influences. I say this with the reminder that all these interactions take place within the general epistemic ambiguity that characterizes the life of finite human beings. It must also be recognized that although God, like other entities, relates internally, God *qua* God is still Other. God is Other in the unique ways that makes God God rather than anything else no matter how intimate God is to the life processes of that which is not God.[130]

What I promote as rationally grounded, consistent with the Scriptures, and supportive of the integrity of human freedom, is a Caring and imaginatively creative God that, given her character, has always been creative. While my proposal acknowledges the categorical distinction between that which is creator and that which is creature, there is the insistence that the notion "God" is inextricable from the notion "world" (of some kind). With the movement from a metaphysic of substance to that of process, any relation between God and a world will be internal on both sides. Equally important is that the creativity that is at the heart of God's character, which is the ultimate principle accountable for God's self-expression (this being true whether God is good and loving or not) and the existence of a world, is equally at the heart of the world's processes. These features point to nothing less than a dynamic relationship between creator and creature, especially the human being that has emerged from a complex evolutionary process with the highest level of subjectivity and volitional ability—exercised in the midst of others whose exercise of similar qualities necessarily affect both process and outcomes. It is in the midst of all this that God seeks to influence the creature in light of God's desire for them.

Whatever else God's pursuit of influence might involve, it includes facilitating the human ability to develop our creativity in ways that are maximally beneficial for self and others. So, rather than being a God who dominates existence or who strategically limits self to get what is desired, God is initiator of a creative enterprise that necessarily involves multiple kinds of self-expression by global actualities. And human beings are free enough to pursue the richest possible combination of values associated with being human beings among other beings—this done within the context of a complex and multidimensional communality. In the ongoing creative process, God can be considered the dominant partner and chief enabler of human beings in the cosmic project that is always on the look-out for that which might result from the fascinating dynamics that characterize human life in relation to the lives of other species. This is a radically different God from one who is a controlling sovereign that must organize everything to guarantee the preferred outcomes.

It strikes me that this portrayal is one means of engaging David Hume's characterization of God in his *Dialogues Concerning Natural Religion* as possibly inept and stupid, and who only brought the world into being after many failed starts.[131] Now, one can imagine numerous cosmic processes, even multiple worlds coming in and out of existence, and classify these not as false starts but attribute them to novel combinations of influences and decisions that are in play at any point. That the outcomes are oftentimes negative is attributable, in some degree, to the risk that is intrinsic to every creative process—this having implications for the ways we address natural evil. It is also the case that given creativity, complexity, and the ambiguity associated with finitude, even the best intentioned and well-constructed processes can lead to bad decisions and great human disasters (moral evil). The outcomes from good decisions by multiple persons expressing finite, realistically libertarian, and relational freedom in a healthy way may well conflict in significant ways, resulting in disastrous consequences. This may be called evil as unintended consequence. Then there are the moral evils that are attributable to the fact that human beings have not come to appreciate appropriately the place we hold in the world and the degree to which the fortunes of the world are linked to the decisions we make. In light of this scenario, an important challenge for human beings is to become more aware of the dynamics of life in general, and to be more committed to pursue expressions of freedom that minimizes negative outcomes and maximizes positive outcomes for one's own sakes and for the sake of others.

With this background I will, in chapter 7, explore aspects of the struggle to pursue freedom in concrete situations, especially libertarian freedom as it is dominantly exercised in the general framework of Western culture.


## NOTES

1. Pinnock asserts that "God is capable of acting unilaterally" and is convinced that, however many the disappointments God experiences because of human freedom, God will achieve God's ultimate purpose "a new creation." See Clark Pinnock, *Most Moved Mover: A Theology of God's Openness* (Grand Rapids, MI: Baker Academic, Baker Book House Co., 2001), 52.

2. Augustine of Hippo, *Confessions*, trans. R.S, Pine-Coffin (London: Penguin Books, 1961), [11.1], 253.

3. Ibid., [11.10], 261.

4. Ibid.

5. Ibid., [11.11], 261-262.

6. Ibid., [11.13], 263.

7. Ibid. As Augustine puts it: "I know what it is, provided that nobody asks me; but if I am asked what it is and try to explain, I am baffled." [11.14], 263.

8. Ibid., [11.15], 266.

9. Ibid., [11.11], 261.

10. Schubert Ogden, *The Reality of God and Other Essays* (San Francisco: Harper and Row Publishers, 1977), 152.

11. Augustine, *Confessions*, [11.4], 256.

12. Ibid., [11.14], 264.

13. Ibid., [11.15, 16], 266.

14. Ibid., [11.27], 275.

15. Ibid., [11.26, 27], 275-276.

16. Ibid., [11.27, 28], 276-278.

17. Ibid., [11.19], 268.

18. Schubert Ogden, *The Reality of God*, 152.

19. Delwin Brown, *To Set at Liberty: Christian Faith and Human Freedom* (Maryknoll, NY: Orbis Books, 1981), 46.

20. Pinnock, *Most Moved Mover*, 97.

21. Ibid., 32, 33.

22. Ibid., 96.

23. Thomas J. Oord, *The Nature of Love: A Theology* (St. Louis, MO: Chalice Press, 2010), 91. Oord's reference is Clark H. Pinnock et al., *The Openness of God: A Biblical Challenge to the Traditional Understanding of God* (Downers Grove, IL: InterVarsity Press, 1994), 114.

24. Ibid., 93. Oord's reference is Clark H. Pinnock et al., *The Openness of God*, 157-158.

25. Pinnock, *Most Moved Mover*, 183.

26. Ibid., 147.

27. Ibid., 148.

28. Alexander Campbell, ed. "Response to Mr. D. A. Skeptic," in *The Christian Baptist*, vol. IV (Bethany, VA: Bethany Printing Office, 1827), 70.

29. James Arminius, "Private Disputations," in *The Writings of James Arminius*, vol. II ed. James Nichols (Grand Rapids, MI: Baker Books, 1956), 100.

30. William Lane Craig, "No Other Name," in *The Philosophical Challenge of Religious Diversity*, eds. Philip Quinn and Kevin Meeker (Oxford: Oxford University Press, 2000), 49-50.

31. As mentioned before, this term derives from the Latin *super* and *sedere* (to sit), the term refers to sitting on the seat belonging to another and thus displacing and replacing that other. One could describe the Christians of whom I speak as maintaining a "displacement and replacement" theology.

32. Keith Ward, *Divine Action* (London: Collins Publishing Group, 1990), 20.

33. Augustine, *Confessions*, [12.8], 285.

34. Clark Williamson, *Way of Blessing Way of Life: A Christian Theology* (St. Louis: Chalice Press, 1999), 136, 139.

35. Ibid.

36. Ward, *Divine Action*, 24.

37. Williamson, *Way of Blessing Way of Life*, 107.

38. Ward, *Divine Action*, 35.

39. Michael Miller, *Reshaping the Contextual Vision in Caribbean Theology: Theoretical Foundations for Theology Which is Contextual, Pluralistic, and Dialectical* (Lanham: University Press of America, 2007), 340.

40. Oord, *The Nature of Love*, 91. Oord's reference is Clark H. Pinnock et al., *The Openness of God: A Biblical Challenge to the Traditional Understanding of God*, 114.

41. This scenario in no way necessitates commitment to the strong anthropic principle popular in some circles.

42. Pinnock, *Most Moved Mover*, 32.

43. Charles Hartshorne, *The Divine Relativity: A Social Conception of God* (New Haven: Yale University Press, 1948), 30.

44. Schubert Ogden, *The Reality of God*, 145.

45. Ibid., 157.

46. Ibid., 151.

47. Martin Heidegger, *Being and Time*, trans. John Macquarrie and Edward Robinson (New York: Harper and Row Publishers, 1962), 23.

48. Ibid., 22.

49. Ibid., 26.

50. Ibid., 24.

51. Paul Tillich, *Systematic Theology*, vol. I (Chicago: University of Chicago Press, 1951), 3-4.

52. Heidegger, *Being and Time*, [note 1], 27. The term is also explicated in Martin Heidegger, *An Introduction to Metaphysics*, (New York: Anchor Books, 1961), [note], 8.

53. Heidegger, *Being and Time*, 26.

54. Ibid.78

55. Ibid., 279.

56. Ibid., 293-296.

57. Even though reckoning with death as the uttermost not-yet fuels the anxiety that is at the heart of human existence, it also signals that the structure of *Dasein* transcends the obvious limitations of finitude in the course of its historical self-realization.

58. Ibid., 434-435.

59. Ibid., 436.

60. Ibid., 401.

61. Ibid., 401.

62. I write *Time* in this way to identify it as primordial time and distinguish it from vulgar time, which is written as "time" when I use the term.

63. Ibid., 436.

64. Heidegger, *Existence and Being* (with introduction and analysis by Werner Brock) (Chicago: Henry Regnery Company, 1965), 49-50.

65. Heidegger provides elaborate explanation of these two concepts, including the distinctions between them. See *Being and Time*, 95-107. What is significant at this point is that they both refer to entities that are available to serve some purpose.

66. As a result we end up in a situation where neither Arminius' doctrine of exhaustive foreknowledge in tandem with the promotion of freewill nor Pinnock's refutation of exhaustive foreknowledge for the sake of freewill results in a conception of freedom that honors human beings in their full integrity.

67. I have chosen to use upper case "C" in order to emphasize the importance of this concept for me.

68. My definition is influenced by Heidegger's discussions in the footnotes on pages 83 and 157 of *Being and Time*.

69. Heidegger, *Being and Time*, 274.

70. Ogden, *The Reality of God*, 150.

71. Ibid., 150.

72. Heidegger, *Existence and Being*, 98.

73. Ibid., 99.

74. Ogden, *The Reality of God*, 151-152

75. Ibid., 152.

76. Ibid., 151. Heidegger discusses this notion in division 2, section VI of *Being and Time*.

77. Heidegger, *Being and Time*, 459.

78. Ibid., 465-467.

79. Ogden, *The Reality of God*, 152.

80. Ibid., 151.

81. Ibid., 153.

82. Ibid.

83. Alfred North Whitehead, *Process and Reality (corrected edition)*, eds. David Ray Griffin and Donald W. Sherburne (New York: The Free Press, 1978), 343.

84. Ogden, *The Reality of God*, 153.

85. Ibid.

86. Ibid., 60, 153.

87. Ibid., 155.

88. The significance of death for the definition of time in existence as we know it does not change when it is considered that many people hope for some kind of postcarnate life.

89. This I take to mean that God and the world are not separable entities, but must always be grasped together.

90. Ogden, *The Reality of God*, 60.

91. Paul Tillich, *Systematic Theology*, vol. I (Chicago: University of Chicago Press, 1951), 228.

92. Ibid. 171.

93. Gordon Kaufman, *In the Beginning . . . Creativity* (Minneapolis: Fortress Press, 2004), 22.

94. Ibid., 23.

95. Ibid., 24-25.

96. Immanuel Kant, *Critique of Pure Reason*, trans. Norman Smith (New York: St. Martin's Press, 1965), 268.

97. Kaufman, *Creativity*, 25-26.

98. Ibid., 26.

99. Ibid., 27.

100. Ibid., 42.

101. Ibid., 44.

102. Ibid., 49-50.

103. Ibid., 48, 50.

104. Miller, *Reshaping the Contextual Vision in Caribbean Theology*, 204. The reference for this declaration is P. B. Vidyarthi, *Sri Ramanujah's Philosophy of Religion: A Critical Exposition of Visistadvaita* (Madras: Prof. M. Rangacharya Memorial Trust, 1978), 215.

105. Ibid. The reference for this declaration is David Elton Trueblood, *Philosophy of Religion* (Grand Rapids: Baker House, 1957), 57.

106. Ogden, *The Reality of God*, 151.

107. Hartshorne, *The Divine Relativity*, 35.

108. Alfred North Whitehead, *Process and Reality,* 20-21, 31-32.

109. Ibid., 19, 23-24, 40.

110. Kaufman, *Creativity*, 95.

111. Having indicated that "an eternal object can be described only in terms of its potentiality for 'ingression' into the becoming of actual entities," Whitehead proceeds to say that "'ingression' refers to the particular mode in which the potentiality of an eternal object is realized in a particular actual entity, contributing to the definiteness of that actual entity." See Whitehead, *Process and Reality* , 23.

112. John Cobb, *A Christian Natural Theology—Based on the Thought of Alfred North Whitehead* (Philadelphia: The Westminster Press, 1965), 141-142.

113. Ogden, *Reality of God*, 57.

114. Ibid.

115. Whitehead, *Process and Reality*, 41.

116. Ibid., 43.

117. Ibid.

118. Ibid., 21.

119. Ogden provides a brief discussion of this notion in *Reality of God*, 57.

120. Hartshorne, *The Divine Relativity*, 42-44

121. Ibid., 19-20.

122. Ibid., 21.

123. Whitehead, *Process and Reality*, 45.

124. For a fuller description see Miller, *Reshaping the Contextual Vision*, 126-127, 244.

125. Oord, *The Nature of Love¸* 97. Originally from Pinnock et al., *The Openness of God*, 114.

126. Ibid.

127. Ibid.

128. Ibid., 98. The quotation is from page 134 in Pinnock's *Most Moved Mover.*

129. John C. Moskop, *Divine Omniscience and Human Freedom: Thomas Aquinas and Charles Hartshorne* (Georgia: Mercer University Press, 1984), 73. Moskop's reference is Charles Hartshorne, *Creative Synthesis and Philosophic Method* (LaSalle, IL: Open Court, 1970), 239.

130. Ibid., 244.

131. David Hume, *Dialogues Concerning Natural Religion,*ed. and introduction Richard H. Popkin (Indianapolis: Hackett Publishing Company, 1980), 36.

*IV*

# Struggling for Freedom at Ground Level

# Chapter Seven

# Freedom in Its Negative and Positive Aspects

Western societies generally privilege libertarian freedom and promote it under what is popularly referred to as liberalism. Many who fall under this general category are most committed to the protection of individual freedom, that is, the clearing away of obstacles that might hinder its expressions. However, they are often criticized for being so preoccupied with individual freedom that they do little to ensure that opportunity and resources are not so dominated by the powerful that others, especially the most vulnerable, are denied the opportunity to pursue a meaningful life. Others actively pursue a prescribed form of life, understood to be that worthy of a specific understanding of freedom. Some think that the latter can be so fixated on the privileged understanding of freedom that they become coercive in the name of freedom.

This chapter is fueled by the conviction that, while the latter concern is legitimate, the former is more of a danger in Western societies. A rabid individualism characterizes much of life, which at its extreme suggests an antithesis between pursuits of individual interest and any attempt to foster concern for other global co-inhabitants and global welfare as a whole. I engage in in-depth theological, ethical, and social analysis of these approaches under the categories of negative and positive freedom, and promote the view that it is subscription to some concept of "common good" that can provide protection for the weak and vulnerable from the excesses of the powerful. This pursuit necessarily involves elements of both negative and positive freedom. In order to facilitate the quest for common good, the church needs to renounce its traditional inclination to align with the powerful, and vigorously embrace the plight of the weak and marginalized. With a clear recognition of challenges identified by a number of thinkers, I adopt this challenging posture against the background of a world view which is at its root organismic. This worldview enables me to be quite clear that a viable exercise of individual freedom is pursued with recognition that one is always doing so in community that includes far more than human beings. Indeed, we might well be at a point when it is by giving priority to the global organism as a whole that human welfare might be best catered for.

## INDIVIDUAL FREEDOM AND DEMOCRACY—IS IT ENOUGH?

In the *Coda* near the end of his text on freedom, Orlando Patterson suggests that "at its best, the valorization of personal liberty is the noblest achievement of Western civilization."[1] Elaborating on what this means, he points to the freedom people have as long as they do not infringe on the freedom of others, equality before the law, philosophical support for the inviolability of the individual's separate existence, and the quest for freedom from all internal and external constraints to self-realization. Pointing to what is at the heart of the dominant spirituality, Christianity, he identifies the core position that "the son of God" was incarnated to set people free from "spiritual thralldom and make them free and equal before God." These elements, he says, "all add up to a value complex that not only is unparalleled in any other culture, but, in its profundity and power, is superior to any other single complex of values conceived by mankind."[2]

The listed elements, coming under the popular label libertarian freedom or spoken of as an expression of the liberal tradition, do constitute the dominant understanding of freedom in the West. And, as should be clear by now, it is my view that personal freedom should be part of the experience of freedom everywhere. One immediate point of difference from Patterson has to do with the fact that his examination of the religious component of freedom from the sociological perspective does not require him to explore in any depth understandings religious people have of what grounds declarations about "the son of God" in relation to the ultimate actuality (personal or nonpersonal) which many theologians consider to be the final grounding for freedom. Neither does it require him to engage the philosophical and theological concepts that establish human freedom as finite freedom. With my convictions about God and God's direct involvement in human life, and also my view regarding the necessary connection between individual human beings and the complex interconnected world, I am not able to say that ideally one's desire to liberate one's self should exclude "all internal and external constraints." However, I can more confidently say that any liberation human beings experience will very probably not exclude many of them. All these considerations will be important elements in my evaluation of what is entailed by Patterson's listed elements.

It is not possible to explore considerations on freedom in the socio-political and economic dynamics of Western life without addressing the celebrated essay *On Freedom* produced by John Stuart Mill in the nineteenth century. Mill was convinced "that social harmony and progress were compatible with reserving a large area for private life over which neither the state nor any other authority must be allowed to trespass. . . . To invade this space in any way would be despotism."[3] Given this conviction, Mill argued that the only reason why others should interfere with an individual's exercise of freedom in this private space is self-protection or to prevent harm to others. Intrusion on person's private space on the ground that it is for the sake of that person's own good is not justified. In this case, Mill is not against using various means of persuasion, but is explicit in declaring that a person has absolute independence over those aspects of her/his life that concerns herself/himself directly.[4] Indeed, "the only freedom which deserves the name, is that of pursuing our own good in our own way, so long as we do not attempt to deprive others of theirs, or impede their efforts to obtain it."[5]

For Mill, it is the very character of human civilization that is at stake. Human beings need adequate space: to develop their own self-understanding and their understanding of the world; to engage issues using well-trained powers of reason and with as much knowledge as possible in order to develop their own unique insights in the interest of truth; to become critically aware of the perspective from which they are approaching issues; and to have opportunity to develop and utilize their creative capacities.[6] The desired outcome is that each individual would be capable of responsibly contributing her/his best to free public discourse in which ideas are refined or refuted through interaction with and between diverse minds.[7] Mill has great interest in ensuring that opportunities for the emergence of genius be not stifled. He is of the view that "persons of genius . . . are more individual than other people." Driven by their individual passions, these persons usually operate contrary to custom and might use resources in ways that some view as wasteful.[8] To deny opportunity for these features to emerge and flourish is to ensure that mediocrity will be "the ascending power among mankind."[9]

Mill did not rule out all compulsion in preserving this freedom. "Since justice demands that all individuals be entitled to a minimum of freedom, all other individuals were of necessity to be restrained, if need be by force, from depriving anyone of it."[10] I imagine that the justification for such force would be that an intrusion on the sovereign space of another is tantamount to an act of aggression. As such, the whole function of law is to prevent these intrusions from taking place.[11] More than anything else, the state is to be always on the watch and be ready to employ appropriate coercion for the sake of freedom. Convinced about the "sacredness" of individual freedom, Mill's approach to the defense of freedom consisted in what Berlin characterizes as the "negative goal of warding off interference."[12]

Berlin classifies this negative goal as constituting the liberal conception of freedom, and he claims that in modern times in the Western world it "has informed plea for civil liberties and individual rights; every protest against exploitation and humiliation, against the encroachment of public authority."[13] Richard Bauckham, on the other hand, is quite modest in his estimation of the continued influence of the liberal understanding of freedom in Britain. However, he points to the major revival it enjoyed in British political thought during the 1980s, the decade of Margaret Thatcher's tenure as Prime Minster, and he acknowledges that a permanent impact has been made on that society.[14] Significantly, the Thatcher era overlapped with the presidency of Ronald Reagan in the US, when what is called neo-liberalism emerged as a strong force. Fortunately, while many of those who espouse the liberal approach have a strong tendency to individualism and unfettered capitalism, there has not been a rush to publicly embrace the extreme expression of this trait represented in Thatcher's declaration that "there is no such thing as society."[15]

Berlin informs us that the liberal understanding of freedom is a comparatively modern one. Despite the developments in regard to individual liberty in early Christianity, for which Patterson gives Paul great credit, Berlin suggests that before the Renaissance there is no tradition of strident promotion of the right to have space in which one is left to one's self, or of privacy itself as something sacred.[16] Mill would not have seen this observation as weakening the pedigree of his promotion of individual freedom. He identifies various stages in the socio-political development of the West in the context of which "the struggle between Liberty and Authority" would have been pursued. And the focus of his essay presumed that a stage had been reached in Western life when constitutional and organizational provisions could be put in place to protect the individual "against the tyranny of political rulers." Among the features mentioned are "elective and temporary rulers" who are "regularly accountable to the community"[17]—these being basic features of modern democracy.

While sympathetic to Mill's overall project, Berlin is critical of certain elements of his discussion. He sides with Mill's detractor James Stephen,[18] and claims that history has shown that freedom of thought and the valuing of truth have thrived "at least as often" in the midst of great rigidity and repression as they have in more tolerant settings.[19] Indeed, freedom in the sense promoted by Mill "is not incompatible with some kinds of autocracy, or at any rate with the absence of self-government." This is because Mill's approach "is principally concerned with the area of control, not its source."[20] Berlin is convinced that "a liberal minded despot would allow his subjects a large measure of personal freedom." This despot, he suggests, "may be unjust, or encourage the wildest inequalities, care little for order, or virtue, or knowledge; but provided he does not curb their freedom, or at least curbs it less than many other regimes, he meets with Mill's specification." He gives as examples the rule of Frederick the Great in Prussia and Josef II in Austria. Under both regimes "men of imagination, originality, and creative genius, and, indeed, minorities of all kinds, were less persecuted and felt the pressure, both of institutions and custom, less heavy upon them than in many an earlier or later democracy."[21] As such, Berlin suggests that Mill's argument for freedom as a necessary condition for the growth of human genius falls to the ground.[22]

Berlin's critique is not unreasonable, especially since Mill claims that he regards "utility as the ultimate appeal on all ethical questions." However, I embrace the elements of Berlin's critique so far identified not only because they address the adequacy of Mill's explication of freedom, but because they pose questions about the integrity of claims I and others make about freedom as a highly prized value. Berlin is correct: "The answer to the question 'Who governs me?' is logically distinct from the question 'How far does government interfere with me?'"[23] And in my framework of thought, the former is as important as the latter. In the very first chapter of this project I did claim that inner freedom, with the exercise of ontological freedom at its core, is the grounding for the most fulsome expression of freedom. Therefore, I am able to celebrate the fact that in situations characterized by severe injustice and vulgar inequality, and where despotic leaders "care little for order, or virtue, or knowledge,"[24] the exercise of ontological freedom can produce a sense of meaning when the situation is evaluated in terms of that which is considered ultimate. This view of ontological freedom is linked directly with the claim I will make in chapter 8 that, in the most oppressive situations, freedom in imagination proves to be a bastion of freedom. However, beyond personal freedom, social freedom is also vital for fulsome freedom.

As I also mentioned in the first chapter, among the features of social freedom is the opportunity to express personal freedom in public ways within a pluralistic setting where diverse persons struggle to balance "a complicated dialectic of ways of life" or social styles.[25] How does this process work if there is one person or a group of people ruling with dominating power and claims the right to decide how every aspect of public life should operate? This feature of despotic rule violates a crucial expression of social freedom in political (civic[26]) freedom, characterized by the opportunity people have "to influence the conditions under which decisions are made that affect their way of life."[27] I, therefore, assert that, with social freedom constricted and highly regulated, it would not be long before the permitted space for personal freedom would lose any appearance of vibrancy and life-giving capacity because it lacks nourishment from the broader social dynamics. It would take enormous effort on the part of individuals to keep themselves from withering away in the suffocating space provided for self-expression.

In what I consider the most significant element of Berlin's critique, he exposes what might be characterized as Mill's naive enthusiasm for democracy, which caused him to overlook the potential dangers it poses for individual freedom. Jonathan Riley hints at what might be informing this apparent naivety when he indicates that Mill is very concerned about a stage of social development in which a "popular majority," the commercial middle class, had "vastly expanded power to ensure, by means other than legal punishment, that all conform to its opinions and customs."[28] Therefore, Mill suggests that those committed to individual freedom should not only be wary of representatives of a government, but also "the tyranny of prevailing opinion and feeling," whereby the values of the popular majority come to dominate a society, "penetrating . . . deeply into the details of life," so that "society is itself the tyrant . . . over the separate individuals who compose it," crushing dissenters.[29] Berlin, however, points us back to Mill's own recognition that "government by the people was not . . . necessarily freedom at all. For those who govern are not necessarily the same 'people' as those who are governed, and democratic self-government is not the government 'of each by himself' but, at best, of 'each by the rest.'"[30] As such, where democratic government is concerned, it is not just particular representatives that are dangerous but the very possibility of the accumulation of inordinate power by any government or political system. Democracy, Berlin suggests, "may disarm a given oligarchy, a given privileged individual or set of individuals, but it can still crush individuals as mercilessly as any previous ruler. An equal right to oppress—or interfere—is not equivalent to liberty."[31]

It is striking that, when Mill is specific about those who controlled public opinion in his time, he points to "chiefly middle class" in England and "the whole white population" in the US.[32] Therefore, we should take with utmost seriousness the fact that the slave system in the US and the apartheid system that followed occurred under a democratic form of government controlled by white Americans. And is it not the case that what was in Mill's England the commercial middle class has, in our era, become the dominant upper class in many places that wields inordinate influence on governments that are ostensibly democratic?


## THE LIBERAL TRADITION NEEDS A COMMITMENT TO THE COMMON GOOD


I now turn more directly to the character of the liberal approach to freedom, with implications for the socio-political life of individuals and communities. In doing so, it is worthy of mention that Berlin was able to critique Mill's ideas for which he had strong sympathy because he was convinced that there was no perfect or final understanding of freedom. Significantly, Berlin recognized that even the negative goal, if absolutized, would invariably lead to coercion, and the opposite of freedom. However, many of those who, like him, privilege negative freedom operate as if the Western liberal tradition, informed primarily by Mill-like ideas and allied to capitalism, is the only legitimate approach to freedom. Thus, in most dominant Western societies, socio-political and economic structures have been fostered that deserve Bauckham's charge that "the central difficulty with the libertarian concept of freedom is that it has no concept of the common good and it defines the freedom of the individual in such a way that it has no necessary relation to a concern for the common good."[33] I take "common good" to mean, conceptually, those elements of a community's life that motivate individual members of that community to thoughts and actions that are not geared toward their own immediate benefit, but, instead, have the welfare of the larger community as the primary focus.

In the determination of what constitutes common good, one ought not to easily dismiss the concern Mill had for the tyranny of the majority. Then there is Berlin's concern over the capacity of democratic governments to be oppressive. Mill is certainly not unmindful of concerns that inform the consideration of the common good. Against the background of his emphasis on individual freedom, he suggests that "instead of a diminution, there is need of a great increase of disinterested exertion to promote the good of others." At the same time, he insists that "disinterested benevolence can find other instruments to persuade people to their good, than whips and scourges, either of the literal or the metaphysical sort."[34]

Berlin's discussion of negative freedom suggests that he would ask that we consider seriously who exactly would decide on behalf of a community what constitutes the common good for them, and who would monitor its concrete expressions to ensure that it serves the interests of all and not just some. He would remind us of the ever present threat that in this process, excessive power would fall into the hands of some as they represent and/or administrate on behalf of the community. The issue for him is not just the good or bad intentions of those who gain inordinate power; it is that there is a level of power that no human can handle properly. Influenced by Benjamin Constant, he declares tellingly: "'It is not the arm that is unjust . . . but the weapon that is too heavy for the human hand.'"[35] Berlin might well agree that the notion of "common good" could be informed by the principle that members of a community should not deliberately make arrangements by which some members are prevented from acquiring the things they consider needful for their welfare, so long as these acquisitions are not unlawful or hinder the ability of others to cater for their well-being. He would definitely understand it to involve a questioning tolerance of the "complicated dialectic of ways of life" to which Robert Neville refers.[36] However, he would probably be wary about going further.

Both Mill and Berlin are wise in their respective concerns. As a Christian theologian, I suggest that Christians should take their concerns seriously and then, with awareness of the risks involved, move beyond them. This move would begin with facing up to the stubborn fact that we operate in an interconnected world in which our welfare and that of our progeny is inextricably linked to that of all other global entities, and the state of the cosmos as a whole. Further, there will be appreciation that the imaginatively creative God who is internal to our individual lives is also the God who is internal to every other life. This God loves the world as a whole and each particular entity within it, and desires to enable each and every entity into the fullest possible expression of their own creative selves, so that together with others they contribute to the best possible world. These considerations would open the way for considerations relevant to the common good.

In the course of my explorations, the best terms I have found that most meaningfully characterize what I understand to be the purpose of this global interaction, with God as a direct participant, are Alfred North Whitehead's notions of "intensity of experience" and "strength of beauty." The former, developed in *Process and Reality*, has to do with the capacity of an entity to synthesize the greatest possible number of elements of varying sorts into a harmonious whole. Here Whitehead's expression "balanced complexity" helps flesh out the character of intensity of experience, even though it does not provide the specific content of any particular experience. Whitehead suggests that "complexity means the realization of contrasts, of contrasts of contrasts, and so on,"[37] and balance means that there is not at some point in an entity's experience the inclusion of a contrast, which because of its incompatibility with any previous contrast or contrasts, undermines the capacity for desirable contrasts in the future. It should be recognized that "contrast" is not used in the sense of one thing being set over against another, but the creation of a complex unity from an array of factors, and "balance" emerges from "the adjustment of identities and diversities for the introduction of contrast with the avoidance of inhibitions by incompatibilities."[38]

The quality of intensity is influenced by the level of anticipation an entity has in regard to its influence on future entities; that is, it is influenced by "the transcendent future in relation to its immediate fact."[39] Put in ordinary language, intensity of experience results from a situation in which an entity has access to the widest range of opportunities for experiences of the richest and most diverse sorts and for the most complexly integrated development; that is, it results from the actualization of as many relevant possibilities as are accessible. The entity will be able to conceive of as wide a variety of ways as is reasonable to consider in which its self-development can contribute to the development of other lives. This flows directly into the concept "strength of beauty," developed by Whitehead in *Adventures of Ideas*, which refers to the mutual adaptation of the richest possible variety of elements into effective contrasts. The closer we are to a situation in which there is the absence of component feelings that mutually inhibit each other so that neither rises to the strength proper to it, the greater the potentiality of realizing "perfection of beauty."[40]

All of this should make it clear that a vision of common good should be as comprehensive and multidimensional as possible in its most fundamental character. Furthermore, if, as I am convinced, God's concern for human beings comes in the context of concern for the world as a whole, the process of ascertaining factors more relevant to the good of individuals and groups will probably involve conflicting situations in which it will be difficult to fashion relevant contrasts that engender intensity of experience for the whole world that God loves. Those to whom I am seeking to communicate through this project, fellow human beings, being finitely free do not have the capacity to be aware of all factors relevant to the good of the earth as a whole, nor do we even have the capability to address all aspects of the factors that we are aware of at any particular moment. Nevertheless, there is the unmistakable challenge to pay as much attention as possible to the needs of self and others—more properly, self in relation to others. Further, we are being lured toward the serious consideration of whether any attempt to determine human needs ought not to be carried out in terms of that which is good for the organism of which we are but a part, the earth, rather than the other way around.

Together, these concerns link directly with the discussions of chapter 6 in which I argued, employing Heidegger's concepts, that "Care" is the disposition most appropriate to the human being as Being-in-the-world. While the situation of the most vulnerable (human and non-human) in our world disposes one to express the negative side of the term, that is, "being worried about," the reasons for that disposition will only be addressed by an intense focus on the positive expression "taking care of." It is ways of life structured in terms of the recognition that it is creative imagination informed by Care that reflect what it means for human beings to be *Da-sein* and to reflect the *Imago Dei*. We display commitment to the realization of "intensity of experience" and "strength of beauty" in the organism of which human beings are a part, the earth, when we take every decision with the appreciation that each individual is part of a web of influence that is cosmic in scope, and has consequence in the inner depths of other lives.

Here we have a clue regarding what should inform the ethical frameworks that are fashioned to guide our approach to common good. Expressing Care is not about operating in terms of rigid moral strictures. Nor is it about attempting to approach all situations and every entity with a fixed template, regardless of how intricate that template is. We do need general guidelines, but these should be developed in a way that invites contextually relevant engagement. At the same time, I am inclined to the view that in this epoch, any framework of guidelines should be biased toward orienting human decisions and actions toward the protection and enhancement of the earth's welfare, rather than a disposition that views the earth with its resources as simply available for the sake of human welfare. These concerns constitute the attitudinal substructure of the explorations that follow that will address common good primarily as it pertains to human beings.

I want to believe that some elements of the spirit that have fueled my general leaning in regard to common good have also inspired Richard Bauckham's apparent inclination toward activism for the sake of the common good. Being committed to the concept of realistically libertarian freedom, I take very seriously his claim that the libertarian concept of freedom as promoted in Western societies is so constituted that it is purely accidental if the individual's choice benefits others. Bauckham indicates that libertarianism has two ways of resolving the tension between individual good and the common good. Describing the first as "astonishing," he lists it as the position that "the pursuit of individual self-interest automatically ensures the common good."[41] Usually applied to the economic sphere, "it means that the free market makes everyone better off." Having disputed this position on empirical grounds, claiming that globally free-market economics has widened the gap between the rich and the poor, he suggests that it seems more like an article of faith than a sober economic position.[42]

I agree with Bauckham that "as an article of faith," this position expresses, "an odd kind of theology. It combines an excessively pessimistic view of human nature (most human beings are expected to act largely from self-interest) with an excessively optimistic view of the world (self-interest coincides with the good of all)."[43] Bauckham further dramatizes the incongruity of popular Western libertarianism by suggesting that "it seems to require us to believe that God has so written the laws of economics that the most determined pursuit of one's own economic gain is the best way to provide for the poor."[44] The second way in which libertarianism reconciles individual freedom and the common good is to leave the common good to private charity. The position of those who support this way is that "unlike . . . funding of public services from taxation, private charity does not infringe the freedom of individuals to do as they wish with their own money." They may or may not choose to be charitable. This approach, Bauckham suggests, exposes the fundamental weakness in the libertarian notion of freedom which is promoted in the socio-political and economic life of the West.

> If freedom is defined simply as freedom to choose, no matter what choice is made, then promoting the common good is just one possible way of exercising freedom. Those who care about the common good may regard it as a better use of freedom than a wholly selfish way of life, but is not, on this view, greater freedom. The good person is no freer than the bad.[45]

I remind the reader that freedom of choice, undergirded by freedom of will, is not only about making choices but making right choices, and I find Bauckham very helpful in this regard. At the same time, the range of my discussion on the issue of freedom should make it not a surprise when I claim that the ability to choose is indeed a good in itself. Considered in this way, there is a sense in which freedom "is what it is,"[46] and the process by which one chooses or what one chooses does not change the goodness of choice *per se*. In this light, the good person who chooses is not freerer than the bad person who chooses, and promoting the common good is indeed just one way of exercising freedom, even if, as I believe, it is the better way.

If we then (as we should) move to consider the character of persons making choices (that is, whether they are good or bad), one has to acknowledge that there is nothing obvious in the mere characterization "good" that necessarily entails "free," or "the ability to make choices that enhance freedom." At the empirical level, it is not unusual for morally good persons to make bad choices that are detrimental to many; and it is not unknown that morally bad persons make choices that benefit many. So, I enthusiastically support Bauckham's orientation toward common good, with the acknowledgment that I am able to do this primarily because I subscribe to the ontological dimension of freedom. It is because this dimension has to do with how people employ all the elements of natural freedom to relate to God (as portrayed in chapter 6) in relation to the world as a whole and to self as linked to both, that I can maintain hope of the possibility of movement toward agreement on general understandings of what "common good" might look like in different epochs and in varied contexts. It is also because of my views regarding the elements and dynamics of ontological freedom that I am inclined to hold that openness to facilitate and experience aspects of life that are not of immediate personal benefit is a sign that one person has greater freedom to experience more dimensions of life and to be influenced by a wider array of affects than those who are less open. Finally, because I am very aware of the probable consequences when certain kinds of choices are not made, I can suggest that those who do not make choices that pertain to common good, as defined above, will very likely contribute to local and global life that is characterized by severely diminished freedom for others and for themselves.

I light of this disposition, I support the view that unrestrained embrace of libertarian freedom easily "contributes to the decay of public values and discourages the emergence of public values."[47] Recalling Bauckham's suggestion that the attitude influencing this decay in Western societies is linked to a Thatcher-like assumption that there is no such thing as society, I suggest that there is a probable consequence that could easily lead to the dismantling of Western societies as we know them. Bauckham's statement of this consequence is framed by the following concerns. There has been a rapid diversification of many Western capitalist societies, with an accompanied pluralistic approach to life in general and human welfare in particular. Accompanying this diversification has been a progressive dismantling of local communities with their historic ties grounded in inter-family connections, fairly homogenous religious commitments with attendant social values, and local economic interdependence. These features of local communities have often been linked to an overarching nationalism fueled by a dominant meta-narrative. In the past, this meta-narrative has provided guidelines for cooperation and informed value-systems that set standards for personal and communal aspiration and evaluation—for good or for ill. Given the changes just described, an unmitigated liberal approach to freedom cannot contribute to the requisite consensus, which ensures that we actually have societies characterized by Care and have criteria to guide accountability, rather than a motley array of groupings of persons operating in settings effectively ruled by the devices of those who happen to have control of the resources on which others depend.

I am of the view that the present economic crisis in the US is giving a hint of what happens when individual freedom and personal aggrandizement are pursued without commitment to the common good. Associated with this deficiency is an inadequate recognition of the ethical considerations identified by Michael Walzer and Bauckham to be appropriate under-girding for the pursuit of justice. It is clear to me that, with the separation of individual interest from a commitment to common good, guided by ethical evaluation, freedom easily becomes a license for excess and abuse. While the militant individualist might make lofty pronouncements about the rights of others to similar freedoms as theirs, oftentimes the overriding interest is to create ever-increasing space to express their own desire to do as they please without hindrance and accountability. This is certainly inconsistent with the ideal situation portrayed by Mill and Berlin, but it is often the way things work themselves out.

There are many examples around the world of how this attitude easily sets the stage for the corruption of civic freedom, as self-interested individualists gain influence in a society and seek to sway legal structures, social conventions, economic processes, and even religious institutions to benefit their particular interests. The larger significance of this concern emerges when one considers that in the contemporary era, the most powerful forces in many societies are not governments and other state apparatus but multinational and transnational corporations that are outgrowths from the commercial class Mill was anxious about in the nineteenth century. As such, they have the greatest capacity to exercise freedom most akin to what Patterson calls sovereignal freedom. My assessment is supported by Rebecca Peters in her text *In Search of the Good Life*. There she points out how contemporary proponents of neoliberal philosophy, in tandem with big business, vigorously promote the idea that freedom is the preeminent marker of human flourishing. She suggests that freedom, as promoted by neoliberals, "does not merely refer to the democratic value that all people have the right to be free: to govern themselves, and to make their own decisions under the rule of law." Instead, "the neoliberal interpretation of freedom goes one step further and is more closely aligned to the notion of liberty concerned primarily with individual freedom to act as one chooses, that is, freedom from constraint and control."[48] Here they seem to have embraced the personal benefits identified in Mill's discussion on freedom and ignored the obligations he associated with being an individual in society.

Peters' evaluation immediately brings to the fore some of the challenges associated with the network of values that fuels this project on freedom. Therefore, I will be explicit in declaring that, along with the appreciation that all human freedom is finite freedom and that cosmic existence is fundamentally organismic, there must be recognition that space for the effective exercise of individual freedom is fundamental to healthy human life. Further, given my convictions regarding human frailty, I am quite convinced that one should always be careful of any accumulation of power by governments and politicians; this is always a potential threat to the viable exercise of individual freedom. At the same time, one should also be very wary when the economically and socially powerful, and their neoliberal supporters, trumpet against any type of government intervention, especially when one learns of the types of intervention some of them perceive as inimical to freedom.

As a first example, we learn from Bauckham that according to the Thatcherist ideal, as it was promoted in the 1980s, funding for public transportation was incompatible with the notion of freedom.[49] We also hear from Peters of the types of government intervention seen as hostile to freedom in the USA, by Milton Friedman who was one of the very influential spokespersons for neoliberalism in this nation. He would have eliminated social security because "citizens are forced to contribute to a fund that is administered entirely outside of their control." Friedman opposed "price support for agriculture, minimum wage laws, national parks, and public housing, among other things." He did, however, believe there are some areas in which government oversight is necessary. These areas include "national defense, the maintenance of law and order, enforcement of contracts and property rights, and a monetary system regulated by the government."[50] It could be justifiably argued that these areas are necessary to promote and protect individual or negative freedom as Mill promoted it. However, Peterson is not surprised that each of these areas relates to establishing a safe environment in which people can function as capitalists.[51]

With my perspective on these matters influenced heavily by experiences in the Caribbean, I acknowledge a further level of anxiety when considering the multinational and transnational nature of the corporations Peters has in mind—these having as their primary interest the maximization of profit. This interest is often pursued by means of the ability to undermine the capacity of "sovereign" governments to regulate the operation of business organizations, to set minimum working conditions for workers, to ensure that citizens are not forced to work for salaries that are not far from slave conditions.

These examples make it clear to me that any promotion of freedom, understood to have adequate ethical foundations, cannot be simply concerned with the establishment of a frontier between the area of private life and that of public authority. This approach would unwittingly or intentionally ignore the actual details of life as many citizens of the world actually live it.

## The Church Is Found Wanting

Unfortunately, these details include the fact that despite the commendable attempts at critical analysis by Christian thinkers like Bauckham, Peters, and others, when considered institutionally, the church has often not served as a liberating agent for those who are most victimized by the structures of social and economic exploitation. The most striking example for me is the church's complicity in colonialism and slavery in many parts of the world, including the Caribbean. Liberation theologian Leonardo Boff is of the view that, throughout its history, the church has been for the most part absent from the struggle for human rights. Pointing, I suspect, to his own tradition (Roman Catholicism) that is still the dominant Christian communion, he claims that practically everything the Western world regards as a basic human right today was once rejected by the official church. Freedom of conscience was called an "erroneous opinion" and even, "madness." Freedom of opinion and expression was qualified as a "most pestilent error."[52] The churches, in general, were hardly present during the debate and passage of the Universal Declaration of Human rights by the United Nations in 1948. From his tradition, there was only representation from groups "on the fringe of officialdom": the World Organization of Catholic Women and the International Confederation of Christian Unions. In answering the question "Why?" he speaks tellingly of the ensnarement of the churches over the centuries. "[T]he church was tied to the dominant secular power. The altar was lashed to the throne."[53]

Clark Williamson helps to highlight the grievous nature of Boff's claims. He reminds us of Jesus' radicalization of the notion of the "Kingdom of God" to mean, not a framework "of domination, but of service, one of welcome for the destitute and marginalized, and in which is included the poor and homeless." In light of this position, Williamson uses the term "communitarian egalitarianism" to characterize life in the earliest Christian community in which "the nobodies of Galilee acted out a new way of being human."[54] Patterson might say that this was exactly the framework in which the further revolutionizing of the understanding of freedom was fostered by Paul. Yet, I remind the reader of my evaluation in chapter 4 in which I suggest that beneath the performance of servanthood was hierarchicalism and an understanding of power in the mode of domination and control, learned from the very society that oppressed the early Christians and encoded by expressions such as Kingdom of God.

Therefore, Williamson's claim that "the church gradually lost this vision and became increasingly allied with the rich and powerful" is not surprising.[55] Having become established under Constantine, the church eventually became aligned with the rich and powerful, and became complicit in the entrenchment of socio-economic inequalities. I do not dispute Williamson's claims that "the church was attacked and conquered by its surrounding culture. Persecution could not kill the church. Acceptance and establishment could. This attack proved irresistible."[56] However, it is my view that the church was able to move with ease toward the mode of domination and control because the early disposition of communitarian egalitarianism that reflected their perception of the way Jesus lived his life was probably incongruous with deep-seated convictions about the character of the God of Jesus Christ. As I have alluded to in many ways over the course of this text, the foundation of these lingering convictions is characterized by a strict hierarchy headed by a selectively benevolent but capricious despot who, exercising sovereignal freedom, is answerable to no one and is not obliged to operate by any standard deemed of high value in human calculation. Whitehead points to the idolatry of the church in which, among other things, "it gave unto God the attributes which belonged exclusively to Caesar."[57] I suggest that this was easy for the church to do because, in important respects, Caesar was in many ways like the God of Israel and even more like the God that resulted from the early Christian synthesis of Hebrew and Greek conceptions. Thus, at least in part, it was the despotic, capricious God that is portrayed in some parts of Hebrew Scriptures that became the Church's Caesar-God.

Having taken on the identity as the chosen representative to the sovereignly free and eternal God to guarantee the spiritual welfare of the earth, who else could be the church's peers but those others, allowed/determined by God to occupy seats of power in their own spheres?[58] Surely, as much cooperation as possible is expected, and it would be even better if the movers and shakers of society were associated with the church. Without doubt the poor, marginalized, and benighted would be enabled into "salvation" through the church by persuasion or coercion, and, as such, contribute to the numerical dominance of Christianity as a world religion. However, just as "saved" human beings, in general, remain nothing in themselves, so the redeemed poor and marginalized have oftentimes remained insignificant in the hierarchy of the church, even as their lot in the socio-political and economic spheres has remained dismal.

In this regard, it is good to hear Boff as he alludes to the pursuits of liberation theologians, and suggests that "the whole modern struggle of the church has been against "the privileges of the mighty, of the state, of the upper class." He points to churches that have become vigorous defenders of the rights of the poor, facing violence and aggression from the mighty because they are not content to be merely charitable agencies, and instead pursue radical systemic transformation.[59] Regrettably, however, the forceful challenge that was presented to traditional Protestant and Catholic communions by Boff and his fellow Liberation theologians during the decades of the 1970s and 1980s has waned. In a number of quarters within and outside of the church this was replaced by easy criticism of their methodology.

One example of criticism within the church comes from Caribbean pastor-theologian Emmet Weir, who, in his discussion on appropriate Caribbean theology, attempts to set up a contrast with the Latin American Liberation theology. In the process he approvingly quotes Kortright Davis: "Generally speaking, it may be asserted that, whereas Latin American liberation theology tends to be anthropocentric, placing a high priority on human effort in the pursuit of freedom, emancipation theology is theocentric, placing the emphasis on The Right Hand of God."[60] This seems to me an unfortunate contrast, and it does not take much reading of the better representatives of Liberation theology to recognize this. In fact, in the very work of Boff's to which I have already referred, he calls on insights from Jon Sobrino, another distinguished Liberation theologian, as he claims that God's partiality toward the poor is not simply the product of God's free-will but is more fundamentally a reflection of God's very essence. Sobrino suggests that to affirm God's predilection for the poor is simply to acknowledge a concrete reflection of the fact that, by God's very essence, God is a God of life.[61] It is this view of God that has inspired many Liberation theologians to exert great effort and employ a range of theoretical and practical means in their quest to enable the poor and oppressed to experience freedom in multiple dimensions and categories.

What for me is most significant at this point is that Weir's and Davis's reflections actually serve as examples of the complex ways in which the pursuit of freedom (or emancipation as Davis calls it) in their region (the Caribbean) is easily nullified by the free sovereign Caesar-God of Christian tradition. Davis is of the mind that the concept of "freedom" ought not to be limited to the ideological and political because freedom is established by the fact that God is "First Cause" and "Omnipotent Creator."[62] While Davis does not unpack these classifications directly, one gets a clearer sense of what he wishes to convey about God's character when, having defined theology as "the science of freedom," he suggests that emancipation is only properly inspired by the acknowledgment of its grounding in the sovereign free-will of God. Having mentioned various basic definitions of freedom, he proceeds to lament the fact that "ultimate Reality has not always been translated into terms of ultimate and unconditional freedom for God." Here I take "unconditional" to mean that God's freedom is not qualified, limited, or restricted in any way; in other words, God's freedom is absolute. This then, is the omni-qualitied and essentially independent God I have been resisting throughout this project.

I acknowledge that this conception of God seems to give a kind of security to many who are oppressed. At the same time, it is the foundation for theological confusion for contemporary Christians who are committed to systemic transformation that benefits oppressed peoples, on the presumption that their efforts are guided by a God who has no limit in the capacity to give freedom and wants to do so because it is consistent with this God's character. How does this view of God correlate with the persistence of vulgar inequality and the progressive degradation of many in places like the Caribbean that result in severely limited experience of freedom in both its external and internal expressions? That some lament the fact that most of the expectations for transformation harbored by Caribbean peoples have not taken place probably suggests to Weir and other theologians of his orientation that these persons are not sufficiently mindful of God's freedom to operate in God's own time and in God's own way. At the same time, these theologians continue to develop Caribbean theology as if they have some significant clue of what liberation or emancipation can look like in that region when, in the final analysis, this can only be determined by the God who, being unconditionally free, is not obliged to operate in any manner that resembles previous actions classified as freedom-enabling.

Davis claims that appropriate theology is the reflection that takes place during the work of emancipation, regarding what God is understood to be doing through this enterprise. Yet, by what means can one even have any authentic understanding when God's freedom is unconditional? Going to the Bible for insight cannot be helpful; all that the narratives and pronouncements can teach us is that "these are the ways God determined that freedom would look like in such and such situation." Therefore, Caribbean theologians will keep championing that about which they can have no real understanding; and if they operate consistently with Davis's characterization of God, they ought not to claim any authority to determine for themselves what freedom should mean in that region.

Along with the theological confusion just identified, I am convinced that continued propagation of the idea of God with which Davis's characterization is associated—the God who by direct or proximate causation is in charge of all that happens—subtly reinforces a strange alliance between many poor and the powerful. At the heart of this alliance is a high regard for the exercise of power in the mode of domination and control. Thus, in many contexts, in both the global North and South, it has not taken much to woo both powerful and powerless into churches where the quality of a person's spirituality is associated with access to or progressive movement toward the chief symbol of power in contemporary times, that is, material wealth. In some of the fastest growing church communities neoliberal economic principles seem to have been baptized and incorporated into the ecclesial ethos by way of what is often called the prosperity gospel. Associated with this phenomenon is a scenario in which the Christian life is characterized by "spiritual laws" correlated with blessings and curses, favor and disfavor.

Instead of an ardent struggle to arrive at a just, if delicate, balance between the protection of individual freedom in its internal and external expressions and the challenges associated with determining the constitution of common good, there is mostly preoccupation with placating and gaining special personal favor from Caesar-God by mastering formulas of spirituality. That which is declared from pulpits to encourage the faithful in these pursuits is often tantamount to the spiritual indictment of many poor and powerless, who persist in their altruism and commitment to community, even as contemporary global dynamics pushes them further into economic ruin.

Having become convinced that their poverty is the result of spiritual inadequacy, many have been drawn into what David Griffin calls "a spirituality of obedience," which I claim is informed by theologies of subservience and subjugation, instead of what Griffin calls "a spirituality of creativity."[63] Who wants to be involved in risk taking and operate in the ambiguity that comes with being creative if it may cause one to violate some spiritual law, be out of favor with the God who established these laws in eternity, and as a result miss one's blessing? Further, who wants to do anything that might destabilize systems that presently produce abundance for some (and as a result victimize the poor) when there is the dream that one day God will hand over this wealth to the righteous (Isaiah 60: 4-7; Haggai 2:7-9; Revelation 21:24)? Why should one challenge present hierarchies and the exercise of power in the mode of domination and control when the aspiration is to be the powerful and to govern on behalf of the Caesar-God?

I do not expect any handover of wealth and power to the presently poor and marginalized Christian. Neither do I believe that there could be any acceptable justification if this handover took place as a result of the continued increase in disparity between the rich and the poor who are not Christian or even believe in a personal sovereign God. What I encourage is a quest for that responsible and justice-enabling mix of personal freedom and the demands of communal responsibility that is realizable within the general rubric of finite freedom. This being so, I am ever mindful that freedom, as articulated by political and economic libertarians in the West, implies different things to different people, depending of their context of operation and the state of their life. I, therefore, face troubling points highlighted by Berlin as he resists those who suggest that there are actually different types of freedom for different kinds of persons.

An important concern fuelling this issue is the significance of political rights or of safeguards against state intervention in contexts with large or increasing numbers of people "who are half-naked, illiterate, underfed and diseased."[64] As one who grew up in the global South and who is aware of the changing circumstance of a growing number in wealthier nations of the North, I take seriously those who ask whether the espousal of Western-style libertarian freedom does not actually mock the condition of those whose lives are characterized by persistent poverty and chronic lack of opportunity. Indeed, the conscientious cannot avoid putting serious thought to the claim that numerous persons around the world "need medical help or education before they can understand, or make use of, an increase in their [individual] freedom." Further, can we refuse to engage with the troubling questions that follow: "What is freedom [as understood by libertarians] to those who cannot make use of it? Without adequate conditions for the use of this freedom, what is the value of this freedom?"[65]

Berlin is very sensitive to the nature of the challenge being posed by his questions, and he acknowledges that some people at particular periods do need clothes and medicine more than personal liberty. Yet, he is clear that the minimal freedom these persons might need at a particular time and the greater freedom they may need later "is not some species of freedom peculiar to [them], but identical with that of professors, artists, and millionaires."[66] Regarding the extent of freedom that is necessary, I state my agreement with his suggestion that the decline of freedom as a sacred value "would mark the death of civilization, and of an entire moral outlook."[67] For me, freedom that is finite, realistically libertarian, and relational is vital for the continuation of the ongoing humanization process. Thus, whatever might be the other emphases demanded in a context at a particular time there needs to be a minimum standard for what is a meaningful expression of such freedom that is applied in contextually appropriate ways to people everywhere.

Ideas from Amartya Sen, who is originally from the global South,[68] provide important insights on democracy that are relevant to the promotion of freedom that is finite, realistically libertarian, and relational in a range of challenging contexts. Sen acknowledges that, given the extreme conditions under which significant numbers of people live, it is not difficult to feel that economic needs are so urgent that they should outweigh issues of political liberty and civil rights.[69] He identifies an extreme form of this view in what he refers to as the Lee thesis, which suggests that quests for democracy and the insistence on basic civil and political freedoms actually hamper economic growth and development.[70] Admitting that this thesis seems consistent with the situation in places like South Korea, post-reform China, and Lee's own country, Singapore, Sen hastens to suggest that it is based on very selective and limited information, rather than any general statistical testing over the wide-ranging data that are viable. Actually, he suggests that, on the whole, there is little evidence that authoritarian governance and suppression of political and civil rights are really beneficial in encouraging the economic development and associated benefits hoped for.[71] On the other hand, he spends a whole chapter identifying the many benefits of democracy in its intrinsic importance.

Sen believes that by definition democracy requires space for debate, discussion, voting, critique, and protest in response to economic needs. He suggests that democracy has both instrumental and constructive importance. Aspects of its instrumental importance include the fact that the "unregimented formation of our values requires openness of communication and arguments, and political freedoms and civil rights can be central for this process." It is also the case that "to express publicly what we value and to demand that attention be paid to it, we need free speech and democratic choice." Furthermore, "rulers have the incentive to listen to what people want if they have to face their criticism and seek their support in elections."[72] An important element of democracy's constructive role is that it gives people a voice and a role in conceptualizing the economic needs of a society, and also a role in shaping values and norms to inform these needs.[73] Sen has no doubt that it is individual freedom that is at the heart of these activities, and as such, this freedom constitutes the basic building block for the development necessary to provide the improved welfare many seek.

Clearly I am in agreement with Berlin, and more so with Sen, on the importance of protecting the right of free expression, civic or political freedom, and democratic institutions in general. At the same time, having grown up in a context that has been a field of exploitation by colonial and neocolonial powers, I am also inclined to the view that the liberal approach to freedom that is the foundation for contemporary neoliberal ideology, with its crass individualism and rabid capitalism, is not viable in vulnerable regions like the Caribbean where I am from. I am sure there are many who are convinced that it is not good for many other nations and regions. In fact, I am sometimes tempted to believe that the typical espousal of libertarian freedom by many Western thinkers is a ruse. It is but another attempt to undermine those features of social and economic policy that can protect the average citizen from the onslaught of those who have the wherewithal to dominate their thinking and thus orient choices, commandeer markets and thus limit choices, influence leaders and thus undermine representation.

With this concern in mind, I am fascinated that Bauckham, reacting to the excesses of libertarian freedom in Britain and other places, suggests that Western Christians should not overlook the socialist tradition, despite the baggage it carries within many societies. He reminds us that "where economic structures benefit one class at the expense of another, the freedom of the latter is reduced." On the other hand, socialist measures such "as the redistribution of wealth by taxation and the public provision of free health care and education on an equal basis for all are . . . not infringements on individual freedom but the way to enhance the freedom of all."[74] In these and other comments, Bauckham represents socialism at its theoretical best; and at its best, this tradition seems to have one important advantage over political and economic libertarianism as popularly touted: "It recognizes that social and economic structures not only infringe freedom, but also grant freedom. Freedom must be fostered and extended, not only by protecting the individual's rights against infringement by society, but also by creating an equitable social order as the social and economic condition for freedom." At the same time, as one whose teen years were marked by Jamaica's pursuit of "Democratic Socialism," I take seriously Bauckham's claim that "if the classic problem for libertarianism is a tension between freedom and the common good, the classic problem for socialism is a tension between freedom and coercion." There is the telling claim that "those who desire the common good, as embodied in government policy, willingly support the measures designed to ensure it, but others are coerced into contributing to the common good."[75]

More recently, Christoph Schöwbel has reflected on this apparently contradictory situation in terms of the relation between freedom and justice. Writing in the English context and, I suspect, with the wider European situation in mind, he reminds us of the catch-words of the French revolution—liberty, equality, fraternity—and suggests that "liberty has proved to be the dominant and victorious principle." For some time, it seemed as if "demands for justice, understood as equality," were on an equal footing, at least in the political realm.[76] However, the collapse of regimes of state socialism in the last decades of the twentieth century suggests to him that "a notion of equality that is not based on a strong affirmation of freedom has in its practical forms of realization only a limited life-span."[77] With the recognition that what Schöwbel classifies as "freedom" corresponds with what Berlin classifies as negative freedom, and that the quest for equality would have been championed by those exercising what Berlin classifies as positive freedom, we listen to Schöwbel as he declares that "equality is now interpreted almost universally as equal access to the exercise of freedom. Freedom appears as the fundamental principle, justice as equality as a derivative notion."[78]

Despite my reservations in regard to socialism, I hear Schöwbel's declaration with social sensibilities similar to Bauckham's, and, as such, new questions arise regarding the access to the exercise of freedom that has now taken precedence over justice. These are: (1) access to do what, and to live in what state of life?; (2) does it mean that as the poor honors the right of the powerful to do what they choose in the opulence of their private space, the poor are left in their freedom to wallow in misery, to starve, and to die? Questions like these should disturb people of conscience. At the same time, exactly because I have witnessed first-hand the abuse and chaos that can result if the pursuit of common good is not carried out with great care, it is now necessary to wrestle with Berlin's concept of positive freedom, which typically characterizes the approach taken by those who privilege justice, understood as equality.

It is in having identified weakness with Mill's approach to negative freedom that Berlin identifies the significance of positive freedom. As I mentioned before, the notion of positive freedom involves the pursuit of a particular prescribed form of life, understood to model a particular understanding of freedom. Berlin asserts that "the 'positive sense of liberty comes to light if we try to answer the question, not 'What am I free to do or be?', but 'By whom am I ruled?' or 'Who is to say what I am, and what I am not, to be or do?'"[79] These are vital questions for Berlin. For this reason it is striking that Berlin goes to great lengths to dramatize how the pursuit of positive freedom can easily end up as oppression.[80]

The path, Berlin suggests, can begin with very idealistic evaluations that characterize human beings as divided selves consisting of a higher self (in the realm of politics, often identified with reason that frees and empowers) and a lower self (identified with nature, unbridled passion, irrational impulses etc., and seen as enslaving). He shows how the process of realizing positive freedom can easily be perceived as requiring this "lower self" to be brought under control as the dominance/autonomy of the "higher self" (considered the most real self) is enhanced.[81] The danger, he suggests, becomes very obvious when we bear in mind that it is generally not considered strange in many societies to have levels of restraint placed on individuals or groups for the sake of a wider social goals "(justice or public health etc.)"—these being goals "which persons would pursue if they were more enlightened, but do not, because they are blind or ignorant or corrupt."[82] When I imagine what the lot of Black peoples in the West would have been without the abolition of slavery, what the US might have been without desegregation, and add to these my present leanings in regard to the address of "Climate Change," I appreciate how the idea of coercing others for their own good can seem tenable. At the same time, when considered in light of the notion of the divided self, it becomes clear how easily the general disposition translates into a legitimization of the oppression of persons by denying types and levels of self-expressions, in the name of freedom, for the sake of other aspects of themselves, considered their more authentic, virtuous or civilized selves.[83]

Given the previous discussions of this project, and being aware of the long history of Christianity in the West, it would be disingenuous of me to ignore the degree to which the scenario just described could be influenced by elements of the orthodox Christian disposition that I have critiqued. What better justification for coercion can there be than to understand oneself as the special emissary of the absolutely free sovereign God that, in the final analysis, is not answerable to any human being or available to be critiqued on the basis of any human standard? Convinced that the details of one's vision for a community have been given by this God, it is easy to imagine one's self as obligated to promote this vision with the kind of authority that reflects the character of the sovereign ruler of all lands and peoples. What better example is there of the divided self than people who, on one hand, are said to be created in the image and likeness of God and, on the other hand, are now fallen and unable to avoid doing the wrong thing (according to Augustine) in regard to freedom and other crucial matters of human welfare? Who is more eligible to direct these persons to the correct path than those from the community of people saved by submitting to and living their lives in and through the life of Jesus the Christ who (according to Luther) has imputed righteousness to them? If true humanity is only realized by giving over one's self to God through Jesus Christ, should those who have not done so be seen as depraved and inhuman?

Convinced about their rightness in this matter and confident of ultimate justification from the God who is unconditionally free, many religious communities have carried out activities that are consistent with what Berlin considers the most dangerous element of the expression of positive freedom. As he put it:

> One belief, more than any other, is responsible for the slaughter of individuals, on the altars of the great historical ideals—justice or progress or the happiness of future generations, or the sacred mission or emancipation of a nation or race or class, or even liberty itself, which demands the sacrifice of individuals for the freedom of society. This is the belief that somewhere, in the past or in the future, in divine revelation or in the mind of an individual thinker, in the pronouncements of history or science, or in the simple heart of an uncorrupted good man, there is a final solution.[84]

I suspect that, being of Jewish descent, Berlin employed the notion "final solution" with acute awareness of its association with the atrocities inflicted on his people in Nazi Germany. In my exploration, it serves as a powerful reminder that it is not just power hungry politicians and profit driven business people that one must be careful of as freedom is promoted in the processes of everyday engagements. Also quite dangerous are humanists or religious idealists convinced that they have the clearest or even certain vision of what freedom looks like, and what kind of human character is compatible with this state of freedom. I am convinced that these elements are not only responsible for attempts by church authorities to take over the lives of believers, but explain, in part, the history of the Christian sanction for or involvement in wars of various kinds, ventures in empire building, and association with repressive regimes of different stripes.

These concerns, I suggest, are especially significant for those who have been nurtured in contexts where the mentality of their peoples has been influenced by long histories of colonization, slavery, and indentureship by Western Christian powers. Many are still convinced on a number of levels that there is nothing good in them, that their own native dynamics have no resources to foster and nurture their "true" humanity, and that redemption must always come from and through some powerful and discerning Other from somewhere else. In the Caribbean, the region with which I am most familiar, this continues to be a major inhibitor to the development of the contextual theology movement, an important fueling agent for the attraction to foreign-born churches and spiritualities, and a significant contributor to the amazing growth of local church communions in which there is meticulous governance of the lives of members. In politics, it makes for a gullible electorate who are predisposed to fanatical allegiance to one party or another, and who seem to be looking for any opportunity to turn political leaders into messiahs. On the economic and social levels, it feeds the inclination to mimic lifestyles and standards of attainment that are totally inappropriate for the local situation, compounding the challenges associated with being a small, vulnerable economy, and intensifying the speed with which the nation slides into economic and social ruin.

## Redeeming Positive Freedom

Obviously I have sympathy for Berlin's critique of positive freedom. However, the commitment I have to the fashioning of some notion of common good demands that this cannot be my last word on that expression of freedom, on its own, and in its relation to negative freedom. If we were to accept the scenario described by Berlin as inevitable, or be driven to religious cynicism by my depiction of its link to elements of Christian belief, we could easily be lured to view as irreversible the growing disparities between rich and poor and the socially powerful and the socially vulnerable, even the ecological degradation of the planet. Some might be buoyed by the hope that the day will come when God will usher in a new heaven and a new earth, where those who suffer hell on earth will live well. Somehow, however, I cannot imagine that bliss in the after-life or some new world could ever compensate for the hell already endured by multiple generations of "the wretched of the earth," whatever lessons might have been learnt in the process. There is also the fact that I do subscribe to the idea of a God who has ideals for each life in relation to every other life, even the planet as a whole, and to the idea that participation in the Christian faith carries with it a call to cooperate with God as God participates in the world.

As should be clear from chapters 5 and 6, I do not subscribe to the idea of a God who, from and infinite non-temporal eternity, predetermined or foreknew exhaustively that the majority of human beings would be benefited by their persistently abject state, and that a few would bask in opulence and comfort with freedom to dominate, using extreme forms of violence when necessary. I am also not convinced that it was God's anticipation that the human animal, which emerged with greatest insight into the character of the earth and with the capacity to influence its processes, would be so preoccupied with self-aggrandizement that we would systematically undermine the earth's capacity to renew itself and provide for the ongoing sustenance of its inhabitants. Finally, genuine human freedom in the dimensions and categories I have identified is not logically compatible with an omni-qualitied God, even when this God strategically self-limits to get what is wanted, such that there is justification for allowing the weakest to be persistently ravaged by the strongest.

The conclusion that is compatible with the idea of an infinitely temporal and imaginatively creative God for which I have argued, and the reasonable inference from historical and ongoing global experience, is that God cannot unilaterally eliminate the excesses of positive freedom or the abuses of negative freedom, and in the end save human beings and other species from the potentially dire consequences of our failure to express freedom responsibly.

I am now very convinced that, being the species that has evolved to the place we have, it is the responsibility of human beings individually and collectively to organize our lives in relation to all life, for the sake of maximal realization of beneficial outcomes from the exercise of freedom in both its ontological and cosmological dimensions. Accompanying this endeavor should be attempts to minimize debilitating outcomes. In the first place, this means, taking seriously all dimensions and activities of life (as far as we can become aware of them) that pertain to the understanding and expression of human freedom as finite freedom—a consideration that immediately pushes us beyond any analysis that does not give serious attention to the potential benefits associated with the religious expression of ontological freedom. With this approach in mind, and with the concept of an infinitely temporal and imaginatively creative God as background, I assert that recognition of God as initiator and ever-present provider of ideals that facilitate intensity of experience and strength of beauty for the cosmos as a whole gives perspective to all human visions, aspirations, and pursuits. When this doctrine of God is included in analysis of social and political processes, with the recognition that it emerges from the exercise of ontological freedom, it reminds us that there is more to the achievement of human freedom than can be accounted for by political, economic, and other social endeavors, even human efforts as a whole.

Taking this doctrine seriously gives one access to a factor of utmost importance to the majority of the world's global citizens as attempts are made to account for the excesses Berlin identifies in his critique of positive freedom and the abuses identified by others in their evaluation of negative freedom. Therefore, on the basis of my proposal of an infinitely temporal and creatively imaginative God that has coexisted eternally with some world, I am clear that, given the absence of such a component from Berlin's framework of analysis, he cannot be seen as having provided the most comprehensive analysis of the excesses he associates with positive freedom. Neither does it enable him to appreciate the full significance of the critiques of negative freedom that are implicit in the analysis of contemporary Western neoliberalism in the earlier section of this chapter. Berlin's analysis, on its own, cannot provide the best clues on how to negotiate the terrain that includes both negative and positive freedom, in order to promote a more comprehensive kind of common good.

To commence the process by which I show how the theological factor contributes to the best clues for negotiating the terrain that includes both negative and positive freedoms, I face Paul Tillich's ideas on faith, in which he alludes to the socio-political scenarios reflected on by Bauckham, Schöwbel, and Berlin. Tillich recognizes that, along with being "the faith of the fighters for enlightenment since the eighteenth century . . . it was humanist faith of the moral kind which was taken over by the revolutionary movements of the proletarian masses in the nineteenth centuries."[85] This claim could also be made for a number of revolutionary movements in the twentieth century. It was exactly their utopianism, he says, that gave these movements their "tremendous power for good and for evil."[86] By its very nature a utopian vision, as freedom easily is, carries the aura of ultimacy and finality. As such, it becomes what Tillich calls ultimate concern, around which every element of a person's life is centered, claiming total surrender and promising ultimate fulfillment.[87] However, Tillich insists that, while many "things" can become ultimate concern, there is really one legitimate ultimate. Every other concern (including human conceptions of freedom, and means to win and/or nurture freedom) is preliminary. The true ultimate, he suggests, is "unconditional, independent of any conditions of character, desire, or circumstance,"[88] and "ultimate concern must transcend every preliminary finite and concrete concern." Indeed, it "must transcend the whole realm of finitude in order to answer the question implied in finitude."[89]

On the basis of this theological foundation, Tillich might well suggest to Berlin that, as a German who had to flee his homeland during Nazi rule and reside in the US where the market and individual success are highly prized, he understands well from both perspectives the consequences when any human enterprise is treated as ultimate and/or perceived to be the final solution. At the same time, someone else noticing that I am attracted to certain ideas of Tillich's might suggest to me that, while, unlike traditional conceptions, Tillich's ultimate is not a personal being,[90] it has far greater kinship with traditional orthodox Christian ideas of God than with the one I developed in chapter 6. As such, even as it puts in perspective all quests for freedom it also exposes the limitation of the concept of an infinitely temporal God to inform a solution to the problems associated with positive and negative freedom.

The ideas that are most obviously in opposition are "unconditionality" and "independence" in Tillich's formulation as against the combination of "temporality" in the Ogden-Heidegger scheme and "relativity" in the Process-Relational scheme. If temporality and relativity were the only important elements in the latter concepts of God, the detractors would have the day. However, I insist that, just as perfection does not need to be understood as independence and absolute unsurpassability, ultimate concern does not necessarily entail independence *simpliciter* and unconditionality *simpliciter*. Therefore, one needs to take note of the dual-aspect nature of God in the latter schemes: In the Ogden-Heidegger scheme God is temporal and infinite; in the Process-Relational scheme God is consequent and primordial. The combination of qualities in each scheme establishes God as categorically supreme and properly qualified as the concern that establishes as limited and preliminary every other concern, including understandings of the character of freedom and the means by which persons should claim freedom. This is exactly what Charles Hartshorne was referring to when he described God as all surpassing and all inclusive.

I have already shown how the idea of an infinitely temporal and imaginatively creative God saves us from unrealistic expectations regarding what God will and will not do as we pursue freedom, and also how it enables us to address logical and ethical challenges associated with traditional orthodox God-talk. Now I assert that the idea of God as an actual entity enables claims of God-human relations to be more than symbolic. Developed in terms of Hartshorne's "self-surpassing surpasser of all,"[91] it gives a better picture of the dynamics of God's involvement in quests for freedom than Tillich's "power of being" that "is the power of everything that is, in so far as it is."[92]

Against the background of the above discussion, I now make a proposal to religious people who, like Bauckham, still promote socialism. I do so with the conviction that, together, the God-concepts developed in the Ogden-Heidegger and Process-Relational schemes are the best representations of ultimate concern that can undergird authentic expressions of human freedom, while serving as reminders to champions of freedom that their conceptions cannot be final or absolute. The proposal is that, having examined the Scriptures, and identified the ways Israel and the early Christian community, at their best, were expected to protect the rights of the poor and otherwise vulnerable, one can easily promote important values associated with socialism without commitment to all aspects of its traditional dynamics. There is no need to characterize what is being pursued under the rubric "common good" as socialist or as any other brand of socio-economic ideology.

Important to my stance is the recognition that having one's material needs adequately addressed is not equivalent to being free. There is also the appreciation that the promotion of finite, realistically libertarian, and relational freedom requires the protection of a personal, private sphere for the conscientious expressions of the individual autonomy Patterson, Mill, and Berlin privilege. The sphere of autonomy would include the freedom to participate in democratic processes described by Sen, as political freedom by Neville, and as civic freedom by Patterson. These features are not only a challenge to some traditional socialists and those who are excessive in their exercise of positive freedom. They are also challenging for those of us in the West who champion liberalism while basking in the personal freedoms facilitated by economic power gained through direct exploitation or through associations with regimes that deny to their citizens the very freedoms we demand for ourselves.

The combination of listed elements, which are expressions of Neville's category of natural freedom, should be associated with the encouragement of a vigorous internal life grounded in ontological freedom that, among other ways, would be exercised in fashioning world-views that are religious and non-religious in nature. These world-views would include, among other elements, an understanding of what "common good" entails as a formal construct, with the details of particular configurations reflecting a creative tension between the demands of local situations and considerations of what is the most wholesome way to operate as participants in one world with multiple contexts and kinds of co-inhabitants. It is operating in light of this creative tension that those who are concerned with general social welfare and those who are captains of industry would have the incentive to wrestle with what Michael Lerner suggests should be an important goal of an economy. This goal is to "reproduce . . . 'a particularly human form of life;'" that is, "to help produce and sustain human beings who are capable of realizing their highest capacities for love; creativity; intelligence; mutual recognition; solidarity; productive work; freedom; caring and nurturing; intimacy; commitment; trust; vitality; and aesthetic, ethical, spiritual, and ecological sensitivity."[93]

It is also with this creative tension in mind that the reader should engage the suggestion, informed by ideas of Leonardo Boff, that the pursuit of common good should privilege the most oppressed people of the world who, being at the mercy of the powerful, are repeatedly violated and exploited by them. Therefore at its center would be efforts to defend and enhance their welfare, "moving outward from these poor and oppressed" to concern for "the dignity of all women and men."[94] This being the case, the pursuit of the common good cannot but be linked to endeavors for human rights, which, in keeping with Berlin's concerns, would be pursued with scrupulous consideration of what is the most realistically libertarian and relational way for freedom to be pursued by each and all in particular contexts. As Boff suggests, when we proceed in this way, there would be the quick appreciation that there is urgent need to prioritize human rights such that the more basic ones: "physical integrity, health, housing, employment, social security, and education come first." Less urgent rights, "will be human rights indeed, but they will be defined from a point of departure in the more basic rights."[95]

Here I suggest that without labeling this endeavor as one "ism" or another, and being always conscious of the complexity of life-situations within the world, there would be appreciation "that human rights actually coincides with a limitation on the privileges of the powerful in order to safeguard the rights of the weakest. In order that all together may be able to create and enjoy a life of justice and communion, some limitations must be placed on the rights of the mighty."[96] Without reiterating points made at various points in this chapter, I give the reminder that all this should take place within a wider circle of concern informed by the recognition that nature is among the rank of the new poor.

## NOTES

1. Orlando Patterson, *Freedom in the Making of Western Culture* (New York: Basic Books, 1991), 402.

2. Ibid., 402-403. Patterson put much effort into tracing this idea through the medieval period, and we await the second volume to see how he charts its path into the contemporary era.

3. Isaiah Berlin, "Two Concepts of Liberty," in *Four Essays on Liberty* (1969; reprint, Oxford: Oxford University Press, 1990), 127.

4. John Stuart Mill, "On Liberty," in *On Liberty and other Essays* (New York: The McMillan Company, 1926), 13.

5. Ibid., 16.

6. Ibid., 14-15, 40-43.

7. Ibid., 61-64.

8. At this time in the USA, a striking contemporary example of the latter would be how much resources ought to be used for certain kinds of scientific experimentation in a time of recession, and also at a time when there is concern that many millions of Americans do not have medical insurance or are inadequately insured.

9. Ibid., 78.

10. Berlin, "Two Concepts of Liberty," 127.

11. Ibid.

12. Ibid.

13. Ibid., 128.

14. Richard Bauckham, *God and the Crisis of Freedom* (Louisville: Westminster John Knox Press, 2002), 27.

15. Ibid., 28

16. Berlin, "Two Concepts of Liberty," 129.

17. Mill, *On Liberty*, 3-6.

18. Stephen's critique was made in the text *Liberty, Equality, Fraternity*. According to Professor Stuart Warner this work "appeared first in periodical form—anonymously, although its author was no secret—in the Pall Mall Gazette from November of 1872 through January of 1873. It was published in book form in March of 1873 and followed a year later by a second edition which included some minor substantive changes, a lengthy second preface, and additional footnotes in the text responding to some of its critics." See: http://oll.libertyfund.org/index.php?Itemid=278&id=571&option=com_content&task=view (Accessed on July 3, 2012).

19. Berlin, "Two Concepts of Liberty," 128. Along with the examples given, there is no denying that in recent times, the former Soviet Union and present-day China, considered by many Westerners to be quite repressive, have produced an impressive number of intellectuals and an array of other expressions of creative genius. It must also be taken into consideration that greater opportunity to express personal freedom opens the way for more persons to choose not to pursue the lifestyle necessary for their genius of any type to flourish.

20. Ibid., 129.

21. Ibid., note 3.

22. Ibid.

23. Ibid..

24. Ibid., 129.

25. Robert Neville, *A Theology Primer* (Albany: State University of New York Press, 1991), 82.

26. This is Orlando Patterson's classification that he defines as "the capacity of adult members of a community to participate in its life and governance." See Patterson, *Freedom*, 4.

27. Neville, *A Theology Primer*, 82.

28. Jonathan Riley, *Mill on Liberty* (London: Routledge, 1998), 42.

29. Mill, *On Liberty*, 7.

30. Berlin, "Two Concepts of Liberty," 163. In the 1926 edition of *On Liberty*, which I have access to, this reflection is found on page 6.

31. Ibid., 163-164.

32. Mill, *On Liberty*, 78.

33. Bauckham, *God and the Crisis of Freedom*, 29-30.

34. Mill, *On Liberty*, 89.

35. Berlin, "Two Concepts of Liberty." 163.

36. Robert Neville, *A Theology*, 82.

37. Alfred North Whitehead, *Process and Reality (corrected edition)*, eds. David Ray Griffin and Donald W. Sherburne (New York: The Free Press, 1978), 278.

38. Ibid.

39. Ibid.

40. Alfred North Whitehead, *Adventures of Ideas* (New York: The Free Press, 1961), 252-256.

41. Bauckham, *God and the Crisis of Freedom*, 30.

42. Ibid.

43. Ibid.

44. Ibid.

45. Ibid.

46. I adopt this expression from Berlin — see "Two Concepts of Liberty," 125.

47. Bauckham, *God and the Crisis of Freedom*, 29.

48. Rebecca Todd Peters, *In Search of the Good Life: The Ethics of Globalization* (New York: Continuum International Publishing Group, 2005), 63-64.

49. Bauckham, *God and the Crisis of Freedom*, 28.

50. Peters, *In Search of the Good Life*, 64. Peters's reference is Milton Friedman, *Capitalism and Freedom* (Chicago: University of Chicago Press, 1962). 35-36.

51. Ibid.

52. Leonardo Boff, *When Theology Listens to the Poor*, trans. Robert Barr (San Francisco, Cambridge: Harper and Row Publishers, 1984), 50-51.

53. Ibid.

54. Clark Williamson, *Way of Blessing Way of Life: A Christian Theology* (St. Louis: Chalice Press, 1999), 269.

55. Ibid.

56. Ibid., 270.

57. Whitehead, *Process and Reality*, 342.

58. I have little doubt that this disposition informed the emergence of the notion of the divine right of kings and was behind Luther's denunciation of the peasant rebellion in Germany during the sixteenth century.

59. Leonardo Boff, *When Theology Listens to the Poor*, 51.

60. J. Emmette Weir, "Toward a Caribbean Liberation Theology," *Caribbean Journal of Religious Studies*, vol. 12 #1, April 1991 [41-53]: 49. Weir's reference is Kortright Davis, *Emancipation Still Comin': Explorations in Caribbean Emancipatory Theology* (New York: Orbis Books, 1990), 144.

61. Leonardo Boff, *When Theology Listens to the Poor*, 61. Boff's reference is Jon Sobrino, "Dios y los procesos revolucionarios," in *Apuntes Para Una Teologia Nicarguense* (San Jose, Costa Rica: Departamento Ecumenico de Investigaciones, 1980), the entire third part.

62. Kortright Davis, *Emancipation Still Comin': Explorations in Caribbean Emancipatory Theology* (New York: Orbis Books, 1990), 8-9.

63. David Ray Griffin, "Creativity and Postmodern Religion," in *God and Religion in a Postmodern World: Essays in Postmodern Theology* (Albany: State University of New York Press, 1989), 29.

64. Berlin, "Two Concepts of Liberty," 124.

65. Ibid.

66. Ibid., 125.

67. Ibid., 129.

68. Originally from India, Sen lived in England for many years and had a distinguished career as professor of Economics before moving to the US. In 1998 he was recipient of the Nobel Prize in Economics.

69. Amartya Sen, *Development as Freedom* (New York: Anchor Books, 2000), 146.

70. Ibid., 148. Lee Kuan Yew is a former prime minister of Singapore.

71. Ibid., 149-150.

72. Ibid., 152.

73. This is chapter six, 146-159.

74. Bauckham, *God and the Crisis of Freedom*, 31

75. Ibid.

76. Christoph Schöwbel, "Imago Libertatis: Human and Divine Freedom," in *God and Freedom—Essays in Historical and Systematic Theology*, ed. Colin E. Gunton (Edinburgh: T& T Clark, 1995), 57.

77. Ibid.

78. Ibid.

79. Berlin, "Two Concepts of Liberty," 130.

80. I suspect that this attitude is, among other influences, informed by his intimate awareness of the Bolshevik revolution, which commenced as resistance to Czarist oppression and which benefited from the astute analysis of Karl Marx, but, over time, developed into Soviet communism that involved activities considered by many to represent the most extreme forms of tyranny in the twentieth century. As a scholar, Berlin would also have carried out in-depth analysis of other examples in the history of European activism in the name of freedom, including the French revolution, referred to by Schöwbel and which ended up in Jacobin tyranny. He would rightly be anxious about any hint of an attitude resembling that of Maximilien Robespierre who was of the view that the terror perpetrated by the Jacobins was the despotism of liberty against tyranny, and of that of his lieutenant Luis de Saint-Just, who was convinced that the people had to be forced to be free.

81. Berlin, "Two Concepts of Liberty," 132. It is not difficult to see how the scenario would be compounded when note is taken of Berlin's suggestion that often the selves may be represented as divided by an even larger gap than is suggested when considered at the personal level. "[T]he real self may be conceived as something wider than the individual (as the term is normally understood), as a social 'whole' of which the individual is an element or aspect: a tribe, a race, a church, a state, the great society of the living and the dead and the yet unborn." This entity, he suggests, "is then identified as being the 'true' self which, by imposing its collective, or 'organic,' single will upon its recalcitrant 'members,' achieves its own, and therefore their 'higher' freedom."

82. Ibid.

83. Ibid., 132-133. I take seriously Berlin's indication that those pursuing positive freedom might even claim that persons resisting their coercion would not do so if they rightly under-

stood what was in their best interests. It might, therefore, be declared that the oppressor is "actually aiming at what in their benighted state they consciously resist, because there exists within them an occult entity—their latent rational will, or their 'true' purpose—and that this entity, although it is belied by all that they overtly feel and do and say, is their 'real' self, of which the poor empirical self in space and time may know nothing or little; and that this inner spirit is the only self that deserves to have its wishes taken into account." We are reminded that, once this view is adopted the coercer is "in a position to ignore the actual wishes of men or societies, to bully, oppress, torture them in the name, and on behalf, of their 'real' selves, in the secure knowledge that whatever is the true goal of man (happiness, performance of duty, wisdom, a just society, self-fulfillment) must be identical with his freedom—the free choice of his 'true,' albeit often submerged and inarticulate self."

84. Ibid., 167.

85. Paul Tillich, *Dynamics of Faith* (New York: Harper and Rowe Publishers, 1957), 69.

86. Ibid.

87. Ibid., 1, 2, 8.

88. Paul Tillich, *Systematic Theology*, vol. I (Chicago: University of Chicago Press, 1951), 12.

89. Ibid., 211.

90. On the other hand, the ultimate (God) is the power of being, and while transcending every being that participates in it, is the power of everything that is, in so far as it is. God as ultimate is, therefore, the ground of all things finite and temporal, but cannot be included under any of these categories.

91. Charles Hartshorne, *The Divine Relativity: A Social Conception of God* (New Haven: Yale University Press, 1948), 20.

92. Tillich, *Systematic Theology*, vol. I, 231.

93. Michael Lerner, *The Politics of Meaning: Restoring Hope and Possibility in an Age of Cynicism* (Reading, MA: Addison-Wesley Publishing Company, 1996), 238.

94. Boff, *When Theology Listens to the Poor*, 52.

95. Ibid., 55.

96. Ibid.

*Chapter Eight*

# Freedom in Imagination

Chapter 7 clarified how challenging it is to translate freedom as a concept and ideal in concrete circumstances, with their complex demands and limitations. These situations often afford only degrees of freedom in particular dimensions and categories, and there are circumstances in which restrictions are so severe that some of the more obvious signs of freedom might not be evident. This chapter is inspired by the conviction that, when other opportunities for the expression of freedom have been denied or severely minimized, there is one bastion of freedom that remains—the imagination. This phenomenon, which is fundamental to the construction of a self, involves the capacity to fashion pictures of reality, construct scenarios that represent ways to negotiating reality, decide what our experiences mean, and make connections between what is at hand and what is envisaged in the future. One might say that imagination has to do with the creation of images: of the self, the world, the significance of the self in relation to the world, and the potential outcomes from these interactions. Imagination is, therefore, a key factor in the irrepressibility of the human spirit, whatever the external circumstances.

Ruth Byrne's insights helps me link imagination to counterfactual reasoning by which, in the normal course of our lives, we develop scenarios that go contrary to established facts. This being said, there are formidable difficulties involved in orienting the imagination of the oppressed toward a wholesome sense of self and constructive pursuits of freedom. Grasping the hope provided by Kwok Pui Lan's suggestion that there are always spaces in the most oppressed mind for creative departures from what is normative, I explore the character of imagination and its link to selfhood. I also argue that conceptions of selfhood which privilege external relations of recognition are not adequate for the persistently oppressed. For these people, the significant human Other is either fellow-oppressed, who have been equally dehumanized, or the oppressor with dehumanizing intention and who represent dehumanizing systems, which have their own unique transcendence. It is shown that the adequate counter to these forces is a God that, as the ultimate Other, has the oppressor's best interest at heart and is open to an engagement of mutual recognition with the oppressed.

Focusing on the Process-Relational concept of "perception in the mode of causal efficacy" that pushes beyond what Byrne calls normal into the interior depths of the self, I imaginatively explore the development of selfhood. This development involves God's offering of ideals that lures persons to visions of self in relation to God and a world of others that can have revolutionary freedom-enabling consequences. It is attunement to this multifaceted dynamic that can be fuel for visions of freedom, plots for freedom, and new expressions of freedom. Heightened appreciation for the significance of imagination in general, and also its theological significance, should make persons more willing to exercise it in more purposeful ways as a form of freedom.

## DEFINING IMAGINATION

Immanuel Kant hints at the challenge associated with exploring the phenomenon of imagination when, in the process of explicating his complex epistemological scheme with a well-defined structure of *a priori* categories, he indicates that imagination is as "a blind though indispensable function of the soul"[1] which constitutes the subjective ground for the link between understanding (cognitive functions of the mind that include *a priori* categories) and sensibility (sense perception) such that experience is synthesized and knowledge is constructed.[2] While imagination is not part of the rational structures through which categorizations are made and we come to know anything about the world, there would be nothing beyond bare sense data to which categories can be applied without some synthetic process from which images emerge. This interpretation is consistent with Kant's claim in the *Critique of Judgment* that "a representation whereby an object is given, involves, in order that it may become a source of cognition at all, imagination for the bringing together the manifold of intuition, and understanding for the unity of the concept uniting the representation."[3]

Applied to the central concern of this chapter, the discussion so far leads to the question: what constitutes the most effective process by which the oppressed of this world can develop wholesome images of themselves and claim the space to engage in considerations that potentially result in meaningful efforts to liberate themselves and others to live purposeful lives? In the process of addressing these questions it will be shown that there is more that can reasonably be said about the character of imagination than Kant's conceptual framework permits, and that imagination is vital for self-understanding and understanding of the world that engenders and expresses human freedom.

It is not surprising that contemporary scholars like Kwok Pui Lan, Gordon Kaufman, and Garret Green presuppose Kant's epistemological framework in their considerations on imagination. Kwok Pui Lan takes up the German term for imagination, *Einbildungskraft*, and indicates that it means the power of shaping into one.[4] She proceeds to suggest that as natural, physical beings we are bound by laws of nature, as moral agents by the law of practical reason, but as imaginative creatures we are constrained by neither and thus have creative power.[5] Gordon Kaufman fills out our understanding as he suggests that imagination has to do with the ability to envision possibilities which do not *actually* exist. "This power to entertain the merely possible, the not-now-actual, and then to work to make these possibilities into actualities has enabled creation of the whole distinctively human world of culture and history; it has freed humanity from being bound to the actual, the given."[6]

Green suggests that "common to various uses of the term imagination (including a family of related terms like fantasy, fanciful, image, imaginary) is an image or picture representing some object that is not directly accessible to the imagining subject."[7] He identifies three levels of inquiry into imagination. There is "transcendental inquiry," exemplified in Kant's approach, which has to do with *a priori* structures of experience. At this most basic level "imagination refers not to any part or aspect of experience itself but rather to the conditions necessary for there to be any experience in the first place."[8] There is "imagination at the level of perception," which reflects the recognition by gestalt psychologists that "we perceive not by means of cumulative association of atomistic sense data but rather by grasping a whole pattern (*Gestalt*) in a single perceptual act."[9] It is the third level that distinguishes Green most from Kant. This level presupposes the previous two, and Green suggests is immediately relevant to theological endeavor. In interpretation "a subject matter that is not available to direct observation is mediated by selective and integrating images, which are themselves of necessity drawn from our experience of reality that is immediately accessible."[10] "This kind of inaccessibility is logical" because that about which we theologize "is not subject to direct observation."[11] I have dramatized, especially in my exploration of God-concepts, that "such objects are frequently imagined in spatial or temporal metaphors."[12] Here I embrace Kaufman's reminder that the very biblical framework from which Christian thinkers find justification for one framework of metaphors or another is itself the outcome of complex processes of mythic imagination.[13]

Kaufman explicitly supports my view that imagination is not only important to having a world, but to being a self with ontological freedom as a key component of any expression of freedom. Imagination may be unique to the human being as Kaufman suggests, or it may not be. It is, however, crucial in identifying the self that makes knowledge-claims, as he suggests. By means of an impressive analysis of the word "I" Kaufman shows that, while it refers to this present self using it, it also has reference to the remembered past and the anticipated future, "sketched as it is in my plans and projects, my hopes and fears." While not *actually* present, both past and future are present symbolically "in the form of memory and imagination." I add that it is not only the future that is imagined; the past is also remembered imaginatively as they both contribute to the sense of who one is and what one is doing. Thus the word "I" is not simply a label for the human entity that is present and visible, "it is a complex symbol which binds together the conceptual and imagistic realities of past and future with the presently existing physical organism and all its needs, binds them to the psycho-physical unity we call a self."[14] Given this dynamic, Kaufman proceeds to claim "that symbolic elements—images, concepts—are constitutive for every instance of human self-consciousness and that in this sense conceptual and imaginative activity is in at the very ground floor of selfhood."[15]

## TOWARD THE RESTORATION OF DEBILITATED SELFHOOD

For those who have operated under the bludgeoning force of oppressive powers that have left them feeling worthless, insignificant, and almost non-persons it is at this "ground floor of selfhood" that the exploration of imagination must begin, in order to encourage its exercise for the sake of freedom. Given my background and his importance for some post-colonialists, I go first to discussions by Frantz Fanon, who, from his experiences growing up in Francophone Caribbean and his later life in Africa, gives us a hint of the debilitating legacy many are locked into as they continue to struggle for survival. He described a relentless process of dehumanization by colonizers, or, more specifically and bluntly, efforts to turn the colonized into animals.[16] Fanon speaks of a cult of inferiority "created by the death and burial of . . . local cultural originality," and the imposition of the language and culture of the "civilizing" nation (mother country) by which the colonized "is elevated above his jungle status in proportion to the adoption of the mother country's cultural standards."[17] The reader might recall that in chapter 4 I employed statements made by Bill Watty many years later to describe this debilitation in Anglophone Caribbean.

We get a glimpse of the religious ideology that helped to justify the process that led to the situations Fanon and Watty describe as Puerto Rican Mayra Rivera quotes the directive from a missionary at the time of the US invasion and occupation of her home country. The missionary declares: "To know the mind of God is the first requisite of the missionary, but next to that he must come to knowledge of the mind of the people over whom he shall be placed by the Holy Spirit."[18] This portrayal is telling. Here we have justification for domination and control based on a vision of self as gifted with the capacity to know the mind of God and the mind of the dominated—even more, to be convinced that God has placed the dominated in one's hand to do as one deems fit. This is, in effect, a nullification of the personhood of the dominated. As such, an appropriate remedy requires restoration of personhood from the root upward that involves radical re-imagining of sociological, psychological, and religious stances in the spirit of freedom that is finite, realistically libertarian, and relational.

## Interpersonal Recognition — Necessary but Not Enough

Having gotten this far in this text the reader should be clear that I do not support the view that selfhood can be gained or reclaimed by escaping to an internal world that is unaffected by external situations or by connecting with an immutable essence that constitutes the real self. I repeat Herman Daley's and John Cobb's declaration that, while the individual does contribute to the self that she/he becomes, "persons are constituted by their relationships and have no identity apart from them."[19] However, it is not to thinkers like Daley and Cobb that post-colonialists have typically turned in order to explore this matter. As part of his analysis, Fanon takes up ideas from Hegel and suggests that "in its immediacy, consciousness of self is simple being-for-itself. In order to win the certainty of one's self, the incorporation of the concept of recognition is important."[20] This has to do with the desire of every self to be acknowledged: to have her/his character as being-for-self recognized by the Other.

With the Jewish Holocaust in mind, this idea of recognition was explored in great detail by Emmanuel Levinas, whose considerations have influenced some contemporary postcolonial theorists and liberation theologians.[21] Levinas advises us never to take outward manifestation for a thing itself. "The who involved in activity is not expressed in the activity . . . but is simply signified in it by a sign in a system of signs, as a being who is manifested precisely as absent from their manifestation." While I am of the view that "being" and "doing" are not as disjoined as Levinas's claim seems to suggest, I agree that a person's life and labor masks her. "As symbols they call for interpretation."[22] Levinas displays his ambivalence toward the idea of an interiorized subjectivity in his claim that interpretation by an Other is not of what is already known to a self. At the same time, he insists that this does not mean that the existence of a self is constituted by the thought of the Other. What he seems to be suggesting is that the human self is inter-subjective. As such, it is exposure to the Other, even by virtue of that Other having a face that is both enigmatic and expressive of beckoning desire, that one is exposed to the questioning of an Other. "The face I welcome makes me pass from phenomenon to being . . . in discourse I expose myself to the questioning of the Other, and this urgency of the response—acuteness of the present—engenders me for responsibility; as responsible I am brought to my final reality."[23] In this process the "transcendence" of the self is appreciated with the recognition that the self is always more than it can draw from itself and contains more than can be drawn from it in the dynamics of recognition.[24]

It is certainly an attractive idea that this dynamic of recognition is the context in which the conceptual and imaginative activity Kaufman associates with the ground floor of selfhood takes place. In fact, it is not farfetched to suggest that the whole process of questions and responses is one in which the imaginative capacity of a self, at any degree of its fulfillment, is at work weaving together external and internal elements in the progressive development of selfhood. This is not only consistent with Kwok Pui Lan's and Kaufman's ideas, but partly explains Levinas's view that "to be I is, over and beyond any individuation that can be derived from a system of references, to have identity as one's content." The "I," he suggests, "is not a being that always remains the same, but is the being who's existing consists in identifying itself, in recovering its identity throughout all that happens to it."[25] Here the reader should recognize that, considered as a general claim, Levinas's position is not inconsistent with the Process-Relational position that a human being is not merely the final product of a long evolutionary process, but is able to contribute to her/his development.

However, with these considerations comes the appreciation that the most significant human Other, in relation to which the oppressed must wrestle with their personhood, is the very oppressor committed to the destruction of their sense of humanity.

In further reflecting on the Caribbean, Fanon paints a vivid picture of the extent of this dilemma: the severe disfigurement of the dynamics of recognition in a context of persistent oppression. He suggests that "the Antilleans have no inherent values of their own; they are always contingent on the presence of the Other." In describing the unhealthy character of the Antillean's desire for recognition he indicates: "Everything the Antillean does is done for the Other."[26] Indeed, the pernicious character of the situation is made stark by the claim that the Antillean in his inferiority compares himself not "with the white man [Other] qua father, leader, God." Instead "he compares himself with his fellow against *the pattern of the white man* (italics mine)."[27] The suggestion seems to be that the Antillean had embraced a model of personhood that was grounded in the image of the white colonizer-oppressor—this image represented by, but transcending every particular white person.

Therefore, it challenges those who, consistent with Levinas's existentialist orientation, would be of the view that the subjectivity of an Antillean could be brought to "final reality" and her transcendence appreciated by means of external encounters of a person-to-person type with representatives of her most dominant Other, the white colonizer. Any one adopting such a position would have had to overlook the fact that the oppressed Antillean, and others like her, is encountered by other individuals in the context of a dominating structure of whiteness that, without an adequate countervailing agent, determines that interpersonal encounters will only perpetuate degradation, destroy selfhood, and kill the capacity of the oppressed Antillean to imagine in freedom for freedom.

There are a variety of contemporary situations in which the dehumanization project Fanon identifies in Africa and the Antilles continues to be evident. Many interactions in contemporary societies are guided by an assessment of worth primarily in terms of the capacity of persons to produce some commodity or provide some service for others. Martin Buber characterized these relations as "I-it" relations, and Fanon, along with others, would use the expression "objectification." The most obvious others will be individuals or groupings of individuals. However, these individuals and/or groups reflect the values of social and/or economic systems that over time have developed characters that supersede the sum-total of those who represent them. Using Levinas's words, their own "surplus" becomes evident. A quite egregious expression is the long-standing global scenario in which, rather than be "recognized as persons," females are lumped under the category "woman," that is, constructed as a negative image of the male subject. Here we have a situation in which it is not merely individual men that are the debilitating Others for women, but the prevailing system of patriarchy that continues to dominate, even if many men resist it. As is the case with other systems of domination, it is often the case that even members of the oppressed group become its representatives.

While Rivera does not make a distinction between systems of oppression as systems and their representatives, her discussion of the virulence of patriarchal oppression of woman is quite applicable to other forms of oppression. In engagement with Catherine Keller's explication of the "separative self," she suggests that wanting to portray an appearance of self-sufficiency and independence, the male subject denies the influences others have in it. This can only be achieved by domination, for "only by subduing and possessing the Other can [the self] feel truly in possession of itself."[28] It is suggested that the success of this gesture "depends on what it hides: the subject's dependence on others to carry the burdens said ego refuses." Under patriarchal oppression, "woman as man's most intimately threatening and yet most comfortingly controlled Other, is there to fill his lack . . . of intimate connections."[29] Significantly, Rivera argues that, while this analysis focuses on the functioning within patriarchal societies, it also illuminates the present dynamics between First and Third world economies. "Pursuing progress without restraint, the First world asserts its control and possession of the Third world, which carries the burden of the physical labor and ecological devastation, all while the first World refuses the vulnerability of intimate connections, interdependence and mutuality."[30]

I now move to another vital component of recognition that has implications for the emergence of personhood that reinforces my view that framing the dynamics of recognition primarily in terms of an external person-to-person interaction is woefully inadequate for producing freedom-enabling imagination. Continuing in conversation with Hegel, Fanon suggests that "there is an absolute reciprocity which must be emphasized."[31] It is in the degree to which recognition is in two directions that full personhood is fostered. He speaks directly to the disposition of the typical colonizer, promoter of patriarchy, and hierarchicalist when he declares that "if I prevent the accomplishment of movement in two directions, I keep the other within himself." Ultimately, the other is deprived of her "being-for-itself." Authentic personhood will be denied on both sides because "what is to happen can only be brought about by means of both"; "they recognize themselves as mutually recognizing each other."[32]

Considered at the interpersonal level, it is obvious that in colonial and neocolonial situations, patriarchal frameworks, and other frameworks of oppression, the disruption of mutual recognition is severe. Those who are dominant have concluded that they know the dominated without having had a real encounter of recognition. Further, the dominator is not available for mutual encounter because they either do not recognize the need for it or do not wish for it to take place. In fact, it serves the purposes of the dominator to keep prevailing images (of self and other, and of self by the other) in place as they justify continued oppression and make the oppressed susceptible to the machinations of the oppressor.

The full gravity of the situation becomes more evident with the appreciation that looming over an individual oppressor (or a group/community of oppressors) is a system to which he is devoted (e.g., Christendom, capitalism, racism, patriarchy etc.), with this system informing the character of relations in which individuals are involved. Thus it is not merely that the oppressor is unavailable to the oppressed for mutual recognition, it is also that there is a transcending system in the name of which he operates, which also infiltrates the life of the oppressed even when she despises individual oppressors or the sum total of oppressors. While omnipresent in a framework of oppression, a system of oppression can never be involved in an authentic process of recognition. Therefore, everyone will be denied the opportunity to achieve full personhood. This, however, does not change the fact that the dominated and oppressed will remain in a situation of unfreedom and degradation, and will not achieve the level of subjective fulfillment that nurtures imagination in freedom for freedom.

## GUIDANCE BEYOND THE OBVIOUS AND INTO THE DEPTHS

Without doubt, formation and/or restoration of the self are, in part, determined by the external interactions of recognition. However, structures of relations such as those just discussed strongly suggest that, especially for the oppressed, there also must be robust exploration of a process that is internal to persons, from which emerges meaningful images of wholesome personhood and constitutes a space for radically re-imaging how the self relates to others. This internal process must involve the kind of recognition that is able to address the depersonalizing impact of individual oppressors, communities of oppression, and also systems of oppression.

I suggest that the way is opened by the explication of a process that involves imaginative embrace of the recognizing presence of the infinitely temporal and imaginatively creative God that is internally related and all-inclusive explicated in chapter six. An encounter with God in the secret depths of the soul does not by itself result in a fully formed and wholesome self; there is still need for recognition by human others. At the same time, confidence that one is engaged with an actuality that (as God) is the ultimate Other, and yet is open to genuinely mutual relations of recognition, can go a far way in countering the power of destructive images that results from person-to-person interactions. This interaction of mutual recognition with God opens the way for the oppressed to imagine themselves differently, imagine their prospects adventurously, and imagine the process by which they can participate in changing their external circumstances. I will work my way slowly toward deeper exploration of God's role by discussing the status and structures of imagination.

## The Status and Dynamics of Imagination

The oppressed, who are besieged by those who keep them under control and would discredit any unconventional insight they entertain, are faced with a major challenge: learning to trust their internal processes and the novel possibilities that emerge from them without becoming disconnected from the facts of the external circumstance that has warped their self-understanding. With this challenge in mind, I am careful in my agreement with Green's claim that objects of imagination may be either realistic or illusory. He suggests that the imaginary is related to the fantastic—departures from the real world such as is expressed in play, daydreaming etc., even the deceitful—"including all attempts to falsify, distort, or misrepresent reality for the purpose of misleading oneself or others."[33] Like other forms of imagination, deceit does not need to be either deliberate or conscious, and so Green suggests that this is what is implied in the atheistic representation of religion as "a variety of unconscious deceitful imagination."[34]

I quickly acknowledge that, understood as a form of self-deception that leads to the deception of others, the capacity to nurture the fanciful should be monitored carefully. Gerald Boodoo is correct that those who most yearn for freedom easily become susceptible to conceptions and schemes that presume expressions of freedom that do not actually exist and promote capacities for freedom that are not realizable.[35] At the same time, everyone who takes stances on what is realistic or unrealistic should also ask: Whose interpretations have determined what is seen as constituting the realistic? What influences govern the *gestalt* which is their and our image of the world or a particular situation? What criteria have determined the images chosen for the sake of interpretation? Is it not the case that most often a prevailing understanding of reality will reflect the perceptions and interpretations of powerful groups and communities whose self-understanding and status is linked to the maintenance of the *status quo* from which they benefit? Will the powerful, for the sake of their own interests, not always seek to convince those with alternative visions that these visions are misrepresentations of reality?

There is virtue in Green's elaboration of what is appropriate employment of imagination that begins with his claim that terms such as "imaginative" imply a realistic use of imagination. What he means becomes clear in his claim that "when we seek 'imaginative leadership' we are not looking for a leader who tells tales or sees things that aren't there, but rather for one who is especially gifted at seeing what is there and able to envision new possibilities for realistic action."[36] My strong conviction is that significant developments in the ongoing quest for freedom will not take place until those who are classified as unrealistic in light of sociopolitical assessment and impious in light of theological assessment claim the freedom to fashion new visions of the world, including what constitutes a life of freedom within it. While there is always the risk of misrepresentation, careful, disciplined pursuits in imagination should be boldly classified as re-presentations of reality, and much like a re-working is a reconfiguration of something already in place, so would a re-presentation be a reconfiguration of what constitutes reality.

A good way to start is with insights from Sharon Parks, utilized by Kwok Pui Lan as she proposed ways oppressed women might navigate the Bible with its androcentric perspective. Appropriating her proposals in light of our emphasis, it involves recognizing that there is a conflict between what is being paraded as freedom and how one is actually experiencing life. This should lead to a process of creative imagination expressed in the quest for a new image; to repattern reality, and the pursuit of new interpretation.[37] Processes like this are grounded in the dynamics of inner freedom than can never be totally hindered by any attempts at external domination and control.

That this process can be a quite sophisticated enterprise is dramatized by consideration of what Ruth Byrne calls counterfactual imagination—a notion used to characterize the common every-day procedure by which changes are made to aspects of our mental representation of reality. Counterfactual imagination involves the creation of scenarios explaining how events could have turned out differently if particular facts or configuration of facts were different. As imaginative reasoning counterfactual thought operates much like deductive reasoning in general,[38] as it proceeds by considering "sets of true possibilities" or "conditionals"[39]—this associated with examination of the relation between antecedents and consequents.[40]

According to Byrne the crucial difference between imaginative thought and ordinary conditionals is that the former involves the consideration of a wider set of possibilities that seem to be inferences from ordinary conditionals. This process includes the utilization of a subjunctive mode of thinking.[41] Interestingly, people tend to change particular kinds of facts so consistently that they can be characterized as constituting "joints" or "fault lines" of reality. Clues on what these are can be detected by the fact that as people struggle with questions regarding how things might have been different and what should have happened, they tend to imagine counterfactual alternatives to actions, controllable events, socially unacceptable actions, causal relations, and actions that come last in a series.[42] There are even fault lines in categories and concepts just as there are in events and episodes—allowing for the invention of new instances of a category.[43]

Kwok Pui Lan's general insight and Byrne's detailed investigation are quite encouraging as we consider the power of imagination to fashion scenarios that can foster the pursuit of external freedoms. Byrne claims that in imagining how things might be different, the way is opened to learn from mistakes, and we are assisted in plans to prevent certain things from happening in the future.[44] It seems to me that, building on these features, people should move easily to the "what if" questions that open up constructive scenarios. However, if the only factors that are eligible to be engaged counterfactually are those provided by the empirical circumstance characterized by oppression, it is quite probable that imaginative exercises will be ones in which deck chairs are creatively rearranged, and even decks reconfigured, but the general conceptual paradigm in which one operates is left unchanged. This is because there is nothing explicit in the elements listed by Byrne that necessarily pushes one who operates in situations of longstanding social and cultural domination to go beyond the reconfiguration of what, in Kwok Pui Lan's language, would be the range of available images and image-making orientations that quite probably reflect dominant cultural patterns. Using Byrne's own language, adjustments could be made that do not deviate too far from facts as they are known, that is, portrayals of the situation in official sources.[45]

Having said this, Byrne is pointing us in a direction that enables us to appreciate Kwok Pui Lan's explanation of the way she went about modifying her thinking after many years of pursuing her vision of a post-colonial feminist approach to theologizing in Asia. Kwok Pui Lan informs us that in her earlier considerations not enough attention was given "to the analysis of the fragmented subjectivity or the multiple fractures of the colonized subject's mind and psyche in the imaginative process."[46] Recalling the evaluations of Fanon and Rivera, I suspect that this condition would have included, among features identified before, the internalization of theological ideas from mainstream Christianity that left many Asian women with the conviction that they have no freedom, cannot handle freedom, or that to pursue freedom is an act of *hubris*. Against this background, Kwok Pui Lan is luring us toward radical appropriation of Byrne's suggestion that there are "joints" or "fault lines" of reality when she points out that, in her consideration of the dynamics of imagination, she moved to the point where she gave more attention to "the cracks, the fissures, and the openings, which refuse to be shaped in any framework, and are often consigned to the periphery."[47]

Kwok Pui Lan displays her emancipation from Kantian epistemological structures as she suggests that these disparate elements "staunchly refuse to follow the set pattern, the established episteme, the overall design that the mind so powerfully wants to shape."[48] And it is the vision provided by Process-Relational ideas that enables us to see from the underside what Kwok Pui Lan refers to as "cracks, the fissures, and the openings." This vision is of a teeming life of interactions in the deep-structure of electrons, molecules, and cells that make up the human being, and is characteristic of every facet of perception and conceptualization in the human brain-mind, from which God is never absent. The powerful developments in Kwok Pui Lan's theology over the years seem to support the view that imaginative attention to these "spaces" and the processes beneath them has the "the potential to point to another path, to signal radically new possibilities."[49]

Significant thinkers through history have alluded to this deeper level, and I now give an idea of the way two modern scholars represented it. William James speaks eloquently as he attempts to relate findings from psychological exploration to the phenomenon of religious experience. He suggests that in the final analysis the dynamic of the religious life is far deeper than even the notion of the subconscious can explain. In the first place, the subconscious only accounts for the "hither" side of the "more" to which we feel connected in religious experience.[50] There is another side, he suggests: "The further limits of our being," which "plunge . . . into an altogether other dimension of existence from the sensible and merely 'understandable' world."[51] Before him Rudolph Otto pointed us beyond the rational structures of mind where impulses from "the deep" come under the influence of categories by which ideas and symbols of religion are formally structured.[52] He calls this deeper place "the fundus animae, the 'bottom' or 'ground of the soul.'"[53] In my framework of thought, what Otto refers to as "bottom" or "ground," represents recognition of the capacity of the human brain-mind to discern the presence of the all-inclusive and internally relating God who is the ultimate Other. From this discernment, insights about self and world emerge, which can counter the forces that would destroy peoples' capacities to imagine and pursue freedom.

## MUTUAL RECOGNITION WITH THE ULTIMATE OTHER— CAUSAL EFFICACY AS A DIVINE PORTAL

Considerations from Alfred North Whitehead have helped me recognize that Kant's inability to go beyond his declaration regarding the mysterious character of imagination was influenced by an approach to perception that was dominated by sense data.[54] Whitehead classifies this mode of perception as presentational immediacy. As should be evident from my earlier discussions, I am convinced that it is the privileging of what he named perception in the mode of causal efficacy that enables important attention to dynamics in the subterranean depths of a person's inner life. Causal efficacy highlights the recognition that there is an inside to every actual entity and process with dynamics. Given our consideration of personhood and imagination, I focus on what Otto referred to as the soul and I call the brain-mind. Indeed, with the recognition that processes within the mind-brain are either electrical or chemical, the picture I have in mind is of conglomerates of interactions within and between actual entities (atoms, electrons, and other subatomic particles).

To prepare for specific discussions of the brain-mind, the reader is asked to imagine processes within any actual entity in the following way. The actual entity internalizes influence from various sources (physical prehension), synthesizes these influences (conceptual prehension), and from this synthesis in which they realize themselves (concrescence), contribute to the development of other processes (superjection). Movement toward application to the human brain-mind is taken with the recognition that it is a complexly ordered intertwining of societies of occasions. Thus, I am able to portray imagination as the picture of a self and world (all that pertains to the life of the self) that emerges from a vast complex of processes at multiple levels of brain-mind dynamics. Of relevance is Marjorie Suchocki's description of a three-phase movement that leads to self-consciousness. There is that mode of existence which "is immersed in the sheer physicality of existence responding to its inner drives and outward circumstances." While thought may occur, it will not be self-conscious thought. The second stage "is more than simple response to otherness; it is response to other as other." In other words, self-consciousness emerges and Otherness is acknowledged. However, self-consciousness "is not yet at home with itself, not yet fully self-conscious." Full self-consciousness arrives when "the knowledge of otherness moves beyond simple differentiation, mediating to the self a knowledge of the unifying bond of rationality which connects other to self, self to other, in an interdependence, which is finally known to be the truth of existence."[55] What we have is a process that involves imagination as the emerging self develops a picture of itself as a particular actuality in relation to other actualities. And what in the simplest entities would probably be felt as a raw drive toward concrescence, leading to superjection, emerges in the movement toward self-consciousness as the growing desire of a self for self-realization and as the anticipation of contributing to a world of others. Anticipation is a form of imagination that intensifies with full self-consciousness, as the self further imagines with greater complexity the specifics of her contribution and the kind of world that could emerge from her/his contribution.

There is never a human self that has no imaginings. However, influenced primarily by an oppressive Other, there will probably not be viable selfhood (Robert Neville's weak image of self) with the capacity to imagine one's self as capable of freedom in any of its dimensions and categories. It is as we consider the debilitated self-consciousness and deformed imagination of those subjected to persistent oppression that the importance of the Process-Relational understanding of God's place in the development of selfhood becomes most striking. The understanding is that the infinitely temporal and creatively imaginative God is involved at every stage, and provides options for the best way to synthesize diverse influences. The ideals God envisages for each person in relation to ideals for others serve as a lure toward the realization of the best possibilities for one's life in relation to other lives. These possibilities are addressed in light of the subjective purpose adapted from the initial aim that inaugurated one's very emergence. Also vital is the appreciation that the ideals God proposes will be the outcome of God's internalization (prehension) and transmutation (synthesizing) of outcomes from other decision making processes carried out in the process of one's becoming and by other related processes of decision making.

The powerful significance of this picture of God-human encounter is appreciated when it is recalled that God, as imaged in Process-Relational thought, is not the perfect absolute of classical theism who, as perfect Being, is characterized by a fixed-final maximum of all values, and thus incapable of growth. It would be a most grotesque contradiction to imagine that God experiencing subjective fulfillment (final reality) through interaction with human beings and the rest of the world. Instead, using a combination of language from Anselm and Hartshorne, God is that being than which no other being could conceivably be greater. But, being unsurpassable in social relatedness, God is capable of entertaining all possible states and values and of experiencing unending increase/growth. As I have said more than once God is "the self-surpassing surpasser of all."[56]

With this God imaged as present to the deepest-depths of the self and involved in every process of emergence toward self-conscious selfhood, I ask: What more authentic and well-informed recognition can the oppressed have than from encounter with an ultimate Other that is as open to being influenced as to influence? Is this not a form of the mutual recognition that Fanon claims the oppressor denies the oppressed? The dynamics of developing selfhood is certainly part of the scenario being referred to when Whitehead declares that "it is as true to say that God creates the World, as that the World creates God."[57] Having said this, it is Hartshorne's picture of God as an everlasting succession of divine occasions with personal order that best portrays the significance of the world's influence on God. With the recognition by an oppressed person that, as human, she represents that aspect of the world with the greatest level of subjectivity, it should be most empowering for her to imagine God experiencing God's own subjective fulfillments (concrescences), with her influence—this corresponding to sequential moments of divine life.[58] The affirming capacity of this picture for the oppressed is compounded by the claim that, when a person's life is complete (at death), that Other who has been present to and affected by every stage in the emergence of personhood will prehend that person in her full subjectivity; that is, her completed personhood will be included in God.

This ultimate Other is anything but the God of traditional Christian theology whose character is imaged with the influence of understandings of sovereignty informed by ancient kings, emperors, and lords, who, in many respects, looks like the absolutization of earthly tyrants and despots. Instead, we have a picture of a God that relates to each person and the world as a whole "with a tender care that nothing is lost."[59] This God is not only "the fellow-sufferer who understands,"[60] but the one who by communicating self tenderly and persuasively for the good of each oppressed, in relation to the good for all else, establishes a certain pattern of self-other relating as ideal. Whitehead suggests that it is a way, which does not emphasize "the ruling Caesar, or the ruthless moralist, or the unmoved mover," but "dwells upon the tender elements in the world, which slowly and in quietness operate by love; and finds purpose in the present immediacy of a kingdom not of this world."[61]

Even as I imagine this pattern of relations engendering in the oppressed a yearning for a world that is structured in this way, I hasten to add that it is not an attempt to diminish revolutionary fervor, nor is it an invitation to apathy. Instead, it is quite consistent with the attitude that appeared to have fuelled Jesus' ministry. As such, it challenges those who would pursue freedom with or for the oppressed to be always concerned with the "spirit" that fuels their activism, the actual goals that are being pursued, and the methods employed to achieve freedom.

Potential discernments generated by perception in the mode of causal efficacy, which would fuel new departures in one's sense of self and the world, seem to correspond with what Thomas Honsinski classifies as "ontological knowing." He suggests that this knowing serves as vital force for the final integration of conceptual and physical prehensions by which abstract possibilities are related to particular concrete facts.[62] I prefer to speak of "ontological awareness" rather than ontological knowledge. Nevertheless, I embrace Hosinski's claim that ontological "knowledge" is the most primitive form of awareness. Admittedly, this awareness will, at the simplest microcosmic level be, at best, fleeting and negligible impressions. It must also be acknowledged that human cognitive structures, as they have evolved, establish epistemic distance that places limitations on our appropriation of divine influence.[63] Still, having emerged from the most basic level of the self (the bottom of the soul), ontological awareness will mark the character of everything that follows from it. As such, negligible impressions are seeds for adventurous imaginings about freedom, even complex conceptual explorations on freedom. So then, it does not matter how secure structures of oppression seem and how prolonged is the enslavement of the oppressed to cults of inferiority, God's vision of and for each oppressed person in relation to God's vision for all others, can never be eliminated from the human brain-mind/soul.

The oppressed need to be enabled to develop the kind of disposition, with relevant theological support, which fosters attunement to their internal processes by which they might discern who they are as selves, even catch a glimpse of God's ideal for them. Here it must be said that the recognition that conceptual schematization is fundamental to mental processes requires the acceptance that impulses for freedom can be carried by an array of religious forms, and also social and ethical frameworks that are not religious. Of utmost importance is not the schematic garb but the sense of call to embrace a drive for freedom that sometimes seems to emerge from an unplumbed place in the depth of their being. At the same time, the acknowledgement that epistemic distance excludes one-to-one correspondence between what human beings discern and God's actual ideals should temper inclinations to grandiose claims about any quest for freedom. It should also make the enlightened among the oppressed willing to engage each other in critical solidarity to arrive at meaningful understandings of what is appropriate in different settings.

Here I recall that, in Green's discussion of levels of imagination, there was the clear impression that whereas the exercise of will is present to some degree at the level of perception, it is present in much greater degree at the level of interpretation.[64] Against the background of my view that perception and interpretation are not discrete steps in cognition, I take the position that any exercise of will on the part of the oppressed will occur in the context of an ongoing tension between what is occurring at the level of conscious awareness and more "primitive" expressions of ontological awareness. It is when ontological awareness lures the will away from its accustomed willings that are guided by conventional understandings of reality that one develops the daring that is associated with revolutionary processes. Ontological awareness also accounts for the conflicted will that often besets those who confront a prevailing *status quo*. As is suggested by experiences like that of fifteenth-century Italian astronomer Nicholas Copernicus, who, fearing the reaction of the Church, chose to hide his heliocentric model of the universe until he was old, the persisting inclination to go against what is taught to be the will of God can sometimes be the best possible expression of freedom. And, as is evidenced in the life of German pastor-intellectual Dietrich Bonheoffer, Jamaican national heroes Paul Bogle, Sam Sharpe, and Marcus Garvey, African American Rosa Parks, and many others, those who choose to heed the call of and to freedom from the primitive depths have no certain idea how things might turn out. It is always a risk. Nevertheless, imagination represents a vital sphere of freedom for those who are battered and bruised in situations of external oppression and unfreedom, where ideational schemes and emotional tones are intentionally designed to keep the adventurous mind in check.

At one level, freedom as imagination is freedom in the form of a retreat from the harshness of direct involvement in external situations over which one has little or no control. As is suggested by Ruth Byrne's discussion of counterfactual imagination, in the space of imaginative retreat one is actually involved in evaluation and critique of self and others, even when the latter is not permitted in the external sphere. Finally, imagination serves as preparation for the future by being a process of experimentation and strategizing in which possibilities are tested for their potential viability. I therefore encourage the oppressed and all who desire a different-better world to intentionally and carefully nurture imaginary scenarios that some might classify as mere fantasy. This endeavor should be pursued as both an act of defiance and as a way to prime the well-spring of ideas and drives that could result in concrete expressions of freedom.

Many have not even begun to fathom their capacity for purposeful imagination, because their vision is dominated by the external circumstance in which they operate or prohibitions associated with particular types of self-understanding. All this has significance for the inclinations of one's will discussed earlier. I now suggest that an important aspect of the struggle for freedom might well involve the reorientation of a "conflicted will" toward becoming a "liminal will." This reorientation would involve serious engagement with what is considered conventional wisdom, while practicing the capacity for attunement to the nudgings and/or eruptions of ontological awareness. It is operating in this threshold state (in-between place) that one develops trust that at the heart of existence is the power of creative transformation. One also becomes more efficient at "fantasizing" in a way that benefits the quest for freedom in a particular context in relation to God's intentions for freedom in the whole cosmos. It is this image of existence in the liminal, in-between place that will influence my upcoming attempt to explore imaginatively ways in which Christian churches might orient themselves to be more effective agents of freedom for their constituents and the wider communities in which they operate.

## NOTES

1. Immanuel Kant, *The Critique of Pure Reason*, trans. Norman Kemp (New York: St. Martin Press, 1965), 112.
2. Ibid., 143-145.
3. Immanuel Kant, *The Critique of Judgment*, trans. with analytical indexes by James Creed Meredith (Oxford: Clarendon Press, 1992), 58.
4. Kwok Pui Lan, *Discovering the Bible in the Non-Biblical World* (New York: Orbis Books, 1995), 13.
5. Ibid., 52.
6. Gordon Kaufman, *The Theological Imagination* (Philadelphia: The Westminster Press, 1981), 60-61. At that time Kaufman was of the view that "this same power of imagination opens us to the awareness of unhappy and destructive possibilities. And our knowledge of human finitude and failure, of sin and death, makes it impossible for us to rest absolutely secure in any of our human attachments."
7. Garrett Green, *Imagining God: Theology and the Religious Imagination* (San Francisco: Harper and Rowe Publishers, 1989), 62.
8. Ibid., 65.
9. Ibid.
10. Ibid., 66.
11. Ibid., 65.
12. Ibid.
13. Kaufman, *The Theological Imagination*, 26.
14. Ibid., 64.
15. Ibid., 66.
16. Frantz Fanon, *The Wretched of the Earth*, trans. Constance Farrington (1963; reprint, New York: Grove Weidenfeld, 1991), 42. "In fact, the terms the settler uses when he mentions the native are zoological terms. He speaks of the yellow man's reptilian motions, of the stink of the native quarter, of breeding swarms of foulness, of spawn, of gesticulations. When the settler seeks to describe the native fully in exact terms he constantly refers to the bestiary."
17. Frantz Fanon, *Black Skin, White Masks*, trans. Charles Lam Markmann (1962; reprint, New York: Grove Press, Inc., 1967), 18.
18. Mayra Rivera, *The Touch of Transcendence: A Postcolonial Theology of God* (Louisville: Westminster John Knox Press, 2007), 10. Rivera references Robert McLean, *Old Spain in New America* (London and New York: Routledge, 1994), 4.
19. Herman Daley and John Cobb Jr., *For the Common Good: Redirecting the Economy toward Community the Environment and a Sustainable Future* (Boston: Beacon Press 1994), 161.
20. Fanon, *Black Skin, White Masks*. 217. Fanon references G.W.F. Hegel, *The Phenomenology of Mind*, 2nd rev. ed. trans. J. B. Baillie (London: Allen & Unwin, 1949), 230, 231.
21. See Rivera, *A Touch of Transcendence* for good examples.
22. Emmanuel Levinas, *Totality and Infinity*, ed. André Schuwer (Pittsburg: Duquesne University Press, 1969), 178.

23. Ibid.

24. Ibid., 180.

25. Ibid., 36.

26. Fanon, *Black Skin, White Masks,* 211-12.

27. Ibid., 215.

28. Rivera, *Touch of Transcendence,* 7. Rivera's source is *From a Broken Web: Separation, Sexism, and Self* (Boston: Beacon Press, 1986), 27.

29. Ibid.

30. Ibid.

31. Fanon, *Black Skin, White Masks,* 217. For the one not allowed to exercise reciprocating recognition it means, on one hand, that she has been deprived of the opportunity to express self in way that enables her to be known beyond the image in someone else's mind. On the other hand, it hinders movement from being simply a member of a general category (even if that is "human") with certain capacities, to exercising self as an actual person, that is, as a questioning, commanding, influencing agent. For the one denying reciprocation, it means that, while they might have power, she will not have wrestled with self as commanded by the question of the other — thus enabling their subjectivity to come to full reality.

32. Ibid.

33. Green, *Imagining God,* 63.

34. Ibid.

35. Gerald Boodoo, "Faces of Jesus," 7-9. This is an unpublished paper written in 1998. Speaking about The Caribbean, Boodoo portrays the basic characteristic of the its theological framework as "forced." For Boodoo this means that one does not have the luxury of "choices." The only options being those "handed out by the structures of exploitation." The forced individual, he suggests, is in the position where freedom is not dependent on will, and the so-called choices made by the will. He suggests that in the situation of oppression there is a "forced" yearning for alternatives, but these alternatives and the means by which they are pursued are themselves conditioned by the situation.

36. Ibid., 66.

37. Kwok Pui Lan, *Discovering the Bible in the Non-Biblical World,* 13. She references Sharon Parks, *The Critical Years: The Young Adult Search for a Faith to Live By* (New York: Orbis Books, 1984), 25.

38. Ruth M. J. Byrne, *The Rational Imagination: How People Create Alternatives to Reality* (Cambridge, Mass: MIT Press, 2005), 29. "Rational thought is thought that leads to reasonable conclusions—for example, deductive rationality is thought that leads to conclusions that must be true whenever the premises are true . . . Deductive reasoning is rational because people have the underlying competence to think of all the relevant possibilities so that they could search for counterexamples . . . Their performance is sometimes not rational because of the limits to the possibilities they can consider."

39. Ibid., 17-20. Byrne indicates that "within the domain of deductive inference, center stage has been occupied by reasoning about conditional relations, often expressed using 'if' . . ."

40. Ibid., 18, 20ff.

41. Ibid. As suggested on pages 30-31 and 157-159, the subjunctive mode is represented by verbal expressions such as "if," "had/had not" instead of "did/did not," "would have/would not have" instead of "did/did not," "if only," and "only if." As suggested in pages 137-143, there are also "even if" scenarios or semifactual alternatives that address the question: What if the [known] cause did not happen, but the outcome did?

42. See relevant discussions on pages 3 and 8. I find quite striking Byrne's indication on page three that "[t]here are points at which reality is 'slippage.'"

43. Ibid., 191-192.

44. Ibid., 10-11.

45. It is Byrne's view that "people create counterfactual alternatives by making minimal changes to their mental representation of the facts because the facts must be recoverable from the imagined possibility and there is the indication that persons tend to invent instances of a category . . . by relying heavily on their knowledge of the existing category." See Byrne, *The Rational Imagination,* 211.

46. Kwok Pui Lan, *Postcolonial Imagination and Feminist Theology* (Louisville, Westminster John Knox Press, 2005), 39.

47. Ibid., 30.

48. Ibid.

49. Ibid.

50. William James, *Varieties of Religious Experience: A Study in Human Nature* (New York: Longmans, Green and Co., 1925), 512.

51. Ibid., 515.

52. Rudolph Otto, *The Idea of the Holy*, trans. John W. Harvey (Oxford: Oxford University Press, 1973) 61.

53. Ibid., 112.

54. Michael Miller, *Reshaping the Contextual Vision in Caribbean Theology: Theoretical Foundations for Theology Which is Contextual, Pluralistic and Dialectical* (Lanham: University Press of America Inc., 2007), 196. Kant's view is stated on page 183 of the *Critique of Pure Reason*.

55. Marjorie Hewitt Suchocki, *The End of Evil* (New York: State University of New York Press, 1988), 41-42.

56. Charles Hartshorne, *The Divine Relativity: A Social Conception of God* (New Haven: Yale University Press, 1964 [1948]), 20.

57. Whitehead, *Process and Reality (corrected edition)*, ed. David Ray Griffin and Donald W. Sherburne (New York, London: The Free Press, 1978), 348.

58. For Whitehead this God is a single entity that is continuously and progressively being enriched by God's everlasting process of concrescence or development in relation to the cosmos.

59. Ibid., 346.

60. Ibid., 351.

61. Ibid., 343.

62. Ibid. From Thomas Hosinski, *Stubborn Facts and Creative Advance* (Lanham: Rowan and Littlefield Publishers, Inc., 1993), 120-122.

63. Miller, *Reshaping the Contextual Vision*, 201.

64. Green, *Imagining God*, 65-66.

*Chapter Nine*

# Modest Imaginings for Freedom-Oriented Ecclesiology

With all its deficiencies, it is the church which, more than any other organization I know in the Western world, has the potential to facilitate focused activism for external manifestations of freedom along with the nurturing of a rich internal life of contemplation and concept formation on the issues addressed in this project. Therefore, central to the life of this complex community of communities should be the facilitation of ongoing examination and reexamination of its structure, beliefs, and practices to ensure that its members are encouraged to operate in ways that reflect freedom that is finite, realistically libertarian, and relational. Being an important element of what I classify as freedom-enabling ecclesiology, this endeavor should include the formulation of language associated with the concept of partnership to counter the debilitations associated with the language of sovereignty and servitude that has guided life in many churches. Accompanying the new language would be imaginative experiments in administrative structures, styles of leadership, and frameworks of relations that reflect considerations on the nature of community explicated near the end of chapter 7.

In the paper "Eschatology and Ecclesiology," I described a principle that I now suggest should inform the freedom-oriented ecclesiology I am proposing. It is that "the church ought to be the sphere in which the integrity of each participant is nurtured, with the recognition that this integrity depends on the exercise of freedom to process the personal individual address of God in relation to communal influence, for the sake of both personal and communal good."[1] As a result of this dynamic, the church is enabled to be an effective collaborator in God's activities in the life of individuals and the cosmos as a whole.

This role of facilitator would be pursed as the church operates in the midst of a creative tension. On one hand, there is the recognition that the quality of the life and work of the whole Christian community or church catholic is determined by the internal dynamics of local groupings of Christians, as individuals interact with each other. On the other hand, there is Alfred North Whitehead's reminder that the quality of "a structured society as a whole" (in this discussion, the church catholic) is by the way it provides a favorable environment for its component societies,[2] which, for this discussion, are congregations with the individuals that comprise them. Together, these considerations point to a network of interactions in which God is at one and the same time immediately present to individuals, particularized groups, the church as a whole, in relation to God's presence at the heart of the cosmos as a whole. They also call for us to respect the integrity of each and every pursuit of ideal aim, and require that Christians develop relationships that engender flourishing of the other in the most comprehensive way possible. It is in light of my commitment to contribute to the church's ability to be a significant facilitator in this complex endeavor, especially in ways by which those who are most unfree are provided with space and opportunity to pursue wholesome development for self and others, that I proceed to imaginatively engage a range of traditional and nontraditional ideas.

Even as I use ideas from thinkers like Martin Luther, Hans Küng, Jürgen Moltmann, and Letty Russell in the process of developing my ecclesiological proposals, I acknowledge that, as far as I know, none of them made the kind of departure from traditional God-talk that is even close to that which I have pursued in this project. Therefore, as radical as some of their ecclesiological ideas are, they have not led to sustained reorientations in the dynamics of power and the structure of authority within our churches. I am convinced that when their ideas are embraced within the theological structure grounded in the idea of an infinitely temporal and imaginatively creative God that is internally related and all-inclusive and applied in light of the privileging of freedom that is finite, realistically libertarian, and relational, they stand a reasonable chance of having significant ecclesiological impact in our time.


## DEFINING CHURCH


I enter this definitional process with the help of ideas from the most complexly ecumenical body I am aware of, the World Council of Churches. In one of this organization's historic documents, *Baptism, Eucharist, Ministry*, we are told that the church is called to proclaim and model the "Kingdom of God" by the way it operates in the world, and the famous declaration attributed to Jesus in Luke 4:18 is utilized in the explanation of what this means. In the midst of activities such as those described in this declaration, the church is to point people to God through Christ and its members are to testify of their faith is God as the ground of their hope, even as they relate to each and all with compassion and love. Further, "The members of the body are to struggle with the oppressed toward that freedom and dignity promised with the coming of the kingdom. And his mission needs to be carried out in varying political, social and cultural contexts."[3] There is also the challenge to pursue its witness in contextually relevant ways, seeking "to bring to the world a foretaste of the joy and glory of God's kingdom."[4]

This document is a general statement that is expected to allow for a range of interpretations by the constituent members. At the same time, it would be inappropriate for me to give the impression that what it declares is compatible with all aspects of the positions I have taken in this project. In fact, the line of argument I have developed in this project makes me hesitant to embrace the notion "Body of Christ," popularly used to characterize the community of Christians. As used in 1 Corinthians 12:12-26, this metaphor encourages a vision of the church as a complex, caring, and unified community under the authority of Jesus the Christ.

On the other hand, it easily fixes the church to Jesus as the Christ and limits emphasis on his claim that his purpose was to facilitate access to God. Further, the employment of the notion "Body of Christ" along with conceptions of the church like "the extension of the incarnation" results in the over-emphasizing on the church's corporate nature and the supernaturalizing of its institutional character. I prefer to use expressions like "people of God," "fellowship of believers" and "a pilgrim people." The first focuses the conviction that the church emerged as a result of God's gracious presence at the heart of human life and that as a community of persons who have been drawn into a unique revelatory constellation linked to the life and work of Jesus they are called-out and set-apart by God for special work often described in terms of setting people free. Together, the other two remind us that the church is also characterized by the active participation of people in intentional relationship with God and with others inspired and guided by Jesus' relationship with God and others. All these people are involved in an ongoing process that is guided by the vision of each and all becoming progressively better at choosing and acting in ways that are consistent with God's ideals and growing in their depth of intimacy with God and others. In light of my ecclesiological intentions, I will proceed to explore the dynamics of and the means toward this intimacy in terms of the idea of partnership. In the process I will explicate the kind of partnership I consider necessary at all levels of the church's life for it to be truly freedom enabling.

Throughout this project, I have been laying the broad conceptual foundation for this partnership by means of the organismic worldview I've privileged and the notion of a fundamentally relational God who is infinitely temporal and imaginatively creative. My vision of what healthy partnership looks like was hinted at in my engagement of Dick Hamm's ideas in the very introduction of this project. This is a situation in which each party in a network of interactions brings something that they can claim as theirs to give, so that each and all in the network will be benefitted, and on which others can rely for the realization of a common goal. It is not unusual that members of inter-human arrangements called partnerships exercise coercive and manipulative power in order to get others to do what they prefer and to gain most benefits from the arrangement. However, in partnerships where freedom such as I have explicated is privileged, the kind of power exercised by each and all needs to be persuasive and designed to enable all partners to discover and nurture their best gifts for self and other. This will be so even when one party, which in the case of the church will be God, is superior to all others.

## CHRISTOLOGICAL CONSIDERATIONS TO SUPPORT AN ECCLESIOLOGY OF PARTNERSHIP

It was through Karl Barth that I was first introduced to partnership as a concept that was appropriate for describing the relation between God and human beings, grounded in what he classified as the humanity of God. Without doubt, it was a step in the right direction when Barth moved from the conception of God as "wholly other" that is "isolated, abstracted and absolutized," and from his emphasis on the "infinite qualitative distinction between God and man," with these together representing God's independent and unique character.[5] There is much to be said for Barth's theological reorientation, which involved an emphasis on God "turning toward human beings and operating in togetherness with humanity, proving and revealing deity, not in a vacuum as a divine being-for-Himself, but precisely and authentically in the fact that He exists, speaks, and acts as the partner of man, though of course as the absolutely superior partner."[6] This foundational partnership, Barth claims, results in a new valuation of what it means to be human *qua* human. However, a challenge emerges for me with Barth's position that this partnership actually occurs representatively in the person of Jesus Christ in whom, as the true human, "there is no isolation of man from God or of God from man." Barth further declares: "Jesus Christ is in His one Person, as true God, man's loyal partner, and as true man, God's."[7] Here another outgrowth of my earlier discussion regarding the inability of Adam and Eve to be representative human beings becomes evident. I now declare that if, as is the case in orthodox thought, Jesus' person is understood to be the incarnation of the preexistent logos (John 1:1-2, 14) or produced by a supernatural visitation of the Holy Spirit (Matt. 1:18) without the full involvement of two human parents, then he also cannot be representative of human beings who actually inhabit the earth.

Those who have spent time exploring the Christological debates of the first five centuries of the Common Era, especially the controversies that emerged after the Council of Nicaea on what hypostatic union entails, would appreciate why many find it well-nigh impossible to make sense of the formulations the church required the faithful to embrace. It is no wonder that Clark Williamson, while affirming the good intention of attempting to make sense of the saving presence of God in Christ, recognizes that "classical christology collapsed under its own weight" and that at the end of the day it was Jesus' humanity that was undermined.[8] With an emphasis on the role of the logos taking on human nature through hypostatic union, Barth does use impressive language to articulate his position that Jesus Christ represents "man taken up into communion with God,"[9] with this resulting in language that is quite affirming on human beings *qua* human beings.[10] However, the inapplicability of this approach for my understanding of God-human partnership comes to a head in Barth's view that, in the final analysis, what singles Jesus out from the rest of humanity is that "as elected man he is also the electing God, electing them in His own humanity."[11] This claim, most probably, reflects Barth's commitment to the doctrine of Trinity. However, Jesus as God incarnate cannot be said to portray what partnership might look like between God and human beings who are not also the incarnation of God and never will be anything but human; nor can human beings look to Jesus' life to find relevant examples of what ought to outflow from such a partnership so that this might guide partnerships within the Christian community made up of persons who are human beings born of other human beings. The concept of *theosis* (deification), for which early thinkers like Irenaeus laid the foundations and is now most emphasized in the Orthodox streams of Christianity, has promise in regard to what is possible for human beings in partnership with God. However, as it has been explicated historically, it presumes the Christological ideas that I have been criticizing.

The foundation for a more authentic ecclesiology of partnership begins to emerge when Jesus is understood to be a human being born of man and woman, and who, as a result of choices made, developed such a relationship with God that God's presence in his life was evident in an especially vivid way. I celebrate the fundamental intuition, developed narratively in the gospels and subject to further explication and application by the apostle Paul and others, that there was something unique and inimitable about the person of Jesus of Nazareth such that he would be disposed to God and related to his contemporaries in ways that transformed their lives profoundly. As such, I would never claim that any other human being can emulate fully that which characterized Jesus' relationship with God. Nevertheless, it was as a human being with his own unique combination of qualities that Jesus gave active attention to the presence of God in his life. Thus, as is represented by the story of his temptation in the wilderness, he can be said to have been genuinely tempted over the course of his life and was capable of making choices that were contrary to God's ideals for his life. Yet, in the final analysis, he remained faithful to his covenant relationship with God. Therefore, while desperately wishing that the situation were other than it was, he could, in the garden of Gethsemane, say "never-the-less"—this leading to the cross.

We who are part of the community that emerged as a result of the partnership between Jesus and God live in the grasp of its influence as appropriated and interpreted in light of concepts and categories handed down through the centuries. It is the concept of grace that best expresses our sense that it is God who took the initiative in establishing the conditions for a partnership God desires for our sake and God's sake. As a result of the ongoing presence of God at the heart of our lives we develop insight into the opportunities and challenges associated with a partnership with God, and we experience a sense of empowerment by and for our pursuit of this partnership. This insight is gained as we operate as partially self-creating human beings who being able to exercise realistic libertarian freedom must take decisions on how we respond to what we discern in ambiguity about the infinitely temporal, imaginatively creative and self-giving God who desires intimacy and partnership with us.

Jesus the unique Jewish man, who would be the Christ for his followers, was persistent in his quest for intimacy and partnership with God. As such, I will not claim that he would have valued every aspect of the finite, realistically libertarian, and relational freedom I promote. However, I will claim that the freedom Jesus experienced as a result of his partnership with God enabled him to resist the lure of selfishness and greed. It also fueled actions by him that fostered in others a desire for freedom and openness to enter into authentic relationships with God and other human beings. In the relations I consider meaningful partnerships between God and members of the community of faith it is not merely, as Barth suggests, that "God speaks to us in promise and command" or that we are assured of "God's existence, intercession, and activity for human beings."[12] Instead, the recognition that human beings have real freedom, and that genuine novelty results from our exercise of freedom, opens the way for us to appreciate God's ongoing growth as a result of involvement in the cosmos, and consequently that God's relevant participation in each life is partly facilitated by the decisions we and others take and the activities that are pursued.[13] This is so, even as God the all-inclusive and internally related self-surpassing surpasser of all contributes to each stage of human development in light of God's ideals for each and all. God is, without doubt, the superior partner, but clearly human contributions are in no wise insignificant to God.

It should make a radical difference in the attitudes we have toward each other in the church if we assumed that each person were involved in some kind of partnership with God. It would be far more difficult to view them simply as fallen, inferior, hapless, undereducated, incompetent, etc. Instead it would be recognized that it is as people are given opportunity to exercise participatory freedom within the churches and are enabled to contribute to a range of processes in the wider society that they become better partners of God and others, even as they develop themselves, the church, and the wider community in which the church operates. In such a scenario the terms "fellowship of believers" and "pilgrim people" take on a new layer of significance, and the church is recognized as a setting for the celebration and responsible exercise of finite freedom that is realistically libertarian and relational. On the other hand, churches could not be perceived as mere aggregations of like-minded persons who have a relationship with God, but as organisms held together and fueled by the complex web of relations that has at its center a God whose partnership with Jesus has universal efficacy and whose relation to each members of the church is informed by the relation to all and whose vision for the whole is linked to the desire for each.

## PARTNERSHIP AMONG THE PEOPLE OF GOD, WITH IMPLICATIONS FOR MINISTRY

In the ecclesiological paradigm I am seeking to encourage, the vision for ministry and the actual processes of church organization, fellowship, and service would be guided by the ongoing recognition that each partnership with God is inseparable from all partnerships with God and that the way we pursue partnerships within the church has implications for the quality of our contributions to God, self, and world. This is indeed solidarity in the "Spirit of Christ" because it is the revelatory orbit that emerged from Jesus' partnership with God that spawned the complex community of faith called the church, and it is the dynamics of Jesus' life as portrayed in the Scriptures that serve as the prime inspiration for our contemporary pursuits. Thus the Spirit of Christ, which represents that which resulted from Jesus' openness to and engagement with the creative presence of God in his life, serves to focus cooperative efforts in the church and water our imaginations regarding what is possible.

Jesus is partner to Christians here, in the sense that he participated in a faith dynamic of the most intimate kind with God (as signified by *Abba*) into which we have also been drawn. This is also in the sense that Jesus gave unique focus to that which in Judaism was envisioned to be *summum bonum* of the human quest for communal and individual fulfillment, that is, what the *Baptism, Eucharist, and Ministry* document referred to as the Kingdom of

God and which a growing number of scholars refer to as the Realm of God.[14] The conviction that what is expected to come to full expression in the *eschaton* should already be evident in the ongoing life of the church in this world, has resulted in the modern characterization of the Realm of God as the "the already and the not yet."

With this in mind, and given my view that the notion Kingdom of God is easily linked to portrayals of God that have been informed by images of rulership patterned from ancient Kings, Emperors, and Lords who were quintessential despots, I identify with those who use Realm of God. I also seek after nomenclature that not only focuses on whose realm it is, but points to the character of relations in the realm. This being so, I embrace "Realm of God" in conversation with Mujerista theologian Ada Maria Isasi-Diaz's claim that the political metaphor "kingdom of God" should be replaced with the more personal and relational "kin-dom of God." The metaphor "Kingdom," she suggests, refers only to male sovereigns and reinforces the male image of God still prevalent in churches. It is dangerous "because it is elitist, hierarchical, patriarchal, and supports all sorts of systemic oppressions." Further: "The idea of kin-dom of God, or the family of God . . . is a more relevant and effective metaphor today to communicate what Jesus lived and died for."[15] Influenced by Whiteheadean ideas I claim that the notion Realm of God actually represents God's presence to and ideals for each life in relation to the ideals for every other life, and the cosmos as a whole. It is the deep-seated if ambiguous awareness of this presence in all human beings that has enabled some in the past and present to be drawn toward the form of life that resulted from Jesus' own unique awareness of God's presence and ideals, to have their lives guided by this awareness, and to look toward a time when there will be full expression of God's presence and ideals.

These considerations have direct implications for our understanding of what constitutes ministry and leadership within the churches and as such determines how we interpret the well-used declaration in 1 Peter 2:9[16] taken by many as central to the identity of the Christian community. There was a brief period in my late teens when, in the self-centered euphoria of recommitment to Christianity, I joined others in using this passage to support my self-characterization as "The King's kid." Fortunately it was not long before my focus was turned to the more legitimately theological concept of "the priesthood of all believers."

While my position on the freedom-denying implications of Luther's position on the status of the human being in relation to God still stands, the radical nature of the concept of priesthood of believers begins to be appreciated with embrace of language from his letter to the Christian nobility in Germany.[17] Here he asserts that baptism places everyone on level ground. As such, "whoever comes out of the water of baptism can boast that he is already a consecrated priest, bishop, and pope." At the most fundamental level of consideration all Christians "have equal authority."[18] In "The Freedom of a Christian" Christians are admonished that as priests they should pray for each other and teach each other about the things of God and do all the things done by priests in Israel.[19] This designation also includes the right to preach the Word and administer absolution and discipline.[20] The character of priesthood becomes more striking when, with the help of the theological and anthropological proposals I have made, each member of the Christian community is seen not as a sinful nobody to whom righteousness has been imputed, but as a person who is pursuing partnership with God and other global co-inhabitants in light of an ongoing desire to live consistently with ideals they sense are reflected in Jesus' life as portrayed in the Gospels.

I embrace this understanding of priesthood as an important element of my ecclesiology, being very mindful of Hans Küng's indication that in the New Testament the word priest is not used anywhere for someone who holds office in the Church, and that as portrayed in the Scriptures, Jesus does not use the image of the priest in any of his declarations. I also endorse wholeheartedly Küng's claim that in the church priesthood is an attitude not an office and that this attitude links the church with Israel in its most fundamental calling as a people (Exodus 19:6 [Isa 61:6; 56:6]).[21] Küng elaborates on the notion of priesthood utilizing orthodox terminology, but does so in a way that reflects the spirit of partnership I wish to communicate. He asserts that it consists in the calling of each faithful to witness to God and God's will before the world, and to give themselves in the service of the world.[22] I take a step beyond his view that it is God who creates this priesthood and that God creates fellowship among believers. I suggest that, as an attitude, priesthood also represents the decisions and actions members of the Christian community take to nurture their best selves and fashion an ethos that enables each individual to pursue their freedom and, at the same time, facilitate the freedom of others.

In keeping with Luther's understanding of priesthood, Küng suggests that it means, on one hand, in the one Spirit every believer has direct access to God (Eph 2:18), that is, there is no need for a holy middleman. On the other hand, each believer has a responsibility to appear before God on behalf of others, even as she is aware that others appear before God on her behalf. Further, there is the function to "mediate between God and the world, by revealing the hidden works of God and making effective [God's] acts of power."[23] I hastily declare that this power would not be coercive, and that those involved are not people who have somehow been freed from the ambiguity that characterizes human existence in finitude. Still, each is challenged to be responsible for other brothers and sisters, "share in [their] struggles and in [their] difficulties," "bear [their] sins with them and to stand by them in everything." So then, the priesthood of all believers "is a fellowship in which each Christian, instead of living for herself, lives before God for others and is in turn supported by others."[24] Here I make an addition to this claim with support from Galatians 6:1-6 where to the admonition to "carry each other's burdens" is added the charge that "each one should carry his own load." As such, it is the creative mix of responsibility to and for self and others that makes for fruitful partnership between members of the church, distinguishing partnership from spiritual co-dependency.

When one claims space and uses opportunity to take responsibility for one's own life in light of one's unique relationship with God and other human beings, one has freedom to express one's uniqueness and also freedom to be with and for others. In this framework the more obviously "spiritual" expressions come to be seen in their necessary association with a wide range of every-day expressions of belonging, care, representation and facilitation. In this matter, it is not simply that the believer "lives before God for others and is in turn supported by others."[25] She also encourages others to claim themselves as authentic participants in a network of relations that includes the internally related, all-inclusive God and all actualities that inhabit the earth. This recognition enables realization of the rich significance of Küng's claim that "the worship of this priesthood thus develops from being worship within the community to being worship within the everyday secular world."[26] Küng, along with Jürgen Moltmann, says more to whet the imagination regarding the radical implications of the notion of the priesthood of all believers for life in our churches.

Taking Matthew 28:19 to apply not only to the first apostles, but to the whole church, Küng suggests that "the entire Church is given the power to baptize . . . and . . . every Christian has the power to baptize (and to teach)." Informed by Matt 18:18, he suggests that "the whole church has the power to forgive sins; and in communion with the Church, which exists in the communion of forgiveness of God and of Christ, every Christian is fundamentally empowered to take an active part in forgiving of sins."[27] Finally, regarding the Lord's Supper, he indicates that although it first occurred in the limited circle of the twelve, "the command 'do this in remembrance of me' (Lk 22:19), is a charge laid upon the whole church. The whole church is given the power to eat the lord's body and drink his blood."[28]

At this point Moltmann takes us to an interesting place in our consideration of church dynamics and the complex nature of partnerships we are invited to nurture. Whereas Küng seems concerned to move eligibility beyond an "inner circle" within the church, Moltmann is concerned for us to recognize that Christ's prevenient and unconditional invitation goes beyond those "faithful to the church."

> The meal is not for the particularly righteous or those who think they are particularly devout, but is for "the weary and heavy-laden, who have heard the call to refreshment. Jesus' meal with tax-collectors and sinners is also present

in the lord's supper. . . ." Therefore, the open invitation to it should be carried "into the highways and byways." It will then lose its "mystery" character, but will not become an ordinary everyday meal for all that, because the invitation is a call to the fellowship of the crucified one and an invitation in his name to reconciliation with God (1Cor. 11.27).[29]

While being enthusiastic in my identification with Küng's and Moltmann's dispositions, I am quite aware that many concerned about good order and efficient processes within churches would have great difficulty with their stridently democratic approach to ministry. The authors of the 1986 Church of England document on "The Priesthood of the Ordained Ministry" acknowledge that the earliest Christian communities had a fairly open structure with "little central direction to church's mission, and considerable variety in the organization of local communities."[30] They remind us, however, that bishops-presbyters and deacons are certainly to be found in some churches, and that by the time of the Pastoral Epistles an ordained ministry with full authority had appeared. I am doubtful about their suggestion that the Epistles probably witness to the first beginnings of a monepiscopacy (rule by a single bishop) in some places, but they are on target in their claim that by the end of the New Testament period a clear distinction had been developed between the members of the community and its leaders. While all baptized believers possessed the same status as members of Christ, the emergence of established ministerial leaders did lead to a distinction of status—this exampled in 1Peter 5:2-4, where the leaders are warned not to dominate the community.[31] However, I am more restrained than they are in classifying the foundation of the status of these leaders to be "ordination" as understood by Episcopalians or even non-Episcopalians.[32]

The authors of the Anglican document attempt to give the impression that the threefold pattern of ministry, of bishop assisted by presbyters and deacons, had early acceptance among churches when he claims that Ignatius of Antioch's referred to it in a way that hinted at acceptance in Syria and Asia Minor. However, in the *Encyclopedia of the Early Church* we are informed that it is in Ignatius' letters, intended to deal with dissenters in the churches, that there is the first evidence of this threefold hierarchy.[33] This difference of viewpoint does not rule out the Anglican's additional claim that the patterns would soon be found in other places, and allowed for a succession of bishops. Succession, they suggest, "became one of the ways, together with the transmission of the gospel and the life of the community, in which the apostolic tradition was expressed. This succession later came to be understood as serving, symbolizing and guarding the continuity of the apostolic faith and fellowship."[34]

I do support the basic understanding of the role of the ordained articulated in the Anglican document. While the entire church has a ministry—the basic elements of which are set out in the *Baptism, Eucharist and Ministry* document—"not all baptized Christians have the same responsibility to shepherd the flock, to care for the Word and Sacraments, to perform defined specific acts in the name of Christ for the service of his people and to lead the mission."[35] I also take seriously their admission that the movement toward a structured hierarchical ministry was influenced by particular historical circumstances like the death of the first apostles, the fall of Jerusalem, and the onset of persecution, exerting pressure for a more cohesive structure.[36] I also get the distinct impression from the *Encyclopedia* that Ignatius' promotion of the threefold hierarchy came as part of an attempt to counter dissention by Sabbatists and Docetists. In the process of encouraging allegiance to bishops he classified them as "vicar of God" and "vicar of Christ," apart from whom nothing should be done in the churches.[37] Together, these are clear signs of the leadership of the early church responding to drastic situations with which they were faced in their time. It points to the need for churches in each era and in different contexts to exercise the freedom to determine what structures and functions are necessary for their viability and integrity. It is, therefore, unfortunate that what were probably reactions born of anxiety led to a fixed structure, antithetical to what I consider freedom-oriented Christianity.

Küng enables further insight into the movement from expressions of freedom to structures of domination. We learn from him that "in the post-Constantinian period the biblical distinction between (priestly!) 'people' (*laos*) and 'non-people' (*ou laos*, 1 Peter 2:10) increasingly turned into a distinction between 'people' (*laici*) and 'priest' (*clerus*)."[38]

Against this background Küng reminds us that the expression "layman" (*laikos*), which in the Greek sense meant "the uneducated masses," and in the Jewish sense "a man who was neither priest nor Levite," does not occur anywhere in the New Testament.[39] However:

> from the third century onward the word is in current use in the Church. In this way the tension between the Church and the world (which had itself now become "Christian") was transferred to within the Church itself, and had become a tension between "*clerus*" (secular priests and monks) and laity. The "clergy" was accorded an increasingly privileged position and grew into a new sociological class on its own, with its own privileges, immunities, dress, titles, duties (celibacy, breviary, etc.) and its own (Latin) culture ad its own (Latin) liturgy.[40]

Striking evidence of the continuation of this classism in our era is found in the understanding of "apostolic succession" promoted in Episcopal ecclesiologies. In that framework, succession is understood to take place through the priestly "caste," and bishops in particular, rather than through the priesthood of the whole community of believers. Without doubt, apostolicity is a noble mark of the church, and my own approach to what it means is similar to that of Clark Williamson. He argues that it is rightly grounded in the recognition that the church has been given the apostolic message, which is the gospel of Jesus the Christ, and called to the apostolic function of communicating that message. I understand this apostolic function to have as one of its important components enabling persons to embrace the call to freedom found in Galatians 5:1, which includes the space to struggle on their own and also with others with the content and application of the gospel and to seek after the realization of its promise and challenge in the most comprehensive way possible for the sake of self and others. The point of apostolic succession, we are told, was "to emphasize the public and known character of the church's teachings, thereby distinguishing them from 'new' heresies."[41]

I am confident that my approach to the determination and address to what is considered heresy might differ from Williamson and even more so from strident defenders of Christian orthodoxy. At the same time, I do support the need for each generation of Christians to publicly recognize and engage traditions of thought and practice handed down to them, guided by established norms and according to agreed-on procedures. This engagement, carried out in light of contemporary concerns and aspirations and utilizing relevant insight from established scholarly disciplines, should result in clear statements on what is considered appropriate belief. I am also of the view that of great importance for the public transmission, exploration, and application of the traditions of interpretations of the gospel are well-prepared persons who are given the authority to identify matters for address and to facilitate adequate address of these matters. However, the setting aside of people for these and other responsibilities ought to be grounded in the *laos tou Theou*, the community of "the people of God." It is indeed the people of God, characterized by partnership with each other and with God, who are the proper bearers of apostolicity.[42] And wrestling with interpretations of the Scriptures, traditions, and processes of doctrinal formulation, the needs of communities, and methods of proclamation should take place on an ongoing basis through interactions at the micro and macro levels of the community.

This discussion of apostolicity directs us back to further exploration on what characterizes leadership and authority in freedom-oriented churches. If all members of the community of faith are priests and, as Luther suggests in his outreach to the Nobility, "a priest in Christendom is nothing else but an officeholder,"[43] how do those officially called priests differ from laypersons? In addressing the question Luther suggests that injustice is done to the words "priest," "cleric," "spiritual," and "ecclesiastic," when they are transferred from all Christians to those few who are called "ecclesiastics." He asserts that in the Scriptures there is no distinction between them, although it gives the name "minister," "servants," "stewards" to those who in his day were called popes, bishops, and lords. We learn that in order to avoid confusion the community entrusts the public service to ordained people, who carry out this duty in the name of the church. These people "according to the ministry of the Word serve others and teach them the faith of Christ and the freedom of believers." [44]

Veli-Matti Kärkkäinen suggests that Luther's pronouncements reflect his stress on the non-institutional character of the church. The church as the communion of saints is called together by the Holy Spirit. [45] Indeed, Luther's most famous definition of the church is that "the church is 'the gathering of all believers, in which the gospel is purely preached and the holy sacraments are administered in accord with the gospel.'"[46] The word and sacraments were the only necessary marks of the church. "Everything else—the structures, ministry patterns, liturgy, and so on—could vary from church to church."[47] In this framework the ordained are members of the community set apart for the specialized public service of ministering, teaching, and administering the sacraments, but the fundamental status of brother/sister priest remains. Not surprisingly Luther contradicts the position articulated by the Anglican document regarding the status of the ordained in his suggestion that the difference between ordained and non-ordained lies purely on the level of service. It is taking someone from a community in which all have like power and charging that person to exercise this power on behalf of the others. [48] It is exactly because all are priests and of equal standing that no one must push ahead to take on a title without the community's approval. "For no one dare take upon himself what is common to all without the authority and consent of the community."[49]

At the same time, there is an identifiable flaw in Luther's thinking that easily enables a modified form of the hierarchicalism identified by Küng to persist in our time. This flaw is evident in Luther's view that, while a community entrusts service to the ordained in the name of the church, the fullness of the authority that comes with ordination is grounded separately in its institution by Christ. In other words, "the office derives directly from its institution by Christ without reference to the universal priesthood."[50] It is claimed that this separate grounding does not nullify the general priesthood as the ordained office is derived from the universal. The fact that public preaching is limited to the ordained that have been called through the community does not nullify the right to preach by the whole priesthood, and this public administration of the ministry of the Word and sacrament is part of the exercise of the priestly office between "brother and brother."[51]

All these declarations would be easily reconcilable if that about the separate grounding of ordination was not intended to establish what distinguishes the status of the minister of word and sacrament from all other ministries within the general priesthood of believers, and instead described a feature common to all members of the community of faith through which the unique ministry of each on behalf of all was established. My own view is that all enabling functions within the church should be seen as equally and directly linked to the priesthood of Jesus, considered the pioneer of faith because of the quality of his relationship with God. Better yet, the greatest emphasis should be on the way these functions are linked to the God to whom Jesus was open and to whom he pointed his disciples. This does not mean that people, even those who sense a leaning to and are set aside for pastoral responsibilities, are called to one responsibility for all time. Instead, it means that capacities that are obvious at a particular point and/or potentials that are discerned should be nurtured and directed toward the internal and external work of church communities.

The foundation for linking this process to Jesus' priesthood so that it supports the kind of partnership I promote is my view that the persuasive and enabling power of God that operated in Jesus also operates in each Christian as God seeks to guide persons toward their most wholesome self-understanding and their best self-expression for their own sake and the sake of others. It is with this understanding that a local Christian community would give approval for individuals to contribute in particular ways in their midst and would stand ready to support these persons for service within the wider church community and the world in general. As it now stands within many churches, even when they claim, as Luther did, that it is the community who gives approval for a pastor/minister/priest to serve in their midst, her/his ordination which is grounded separately and uniquely in the priesthood of Jesus still situates the ordained in an elevated space. The church ends up with two different orders of priesthood: one seen as a function of membership in the Christian community and the other as having a unique character that results from direct-special association with Jesus the Christ.

Letty Russell provides commentary that is relevant to this situation. She indicates that while Paul pointed to the variety of gifts recognized in the congregations (1Cor 12:28), "the way in which the church structured the gifts of ministry so that some are set apart by ordination to serve a need of the church for ordered leadership . . . has had disastrous effects in producing a class division between 'upper-class' and 'lower class' laity." She continues to suggest that "no matter how much we all emphasize that there is only one ministry of Jesus Christ and that we all share in this ministry, the clerical structures continue to reinforce structures of hierarchy and domination, whether or not the particular clergyperson is male or female."[52] Russell's claim that the paternalism is a predominant pattern of authority in many congregations is consistent with this position. And she suggests that this "can be an authority of false love that uses people's need for strength and assurance to dominate them through a relationship of dependence."[53] I venture to say that the oppressive capacity of the clerical hierarchy is heightened when behind it all is the theological hierarchy described in chapter 4 of this work, which begins with the omni-qualitied God that by direct and indirect means is in charge of all things, and whose special representative the ordained pastor becomes.

This situation, I suggest, is not necessarily mitigated by an emphasis on ministry as *diakonia*, supported by the suggestion that Jesus gave radically new meaning to this notion so that service becomes an essential characteristic of discipleship.[54] Williamson's identification of Mark's description of the feeding of the multitude immediately after the description of Herod's banquet (Mark 6: 21-29 vs. Mark 6:30-44) does give an impressive example of how Jesus sought to dramatize this reorientation in the context of its most demeaning expression in Greco-Roman culture, that is, at meal-time.[55] I suggest, however, that similar to the term slave the flavor of inferiority which *diakonia* had in the wider culture was probably not expunged when appropriated later for Christian purposes by people who had been socialized in the Greco-Roman culture and lived out their new faith within that culture. Thus it should not be surprising that those who would be leaders and exercise authority on behalf of the almighty sovereign would be inclined to nomenclature that more properly represent their sense of what they were called by God to do.

Here there is a direct link between Küng's description of the reconstrual of the meaning of the *laos* in relation to *clerus* in the immediate post-Constantinian period and Williamson's view that Eusebius' description of the banquet for bishops hosted by Constantine at the Council of Nicaea signaled that the church had embraced Herod's way of doing things. In Mark's deliberate contrast between Herod's feast and the feeding of the multitude, the rich and powerful reclined to be served in the former and, in the latter, the poor reclined to be served by the disciples. At Constantine's banquet the bishops, who ruled in God's name, were the ones reclining in lavish couches, under the protection of soldiers with swords drawn, and being catered to by the Emperor's servants.[56] In my personal experience as a youngster in the Presbyterian ethos, there was no question that my Scottish and Irish pastors were kings,[57] that elders were ruling princes, and that deacons were lower down in the totem pole. Russell reminds us of the unique challenge facing women as they operate in this framework. While in the general scheme women constitute a third class below clergy and laymen, in some frameworks they are part of the "upper-class clergy." However, "as women they can't measure up to the role of sacred masculinity so they remain 'third-class' according to gender."[58] This point should not be lost, even as we take to heart the following challenge from Küng that:

> The fundamental error of ecclesiologies, which turned out, in fact, to be no more than hierarchologies (where *ecclesia* = *hierarchia*) was that they failed to realize that all who hold office are primarily (both temporally and factually speaking) not dignitaries but believers, members of the fellowship of believ-

ers; and that compared with this fundamental Christian fact any office they hold is of secondary, if not tertiary importance.[59]

## CONCRETE STEPS TOWARD PARTNERSHIP

I am convinced that the attitude recommended by Hans Küng will be most evident when the language, attitude, and practice of partnership are embraced in association with the approach to the priesthood of all believers I have set out above. And vital to this movement is sustained and mutually reinforcing relationship between theological exploration and the modeling of a new approach at the most visible levels of church leadership. Thus I have great interest in John Calvin's instructions regarding the relation between the offices of pastor and teacher. In the *Institutes* he makes it clear that the church can never go without pastors and teachers. He proceeds to establish the difference between the two: "teachers are not put in charge of discipline, or administering the sacraments, or warnings and exhortations, but only of Scriptural interpretation—to keep doctrine whole and pure among believers. But the pastoral office includes all these functions within itself."[60] I support wholeheartedly the recognition that the role of teacher can be independent of the role of pastor, and in keeping with my approach to the priesthood of all believers I envisage that the specialist teacher (what Calvin has in mind) would be a teacher of teachers.[61] At the same time, my emphasis on partnership makes me suggest that there can be congregational frameworks in which one who is primarily teacher might also participate in carrying out the other responsibilities Calvin lists. That being said, I cannot ignore that Calvin's view of the character of the pastoral office is more relevant to the way churches are structured at this time. This makes it all the more important that there should be significant emphasis on preparing congregational leaders to carry out both roles effectively.

The mind-set that is promoted in ministerial preparation should have as an important component the recognition that the purpose of a pastor/minister-priest is to enable members of congregations to develop their capacity to minister to each other through prayer and proclamation and also to operate with the recognition that they are called to care for others not just because they are fellow-believers but because they are human beings and fellow travelers through life. I go beyond Calvin in my exploration of the transaction of both pastoral and teaching functions within the church with my view that, even in situations where these roles are now primarily in the hands of ministerial specialists, the goal should be that it does not remain so. This places a necessary burden on all who are now concerned with the preparation of specialists. This is to give them the highest level of training in the requisite range of disciplines and to orient them away from the controlling approaches church leaders so easily adopt. Emphasis should be on a disposition to foster linkages with others who are capable of contributing to the heightened effectiveness of the process by which as many members of a congregation as possible are prepared to contribute at the highest possible level to the nurture, education, worship, and outreach of that community. Being mindful that members of congregations are usually persons with significant responsibilities in other spheres of life, I do not envisage this process leading to the obsolescence of specialists.

This view is only reinforced when I take into account the fact that, in the denominations with which I am now most familiar, there is increasing reliance on bi-vocational leadership. At the same time, the welfare of local communities ought not to be as dependent on these specialists as has been the case historically. A significant benefit of lessened dominance in any one congregation or group of congregations is that these specialists would have more time and scope to devote to the preparation of teaching materials, the organization of administrative structures and pedagogical tools, and the creation of opportunities by which congregations become intentional learning communities. They would also be more available to make contributions in the wider network of communities that constitute individual denominations and the Christian community at large.

The learning processes that are fostered in congregations ought to reflect the action-reflection model popularized by Liberation theologians in which ongoing education in the intellectual and practical disciplines of faith inform the way people of faith operate in their everyday lives, and the challenges and insights from that wider forum are intentionally fed into further explorations within the church setting. As one interested in how the churches might become champions of freedom in multiple dimensions for the weakest and most marginalized, I take heed to the indication of Leonardo and Clodovis Boff that, before attempts are made to utilize the Scriptures in theological reflection that inform practical engagements with social and political systems, there is need for what they call the socio-analytical mediation. Through this endeavor the church in a context educates itself regarding obvious and underlying structures on which are hinged the relations between the powerful and weak, wealthy and poor, oppressor and oppressed, those who enjoy more freedom and those with less freedom.[62] This pre-theological work would feed into various types of theological reflection at every level of church life with the hope that it would outflow into every area of life in the wider society. The consistent bias should be toward the interest of those who are least able to exercise internal freedom in ways that enhance their capacity to pursue external freedom for personal and communal good. Jamaican theologian and church leader Ashley Smith speaks eloquently about desired consequences for the poor and marginalized in his region and other similar settings. He points out that meaningful social change always begins with significant changes in people's awareness of reality, and he continues to say:

"Whenever those who are traditional victims become conscious of the entities present in the relationships between themselves and the privileged of the existing state of those relationships, they become aware also of powers inside and outside of themselves. With this new awareness of power comes the perception of possibilities for themselves."[63]

Language from Paulo Freire is borrowed as Smith suggests that the church's intention should be to facilitate a situation in which "the consciousness of the poor and marginalized 'ceases to be naïve and becomes problematic.'" As a result, Smith suggests, "their [the poor and marginalized] own history has begun, for they now see themselves as authentically human and therefore no longer as appendages of other people's humanity or mere factors in other people's history. They are now conscious of participating in their own history."[64]

This is a wonderful vision that is in keeping with the proposals for freedom articulated throughout this project. I embrace it with the conviction that any attempted reorientation of consciousness in the poor and marginalized needs to take place as one component of the pursuit of reoriented consciousness in all who participate in the socio-political and economic dynamics of a society. My experience in the island Smith is from, and where he was a significant contributor to a radical attempt at social transformation, makes it clear to me that until those who hold and wield power are themselves enabled into a new vision of reality that includes an enlarged understanding of what it means to be human in a world that they hope will be hospitable to pursuits of freedom by their progeny, the vision he has for the poor will continue to be frustrated.

Bearing in mind explorations in previous chapters, the appropriate theological framework to undergird this process would be informed by appropriation, refinement, and contextual translation of the metaphysical notions explicated in this work that serve as foundation for belief in a fundamentally interconnected and relational world, the processes and end of which are worked out by means of a network of responses to the lure of an infinitely temporal and imaginatively creative God who has desires for each in relation to all. The interpretational orientation and tools developed in this process would be applied in the evaluation of data from the church's socio-analytic meditation, in the analysis of the Scriptures, and in the exploration of doctrinal ideas handed down by previous generations. Having taken seriously that the God who is present to individual Christians and Christian communities is also present to people and communities in other settings (religious and non-religious), there would not be aversion to ideational and practical interactions with them.

In this interaction there would be openness to being influenced in thought and action and willingness to influence the thoughts and actions of others who should be considered partners in the quest for freedom. Within congregations, the results from intra-inter-extra church partnerships would influence every aspect of life, and every effort would be made to expose all member of a community to that which results from these interactions. In these processes, the ministerial specialist would ensure that there are proper linkages between the academic, pastoral and popular expressions of the theological enterprise as she/he contributes ongoing guidance for the development of partnerships within and outside of the community of churches.

As I consider the need for the development of structures and the preparation of personnel through which education, care, and outreach are carried out in congregations, I identify with Letty Russell's claim that "in our time religious orders of vocation, polity, and church law can no longer be understood as static patterns set out by divine order." These, she reminds us, "are gifts rather than givens of God: part of the changing patterns of church life that evolve out of the function of the church in its work of service and witness to God's love and justice in the wider society." Indeed, "ministries of the church are part of the organization of the church as it responds to the Spirit of Christ continually at work in its midst."[65] This spirit leads to a new order of freedom, in which Christ has set us free to be for others. In this understanding, ministry is the response of each and every Christian in the context of community to Christ's call to freedom. Therefore, I insist that congregations and denominations must be structured to ensure that, as a community of priests, it is well able to carry out its calling so that members of the church as members of the wider community of human beings can exercise themselves as ordinary citizens and/or civic leaders to facilitate as much freedom as is attainable. The constitution of "authority" in each place would be guided by perceived requirements for realizing the optimum combination of the dimensions and categories of freedom elaborated throughout this project.

As I indicated in the paper "Eschatology and Ecclesiology," a severe weakness of historic denominationalism has been that in the quest for notable identity and pervasive influence, diverse peoples and groupings have been pressed into suffocating types of uniformity.[66] This suffocation has often been pursued in the name of doctrinal purity, proper order, and maintaining the unity of the faith, among other things. I still maintain that, while these values should not be ignored in freedom-oriented ecclesial frameworks, there needs to be resistance to overbearing communalism or centralized hierarchical authoritarianism, which threatens privacy, suffocates individuality, and undermines personal decision-making and risk-taking. At the same time, with the recognition that Christians live in an interconnected world in which the welfare of each and all is inseparably linked, there should be promotion of the view that the most beneficial exercise of freedom by individuals, particular church communities and networks of communities called denominations, will be better ensured when it is pursued with the awareness of being part of a global network of Christians and an even larger network of global co-inhabitants that are all uniquely related to the internally-related, all-inclusive God.

This approach calls for responsible decision-making in relation to the ongoing struggle to determine what is the common good in particular settings in relation to common good considered in a global sense, and it should contribute to the ability to embrace the catholicity of the Christian community in its complex contextuality. This complex, contextual catholicity allows for identification with Küng's claim that the church is wholly present in every place; that is, each local church is "endowed with the entire promise of the gospel and an entire faith, recipient of the undivided grace of the Father, having present in it the entire Christ and enriched by the undivided Holy Spirit."[67] There would be openness to Moltmann's claim that "'the church' with its structures, organizations, and powers exists exclusively for the sake of the congregation."[68] This responsibility to congregations, I suggest, involves ensuring that they benefit from the services of ministerial specialists who receive the best possible preparation in theological and ministerial disciplines and are disposed to enabling communities of faith to be effective champions of responsible freedom in their context. It also involves providing a framework of checks and balances against potential abuses of freedom and avenues (with guidelines) through which appropriate appeals can be made for assistance in handling situations that undermine the work of freedom in local settings.

Informing the life of congregations within this framework of support could be the qualified embrace of Moltmann's claim that "the congregation is mature to the degree that it no longer experiences itself as being taken care of ecclesiastically and tended to by ordained officials but rather becomes the independent, responsible subject of its own history with God."[69] In my vision this means that final decisions on the organizational structure and dynamics of ministry in a context will be determined locally. At the same time, Christians in a local situation should appreciate that the complex nature of human limitation applies to the ability to interpret the Scriptures, formulate theology, read a context, and identify every consideration relevant to good structure and effective engagement with a local situation in light of more global demands. Local congregations would take seriously concerns that inform the larger ecclesial system with which it is associated, available guidelines for effective operation, along with external analysis of the local situation with insights regarding potential implications for the network of global co-inhabitants. These considerations would inform the way a congregation seeks to constitute itself as "a free zone of the Spirit of God,"[70] which in my scheme necessarily involves the recognition that a congregation is made of persons who, being in unique individual relationship with God, are themselves finitely free zones of the Spirit of God.

These considerations feed into my embrace of the spirit of Küng's reminder that, while the individual local church is an entire Church, the church catholic is not made up by simply local churches being added together and associated externally, "but by being inwardly at one in the same God, lord and Spirit, through the same gospel, the same baptism and sacred meal and the same faith."[71]

My embrace of a complex, contextual catholicity enables the recognition that the signs of unity identified by Küng serve to exclude communities of Christians from the so-called left-wing of the Reformation that, like the Quakers, do not practice water baptism of any kind or set apart one meal as sacred. In pursuing a theological solution to this challenge, I encourage embrace of the suggestion that practices of the church classified as sacraments by some and ordinances by others are grounded in what I call a "primal sacrament," which is God's involvement in cosmic dynamic and human history. As I have written before, "it is God's internal relatedness that enables basic elements of life, represented in bread, wine, and water, to be properly symbolic, which means having the capacity to open us up to the hidden depths of reality, while participating in the power of that which is symbolized." Further, "because of internal relatedness, God is in a sense consubstantial with the sacramental elements exactly because of being consubstantial with all life."[72] Grounded in the gospel of freedom and taking seriously the outcomes from attempts by many generations of Christians to respond to the God who is internal to the life of each individual as well as the cosmos as a whole, contemporary communities of faith would be challenged to explore separately and together ways to dramatize this primal sacrament in the whole life of congregations so that quests for freedom in a context actually promote a complex catholicity and the people of God become more sensitive to the lure of God toward ever-richer and life-enhancing partnerships in the churches and the wider world.

Feminist theologians raise issues that challenge us regarding what a complex contextual catholicity might look like. Some have pursued the development of communities called "Woman Church" as a way to give women space away from male dominated frameworks in which they have been oppressed for generations. Russell is of the view that in the framework of Woman Church feminist styles of leadership would draw their model of behavior from a partnership paradigm that is oriented toward community formation. What she has in mind is captured in the notion of church in the round discussed in her book with that title.[73] Recognizing the virtue in Russell's ecclesial inclination I am able to envisage expressions of Woman Church that operate within existing denominational structures, as Russell promotes it, and those that step away completely as Rosemary Radford Reuther perceives is sometimes necessary. Actually, bearing in mind the example of "Base Communities" within the Roman Catholic Church in Latin America, I am able to imagine the basic model of particularized communities of Christians being the case for a number of historically oppressed groups within all branches of the church. In this matter I have moved from a place where I insisted that each congregation should as much as possible reflect the complex nature of the community of faith, considered in terms of gender, ethnicity, sexual orientation etc. I now accept that there are a wide range of important concerns in different contexts that must be addressed so that the church catholic is able to move to that place of diversity and complexity, which for me is still exemplified in the eschatological vision of the scene around the throne of God in Revelation 7.

While I hold that the churches should as much as possible operate in anticipation of the full realization of the vision captured in Revelation 7, it is now clear to me that there is not one way that churches can or ought to structure themselves as historical and cultural phenomena so that movement toward the ideal is evident in the church as a global community that seeks freedom for both weak and strong oppressed and oppressor. I, therefore, embrace the idea of particularized fellowships in light of Reuther's view that the separation of women ought not to be an end in itself, but a stage in a process. She insists that "this is a stage that is absolutely necessary . . . . a stage toward a further end in formation of a critical culture and community of women and men in exodus from patriarchy." The need for separation is reinforced by her claim that "women, more than any other marginalized group, have lacked a critical culture of their own."[74] I support Reuther's encouragement of the formation of parallel male groups and also the continuation of mixed gender groups in which males of good will might wrestle with what feminism means to them.[75]

At the same time, I am also quite interested to see what would happen if the oppressed female and male descendants of slaves and/or indentured workers in places like the Caribbean took time away from the constraints of externally determined orthodoxy and struggled to develop thought and practice that reflected and contributed to the ongoing struggle with what it means to be the people of God in those contexts. In the imagined scheme, particularized communities of faith who are looking to the day when they will be more diversified would operate alongside those made up of persons who have the capacity to operate in greater diversity, even as they both work to discern what healthy forms of diversity and partnership might look like. I imagine that, wherever possible, opportunities would be sought to fashion engagement under carefully structured conditions between diverse types of congregations so that each learn from the other and the foundation is prepared for that time when things might be different. This ecclesiological scenario points to the component of partnership that can be classified as critical solidarity and is consistent with an approach to theologizing I have elsewhere classified as "dialectical contextualism."[76]

As I imagine the settings in which the ecclesial proposals of this chapter will be pursued, I still hold to the view expressed in "Eschatology and Ecclesiology" that large congregations of the contemporary mega-church type are not ideal. I am still of the mind that the larger a community of faith grows the stronger will be the perceived need to put in place mechanisms to maintain good order viewed as that which will protect the community's status as a single community heading in one direction. This leaning is encouraged when, as is often the case, these churches emerge from the vision of a single charismatic leader whose personality and/or doctrinal pronouncements become the central galvanizing source of the community and the reference point for establishing authority and orthodoxy. "Consequently, beneath the rhetoric of personal faith and excitement from the types of individual expression that are permitted, there is resistance to diversity of opinion as attempts are made to construct single-minded adherence to specific propositions and practices."[77] In order for this to be the case, individuality and unique perspectives on Christian thought must be subordinated, and with the increased possibility of variance that comes with increased numbers, more effective strategies are required to keep persons in their place. These strategies are often pursued using the rhetoric of submission to God through God's uniquely elected and specially gifted representatives. These are associated with standards of piety and quests for holiness that are linked inflexibly to norms for biblical interpretation and theological formulation enforced by a central authority answerable only to God. The outcome I have suggested is "intellectual and psycho-spiritual oppression."[78]

Bearing in mind the previously proposed relation between individual congregations and larger complexes of affiliation, the frameworks I privilege are networks of small to medium sized communities of people in which difference is honored, and which allow for individual adventures of faith with lessened fear of chaos. At the same time there is greater opportunity for concrete expressions of freedom in community as persons engage in cooperate governorship of their spiritual welfare by means of participatory freedom that involves critical solidarity. In this setting there would be greater likelihood of the kind of sensitive and empathetic partnership that emerges when persons enter and participate compassionately in each other's lives.[79] This should lead to theological engagement that links reciprocally abstract conceptual exploration with the specific concerns of individual lives in critical-creative tension with the concerns of a denomination and the wider network of concerns harbored by varying communities of fellow-citizens of the world.

So then, I operate with the expectation that the church in its complex, contextual catholicity will, in its internal life and its relations with other communities and organizations, testify to that which is its raison d'être, that is, the pursuit and championing of freedom in its natural and ontological dimensions, operating in the dialectical tension between individual freedom and the common good. In the process there will be clear indication of the recognition that freedom and justice are necessary for the promotion of wholesome existence for each person in relation to all others, and the cosmos as a whole. In keeping with the example of Jesus the Christ, the church will give special attention to those who have been denied access to resources and opportunity, and thus limited in their ability to nurture their own well-being and the well-being of others, while honoring the dignity of all people. Important to the dignity of each human being is the responsibility to contribute to the determination of what it means to be human, and to nurture the ability to be the best kind of co-inhabitant in a cosmos that is at root organismic. Such a responsibility necessitates imagination regarding what is possible, what is most helpful, and how in each moment of decision-making, the legacy from the past and that which is hoped for can come together in the creative ways for the good of each and all. The Christian community, as one facilitator in this dynamic, will free itself from a preoccupation with self-preservation, and will take the decision to be God's partner as God works for the good of that which God loves, the world.

## NOTES

1. Miller, Michael St. A. "Eschatology and Ecclesiology: Reflections Inspired by Revelation 21:22," *Encounter* 64:2 (2003): [109-138], 132.

2. Alfred North Whitehead, *Process and Reality (corrected edition)*, eds. David Ray Griffin and Donald W. Sherburne (New York: The Free Press, 1978), 99.

3. World Council of Churches, *Faith and Order Paper 111*, 1982 (Reprinted with permission of the Association of Evangelical Lutheran Churches, Suite 80LL, 12015 Manchester Rd. St. Louis MO 63131), 30.

4. Ibid.

5. Karl Barth, *The Humanity of God* (Richmond, VA: John Knox Press, 1963), 42.

6. Ibid., 45.

7. Ibid., 46.

8. Clark Williamson, *Way of Blessing Way of Life: A Christian Theology* (St. Louis: Chalice Press, 1999), 213.

9. Barth, *Humanity of God*, 50.

10. Barth suggests that this gives a definite distinction to humanity as such, this applying even to "the oddest, most villainous or miserable." This, he suggests, has nothing to do with an optimistic judgment of human beings but is grounded in the simple fact that God has chosen human beings to be God's covenant-partner. See *Humanity of God*, 52-53.

11. Karl Barth, *Church Dogmatics—The Doctrine of God* II.2, eds. G. W. Bromiley and T. F. Torrance (Edinburgh: T. & T. Clark, 1982), 177.

12. Barth, *Humanity of God*, 37.

13. I am referring to God's synthesis of prehensions from previous decisions and actions of each in relation to God's prehensions from all other cosmic processes.

14. My colleague Ron Allen in the text *Preaching Luke Acts* suggests that the concept Kingdom of God constitutes the overarching theme that runs throughout these two books. It is his view that we can hear everything that occurs in these two volumes through the notion of the divine reign. Other themes add specificity to this one. See Ronald Allen, *Preaching Luke-Acts* (St. Louis: Chalice Press, 2000), 35.

15. Ada Maria Isasi-Diaz, "Christ in Mujerista Theology," in *Thinking of Christ: Proclamation, Explanation, Meaning,* ed. Tatha Wiley (New York: Continuum Publishing Group Ltd., 2003), 163.

16. "But you are a chosen people, a royal priesthood, a holy nation, a people belonging to God, that you may declare the praises of him who called you out of darkness into his wonderful light."

17. Given that the purpose of the letter was to seek protection against his Catholic foes, some might also question the motives fueling his theological posture.

18. Martin Luther, "To the Christian Nobility of the German Nation Concerning the Reform of the Christian Estate," in *Luther's Works (The Christian in Society),vol. 44,* ed. James Atkinson (Philadelphia: Fortress Press, 1966), 129.

19. Martin Luther, "The Freedom of a Christian," in *Martin Luther's Basic Theological Writings* , ed. Thomas Lull (Memphis: Fortress Press, 1989), 607.

20. Veli-Matti Kärkkäinen, *An Introduction to Ecclesiology: Ecumenical, Historical and Global Perspectives* (Downers Grove, IL: InterVarsity Press, 2002), 43. He references Martin Luther, *Weimarer Ausgabe* 7.57; 11.412.

21. Hans Küng, *The Church* (New York: Image Books, 1976), 466.

22. Ibid.

23. Ibid., 487.

24. Ibid.

25. Ibid.

26. Ibid.

27. Ibid., 485.

28. Ibid.

29. Jürgen Moltmann, *The Church in the Power of the Spirit* (Minneapolis: Fortress Press, 1993), 260-261.

30. Board of Mission and Unity of the Church of England, *The Priesthood of the Ordained Ministry* (London: Church House Publishing, 1986). 18-19. We hear of diverse forms of ministry: *presbyteroi* (elders), *episkopoi* (overseers), *diakonoi* (deacons), *apostoloi* (apostles), *prophetai* (prophets), *evangelistoi* (evangelists), *didaskaloi* (teachers) etc.

31. Ibid., 21.

32. Ibid.

33. Angelo Di Berardino, ed. *Encyclopedia of the Early Church,* trans. Adrian Walford (New York: Oxford University Press, 1991), 404.

34. Board of Mission and Unity of the Church of England, *The Priesthood of the Ordained Ministry,* 21.

35. Ibid., 20.

36. Ibid.

37. Di Berardino, ed. *Encyclopedia of the Early Church,* 404.

38. Küng, *The Church,* 492.

39. Ibid. Kung points out that "layman" is used in the first letter of Clement (40:6) to refer to the simple faithful by contrast to the high priest, priests, and Levites.

40. Ibid., 493.

41. Williamson, *Way of Blessing Way of Life,* 261-262.

42. Ibid.

43. Luther, "To the Christian Nobility," 129.

44. Martin Luther, "The Freedom of a Christian," 608.

45. Kärkkäinen, *An Introduction to Ecclesiology,* 39-40. Kärkkäinen points us to *Weimarer Ausgabe* 7.219; 30.190 as the original source.

46. Ibid. Kärkkäinen references the *Augsburg Confession* 7:1.

47. Ibid.

48. Luther, "To the Christian Nobility," *Luther's Works,* 128.

49. Ibid., 129

50. Ibid., 43. Kärkkäinen points us to *Weimarer Ausgabe,* 50.647 as the original source.

51. Ibid., 43. Kärkkäinen points us to *Weimarer Ausgabe* 12.189 as the original source and acknowledges that he is following Paul Althaus' interpretation in *The Theology of Martin Luther,* 324-325.

52. Letty Russell, *Church in the Round: Feminist Interpretation of the Church* (Louisville: Westminster/John Knox Press, 1993), 50-51.

53. Letty Russell, *Household of Freedom: Authority in Feminist Theology* (Philadelphia: The Westminster Press, 1987), 90.

54. Küng, *The Church,* 498.

55. Williamson, *Way of Blessing Way of Life,* 270.

56. Ibid.

57. Admittedly, the fact that they were white and from overseas had something to do with it.

58. Russell, *Church in the Round,* 51.

59. Küng, *The Church,* 465.

60. John Calvin, *Institutes of Christian Religion* , ed. John McNeill, trans. and index Ford Lewis Battles (Philadelphia: Westminster Press, 1960), [Bk.4.iii.4], 1057.

61. This specialist would participate in the preparation of Bible Study leaders and Church School teachers. As I imagine their preparation, it would begin with a basic Divinity degree with a focus on Historical, Doctrinal, and Biblical studies that would not be tied to a requirement of ordination.

62. Leonardo Boff and Clodovis Boff, *Introducing Liberation Theology* (1987; reprint, Maryknoll, NY: Orbis Press, 2011), 24-32. This mediation is associated with two others: the hermeneutical and the practical.

63. Ashley Smith, *Real Roots and Potted Plants: Reflections on the Caribbean Church* (Williamsfield, Jamaica: Mandeville Publishers, 1984), 27. Smith's reference is Paulo Freire, *The Pedagogy of the Oppressed* (New York: Herder and Herder), 26-27.

64. Ibid.

65. Russell, *Church in the Round,* 50.

66. Miller, *Eschatology and Ecclesiology,* 133.

67. Kung, *The Church,* 121.

68. Jürgen Moltmann, *The Open Church: Invitation to a Messianic Life-Style* (London: SCM Press Ltd, 1978), 115.

69. Ibid.

70. Ibid.

71. Kung, *The Church,* 387-388.

72. Miller, "Eschatology and Ecclesiology," 136. I employ the familiar language of "substance" as a convenient way to indicate that God is present to each entity and all life in the most intimate way that it is possible for any one entity to be so.

73. Russell, *Church in the Round,* 54-63, 67-74.

74. Rosemary Radford Ruether, *Women-Church: Theology and Practice of Feminist Liturgical Communities* (San Francisco: Harper and Row, 1985), 59-60.

75. Ibid., 63.

76. See a description in chapter 5 of Michael Miller, *Reshaping the Contextual Vision.*

77. Miller, "Eschatology and Ecclesiology," 133.

78. Ibid., 137.

79. Ibid.

# Bibliography


Aeschylus. *Prometheus Bound.* Translated by James Scully and C. J. Herington. Oxford: Oxford University Press, 1975.

Altmann, Walter. *Luther and Liberation.* Minneapolis: Fortress Press, 1992.

Anselm. *Proslogion with a Reply on Behalf of the Fool by Gaunilo and the Author's Reply to Gaunilo.* Edited by M. J. Charlesworth. Notre Dame: University of Notre Dame Press, 1979.

Arendt, Hannah. *Between Past and the Future: Six Exercises in Political Thought.* New York: Viking Press, 1961.

———. *The Human Condition.* Chicago: The University of Chicago Press, 1958.

Augustine of Hippo. *City of God.* Translated by Demetrius Zema, Gerald Walsh, Grace Monahan and Daniel Honan. New York: Image Books, 1958.

———. *Confessions.* Translated by R. S. Pine-Coffin. London: Penguin Books, 1961.

———. "Grace and Free Will." In *The Fathers of the Church.* Edited by Roy Joseph Deferrari, Washington DC: The Catholic University of America Press, 1968.

———. "The Predestination of the Saints." In *Four Anti-Pelagian Writings.* Translated by John Mourant and William Collinge. Fathers of the Church: A New Translation (Patristic Series), vol. 86. Washington DC: The Catholic University of America Press, 1992.

———. *On Free Choice of the Will.* Translated by Thomas Williams. Indianapolis: Hackett Publishing Company, 1993.

———. "Treatise on the Grace of Christ and Original Sin." In *Works of Augustine—A Translation for the 21st Century.* Edited by John E. Rotelle, O.S.A. Translated by Ronald J. Teske S.J. New York: New City Press, 1997.

Bagnall, W. R., ed. *The Writings of James Arminius,* vol. III. Grand Rapids: Baker Books, 1956.

Barth, Karl. *The Humanity of God.* Richmond: John Knox Press, 1963.

———. *The Word of God and the Word of Man.* Translated by Douglas Horton. New York: Harper Torchbooks, 1957.

———. *Church Dogmatics: The Doctrine of God* II.2. Edited by G. W. Bromiley and T. F. Torrance. Edinburgh: T. & T. Clark, 1982.

Bauckham, Richard. *God and the Crisis of Freedom—Biblical and Contemporary Perspectives.* Louisville: Westminster John Knox Press, 2002.

Berlin, Isaiah. *Two Concepts of Liberty, Essays on Liberty.* Oxford: Oxford University Press, 1990.

Boff, Leonardo. *When Theology Listens to the Poor.* San Francisco: Harper and Rowe, 1984.

Boff, Leonardo, and Clodovis Boff. *Introducing Liberation Theology.* Maryknoll: Orbis Press, 2011.

Boodoo, Jerald. "Faces of Jesus in a Forced Theological Context." Unpublished paper, 1998.

Boulton, Matthew Myer. *Life in God: John Calvin, Practical Formation, and the Future of Protestant Theology*. Grand Rapids: Wm. B. Eerdmans Publishing Company, 2011.

Brinkman, Martien. *The Tragedy of Human Freedom: Failure of the Christian Concept of Freedom in Western Culture*. Translated by Harry Lecken and Henry Jansen. New York: Rodopi Publishers, 2003.

Brown, Delwin. *To Set at Liberty: Christian Faith and Human Freedom*. Maryknoll: Orbis Books, 1981.

Brueggemann, Walter. *Journey to the Common Good*. Louisville: Westminster John Knox Press, 2010.

Bryne, Ruth. *The Rational Imagination: How People Create Alternatives to Reality*. Cambridge, London: MIT Press, 2005.

Burrell, David. *Faith and Freedom—An Interfaith Perspective*. Malden: Blackwell Publishing, 2004.

Calvin, John. *Institutes of the Christian Religion*, vol. I. Edited by John McNeill. Translated by Ford Lewis Battles. Philadelphia: Westminster Press, 1960.

———. *Institutes of the Christian Religion*, vol. II. Edited by John McNeill. Translated by Ford Lewis Battles. Philadelphia: Westminster Press, 1960.

Campbell, Alexander. *The Christian Baptist*, vol. IV. Bethany, WV: Bethany Printing Office, 1827.

———. *The Christian System*. Cincinnati: Standard Publishing Company, 1839.

Casas, Bartolome de Las. *History of the Indies*. Translated by Andree Collard. New York: Harper and Row Publishers, 1971.

Chardin, Pierre Teilhard de. *The Phenomenon of Man*. New York: Harper & Row Publishers, 1975.

Church of England. *The Priesthood of the Ordained Ministry*. Church House Publishing, 1986.

Cobb, John Jr. *A Christian Natural Theology—Based on the Thought of Alfred North Whitehead*. Philadelphia: The Westminster Press, 1965.

———. *The Structure of Christian Existence*. Philadelphia: Westminster Press, 1967.

Craig, William Lane. "No Other Name." In *The Philosophical Challenge of Religious Diversity*. Edited by Philip Quinn and Kevin Meeker. Oxford: Oxford University Press, 2000.

Daley, Herman, and John Cobb Jr. *For the Common Good: Redirecting the Economy toward Community, the Environment and a Sustainable Future*. Boston: Beacon Press, 1994.

Damasio, Antonio. *Descartes' Error: Emotions, Reason and the Human Brain*. New York: Putnam's Sons, 1994.

Davis, Kortright. *Emancipation Still Comin': Explorations in Caribbean Emancipatory Theology*. New York: Orbis Books, 1990.

Descartes, Rene. *Meditations on First Philosophy*. Translated by Donald Cress. Indianapolis: Hackett Publishing Company, 1979.

Dostoyevsky, Fyodor. *The Brothers Karamazov*. Translated by Richard Peyear and Larissa Volokhonsky. San Francisco: North Point Press, 1990.

Erasmus, Desiderius. "The Free Will." In *Milestones of Thought in the History of Ideas*. Edited by Ernst Winter. New York: Frederick Ungar Publishing Co., 1961.

Fanon, Frantz. *Black Skin, White Masks*. Translated by Charles Lam Markmann. New York: Grove Press Inc., 1967.

———. *The Wretched of the Earth*. Translated by Constance Farrington. New York: Grove Weidenfelt, 1963.

Ferguson, John. *Pelagius—A Historical and Theological Study*. Cambridge: Heffer and Sons, Ltd., 1956.

Gerrish, Brian A. *Grace and Reason: A Study in the Theology of Luther*. Oxford: Oxford University Press, 1962.

Green, Garrett. *Imagining God: Theology and the Religious Imagination*. New York: Harper and Rowe Publishers, 1989.

Griffin, David Ray. *God and Religion in a Postmodern World—Essays in Postmodern Theology*. Albany: State University of New York Press, 1989.

Guthrie, Shirley. *Christian Doctrine*. Louisville: Westminster John Knox Press, 1994.

Hamid, Idris. *Troubling of the Waters*. San Fernando: Rahman Printery Limited, 1973.

Hartshorne, Charles. *The Divine Relativity: A Social Conception of God.* New Haven: Yale University Press, 1948.

Heidegger, Martin. *Being and Time.* Translated by John Macquarrie and Edward Robinson. New York: Harper and Row Publishers, 1962.

―――. *An Introduction to Metaphysics.* New York: Anchor Books, 1961.

―――. *Existence and Being.* Chicago: Henry Regnery Company, 1965.

Hosinski, Thomas. *Stubborn Facts and Creative Advance.* Lanham: Rowman and Littlefield Publishers, 1993.

Hume, David. *Dialogues Concerning Natural Religion.* Edited with introduction by Richard H. Popkin. Indianapolis: Hackett Publishing Company, 1980.

Isasi-Diaz, Ada Maria. "Christ in Mujerista Theology." In *Thinking of Christ: Proclamation, Explanation, Meaning.* Edited by Tatha Wiley, New York: Continuum Publishing Group, Ltd., 2003.

James, William. *Varieties of Religious Experience: A Study in Human Nature.* New York: Longmans, Green and Co, 1925.

Janzen, J. Gerald. *Abraham and All the Families of the Earth: A Commentary on the Book of Genesis 12-50.* Grand Rapids: Wm. B Eerdmans Publishing Co., 1993.

Johnson, Elizabeth A. *She Who Is: The Mystery of God in Feminist Theological Discourse,* Tenth Anniversary edition. New York: The Crossroad Publishing Company, 2002.

Johnston, Carol. *The Wealth or Health of Nations: Transforming Capitalism from Within.* Cleveland: The Pilgrim Press, 1998.

Jones, Joe R. *A Grammar of Christian Faith: Systematic Explorations in Christian Life and Doctrine,* vol. II. Lanham: Rowman and Littlefield Publishers Inc., 2002.

Kant, Immanuel. *The Critique of Judgment.* Translated by James Creed Meredith. Oxford: Clarendon Press, 1992.

―――. *Critique of Pure Reason.* Translated by Norman Smith. New York: St. Martin's Press, 1965.

―――. *Grounding for the Metaphysics of Morals.* Translated by James W. Ellington. Indianapolis: Hackett Publishing Company, 1980.

Kärkkäinen, Veli-Matti. *An Introduction to Ecclesiology: Ecumenical, Historical and Global Perspectives.* Grove: InterVarsity Press, 2002.

Kaufman, Gordon. *In the Beginning . . . Creativity.* Minneapolis: Fortress Press, 2004.

―――. *The Theological Imagination.* Philadelphia: The Westminster Press, 1981.

Kelly, J. N. D, ed. *Early Christian Doctrines,* Revised Edition. New York: Harper San Francisco, 1978.

Kenny, Anthony. *The God of the Philosophers.* Oxford: Clarendon Press, 1979.

Krodel, Gottfried G., ed. and trans. *Luther's Works* Vol. 50 – Letters III. Philadelphia: Fortress Press, 1975.

Kung, Hans. *The Church.* New York: Image Books, 1976.

Kwok, Pui Lan. *Discovering the Bible in the Non-Biblical World.* New York: Orbis Books, 1995.

―――. *Postcolonial Imagination and Feminist Theology.* Louisville: Westminster John Knox Press, 2005.

Lerner, Michael. *The Politics of Meaning: Restoring Hope and Possibility in an Age of Cynicism.* Reading: Addison-Wesley Publishing Company, 1996.

Levinas, Emmanuel. *Totality and Infinity.* Edited by Andre Schuwer. Pittsburg: Duquesne University Press, 1969.

Locke, John. *An Essay Concerning Human Understanding.* Collated, annotated, and with commentary by Alexander Campbell Fraser. New York: Dover Publication Inc., 1959.

Lossky, Vladimir. *The Mystical Theology of the Eastern Church.* Crestwood: St. Vladimir's Seminary Press, 2002.

Lull, Thomas. *Martin Luther's Basic Theological Writings.* Memphis: Fortress Press, 1989.

Luther, Martin. *The Bondage of the Will.* Grand Rapids, MI: Fleming H. Revell Company, 1957.

―――. "The Freedom of a Christian." In *Martin Luther's Basic Theological Writings.* Edited by Thomas Lull, Memphis: Fortress Press, 1989.

————. "Lectures on Romans." In *Library of Christian Classics*, vol. XV. Edited by Wilhelm Pauck. Philadelphia: Westminster Press, 1961.

————. "To the Christian Nobility of the German Nation Concerning the Reform of the Christian Estate." In *Luther's Works*. Edited by James Atkinson, Philadelphia: Fortress Press, 1966.

————. "Two Kinds of Righteousness." In *Martin Luther's Basic Theological Writings*. Edited by Thomas Lull, Memphis: Fortress Press, 1989.

Mill, John Stuart. *On Liberty and other Essays*. New York: The McMillan Company, 1926.

Miller, Michael St. A. "Eschatology and Ecclesiology: Reflections Inspired by Revelation 21:22." *Encounter* 64: 2 (2003): 109-138.

————. "Mission in Pluralistic Contexts—a Caribbean Perspective." In *Chalice Introduction to Disciples Theology*. Edited by Peter Heltzel. St. Louis: Chalice Press, 2008.

————. *Reshaping the Contextual Vision in Caribbean Theology: Theoretical Foundations for Theology Which Is Contextual, Pluralistic, and Dialectical*. Lanham: University Press of America, 2007.

Moltmann, Jürgen. *The Future of Creation—Collected Essays*. Philadelphia: Fortress Press, 1979.

————. *The Church in the Power of the Spirit*. Minneapolis: Fortress Press, 1993.

————. *The Open Church: Invitation to a Messianic Lifestyle*. London: SCM Press, Ltd., 1978.

Moskop, John C. *Divine Omniscience and Human Freedom: Thomas Aquinas and Charles Hartshorne*. Georgia: Mercer University Press, 1984.

Neville, Robert. *A Theology Primer*. Albany: State University of New York Press, 1991.

Nichols, James, ed. *The Writings of James Arminius*, vol. I. Grand Rapids: Baker Books, 1956.

————. *The Writings of James Arminius*, vol. II. Grand Rapids: Baker Books, 1956.

Ogden, Schubert. *The Reality of God and Other Essays*. San Francisco: Harper and Row Publishers, 1977.

————. *Faith and Freedom: Toward a Theology of Liberation*. Nashville: Abingdon Press, 1989.

Oord, Thomas J. *The Nature of Love: A Theology*. St. Louis: Chalice Press, 2010.

Otto, Rudolph. *The Idea of the Holy*. Translated by John W. Harvey. Oxford: Oxford University Press, 1973.

Patterson, Orlando. *Freedom in the Making of Western Culture*, vol. I: New York: Basic Books, 1991.

Peters, Rebecca Todd. *In Search of the Good Life: The Ethics of Globalization*. New York: Continuum International Publishing Group, 2005.

Pinnock, Clark. *Most Moved Mover: A Theology of God's Openness*. Grand Rapids: Baker Academic Press, 2001.

Placher, William C. *Narratives of a Vulnerable God: Christ, Theology, and Scripture*. Louisville: Westminster John Knox Press, 1994.

Presbyterian Church USA. *The Book of Confessions*. Louisville: General Assembly - The Presbyterian Church USA, 1991.

Rivera, Mayra. *The Touch of Transcendence: A Postcolonial Theology of God*. Louisville: Westminster John Knox Press, 2007.

Ruether, Rosemary Radford. *Women-Church: Theology and Practice of Feminist Liturgical Communities*. San Francisco: Harper and Row, 1985.

Russell, Letty. *Church in the Round: Feminist Interpretation of the Church*. Louisville: Westminster John Knox Press, 1993.

————. *Household of Freedom: Authority in Feminist Theology*. Philadelphia: The Westminster Press, 1987.

Schwöbel, Christoph. "Imago Libertatis: Human and Divine Freedom." In *God and Freedom—Essays in Historical and Systematic Theology*. Edited by Colin E. Gunton, Edinburgh: T&T Clark, 1995.

Sen, Amartya. *Rationality and Freedom*. Cambridge: Harvard University Press, 2004.

————. *Development as Freedom*. New York: Anchor Books, 2000.

Smith, Ashley. *Emerging from Innocence: Religion, Theology and Development*. Mandeville, Jamaica: Eureka Press, 1991.

————. *Real Roots and Potted Plants: Reflections on the Caribbean Church*. Williamsfield: Mandeville Publishers, 1984.

Stowers, Stanley. *A Rereading of Romans: Justice, Jews, and Gentiles*. New Haven: Yale University Press, 1994.

Suchocki, Marjorie Hewitt. *The End of Evil*. New York: State University of New York Press, 1988.

Tillich, Paul. *Dynamics of Faith*. New York: Harper and Rowe Publishers, 1957.

————. *Systematic Theology*. vol. I. Chicago: University of Chicago Press, 1951.

————. *Systematic Theology*. vol. II. Chicago: University of Chicago Press, 1958.

Walzer, Michael. *Exodus and Revolution*. New York: Basic Books, 1985.

Ward, Keith. *Divine Action*. London: Collins Publishing Group, 1990.

Watson, Francis. "Christ, Law and Freedom: A Study in Theological Hermeneutics." In *God and Freedom—Essays in Historical and Systematic Theology*. Edited by Colin E. Gunton, Edinburg: T&T Clark, 1995.

Watty, William. *From Shore to Shore: Soundings in Caribbean Theology*. Barbados: CEDAR Press, 1981.

Weir, J. Emmette. "Towards a Caribbean Liberation Theology." *Journal of Religious Studies* 12, no. 1 (1991): 41-53.

Whitehead, Alfred North. *Adventures of Ideas*. New York: The Free Press, 1961.

————. *Process and Reality*. Edited by David Ray Griffin and Donald W. Sherburne. New York: The Free Press, 1978.

Williams, Charles K., ed. *The Bacchae of Euripides*. New York: Farrar, Straus and Giroux, 1990.

Williamson, Clark. *Way of Blessing Way of Life: A Christian Theology*. St. Louis: Chalice Press, 1999.

World Council of Churches. *Baptism, Eucharist and Ministry* (Faith and Order Paper 111), 1982. Reprinted with permission of the Association of Evangelical Lutheran Churches, Suite 80LL, 12015 Manchester Rd., St. Louis, Mo 63131.

# Index